The Resurrection

The Resurrection

*An Interdisciplinary Symposium on
the Resurrection of Jesus*

Edited by
STEPHEN T. DAVIS
DANIEL KENDALL, SJ
GERALD O'COLLINS, SJ

OXFORD UNIVERSITY PRESS

*This book has been printed digitally and produced in a standard specification
in order to ensure its continuing availability*

OXFORD
UNIVERSITY PRESS

Great Clarendon Street, Oxford OX2 6DP

Oxford University Press is a department of the University of Oxford.
It furthers the University's objective of excellence in research, scholarship,
and education by publishing world-wide in

Oxford New York

Auckland Bangkok Buenos Aires Cape Town Chennai
Dar es Salaam Delhi Hong Kong Istanbul Karachi Kolkata
Kuala Lumpur Madrid Melbourne Mexico City Mumbai Nairobi
São Paulo Shanghai Taipei Tokyo Toronto

Oxford is a registered trade mark of Oxford University Press
in the UK and in certain other countries

Published in the United States
by Oxford University Press Inc., New York

ISBN 978-0-19-826985-4

Preface

Every project has its history. This one began with our desire to meet and dialogue on the resurrection of Jesus with scholars in a variety of disciplines. Hence we invited fifteen other specialists, many of whom have already published works on the resurrection. In planning the various papers that are published in this book, we wanted to include contributions from biblical studies, foundational (or fundamental) theology, systematic theology, moral theology, spiritual theology, the philosophy of religion, homiletics, liturgy, the study of religious art, and literary criticism. We managed to secure papers from experts in most of these fields, and in one way or another all these fields have entered this book.

To promote advance discussion and establish stronger connecting threads between the different contributions, we encouraged those presenting papers to circulate them beforehand to all the members of the symposium. In some cases two preliminary drafts had been sent out for such feedback before we met at Dunwoodie (7–10 April 1996) for the Resurrection Summit itself.

This procedure distinguishes our book from other works produced in collaboration like Paul Avis (ed.), *The Resurrection of Jesus Christ* (London: Darton, Longman & Todd, 1993); Stephen Barton and Graham Stanton (eds.), *Resurrection. Essays in Honour of Leslie Houlden* (London: SPCK, 1994); and C. F. D. Moule (ed.), *The Significance of the Message of the Resurrection for Faith in Jesus Christ*, Studies in Biblical Theology, 8 (London: SCM Press, 1968). These works put together contributions from different writers, but did not emerge from any meeting that they held together. In *Resurrexit* (Rome: Libreria Editrice Vaticana, 1975) Eduard Dhanis edited the proceedings of an international symposium on the resurrection that took place in Rome (1–5 April 1970), at which the twenty contributors included such biblical scholars as J. Blinzler, R. E. Brown, J. Coppens, J. Dupont, A. Feuillet, J. Jeremias,

J. Kremer, X. Léon-Dufour, C. M. Martini, and J. Schmitt. The papers for this symposium were not circulated in advance, and it was largely an exegetical exchange. A book coming from G. R. Habermas and A. G. N. Flew, *Did Jesus Rise from the Dead?* (San Francisco: Harper & Row, 1987) followed a debate between the two authors (2–3 May 1985); five other participants and respondents were invited, but not all of them were present for the debate itself. The North Park Symposium on Theological Interpretation of Scripture (held at North Park Theological Seminary, Chicago) produced a whole issue of a journal after their meeting on the resurrection of 8–10 October 1993: *Ex Auditu*, 9 (1993). The contributions coming from the nine papers, one response, and one sermon published in that issue of *Ex Auditu* were mostly, but by no means entirely, of a biblical nature. In recalling these earlier collaborative publications on the resurrection, we are encouraged to think that both the procedure involved and the variety of disciplines represented set our volume somewhat apart from earlier joint works on the subject.

After John Wilkins, in Chapter 1, gives his impressions of the Resurrection Summit, in Chapter 2, Gerald O'Collins first summarizes current debates concerning the essential resurrection claim, the nature of the Easter appearances, the historicity of the empty tomb, and the credibility of resurrection faith. He then proposes questions that invite fuller examination in the historical, systematic, ethical, spiritual, and liturgical areas. In his response the Most Reverend Doctor Peter Carnley argues that one can neither prove nor disprove John Hick's conjecture about the Easter appearances as psychogenic projections. A theology of the resurrection should concentrate more on an epistemology of faith capable of explaining how the presence of the Spirit of Christ today can be identified *as* the presence of Jesus the Crucified One.

In Chapter 3, Janet Martin Soskice proposes explaining Paul's idea of the resurrection through his image of the body (both Christ's and our own) as temple. This is connected with Jesus' own 'temple destruction' saying. Belief in the resurrection for Paul has implications not only for a corporeality (bodiliness) but also for our belonging together in one body (corporateness). Christ's risen body is the new Temple, the place where God dwells with women and men.

In Chapter 4, Carey Newman investigates the narrative, historical, and theological logic standing behind the New Testament's identification of Jesus as 'Glory'. Christians' use of Glory language signals that the eschatological age of blessing has broken in upon this world in the resurrection of Jesus. The New Testament's provocative use of Glory language clearly opens a theological breach in the wall of Jewish monotheism by scandalously identifying Jesus as the divine presence. This use of Glory language as a sign of God's power and presence in the resurrection of Jesus indicates that the parting of ways between Christianity and Judaism occurs quite early, and does so because of a high Christology.

In Chapter 5, Alan Segal sketches the history of expressions of resurrection in biblical thought. As opposed to the young men in Jewish millenarian movements who lose their lives as martyrs in the expectation of bodily restoration at the end of time, Hellenized Jewish intellectuals embraced the Platonic notion of the immortality of the soul, in order to express continuity of consciousness after death. The martyrdom context is crucial for understanding the expectation of Jesus' resurrection among his followers. Although both Rabbinic Judaism and early Christianity affirm resurrection strongly, they eventually subsume concepts of immortality of the soul, each in its own way and in stark contradiction to each other.

In Chapter 6, Stephen Davis discusses the kind of seeing experienced by the witnesses to the risen Christ. Some say that it was 'grace-assisted seeing': the witnesses saw the resurrected Jesus only because God, by a special grace, allowed them to do so. Davis argues against this and in favour of the theory that the witnesses saw Jesus in a normal or fairly normal sense of the word 'see'.

In Chapter 7, William Alston defends the (by and large) historical accuracy of the resurrection appearance narratives in the Gospels. The defence is carried out by displaying the failure of attempts by New Testament scholars to show that a particular feature of the narratives (the appearance of the risen Jesus in embodied, perceptible form) is *not* of historical value. In particular, the contentions of one scholar, Reginald Fuller, are critiqued. To the extent that Fuller's treatment can be taken as representative, this essay, if successful, will have removed a crucial obstacle to the rational acceptance of the appearance narratives as factually correct in the main. It ends by identifying certain disqualifying features of Fuller's treatment that, it is claimed, are pervasive in twentieth-century Gospel criticism. In her response Sarah Coakley accepts

Alston's case as convincing against the dogmatic scepticism of Fuller's treatment of bodily resurrection, while suggesting that Alston has overstated matters in denying significance to the redactional strands of the Gospel writers' thinking. There is also a puzzling continued appeal to the objective historical 'facts', granted that Alston explicitly disavows at the outset anything other than an *intra-Christian* approach. His overriding concern to support a 'literal' bodily resurrection may lead him to understress some important dimensions of the resurrection accounts: the 'atypical' nature of the risen body, the consequent importance of metaphorical speech in discussing it, the epistemic transformation required in recognizing it, and the gender dimensions possibly implicit in such recognition.

In Chapter 8, Richard Swinburne argues that in assessing what happened on some particular past occasions, we have to take into account both detailed historical evidence and general background evidence. In the case of the resurrection we must take into account the detailed historical evidence (for example, that contained in the New Testament) and balance it against our background evidence. The latter will include evidence not only of what normally happens (for example, that humans do not rise from death), but also of natural theology—that there is a God who may be expected on occasion to set aside the laws of nature. An appendix to this philosophical discussion argues that the widespread early Christian practice of celebrating the Eucharist on Sundays provides strong detailed historical evidence, additional to that normally considered in favour of the resurrection.

In Chapter 9, Francis Schüssler Fiorenza develops a fundamental theological approach to Jesus' resurrection that takes seriously the contemporary critique of foundationalism. He first discusses two different contemporary approaches within fundamental theology to the resurrection of Jesus: one emphasizing probability and combining internal and external reasons, the other focusing on the life of Jesus. After analysing two distinct genres of New Testament testimonies, hymnic material and appearances narratives, he treats the importance and function of the testimony not only as an avenue of openness to transcendence, but also as a key for the interpretation of the New Testament texts. He concludes with reflections on the nature of metaphor, historical reconstruction, hermeneutical interpretation, and the relations between the object and ground of faith.

In Chapter 10, William Craig argues that John Dominic Crossan's reconstruction of the events of Easter is based upon idiosyncratic presuppositions concerning sources and methodology which are not accepted by any major New Testament critic. Concerning Jesus' burial, Crossan is unable to make a plausible case for regarding Mark's account as historicized prophecy; nor does he render doubtful the historicity of Joseph of Arimathea's role in the burial. With respect to the empty tomb, Crossan fails to sustain his hypothesis that the Marcan account is rooted in the *Gospel of Peter* and that the female dramatis personae are residue from the prior Secret Gospel of Mark. Crossan is largely silent concerning the appearance traditions, adopting the long-refuted interpretation of the appearance stories as legitimations of authority. Finally, Crossan cannot provide any convincing explanation of the origin of the disciples' belief in Jesus' resurrection. In his response Paul Eddy agrees with Craig's response to Crossan. His critical comments aim at refining and developing Craig's already strong argument. Eddy concludes by raising several issues related to the very important question of presuppositions.

In Chapter 11, Alan Padgett analyses and rejects a powerful and attractive ideology ('myth'): namely, that the best approach to biblical and religious studies is one that brackets off our own faith, based on the assumption that religious faith corrupts scientific research. He recommends instead a post-modern method that is holistic, humble, and accepting of different faiths, and uses the resurrection of Jesus as a focused example.

In Chapter 12, Marguerite Shuster illustrates how the absolute centrality of Jesus' resurrection to Christian faith can be seen clearly articulated by major preacher-theologians from the apostle Paul through Augustine, Luther, Barth, and Thielicke. They all interpreted the resurrection as bodily (a changed body, but a body none the less) and united Christ's resurrection with that of Christians. Though tone and emphasis differed considerably, all combated the forms which doubt of these affirmations took in their own day, and played out the consequences of resurrection faith for the life of the world. The intellectual seriousness with which they engaged the questions of their own time, as well as the intensity with which they related theological affirmation of the resurrection to the perennial threats of sin, death, and final futility, challenge today's theologians and preachers to do likewise.

In Chapter 13, Brian Johnstone begins by pointing out how the resurrection of the crucified Jesus is at the centre of the Christian kerygma. The resurrection ought, therefore, to be at the centre of moral theology and Christian ethics. However, this has not been the case. This chapter describes what a moral theology as reflection on the experience of the resurrection would look like. It would be a practical theology of the resurrection, an ethics of transformation focused on the transformation of Jesus and the transformation of humankind which that makes possible.

As the summaries offered above indicate, this volume contains thirteen presentations from the Resurrection Summit but only three responses. In fact, each of the presentations was followed by a response that initiated the discussion of the particular paper. To avoid making this volume too long, we include only three of the responses. Together with John Wilkins's introductory piece, these three responses reflect the inner dynamics of the symposium. We also decided not to include a bibliography but simply to mention several that are available. The most extensive recent bibliography on the resurrection is provided by G. Ghiberti and G. Borgonovo, 'Bibliografia sulla resurrezione di Gesù (1973-92)', *La scuola cattolica*, 121 (1993), 171-287. See also M. Isidro Alves, 'Ressurreição e Fé Pascal', *Didaskalia*, 29 (1989), 279-537, at 519-37; Barton and Stanton (eds.), *Resurrection*, 231-3; J. Nolland, *Word Biblical Commentary*, xxxv: *Luke 18: 35-24: 53* (Dallas: Word, 1993), 1168-73.

Inevitably, one or two reviewers will query our choice of symposiasts, and even propose names of those we should have asked to attend. Doubtless we could have brought together a different team. To avoid possible misunderstandings, however, let us mention that we did invite some other scholars who, for a variety of good reasons, could not come to participate and contribute. Three further scholars (Martin Hengel, Graham Stanton, and Anthony Ugolnik) accepted our invitation to attend and present papers, but eventually had to drop out.

We are most grateful to the McCarthy Family Foundation and, specifically, to Eugene and Maureen McCarthy, for their generous support of our Resurrection Summit, and to Sr. Miriam Pollard, OCSO, for creating the Summit's logo. Our special thanks go to Bishop Edwin F. O'Brien, Rector of St Joseph's Seminary,

Dunwoodie (Yonkers, NY) for his gracious hospitality and help—he is also leading St Joseph's Seminary in its centennial celebrations. We wish to thank warmly the Catholic Archbishop of New York, Cardinal John O'Connor, for his support and encouragement and, in particular, for offering us a beautiful commemorative concert in St Patrick's Cathedral. Fr. Gerard R. Rafferty, John Hopkins, Antoinette Mecca, and other members of the Dunwoodie 'family' provided us with extraordinarily efficient assistance. We also want to thank Kenneth Woodward, Eric Avram, Bill Blakemore, Mary Ann McRae, and other journalists and representatives of the media for their vivid interest and sincere support. Lastly, we are particularly grateful to all the scholars who participated in and contributed to this symposium on the resurrection of Jesus, as well as to John Wilkins, who accompanied all our proceedings with the skill of a great journalist.

As world history moves towards the third millennium, we offer the proceedings of this interdisciplinary and international symposium to all interested readers. May the volume offer them some little help towards understanding the resurrection of the crucified Jesus, which initiated the story of Christianity.

STEPHEN T. DAVIS, DANIEL KENDALL, SJ, and GERALD O'COLLINS, SJ

26 May 1996

Contents

Abbreviations   xv

Participants in the Resurrection Summit
(Easter 1996, New York)   xviii

1 A Summit Observed   1
   JOHN WILKINS

2 The Resurrection: The State of the Questions   5
   GERALD O'COLLINS, SJ
   Response: PETER F. CARNLEY   29

3 Resurrection and the New Jerusalem   41
   JANET MARTIN SOSKICE

4 Resurrection as Glory: Divine Presence and   59
   Christian Origins
   CAREY C. NEWMAN

5 Life after Death: The Social Sources   90
   ALAN F. SEGAL

6 'Seeing' the Risen Jesus   126
   STEPHEN T. DAVIS

7 Biblical Criticism and the Resurrection   148
   WILLIAM P. ALSTON
   Response: SARAH COAKLEY   184

8 Evidence for the Resurrection   191
   RICHARD SWINBURNE

9 The Resurrection of Jesus and Roman Catholic
   Fundamental Theology   213
   FRANCIS SCHÜSSLER FIORENZA

xiv   *Contents*

10 John Dominic Crossan on the Resurrection of Jesus   249
WILLIAM LANE CRAIG
Response: PAUL RHODES EDDY   272

11 Advice for Religious Historians: On the Myth of a Purely
Historical Jesus   287
ALAN G. PADGETT

12 The Preaching of the Resurrection of Christ in
Augustine, Luther, Barth, and Thielicke   308
MARGUERITE SHUSTER

13 Transformation Ethics: The Moral Implications of the
Resurrection   339
BRIAN V. JOHNSTONE, CSsR

Index of Names   361

Abbreviations

ABD	*Anchor Bible Dictionary*
ANF	Ante-Nicene Fathers
AnBib	Analecta biblica
BBM	Baker Biblical Monograph
BETL	Bibliotheca ephemeridum theologicarum lovaniensium
BK	Biblischer Kommentar: Altes Testament
BNTC	Black's New Testament Commentaries
BzTAT	Beiträge zur Theologie des Alten Testaments
CBQ	*Catholic Biblical Quarterly*
CBQMS	Catholic Biblical Quarterly—Monograph Series
CGTC	Cambridge Greek Testament Commentary
EHS	Europäische Hochschulschriften
FOTL	The Forms of the Old Testament Literature
GLB	De Gruyter Lehrbuch
GP	Gospel Perspectives
H/BNTC	Harper's/Black's New Testament Commentaries
HSM	Harvard Semitic Monographs
ICC	International Critical Commentary
IEJ	*Israel Exploration Journal*
Inter	*Interpretation*
JAAR	*Journal of the American Academy of Religion*
JAARS	Journal of the American Academy of Religion Studies
JBL	*Journal of Biblical Literature*
JR	*Journal of Religion*
JSNTSS	Journal for the Study of the New Testament—Supplement Series
JSOT	*Journal for the Study of the Old Testament*
JSOTSS	Journal for the Study of the Old Testament—Supplement Series

KD	*Kerygma und Dogma*
LEC	Library of Early Christianity
LThK	*Lexikon für Theologie und Kirsche*
LXX	Septuagint
MT	Masoretic Text
NASB	New American Standard Bible
NCBC	New Century Bible Commentary
NICNT	New International Commentary on the New Testament
NIGTC	New International Greek Testament Commentary
NovTSupp	Novum Testamentum, Supplements
NPNF	Nicene and Post-Nicene Fathers
NRSV	New Revised Standard Version
NT	New Testament
NTL	New Testament Library
NTS	*New Testament Studies*
NTTS	New Testament Tools and Studies
OT	Old Testament
OTL	Old Testament Library
QD	Questiones disputatae
RSV	Revised Standard Version
SBLASP	Society of Biblical Literature Abstracts and Seminar Papers
SBLMS	Society of Biblical Literature Monograph Series
SBT	Studies in Biblical Theology
SJLA	Studies in Judaism in Late Antiquity
SNTSMS	Society for New Testament Studies Monograph Series
SPSH	Scholar Press—Studies in the Humanities Series
ST	*Summa theologiae*
SUNT	Studien zur Umwelt des Neuen Testaments
SVTP	Studia in Veteris Testamenti pseudepigrapha
TDNT	*Theological Dictionary of the New Testament*
TNTC	Tyndale New Testament Commentaries
TRE	*Theologische Realenzyklopädie*
USQR	*Union Seminary Quarterly Review*
WBC	Word Biblical Commentary
WMANT	Wissenschaftliche Monographien zum Alten und Neuen Testament

WUNT	Wissenschaftliche Untersuchungen zum Neuen Testament
ZAW	*Zeitschrift für die alttestamentliche Wissenschaft*
ZTK	*Zeitschrift für Theologie und Kirsche*

Participants in the Resurrection Summit
(Easter 1996, New York)

WILLIAM P. ALSTON Born in Shreveport, Louisiana, he earned his Bachelor's degree from Centenary College of Louisiana and his Ph.D. from the University of Chicago in 1951. Currently he is Professor of Philosophy at Syracuse University. Recent books by him include *The Reliability of Sense Perception* (1993), *Perceiving God: The Epistemology of Religious Experience* (1991), *Epistemic Justification* (1989), *Divine Nature and Human Language* (1989), and another book scheduled to appear in 1996, *A Realist Conception of Truth*, all published by Cornell University Press.

PETER F. CARNLEY Born in New Lambton, New South Wales, he obtained degrees at Trinity College (Melbourne University) and St John's College, Cambridge. Since 1981 he has been the Anglican Archbishop of Perth and Metropolitan of the Province of Western Australia. Publications by him include 'The Poverty of Historical Scepticism', in *Christ, Faith and History* (Cambridge: Cambridge University Press, 1972), and *The Structure of Resurrection Belief* (Oxford: Clarendon, 1987, 1993).

SARAH COAKLEY Born in London, she obtained her undergraduate degree (1973) as well as her graduate degree (1982) from the University of Cambridge. Currently she is Edward Mallinckrodt, jun., Professor of Divinity at Harvard University. Writings by her include *Christ without Absolutes: A Study of the Christology of Ernst Troeltsch* (Oxford: Oxford University Press, 1988); 'Why Three? Some Further Reflections on the Doctrine of the Trinity', in S. Coakley and D. Pailin (eds.), *The Making and Remaking of Christian Doctrine: Essays in Honour of Maurice Wiles* (Oxford: Clarendon, 1993), 29–56, and S. Coakley (ed.), *Religion and the Body* (Cambridge: Cambridge University Press, 1997).

M. SHAWN COPELAND Born in Detroit, Michigan, she obtained her Bachelor's degree in 1969 from Madonna College (Livonia, Mich.)

and her Ph.D. from Boston College in 1991. She currently teaches theology at Marquette University. Publications by her include (with Elisabeth Schüssler Fiorenza) *Violence Against Women* (London: SCM, 1994); she co-edits the Feminist Theology series for *Concilium*; and is currently preparing a manuscript entitled 'Suffering, Solidarity, and the Cross'.

WILLIAM LANE CRAIG Born in Peoria, Illinois, he obtained his Bachelor's degree in 1971 from Wheaton College, his Ph.D. from the University of Birmingham in 1977, and his D.Theol. from Ludwig-Maximilians-Universität Munich in 1984. Currently he is Visiting Professor at Talbot School of Theology (California). Books by him include *Reasonable Faith: Christian Truth and Apologetics* (Wheaton, Ill.: Crossway Books, 1994), *Assessing the New Testament Evidence for the Historicity of the Resurrection of Jesus* (Lewiston, NY: Mellen, 1989), and *The Historical Argument for the Resurrection of Jesus* (Lewiston, NY: Mellen, 1984).

STEPHEN T. DAVIS Born in Lincoln, Nebraska, he obtained his Bachelor's degree from Whitworth College in 1962, his M.Div. from Princeton Theological Seminary, and his Ph.D. from the Claremont Graduate School in Philosophy in 1970. Currently he is Professor of Philosophy and Religion at Claremont McKenna College. Books by him include *Risen Indeed: Making Sense of the Resurrection* (Grand Rapids, Mich.: Eerdmans, 1993), *Death and Afterlife* (New York: St Martin's Press, 1989), and *Encountering Jesus* (Atlanta: John Knox Press, 1988).

PAUL RHODES EDDY Born in Minneapolis, he obtained his Bachelor's degree from Bethel College in St Paul. Currently he is a Ph.D. candidate at Marquette University and Instructor of Theology at Bethel College and Theological Seminary. His publications include 'Jesus as Diogenes? Reflections on the Cynic Jesus Thesis', *JBL* 115 (1996), 449–69; 'Religious Pluralism and the Divine: Another Look at John Hick's Neo-Kantian Proposal', *Religious Studies*, 30 (1994), 467–78; and he is co-editor and a contributor to *Directions in New Testament Methods* (Milwaukee: Marquette University Press, 1993).

FRANCIS SCHÜSSLER FIORENZA Born in Brooklyn, New York, he obtained his undergraduate degree at St Mary's Seminary in Baltimore in 1961, and his D.Theol. from the University of Münster in 1972. Currently he is the Charles Chauncey Stillman Professor of Roman Catholic Studies at Harvard University. Books by him include *Handbook of Catholic Theology* (New York: Crossroad, 1995), (with Don Browning) *Habermas, Modernity, Public Theology* (New York: Crossroad, 1992), (with J. Galvin) *Systematic Theology: Roman Catholic Perspectives* (Minneapolis: Fortress, 1991), and *Foundational Theology: Jesus and the Church* (New York: Crossroad, 1984).

BRIAN V. JOHNSTONE Born in Melbourne, Australia, he earned a doctorate in theology (Leuven, 1973). Since then he has taught Moral Theology at Melbourne College of Divinity, Catholic University of America, Fordham University, and the Gregorian University (Rome). Currently he is Professor of Moral Theology at the Alfonsian Academy (Rome). He has published many articles on moral-theological topics, such as 'Eschatology and Ethics', 'Ethical Theory', 'Just War Doctrine', 'Bioethics', and 'Conscience'.

DANIEL KENDALL Born in Miami, Arizona, he obtained his undergraduate degree at Santa Clara University in 1961 and his STD from the Gregorian University in Rome. Currently he teaches theology at the University of San Francisco. Publications by him include (all with Gerald O'Collins) 'On Not Neglecting Hatred', *Scottish Journal of Theology*, 47 (1994), 511–18, 'On Reissuing Venturini', *Gregorianum*, 75 (1994), 241–65, 'Did Joseph of Arimathea Exist?', *Biblica*, 75 (1994), 235–41.

CAREY C. NEWMAN Born in Florida, he earned his undergraduate degree at the University of South Florida in 1980 and his Ph.D. from Baylor University in 1989. Currently he teaches New Testament at the Southern Baptist Theological Seminary in Louisville, Kentucky. Recent publications by him include 'Acts' (in *A Complete Literary Guide to the Bible* (Grand Rapids, Mich.: Zondervan, 1993)), *Paul's Glory-Christology* (Leiden: Brill, 1992), and 'Transforming Images of Paul', *Evangelical Quarterly*, 64 (1992), 61–74.

GERALD G. O'COLLINS Born in Melbourne, Victoria, he obtained his undergraduate degree at the University of Melbourne in 1957 and his Ph.D. from Cambridge University in 1968. Currently he teaches theology at the Pontifical Gregorian University in Rome. Publications by him include *Christology* (Oxford: Oxford University Press, 1995), *The Resurrection of Jesus Christ* (Milwaukee: Marquette University Press, 1993), and *Retrieving Fundamental Theology* (Mahwah, NJ: Paulist, 1993).

ALAN G. PADGETT Born in Washington, DC, he earned his BA from Southern California College (1977), an M.Div. from Drew University

(1981), and a D.Phil. from Oxford University (1990). Currently he is Professor of Theology and Philosophy of Science at Azusa Pacific University (California). Books by him include *God, Eternity and the Nature of Time* (London: Macmillan, 1992) and in the role of editor, *Reason and the Christian Religion: Essays in Honour of Richard Swinburne* (Oxford: Oxford University Press, 1994), in addition to several articles in *New Testament Studies*.

PHEME PERKINS Born in Louisville, Kentucky, she obtained her Bachelor's degree from St John's (Annapolis) in 1966 and her Ph.D. from Harvard University in 1971. Currently she teaches theology at Boston College. Recent publications include *First and Second Peter, James, and Jude* (Atlanta: John Knox Press, 1995), *Peter: Apostle for the Whole Church* (University of South Carolina Press, 1994), and *Gnosticism and the New Testament* (Minneapolis: Fortress, 1993).

ALAN F. SEGAL Born in Worcester, Massachusetts, he earned his Bachelor's degree at Amherst College in 1967 and his Ph.D. at Yale University in 1975. Currently he is Professor of Religion at Barnard College, Columbia University. Publications by him include *The Messiah: Developments in Earliest Judaism and Christianity* (Minneapolis: Fortress, 1992), *Paul the Convert: The Apostleship and Apostasy of Saul the Pharisee* (New Haven: Yale University Press, 1990), and *Rebecca's Children* (Cambridge, Mass.: Harvard University Press, 1988).

MARGUERITE SHUSTER Born in Santa Paula, California, she obtained her Bachelor's degree at Stanford in 1968 and her Ph.D. from the Fuller Graduate School of Psychology in 1977. Currently she teaches Preaching at Fuller Theological Seminary. Her writings include (co-edited) *Perspectives on Christology: Essays in Honor of Paul K. Jewett* (Grand Rapids, Mich.: Zondervan, 1991), doctrinal sermons in *God, Creation, and Revelation* (Grand Rapids, Mich.: Eerdmans, 1991), *Power, Pathology, Paradox: The Dynamics of Evil and Good* (Grand Rapids, Mich.: Zondervan, 1987), and she is editor of *Who We Are: Our Dignity as Human* (Grand Rapids, Mich.: Eerdmans, 1996).

JANET MARTIN SOSKICE Born in Vancouver, British Columbia, she earned her Bachelor's degree at Cornell University in 1973 and her Ph.D. from Oxford University in 1982. Currently she is a University Lecturer in the Faculty of Divinity, University of Cambridge, and a Fellow of Jesus College. Publications by her include (with K. W. M.

Fulford and Grant R. Gillett) *Medicine and Moral Reasoning* (Cambridge: Cambridge University Press, 1994), and *Metaphor and Religious Language* (Oxford: Oxford University Press, 1985), and she is editor of *After Eve* (London: Marshall Pickering, 1990).

RICHARD SWINBURNE Born in Smethwick, England, he obtained his Bachelor's degree from Exeter College, Oxford, in 1957 and his M.A. (Oxon.) in 1961. Currently he is Nolloth Professor of the Philosophy of the Christian Religion at Oxford University. His publications include *Is There a God?* (1996), *The Christian God* (1994), and *The Coherence of Theism* (1993), all published by Oxford University Press.

JOHN WILKINS Born in Cheltenham, England, he obtained his BA degree in Classics and Theology from Cambridge University in 1961. Since 1982 he has been editor of the international Catholic weekly *The Tablet* of London. Books he has edited include *Understanding Veritatis Splendor* (London: SPCK, 1994).

Note: Shawn Copeland, Daniel Kendall, and Pheme Perkins were all active and valuable participants in the Resurrection Summit, but this volume does not include contributions from them.

1

A Summit Observed

JOHN WILKINS

'I would much rather be sitting in my study, working on my next book', said Dr Stephen Davis to the American media at the press conference that concluded the Resurrection Summit, 'than talking to you guys.' But for good or ill, the speculations of the analytical philosophers, biblical theologians, and exegetes are out in the open, and the debates are going on in public.

As an English observer at the summit, held in the archdiocesan seminary of New York from 7 to 11 April 1996, I was astonished to find that all three main-line American weeklies had cover stories on Jesus during that Easter week. *Time* and *US News and World Report* focused on the Jesus Seminar, a group of seventy-five biblical scholars who have popularized their work by their method of voting on the authenticity of Gospel material: a red bead for what sounds to them 'Definitely like Jesus', a pink bead for 'May well be', a grey for 'Doubtful', and a black for 'Definitely not'. The seminar, as scholars at the Resurrection Summit pointed out, uses criteria which are biased towards a negative verdict, so that their version of the Gospels in appropriate shades is coloured mainly black.

Contemplating the controversial results, not a few Christians will agree with Kenneth Woodward, religion editor of *Newsweek*, who wrote in that week's issue that 'after 150 years of scholarly search, there are signs that the quest for the "historical" Jesus has reached a dead end'. For, Woodward went on, 'truth is not always historical, and what seems warranted by historical evidence, does not always turn out to be true'. That implies a caution for anyone who trusts too exclusively in the method of biblical criticism. Some of the papers discussed at the summit argued doughtily and usefully that the early Christians had supplied very good evidence of the truth of what they believed. Nevertheless, their authors were warned during the discussions by one of their number, Francis Schüssler

Fiorenza, Professor of Roman Catholic Theology at Harvard. 'Beware,' he said. 'You may be more like your opponents than you admit.'

Schüssler Fiorenza had his own project: to revalidate testimony. A former pupil of Karl Rahner, he noted how his teacher had sought to uncover the transcendent in the unlimited human drive of willing and knowing. Similarly with testimony, Schüssler Fiorenza suggested. At the deepest level, those who give it uncover the truth of their being to another. One conclusion I drew was that in judging New Testament testimony, one should remember what sort of witness this is before suggesting that it might just be made up as convenient corroborative fiction.

The divisions between the participants in the Resurrection Summit discussions were not between those who thought the resurrection 'happened' and those who did not. Rather, they tended to be between the philosophers of religion and the biblical exegetes. Sometimes I found that I leant to one side, sometimes to the other, so in my case the dividing line went down the middle of myself. For example, I was struck by the postscript which Professor Richard Swinburne, Nolloth Professor of the Philosophy of Christian Religion at Oxford, added to his paper. In it he drew attention to the simple historical fact that from the beginning, everywhere, the Eucharist was celebrated on a Sunday, clear evidence that the early Christians knew that the foundation of their faith lay in a tremendous happening on that day. I thought he had 'seen' something, and the persuasiveness of it remained with me, despite criticism from exegetes during the discussion on the grounds that the Eucharistic formula is already in any case present in St Paul's first letter to the Corinthians.

On the other hand, I was less convinced when Stephen Davis, also a philosopher, argued that if one of the witnesses of the resurrection appearances had had a camera, the risen Christ could have been caught on film. The eye of faith is not a camera's eye, the exegetes objected during the discussion, and this time I felt the balance lay with them. But Davis, of Claremont McKenna College (California), responded with a little sermon from the heart about the suffering and failure in the world which only a full resurrection of the body could overcome: that was itself, in its own way, testimony.

Those present at the summit included Catholics, Baptists, Methodists, Anglicans, and Presbyterians, an Orthodox and a Jew.

I doubt whether in England, despite Christian–Jewish dialogue being well advanced, any Jewish participant could have joined a Christian group with the same ease and assurance as did Professor Alan Segal of Barnard College, New York. It was he who pointed out to us that the Jesus Seminar had succeeded in coming up with a non-Jewish Jesus, a cynic philosopher who would have been at home in the market-place of ancient Athens, whereas other biblical scholars are now agreed—it is the only thing they agree on—that Jesus can be understood only against the Jewish background from which he came and within which he moved and ministered. The Jesus Seminar had confused the man with the audiences to which he was preached, Professor Segal said.

It was also he who pointed out where the real scandal of the resurrection lay. The claim that Jesus had risen would not necessarily have brought about a parting of the ways between Jews and Christians. Enoch and Elijah, for example, had both, according to the biblical account, been caught up into heaven because they were too holy for death to overcome them. Rather, it was the Christian claim that this man who had been executed as a criminal was God, and that his suffering and death told us something new about God—that was the scandal.

In the hall of St Joseph's Seminary where we met, there is a superb copy of the *Pietà* by Michelangelo that stands in St Peter's in Rome. To mark the Easter season, lilies had been placed in front of it. During a break, as I gazed at the depiction of Mary cradling her dead son in her arms, it was as though in the light of Segal's comments I was seeing it for the first time.

The Resurrection Summit, as the essays in this book show, was concerned to do much more than simply offer a riposte to the reductionist conclusions of the Jesus Seminar. Indeed, what originally motivated the co-chairmen, Father Gerald O'Collins, SJ, of the Gregorian University in Rome and Stephen Davis, to plan the summit was their conviction that the full impact of the resurrection had still not been realized in Christian life and ethics. The paper by Janet Martin Soskice of Cambridge University on the corporate dimension of resurrection doctrine, for example, introduced a consideration that American participants agreed was difficult to bring home to their individualist students.

For me as a layman, one of the most suggestive of all the papers was that by Father Brian Johnstone, a Redemptorist priest from

Rome, on the resurrection and ethics. Christian ethical reflection has been based more on natural law, the Ten Commandments, and the theology of the cross. For Johnstone, the impact of a resurrection ethic will be above all in opposition to the view that conflict is the ultimate truth in human affairs, and that violence—nowadays idolized in Western cinema—is the determining characteristic of the human animal.

Here, then, is yet another book on the resurrection. But the story is ever new. We shall never get to the end of telling it.

2

The Resurrection: The State of the Questions

GERALD O'COLLINS, SJ

What is worth asking, knowing, and believing about the resurrection of Jesus? What issues call for particular mention here? Where should attention to the resurrection focus in the closing years of the second millennium? This essay will first reflect on certain present concerns, and then propose some agenda for the future. Four terms gather together many persistent concerns that remain current: the primary claim, the appearances, the empty tomb, and credibility. Let me take them up in turn.

I

(1) *The Proclamation*

What do the authors of the New Testament and subsequent Christians primarily mean by their claim that God raised Jesus from the dead, or that Jesus rose from the dead?[1] One could put together the main-line responses from the New Testament and the post-New Testament tradition as follows: after his crucifixion and burial, through a special divine action[2] that set the ultimate seal of approval on his life and work, Jesus was personally delivered from the state of death; with his earthly body transformed and taken up into a glorified existence, he initiated the end of all things for all human beings and their world. The post-resurrection appearances

---

[1] A prior question is, of course: what did the pre-Easter Jesus understand by resurrection in general (e.g. Mark 12: 18–27) and by the resurrection he expected for himself (accepting a historical nucleus for Mark 8: 31; 9: 31; 10: 34)?

[2] 'Special divine action' is a modern, rather than a biblical, notion. The Scriptures draw no distinction between common divine activity (in upholding and working through the general laws of nature) and special divine acts (manifested e.g. in the miraculous).

(with the mission which they entailed and the new life of the Holy Spirit which they brought) showed how Jesus' resurrection was not only primarily 'for him' (*pro se*) but also secondarily 'for us' (*pro nobis*). This version of the basic Easter claim has often been disputed, both explicitly and implicitly, both in part and in whole.

In his *Metaphor of God Incarnate* we find John Hick slipping from an appropriate question about why the first disciples believed in Jesus as risen from the dead ('what . . . caused the first disciples to believe, after Jesus' crucifixion, that he was now alive as their exalted and glorified Lord?') to a thoroughly dubious equation of their 'experience' with 'the original resurrection event' itself.[3] Hick begs the question here by quietly identifying (i) the experiences that caused the first disciples to know and believe something new after Jesus' crucifixion (= why they believed) with (ii) what they claimed had happened to Jesus himself in 'the original resurrection event' (= what they believed). Why they believed guides us in establishing what they believed and, eventually, in establishing what had happened to Jesus himself. Nevertheless, *why* they believed and claimed all that they did should not be equated with *what* they believed had happened to Jesus himself in 'the original resurrection event': his transformation to new life as their resurrected and glorified Lord. Hick's identification of why they believed (and the changes they underwent) with what they believed is by no means unknown in resurrection literature.[4]

Such revisionist accounts of resurrection language and the primary Easter claim are also developed quite explicitly, above all by those who 'explain' it as amounting to a claim that Jesus rose only 'in the mind and hearts' or 'lives and dreams' of his followers. Thus Sallie McFague assures her readers that what 'really happened' in Jesus' resurrection was 'the awareness of his continuing presence and empowerment. . . . The resurrection is a way of speaking about an awareness that the presence of God in Jesus is a permanent presence in our midst.' This version of the New Testament's talk of

---

[3] J. Hick, *The Metaphor of God Incarnate*, (London: SCM, 1993), 24.

[4] See e.g. Erich Seeberg, who interpreted the resurrection as nothing more than 'the first appearance of Christ' to Peter: 'Wer war Petrus', *Zeitschrift für Kirchengeschichte*, 53 (1934), 571–84, at 581. To put this in terms of Luke 24: 34 ((a) 'the Lord has risen indeed', (b) 'and has appeared to Simon'), Seeberg reduced statement (a) (*what* they believed) to statement (b) (*why* they believed). Like others, he also reduced the post-resurrection appearances to the Petrine one, and hence made (b) read: 'he appeared only to Simon'.

Jesus' resurrection turns it first of all into a claim about the disciples' new consciousness. Three words emerge as central here: 'awareness', 'presence', and 'empowerment'. The disciples became aware, not that Jesus himself had been delivered from death and was living a new glorious existence, but that the divine presence in Jesus was/is 'a permanent presence in our midst'.[5] An end-note (p. 199 n. 2) makes it even clearer that 'the resurrection of Jesus' is merely 'an expression of God's presence in all space and time'. Talk of Jesus' resurrection simply helps us to 'an understanding of creation' and the divine presence in creation; it adds no fresh assertion about what 'really happened' to Jesus himself. At McFague's hands, the second article of the Creed makes no advance over the first: Christological belief adds nothing to belief about God's creation. Another end-note (p. 199 n. 1) explains how the disciples' new consciousness of the divine presence included their 'empowerment': 'the meaning of the resurrection' is their *continuing empowerment* by God (her italics).

McFague quotes the late Norman Perrin[6] to describe what this empowerment 'actually' entailed 'according to the evangelists': 'it became possible to *know* Jesus as ultimacy in the historicity of everyday (Mark), . . . it became possible to *live* the life of a Christian within the church (Matthew), . . . it became possible to *imitate* Jesus in the meaningful life in the world (Luke)', (p. 199 n. 1; my italics). One might very well wonder what on earth Perrin's conclusion about Mark could have meant, why he did not express himself more clearly, and how someone years later could quote sympathetically this statement from him. At all events, one thing comes through clearly. For McFague, talk of Jesus' resurrection was and is only talk of a new possibility for the disciples: they could now (in another, fresh way) know and imitate Jesus, and so live a Christian life in the

---

[5] S. McFague, *Models of God: Theology for an Ecological, Nuclear Age* (Philadelphia/London: Fortress/SCM, 1987), 59. In 'A Naked Pillar of Rock', Maurice Wiles suggests several 'constructive' possibilities for 'a theological treatment of resurrection' which move away from 'more traditional Christian affirmation': in S. Barton and G. Stanton (eds.), *Resurrection: Essays in Honour of Leslie Houlden* (London: SPCK, 1994), 116–27, at 124–5. But the more basic question is: do these possibilities move away from, and seriously distort, what the NT witnesses claimed about the fate of Jesus himself? Is Wiles making the Easter texts from the NT writers 'mean' what he wishes they would have said?

[6] N. Perrin, *The Resurrection Narratives. A New Approach* (London: SCM, 1977), 81; in the USA this work was published with the clearer title of *The Resurrection according to Matthew, Mark, and Luke* (Philadelphia: Fortress, 1977).

Church. Like the awareness of the divine presence in all creation, this new and continuing 'empowerment' brought change only on the side of the disciples, and no change for the dead Jesus himself. McFague proposes that 'to be a Christian is to be persuaded that there is a personal, gracious power [lower case!] who is on the side of life and its fulfillment, a power whom the paradigmatic figure of Jesus of Nazareth expresses and illuminates' (p. 192 n. 37). Despite the fact that he expresses and illuminates paradigmatically this 'power', 'it' does not seem to have been very gracious towards Jesus, and certainly not on the side of his 'life and fulfillment' if for Jesus no resurrection followed his crucifixion.

In eliminating any reference to the personal fate of Jesus, McFague has made the Easter texts say what she wishes they had said. There are at least two points to be raised here. First, in speaking of the resurrection, the New Testament used a variety of idioms to refer to what had happened to Jesus himself: kerygmatic and confessional formulas (e.g. 1 Cor. 15: 3–5), hymns (e.g. Phil. 2: 6–11), Easter narratives (the closing chapters of the Gospels and Acts 1: 1–11), a new attribute for God (e.g. Gal. 1: 1), missionary speeches (e.g. Peter's discourses in Acts), reflective theological argument (e.g. 1 Cor. 15: 12–57), and the language of heavenly vindication (e.g. Mark 14: 62).[7] As Stephen Davis has insisted, any revisionist theory that takes all this variegated language to have referred only to changes in the disciples turns the New Testament writers into either 'obtuse communicators', who were unable to express their intended meaning, or 'deceptive communicators, who intentionally hid their intended meaning behind the words they used'.[8]

Second, the freedom that McFague and others allow themselves in 'explaining' what the New Testament writers wanted to express by their resurrection claims is self-destructing. Readers of such modern, revisionist works are entitled to take the same liberty in exegeting *these* texts: 'McFague appears to be speaking of the first disciples' new awareness and empowerment at the origins of Christianity but *really* she is talking only of current developments in the community where she worships.' If she deals with the New Testament authors with great—even total—reader freedom, surely those who read *Models of God* can in their turn rightly use the same freedom

---

[7] See G. O'Collins, *Christology* (Oxford: Oxford University Press, 1995), 87–90.
[8] S. Davis, *Risen Indeed: Making Sense of the Resurrection* (London: SPCK, 1993), 40.

in 'exegeting' her book. In the post-Bultmannian era Willi Marxsen has proved to be the most notable and challenging revisionist. He 'explains' the resurrection as meaning not that Jesus himself continues in a new, transformed existence, but that the 'cause of Jesus continues'.[9] There is more than an echo of Marxsen's view when McFague remarks that 'Jesus' story . . . continues' (p. 59). Against Marxsen, McFague, and others, it has long been necessary to insist that the primary Easter claim coming from the New Testament witnesses was that Jesus himself continues in a new and glorious existence. These witnesses reported two major (but not exclusive) signs attesting his resurrection: his appearances and his empty tomb.

(2) *The Appearances*

Apropos of the post-resurrection appearances, many issues press for attention. Does my suggestion about 'graced seeing', challenged by Stephen Davis, deserve defence and development?[10] To what extent were the witnesses' powers of perception enhanced by God in a special way? If grace built on nature (= their natural powers of perception), do we place the emphasis here on grace or on nature? Where do we place our emphasis as regards the object they saw: the *risen* body of Christ or the risen *body* of Christ? The former choice emphasizes the element of transformation, the latter that of the material object seen. What of the distinction made by William Craig in clarifying the Easter encounters, when he contrasts the post-resurrection 'appearances of Christ' (which involve 'extra-mental phenomena') with 'visions' (which, even in the case of 'veridical visions sent by God, are exclusively mental phenomena')?[11]

In dialogue with Reginald Fuller, Hans Kessler, and Pheme Perkins, I have argued that the Easter appearances were episodes of revelation that called the recipients to faith through a distinctive experience, which corresponded to their special and non-transferable mission in becoming with Christ founders of the Church, and which involved something visually perceptible.[12] All the items in this

---

[9] See W. Marxsen, *The Resurrection of Jesus of Nazareth* (Philadelphia/London: Fortress/SCM, 1970); on his interpretation see G. O'Collins, *Jesus Risen* (London: Darton, Longman & Todd, 1987), 62-6.

[10] O'Collins, *Jesus Risen*, 11-12, 118-21; Davis, *Risen Indeed*, 23-4.

[11] W. L. Craig, *Assessing the New Testament Evidence for the Historicity of the Resurrection of Jesus* (Lewiston, NY: Mellen, 1989), 68 n. 29.

[12] G. O'Collins, *Interpreting the Resurrection* (Mahwah, NJ: Paulist, 1988), 5-21.

description merit lengthy, full treatment. So too does the initial work that Daniel Kendall and I published on Mary Magdalene and her significance as Easter witness.[13] Here, however, I want to examine a further point, one that recurs in discussions of the appearances: 'the generalizing habit inculcated by the scientific world-view', which takes offence at any assertions of 'special' or once-and-for-all experiences and events. This world-view waters down such claims by generalizing them.[14] This comment from Walker Percy about the way the Christian story as a whole scandalizes the modern mind fits nicely the particular case of the post-resurrection appearances.

In his *The Metaphor of God Incarnate* John Hick tries to tame the specialness of the Easter appearances by generalizing them. The experiences of Peter, Mary Magdalene, Paul, and others could have been 'waking versions' of the near-death experiences which Raymond Moody and other recent authors have reported—experiences of bright light or of a brightly shining figure who is often identified as Christ by Christians who have gone through such experiences (p. 24). A few pages later Hick attempts to generalize the post-resurrection appearances by introducing another (alleged) parallel, but one of a very different kind: bereavement sequences of widows, widowers, and others who have lost their dear ones. He suggests the following reconstruction: 'during the days and weeks after his death', Jesus may have proved vividly present, as is widely reported of recently dead persons who are experienced as 'invisibly present' to comfort, guide, or challenge the living (p. 38). In short, we meet here yet another attempt to generalize away anything truly special and particular about the Easter appearances—by invoking two kinds of experiences that repeatedly recur and have been 'scientifically' studied.[15]

---

[13] 'Mary Magdalene as Major Witness to Jesus' Resurrection', *Theological Studies*, 48 (1987), 631–46; repr. in my *Interpreting the Resurrection*, 22–38. Mention of Mary Magdalene raises the issue of the post-resurrection appearance to Peter (1 Cor. 15: 5; Luke 24: 34) and its significance; on this see also the doctoral dissertation of W. T. Kessler, 'Peter as the First Witness of the Risen Lord: An Historical and Theological Investigation', defended at the Gregorian University, 19 Jan. 1995.

[14] J. Tolson, *Pilgrim in the Ruins: A Life of Walker Percy* (New York: Simon and Schuster, 1992), 473.

[15] In *Religious Experiences* (Berkeley: University of California Press, 1985) Wayne Proudfoot develops a distinction that bears on this scientific world-view: the distinction between descriptive and explanatory reductionism. Descriptive reductionism will not accept accounts of religious experiences coming from the subjects of those experiences. Explanatory reductionism (which we see exemplified in the writings of Hick, McFague, and others) purports to accept the subjects' accounts of their experiences,

There are specific objections to this attempt. Conjecturing that the Easter encounters were 'waking versions' of near-death experiences seems like appropriating to the issue in hand 'data' from a very different context. The whole point in reports of near-death experiences is that the reports come from people who were revived after being clinically dead—something which is certainly not the case with Peter, Paul, Mary Magdalene, and the other original Easter witnesses.[16] Furthermore, the post-resurrection appearances to the eleven (for which the New Testament supplies multiple attestation) and to more than 500 believers (reported in 1 Cor. 15: 6) obviously cannot be illuminated by Hick's analogy. Near-death experiences are attributed to individuals, not groups. Hick's second parallel, which is drawn from the deeply felt presence of loved ones who have recently died, may seem more plausible. It is obviously worth examining scientific reports and evaluations of such experiences. But Hick ignores here two massive items in the story of Jesus and his disciples' grieving process. Unlike the spouse who leaves behind a grieving partner, the pre-Easter Jesus made extraordinary claims to personal authority, which many scholars understand as equivalent to putting his authority on a par with God's. Then he died by crucifixion, a death reckoned to be utterly shameful before God and human beings.[17] In this case the beloved person suffered a totally

but either misinterprets what is reported (by claiming e.g. that the Easter witnesses were simply talking of their own new consciousness) or else offers a causal explanation that is different from the subjects' own (by claiming e.g. that these witnesses were going through a bereavement sequence or suffering from 'cognitive dissonance', which adequately explains everything we need to know about their experiences). See Michael Goulder's psychological version of such 'explanatory reductionism': 'Did Jesus of Nazareth Rise from the Dead?', in Barton and Stanton (eds.), *Resurrection*, 58–68. As Wolfhart Pannenberg remarked years ago, such psychological 'explanations', when carefully scrutinized, turn out to be implausible precisely in psychological terms: *Jesus—God and Man*, trans. L. L. Wilkins and D. A. Priebe (London: SCM, 1968), 95–8.

[16] In *The Unfinished Gospel: Notes on the Quest for the Historical Jesus* (Westlake Village, Calif.: Symposium Books, 1994) Evan Powell uses various traits of near-death experiences to speculate that Jesus himself survived crucifixion (pp. 323–37). Thus Christianity began with a near-death experience! On differing theories about Jesus surviving his crucifixion see G. O'Collins and D. Kendall, 'On Reissuing Venturini', *Gregorianum*, 75 (1994), 241–65; repr. in O'Collins and Kendall, *Focus on Jesus* (Leominster: Gracewing, 1996), 153–75.

[17] In 'The Resurrection of Jesus of Nazareth', in B. Chilton and C. A. Evans (eds.), *Studying the Historical Jesus* (Leiden: Brill, 1994), 423–42, Pheme Perkins questions 'the assumption that Jesus' execution would have automatically been considered shameful. Jesus' death is no more disgraceful than that of John the Baptist' (p. 439; see also p. 431 n. 41). But evidence from Roman sources, in particular, suggests that

humiliating and disgraceful death by public execution. That, as
Paul emphasized in 1 Corinthians and Galatians, makes a huge difference to the religious perception of Jesus' passing from this world.
In short, the prior claims coming from Jesus and the specific nature
of his death separate his case from 'normal' deaths and the bereavement sequences that follow for those who have lost their dear ones.

Quite apart from any specific objections to Hick's two purported
parallels to the post-resurrection appearances, there is an underlying problem. Hick wants to blunt the specialness of the first disciples' Easter experiences by subsuming them under general 'laws'
about near-death experiences and bereavement sequences. He
wants to explain (or explain away) these post-resurrection experiences in 'normal' human and religious terms. Others before him
have done likewise by attempting, for example, to subsume Paul's
Damascus Road encounter and other encounters with the risen
Lord under general 'laws' of mysticism.[18] In the case of Paul such
attempts have been legion: for instance, scientific knowledge of
epileptics and of ruthless persecutors suddenly hit by guilt feelings
are alleged to 'explain' what happened to Paul on the road to
Damascus. Walker Percy saw all this as a generalizing habit encouraged by the scientific world-view. Beneath this habit lies the deeply
rooted modern faith that for any occurrences, no matter how extraordinary or seemingly unique they may seem, it is in principle possible to find a scientific explanation to account for them and even
some very close analogies (for instance, in near-death experiences
and bereavement sequences).

Here I do not wish to go so far as to deny any analogy whatsoever between the first Easter experiences and other religious experiences. Christian mysticism, explored by William Alston in *Perceiving
God: The Epistemology of Religious Experience*[19] could, up to a point,
illuminate the epistemology of the post-resurrection encounters.[20]

---

crucifixion was considered much more shameful than decapitation; see my
'Crucifixion', in *ABD* i. 1207–10.

[18] On such attempts see the doctoral dissertation of Charles Kosanke, published
as *Encounters with the Risen Jesus in Luke–Acts* (Rome: Gregorian University Press,
1993), 5–13.

[19] (Ithaca, NY: Cornell University Press, 1991).

[20] Sandra Schneiders rightly warns that 'visionary encounters of the mystics with
Jesus' should not be taken as 'identical in kind or comparable in significance with
the Easter appearances': 'The Resurrection of Jesus and Christian Spirituality', in M.
Junker-Kenny (ed.), *Christian Resources of Hope* (Dublin: Columba, 1995), 81–114,
at 90–1. The point at issue here concerns possible analogies with the post-Easter

Yet, properly understood, analogy allows for what is unfamiliar and even unique, as Stephen Davis insists.[21] Just as the resurrection itself was in some ways strikingly unique, so too were the post-resurrection encounters. This means that accepting partial analogies to these encounters does not amount to explaining these encounters as largely, or even totally, similar to frequently repeated experiences which we can study 'scientifically'.[22]

(3) The Empty Tomb

The discovery of the empty tomb constituted the second major sign pointing to Jesus' resurrection from the dead. There are many issues to face here. Let me simply draw attention to two persistent challenges. Some writers have encouraged the impression that the historicity of the empty tomb enjoys scant credibility in the academic community. In a posthumous work Norman Perrin wrote as follows of scholarly opinion, presumably referring to those in biblical studies: 'Scholars are coming increasingly to the conclusion that the empty tomb tradition is an interpretation of the event—a way of saying "Jesus is risen!"—rather than a description of an aspect of the event itself.'[23] Three years earlier, in *On Being a Christian*, Hans Küng told his readers: although 'a number of influential exegetes even today [sic!] . . . hold that the empty tomb is historically probable', 'historical criticism has made the empty tomb a dubious fact'. Hence it is 'scarcely possible to refute the assumption [sic!] that the stories of the tomb are *legendary elaborations of a message of the resurrection*'.[24] Later, in his *Credo*, he repeated more or less the same claim: 'the majority of critical biblical exegetes . . . conclude that the stories about the tomb are legendary elaborations of the message of the resurrection'.[25]

appearances. For the event of Christ's resurrection itself and for the resurrection his followers expect, right from the time of St Paul (esp. in 1 Cor. 15), Christians have struggled to find analogies: see C. W. Bynum, *The Resurrection of the Body in Western Christianity, 200-1336* (New York: Columbia University Press, 1995), 'images of resurrection body' (pp. 351-2 in general index).

[21] Davis, *Risen Indeed*, 31.

[22] See D. Kendall and G. O'Collins, 'The Uniqueness of the Easter Appearances', *CBQ* 54 (1992), 287-307.

[23] Perrin, *Resurrection Narratives*, 82-3.

[24] Hans Küng, *On Being a Christian* (1974), trans. E. Quinn (London: Collins, 1977), 364-6; his italics.

[25] Hans Küng, *Credo* (London: SCM, 1993), 104-5.

But was, and is, this assertion about scholarly opinion true? In my *Jesus Risen* (p. 123) I listed thirty scholars (mainly exegetes) who, with greater or less intensity, maintain a historical nucleus in the empty tomb tradition, or at least do not argue that it was a legend created by Mark or by pre-Marcan tradition: I. Berten, J. Blank, J. Blinzler, R. E. Brown, H. von Campenhausen, J. Delorme, J. A. Fitzmyer, R. H. Fuller, W. Grundmann, J. Jeremias, W. Künneth, X. Léon-Dufour, C. M. Martini, C. F. D. Moule, J. Murphy-O'Connor, F. Mussner, W. Nauck, W. Pannenberg, K. H. Rengstorf, E. Rückstuhl, L. Schenke, J. Schmitt, K. Schubert, E. Schweizer, P. Seidensticker, A. Strobel, P. Stuhlmacher, W. Trilling, A. Vögtle, and U. Wilckens. To that list one might add such further exegetical names as P. Achtemeier, J. Gnilka, R. H. Gundry, M. Hooker, P. Perkins, R. Pesch, and C. Rowland.[26] Besides querying the accuracy of what Perrin and Küng report about academic trends, one can very well detect here the ongoing habit of some male writers of minimizing the testimony of the women.[27] By belittling the empty tomb tradition as a later elaboration, they devalue the witness of women; after all, women, and not men, were utterly central to the empty tomb tradition. In *On Being a Christian* Küng contrasts 'the women' with 'the disciples' as if—*pace* Matthew 28: 19; Mark 15: 41; Luke 8: 1–3; John, almost *passim*; Acts 6: 1, 2, 7; 11: 26; and other testimonies—the women did/do not count as 'disciples'. In the same place (p. 364) Küng also toys with the idea of reducing the 'witnesses' of the empty tomb to one woman, Mary Magdalene—something he has resolutely and rightly refused to do in the case of witnesses to the appearances: 'a reduction of all the appearances . . . to the one appearance to Peter, as if the former were merely to confirm the latter, is not justified' (pp. 348–9). A similar dismissal of women's testimony comes from a few like John Dominic Crossan, who also from the outset eliminates the empty tomb tradition by putting down as a Marcan invention the prior story of Jesus' burial at the hands of Joseph of Arimathea. The historicity of the burial story does not stand or fall with the women's testimony to it. But the historical reliability of the tradition of women subsequently discovering Jesus' tomb to be open and

---

[26] See F. Neirynck, 'Marc 16, 1–8 tradition et rédaction', *Ephemerides theologicae lovanienses*, 56 (1980), 56–88.

[27] See C. Osiek, 'The Women at the Tomb: What are They Doing There?', *Ex Auditu*, 9 (1993), 97–107.

empty obviously depends on the essential reliability of the prior story of Joseph of Arimathea having buried Jesus in an identifiable tomb.[28]

A notable contemporary exegete has been setting aside the historicity of the entire empty tomb narrative (Mark 16: 1–8) by proposing that the author of Mark *composed* the passage 'in toto' as a natural way (at that time) of narrating and interpreting the early Christian proclamation of Jesus' resurrection. Yarbro Collins builds her case partly on supposed parallels in stories about various ancient individuals said to have been 'translated' into immortal, heavenly life.[29] A number of serious considerations tell against her hypothesis. First, practically all of the examples she offers concern figures who, unlike Jesus, are obviously non-historical. Second, in responding to Norman Kretzman, she rightly calls for the exercise of 'the historical imagination' when judging what is historically probable (pp. 152–3). In the name of our historical imagination, however, one must ask: is it at all possible that a first-century Christian, deeply committed to the new faith, most probably of Jewish background, obviously steeped in the Jewish Scriptures, and of no great literary talent, like the author of Mark, could or would have consciously drawn on what was, on her own showing, largely a Graeco-Roman mythological scheme about someone's translation (into heavenly existence), to compose a complete 'fiction' (her word) as a way of proclaiming Jesus' resurrection from the dead? Mark 1–15 shows this evangelist setting the story of Jesus in the context of Jewish salvation history; those chapters are permeated with quotations and echoes of the Jewish Scriptures, as Mark goes about illustrating how Jesus fulfilled various Jewish (and not Graeco-Roman) religious motifs. Can Graeco-Roman thought-forms be 'imagined' to prove the master-key to what happened when Mark

[28] See R. E. Brown, *The Death of the Messiah*, ii (New York: Doubleday, 1994), 1201–79; G. O'Collins and D. Kendall, 'Did Joseph of Arimathea Exist?', *Biblica*, 75 (1994), 235–41. Further points could be added to our case for the historicity of Joseph of Arimathea. Having outlined the guilty responsibility of the *entire* Sanhedrin (Mark 14: 53, 55, 64), how could Mark then turn around and invent a Sanhedrinist (15: 43) who generously gave Jesus a respectable burial (15: 46)?

[29] Adela Yarbro Collins, 'The Empty Tomb in the Gospel According to Mark', in E. Stump and T. P. Flint (eds.), *Hermes and Athena* (Notre Dame, Ind.: University of Notre Dame Press, 1993), 107–40. This paper, to which references will be made within the text, had already appeared as 'The Empty Tomb and Resurrection According to Mark', in Yarbro Collins, *The Beginning of the Gospel: Problems of Mark in Context* (Minneapolis: Fortress, 1992), 119–48.

wrote his final eight verses? Yarbro Collins properly recognizes (but does not convincingly respond to) the objection that 'it is hard to find' in Mark much influence from Graeco-Roman literature (pp. 130-1), from which she takes most of her examples for her hypothesis about the evangelist's fictional composition of 16: 1-8. She invokes in her support D. E. Aune, *The New Testament in its Literary Environment*,[30] and V. K. Robbins, *Jesus the Teacher: A Socio-Rhetorical Interpretation of Mark*.[31] Apropos of these two books, one should notice the cautions expressed about the first by John Drury, in the review he wrote for the *Journal of Theological Studies*,[32] and about the second by James Swetnam, in his review for *Biblica*.[33] When reviewing Robbins's work, J. M. Bassler emphasized his recognition of both a Graeco-Roman *and* a Jewish background to Mark's Gospel.[34]

Third, as Hugo Meynell asks,[35] what are we to make of the moral probity of Mark in creating such a fictional narrative (and one that touches on an utterly central theme in the original Christian proclamation) and of the gullibility of the early Christians (including Matthew and Luke) in believing and repeating his fiction as if it were a basically factual narrative? Fourth, many scholars would agree with E. P. Sanders's judgement that, like the early Christian tradition in general, Mark was not 'terribly creative'.[36] Overall, the evangelist shaped and adapted existing material, rather than inventing complete narratives himself. Can we suppose that he suddenly did that for the first time when he came to the resurrection of Jesus? Fifth, such standard recent commentators on Mark as Ernst, Gnilka, Gundry, Harrington, Hooker, Pesch, and Schweizer agree that Mark 16: 1-8 drew on a source (or sources), whether or not they suppose that this material belonged to or was connected with a (hypothetical) pre-Marcan passion narrative. Even Gerd Luedemann agrees that the author of Mark drew on some previous unit(s) of tradition when composing Mark 16: 1-8.[37] Here he dis-

[30] (Philadelphia: Westminster, 1987).   [31] (Philadelphia: Fortress, 1984).
[32] 41 (1990), 204-6.   [33] 66 (1985), 136-9.
[34] *JBL* 106 (1987), 339-41.
[35] 'On New Testament Scholarship and the Integrity of Faith', *New Blackfriars*, 76 (1995), 127-40, at 135.
[36] E. P. Sanders, *The Historical Figure of Jesus* (London: Penguin, 1993), 218.
[37] G. Luedemann, *The Resurrection of Jesus: History, Experience, Theology*, trans. J. Bowden (Minneapolis: Fortress, 1994), 111-21, 231. For my assessment of Luedemann's book see *Gregorianum*, 77 (1996), 357-9, and *Theological Studies*, 57 (1996), 341-3.

agrees with J. D. Crossan, who back in a 1976 essay had anticipated Yarbro Collins in arguing that these verses were *in toto* a Marcan composition.[38] Sixth, Yarbro Collins, while alluding to Crossan's 1976 hypothesis (pp. 134–5), does not seem to have been aware of the way in which Paul and Linda Badham had already (unconvincingly) argued (in 1982) that the author of Mark invented the whole of 16: 1–8.[39] Her own, fresh attempt to interpret these eight verses as 'fiction' is no more convincing.

(4) *Easter Faith*

The challenge of verifying faith in Jesus' resurrection has retained its vitality from the time of the New Testament. In particular, for more than two centuries now, Enlightenment and post-Enlightenment debates have scrutinized the meaning, factuality, and credibility of the resurrection.[40] The case for Easter faith has frequently highlighted one or more of the following elements: (i) historical evidence, (ii) present testimony and experience, and (iii) the grace needed to appropriate the Easter mystery.

(i) What I have just been saying about the post-resurrection appearances and the discovery of the empty tomb obviously focuses on clarifying the historical grounds for Easter faith. Without expecting too much from the strategies of secular and 'scientific' historiography, as if they alone could vindicate in a scholarly way belief in Christ's resurrection,[41] we should not avoid historical questions and debates. The Jesus Seminar, for instance, has revived the thesis proposed long ago by the history-of-religions school that Paul and the Gospel writers developed 'the view of Jesus as a cult figure analogous to others in the hellenistic mystery religions' and 'understood as a dying/rising god'.[42] In *Jesus Risen* I summarized the standard

[38] Crossan's essay, 'Empty Tomb and Absent Lord (Mark 16: 1–8)', appeared in W. H. Kelber (ed.), *The Passion in Mark. Studies on Mark 14–16* (Philadelphia: Fortress, 1976), 135–52.

[39] For a rebuttal of the Badhams's thesis see my *Interpreting the Resurrection*, 54–8; for their thesis see P. and L. Badham, *Immortality or Extinction?* (Totowa, NJ: Barnes and Noble, 1982).

[40] See my 'Resurrection', in A. E. McGrath (ed.), *The Blackwell Encyclopedia of Modern Christian Thought* (Oxford: Blackwell, 1993), 553–7.

[41] See Sarah Coakley's critique of W. Pannenberg's apologetic for the resurrection: 'Is the Resurrection a Historical Event?', in P. Avis (ed.), *The Resurrection of Jesus Christ* (London: Darton, Longman & Todd, 1993), 85–115.

[42] R. W. Funk, R. W. Hoover, and the Jesus Seminar, *The Five Gospels. The Search for the Authentic Words of Jesus* (London: Macmillan, 1993), 4, 7.

arguments that demolish the thesis about the first Christians imposing on Jesus the scheme of a dying/rising god which they had drawn from Hellenistic religious thought. What I should have pointed out as well was the way such a thesis runs against the present tide of main-line scholarship, which—now drawing on extensive data from the Dead Sea Scrolls, recent archaeological discoveries, and other sources—insists that Jesus and the first Christians must be interpreted primarily against a Jewish and not a Hellenistic background. Historical debates also concern the hypothesis of Q, the common source apparently used by Matthew and Luke along with the Gospel of Mark. Q contains no passion and resurrection narratives—something which suggests to certain writers that Jesus' resurrection did not matter to the community (or communities) behind Q; they were interested in Jesus only as a counter-cultural teacher and leader.[43] In his *Death of the Messiah* Raymond Brown, however, rightly criticizes the 'dubious confidence' of those who fondly imagine that the total knowledge/faith of the Q author(s) can be known from contemporary reconstructions of the document.[44] John Meier warns against the extraordinarily tenuous positions and conclusions reached by those who turn their creative fantasies loose on the Q hypothesis.[45]

(ii) In Peter Carnley's *The Structure of Resurrection Belief*[46] the present experience of God's Spirit bulks large, and reduces somewhat the importance of the initial apostolic encounters with the risen Christ himself. In Carnley's view the experienced reality of Easter revelation and faith seems to have been, and to remain, largely confined to the experience of Christ's Spirit.[47] In his contribution to the present volume Francis Schüssler Fiorenza develops the hermeneutics of testimony, rightly stressing the intersubjectivity and trusting self-transcendence involved in accepting Easter testimony as veracious. Yet one also needs, I think, to ask: what

[43] See Burton Mack, *The Lost Gospel. The Book of Q & Christian Origins* (San Francisco: HarperSan Francisco, 1993); see also H.-D. Betz, 'Jesus and the Cynics: Survey and Analysis of a Hypothesis', *JR* 74 (1994), 453-75.

[44] Brown, *Death of the Messiah*, i. 478 n. 23.

[45] J. Meier, *A Marginal Jew. Rethinking the Historical Jesus*, ii (New York: Doubleday, 1994), 177-81; see also D. C. Allison, 'A Plea for Thoroughgoing Eschatology', *JBL* 113 (1994), 651-68, at 661-3.

[46] (Oxford: Clarendon, 1987).

[47] See Robert Scholla's doctoral dissertation, published as *Recent Anglican Contributions on the Resurrection of Jesus (1945-1987)* (Rome: Gregorian University Press, 1992), 196-258.

makes me/us open and disposed to accept the testimony of others and trust their message? To adapt Karl Rahner's famous title, what makes us hearers of the Easter word? Do the internal dynamisms and expectations of the human spirit deserve to be noted at this point by those who wish to offer a complete account of what accepting testimony entails? In *The Resurrection of Jesus Christ: Some Contemporary Issues* I argued for public testimony 'from the outside' meshing with our deepest questions 'from the inside' in the making of resurrection faith and hope.[48]

(iii) As Sarah Coakley recalled in her critique of Pannenberg, Easter is the paschal *mystery*. The dimension of mystery and grace might seem to be ignored in Richard Swinburne's *Revelation: From Metaphor to Analogy*[49] when he describes the resurrection as 'the original miracle' (p. 145) or 'super-miracle' (p. 219; see pp. 110-12). But he does add that the Church has always regarded the resurrection as 'vastly more mysterious and of vastly greater significance' (p. 112) than a 'mere' miracle like the resuscitation of a corpse. *Time* magazine for 10 April 1995, when running the cover story 'Can We Still Believe in Miracles?' (pp. 64-73), played down this 'vast' difference between miracles and the resurrection by referring to 'Miracles' in the article's title but featuring on its cover Noël Coypel's painting of Jesus' resurrection. The article understood the resurrection to be the most important of miracles (p. 70). As regards the grace-guided acceptance of Easter faith, surveys and reports on why people believe specifically in Jesus' resurrection (or in Jesus as gloriously risen from the dead) might illuminate the question. As far as I know, such 'empirical' research in this sector has never been attempted in a scholarly way. Yet it has always struck me as more interesting and informative to discover a posteriori why people in fact believe, rather than insisting a priori why they ought to believe. With this suggestion, however, I have reached the second part of my essay and some proposals for the agenda in resurrection studies.

II

What agenda would I encourage in resurrection studies? My proposals touch (1) historical, (2) theoretical, (3) practical, and (4) liturgical matters.

---

[48] (Milwaukee: Marquette University Press, 1993), 33-5.
[49] (Oxford: Clarendon, 1992).

(1) *Historical Questions*

Biblical and historical accounts of resurrection belief are still far from covering all the major areas and issues. We are indebted to Cavallin, Martin-Achard, Nickelsburg, Perkins, Segal, and above all Émile Puech[50] for clarifications of first-century Jewish language and ideas about resurrection and exaltation. Apocalyptic imagery of eschatological ascents to the heavenly world of God's angels establishes one important notion that was current at the time: resurrection as exaltation to angelic status. Just by themselves, contemporary notions of resurrection do not decide the question discussed above as to whether Mark simply composed 16: 1–8 as a 'fiction'. In any case, this research rightly focuses attention on Jewish sources rather than on the Graeco-Roman material that bulks largely (albeit not exclusively) in Yarbro Collins's hypothesis. An even better-founded account of first-century ideas of resurrection and exaltation at the end-time will come only with the fuller use of the Dead Sea Scrolls.

Caroline Bynum's magisterial *The Resurrection of the Body in Western Christianity* covers a long period (200–1336), even if it does not attend much to the early Middle Ages. It concentrates on ideas and images of our bodily resurrection, rather than taking up precisely ideas and images of Christ's own resurrection. The book reminds us that we still lack substantial studies of the whole story (from the New Testament to the twentieth century) of Christian belief in, preaching of, and theology about Jesus' resurrection from the dead. We also continue to lack full studies of how Jesus' resurrection was assumed and expressed by Christian liturgies down through the ages—in both East and West. What I offered in the first three chapters of *Jesus Risen* was a mere sampling of all that patristic and later writers have to say about his resurrection.[51] Hopefully, Marguerite Shuster's essay will encourage others to study further

---

[50] *La Croyance des Esséniens en la vie future: immortalité, résurrection, vie éternelle?*, Études Bibliques, 21/22 (Paris: Gabalda, 1993).

[51] See also my 'Augustine on the Resurrection', in F. LeMoine and C. Kleinhanz (eds.), *Saint Augustine the Bishop* (New York: Garland, 1994), 65–75; also A. Hamann, 'La Résurrection du Christ dans l'antiquité chrétienne', *Recherches de Science Religieuse*, 49 (1975), 292–318; 50 (1976), 1–24. Two articles in *TRE* offer some information and bibliographical help on the history of the resurrection doctrine: R. Staats, 'Auferstehung II/2 Alte Kirche', iv. 513–29; F. Wintzer, 'Auferstehung III. Praktisch-theologisch', iv. 529–47.

how great theological preachers down through the centuries encouraged and expressed faith in the resurrection, dealt with doubts, and spelled out the implications of Easter faith for daily life.

None of these remarks about the need for more biblical and historical research should be construed as encouraging a retreat into 'merely' historical reconstructions of the genesis and 'original' significance of Easter texts and artefacts coming from biblical or later times. In any case, good scholarly work about the past continues to raise religious questions for today. Shuster's study, along with others in this volume, illustrates the way historical scholarship serves, rather than evades, the never-ending quest for meaning, truth, and faith.

(2) *Theoretical Questions*

On the 'theoretical' level we continue to lack any specific and appropriate treatment of Christ's resurrection as an (or rather the special) act of God. Those theologians and philosophers who have been exploring God's interaction, whether extraordinary or ordinary, with creation normally reflect on divine activity in relation to the world without developing a specific treatment of Christ's resurrection. They may mention in passing his resurrection from the dead, but have little or nothing to suggest about how the divine agency worked there.[52] There are, of course, several massive challenges to face: nothing that I say about divine action can possibly be an adequate description. Modern philosophy has not come up with any agreed theory of action and personal action; some current accounts of divine action exclude not only the resurrection but also any other special, divine interventions.[53] Let me at least take a stand here by making three points.

First of all, I recognize that in speaking of God's activity I refer to a personal, incorporeal agent of a radically different kind from any

---

[52] The following, representative works on divine activity rarely or never refer to the specific case of the resurrection: B. Hebblethwaite and E. Henderson (eds.), *Divine Action* (Edinburgh: T. & T. Clark, 1990); T. V. Morris (ed.), *Divine and Human Action* (Ithaca, NY: Cornell University Press, 1988); R. J. Russell *et al.* (eds.), *Quantum Cosmology and the Laws of Nature: Scientific Perspectives on Divine Action* (Vatican City: Vatican Observatory Publications, 1993).

[53] See e.g. G. D. Kaufman, 'On the Meaning of "Act of God" ', *Harvard Theological Review*, 61 (1968), 175-201; M. Wiles, *God's Action in the World* (London: SCM, 1986).

or all temporal, created agents, whether personal or non-personal. The invisible, direct actions of God are unlike any created causality and, in particular, very different from those engaged in by corporeal, personal agents like ourselves. The omnipresent, non-embodied God is located and active everywhere, acting from within, and independently of our observation. We human beings normally act from without, and through movements of our bodies; as corporeal agents we are open to observation (the great exception being our mind–body interaction). Human activity's closest analogy to divine action comes in the way we bring about changes in our world by our intentions and decisions (which we then translate into action). The divine intentions as such immediately cause effects, without any need to be translated into action by some bodily movement. Moreover, by insisting on such special divine interventions as the resurrection, we are certainly not proposing that God comes on the scene to act for the first time. By creating and sustaining everything in existence, God already acts through the founding relationship of creation, so as to be always dynamically and intimately present everywhere, to everything, and in every situation of creation. We are speaking, rather, of special situations in which God is differently engaged and intentionally produces various qualitatively distinct effects; particularized intentions of God bring about particular states of affairs at particular times and places within the created world.

As regards the case in hand, the quality and nature of the effects (the resurrection of Jesus from the dead and the sustaining of his salvific impact on the world) point to effects rather than to the divine cause that brings about these effects. Our greater clarity about effects holds true of created causality and, even more, of divine causality and how it works, right from the most basic divine causality at work in creating and sustaining the universe that we continually experience. Hence, with reference to Jesus' resurrection and its subsequent impact, we should expect that the precise way in which God brings about these effects will remain as mysterious or more mysterious than the creation of the world.

In a real sense the divine 'action' *is* the finite, observable effect: the risen, glorified Jesus who appears to the disciples and is ceaselessly active in the visible Church and the world. This brings me to my second point. The classical adage that 'every agent brings about something similar to itself' (*omne agens agit sibi simile*) suggests the various ways in which effects will have a special relationship to, and consistently resemble, their causes. In our case the divine Agent leaves a personal impression on the effects, and is known through these effects: the risen Christ and the world-wide impact he has enjoyed. The Word of God, hypostatically united with the risen humanity, is actively and personally present in *this* glorified existence; it participates in God, and leads others to participate in the divine life. What God has brought about as *sibi simile* (the risen existence of Christ) in its turn works to make all men and women 'similar' to God through the life of grace and glory. The classical adage I have appealed to helps to illuminate both Christ's original passage from death to glorified life and the endlessly repeated passage to grace and glory in those who experience his spiritual power.

Third, such special, direct actions of God as the resurrection, far from being random or even arbitrary events, are related to a wider, unified project that gives point and purpose to their occurrence: the future completion of all persons and things in Christ. Another adage, 'the end commands all', proves its worth here. Both in raising Jesus from the dead and then empowering his saving impact on the entire world, God has in view his final goal: the progressive assimilation of humanity and the universe to Christ. The goal of the resurrection is nothing less than that of moving the whole of creation to participate as fully as possible in the life of God.

Points two and three call attention to the salvific aim of God's special acts: they occur for our benefit, and promote a privileged communion with God. My second point, in using the language of 'knowing' and 'experiencing', brought up the *revelatory* dimension of the divine acts—in particular, the resurrection of Christ. Along with their saving scope, special divine acts like the resurrection are eminently personal events of God's self-revelation.[54]

After developing these three points that should shape a fuller account of Christ's resurrection as the act of God, let me list more quickly other theoretical questions that deserve examination today. (i) A traditional axiom holds that all three persons of the Trinity are inseparably involved in every external action (*opus ad extra*). Yet the

---

[54] In his chapter in this volume Francis Schüssler Fiorenza several times recalls how 'background theories' can be open or closed to God's creative activity in history. As he properly insists, it should not simply be assumed that God does so act. This, in fact, was the reason I developed my own background theory on this issue in 1987 (*Jesus Risen*, 136, 186–7), 1993 (*The Resurrection of Jesus Christ. Some Contemporary Issues*, 39–50), and in 1995 (*Christology*, 106–12), and here.

'term', or objective effect, within the finite, world nexus can be special to one or other divine person: for instance, the incarnate life of God the Son. All three persons were involved in bringing about the incarnation, but the 'term', or visible point of arrival, the incarnate Word with his mission, is peculiar to him. Can, or should, we introduce a similar distinction in the case of the resurrection? While the causality exercised in the resurrection is common to all three persons, does the 'term' (the risen, 'spiritual' Christ) belong in a 'proper' way to the 'economic' mission of the Holy Spirit? Can Romans 8: 9–11 and Paul's reflections on the 'spiritual' body in 1 Corinthians 15 encourage us in this way to ascribe the 'term' of the resurrection to the Holy Spirit's proper role in the whole 'economy' of salvation? This ascription would be further encouraged by 1 Timothy 3: 16, if we translate *edikaiōthē en pneumati* as 'vindicated by the Spirit'.

(ii) This brings us to the vexed question of the nature of the risen body[55] and the link between Christ's earthly body and glorified body. How might my suggestions about the bond between being historical and being bodily and about Christ's history rising with him (*Jesus Risen*, 179–86) be developed further? Caroline Walker Bynum's *The Resurrection of the Body* illustrates extensively the persistent conviction of Christians that resurrection will preserve for all eternity their gender, personal experience, and other personal characteristics. What then of the theories that break the link between the pre-Easter and the post-Easter Christ by maintaining the transmigration of his soul (in which his 'real' identity is lodged) to a brand-new, 'pneumatic', body?[56] What of the views of those who revive Gnostic-style talk of Jesus living 'male' but rising 'human'?[57] (Such views can hardly accept that the glorified Jesus, who appears to his disciples, is, and is recognized as, the same, numerically iden-

---

[55] See Maurizio Teani, *Corporeità e risurrezione. L'interpretazione di I Corinti 15, 35–49 nel Novecento* (Rome: Gregorian University Press, 1994).

[56] See H. Häring and J.-B. Metz (eds.), *Reincarnation or Resurrection?*, Concilium, 5 (London: SCM, 1993).

[57] V. R. Mollenkott, *The Divine Feminine: The Biblical Imagery of God as Female* (New York: Crossroad, 1983), 70–1. On earlier versions of gender differences vanishing at resurrection with unisex, spiritual bodies see Bynum, *Resurrection of the Body*, 141–55. Such views detach the risen Jesus from the particular characteristics and circumstances (especially the sexual, racial, religious, and geographical ones) that shaped his history as a first-century Jewish male who lived in Palestine. Since his particular history is thus not supposed to rise with him, what he was, did, and suffered during his earthly life no longer matters—at least *sub specie aeternitatis*.

tical, personal agent who died on the cross.) How can the visual arts, literature, and—in general—our imagination lend credibility to the risen Jesus' glorified, bodily existence? To what extent can modern science illuminate the nature of future, risen bodiliness (as well as the nature of a transfigured world to come)?

(iii) Since Pannenberg's classic *Jesus—God and Man* appeared,[58] several other Christologies have centred on the resurrection. But has an appreciation of Christ's resurrection and of his risen presence been sufficiently effective so far in structuring many, major works in Christology? Could it be that none of these latter-day Christologies have been adequately built around the heart of the risen Christ's ongoing presence: his presence through the sacraments in particular and the liturgy in general?

(iv) Further, the links between Christ's resurrection, the recognition of his divinity, and orthodox Trinitarian faith need further exploration. Reductionist versions of the resurrection, not to mention outright denials of it, inevitably bring rejection of Christ's divine identity, the 'economic' mission of the personal Holy Spirit, and belief in a tripersonal God. At best the revisionists and deniers leave us with a modalism that can hardly be distinguished from straight Unitarianism. Such tampering with Trinitarian faith is exemplified by John Hick in *The Metaphor of God Incarnate*: 'God is humanly known—as creator, as transformer, and as inner spirit [all in lower case]. We do not need to reify [sic!] these ways as three distinct persons' (p. 153).

(v) As soon as I read his *Diskussion um Kreuz und Auferstehung*,[59] I was impressed by Bertold Klappert's version of the resurrection's 'multi-dimensionality'. He elaborated a scheme that highlighted the resurrection as the event that reconciles, opens the future in hope, launches the kerygma, and grounds faith. What I missed, however, was a sense of the resurrection as the effective revelation of divine love. That led me to develop this theme in a 1984 article in the *Heythrop Journal*[60] and then three years later in *Jesus Risen* (pp. 188–200); yet this provisional exploration of the resurrection as mystery of love has so far failed to stir up any debate or even much comment. In *She Who Is* Elizabeth Johnson writes of the resurrection

[58] German original 1964. (London: SCM, 1968).
[59] (Wuppertal: Aussaat Verlag, 1967).
[60] 'Christ's Resurrection as Mystery of Love', *Heythrop Journal*, 25 (1984), 39–50.

as the powerful victory of 'compassionate love',[61] but she is almost alone in doing so. In *Der auferweckte Gekreuzigte*[62] Ingolf Dalferth has much to say about Christ's resurrection (especially pp. 52–84), repeatedly invokes God's love, refers to my *Jesus Risen* (p. 66), but never comments on the proposal to explore the resurrection as mystery of love. This silence leaves me with the question: should I explore further the resurrection as mystery of God's love, or should I remain content with Klappert's scheme, which draws from some of the best twentieth-century writing on the resurrection but has nothing specific to remark about love?

(3) *Practical Questions*

The resurrection of Christ invites much more reflection on the way it serves as a critical, liberating, and constructive response to universal evils and endless injustices. Jon Sobrino and other exponents of liberation theology have led the way here: the whole history of human suffering and human longing for justice provides an essential context for understanding and interpreting the resurrection. Jürgen Moltmann's *Theology of Hope*[63] has prepared the ground for a 'practical' approach to the Easter mystery, presenting it as the event *par excellence* of divine promise that arouses human hope. The serious attempt, in the light of the crucified Christ's victory over death, to implement justice, peace, and human solidarity will enable us to participate in and verify his resurrection. Apropos of liberation Christology, one must admit, a little sadly, how little the theologians of that school have reflected on Christ's resurrection. This neglect seems, in general, to have been motivated by the proper desire to avoid ideological and triumphalistic interpretations of the resurrection that 'mystify' human suffering. Whatever the reasons, liberation theologians are relatively silent about Jesus' rising from the dead.

After devoting two chapters to the theme in his *Christology at the Crossroads*,[64] Jon Sobrino, for instance, gave the resurrection only one chapter in his *Jesus Christ in Latin America*[65] and only a few pages in his *Jesus the Liberator: A Historical-Theological Reading of Jesus of Nazareth*.[66] The crucified people Sobrino has spoken for and

[61] (New York: Crossroad, 1993), 159.   [62] (Tübingen: J. C. B. Mohr, 1994).
[63] German original 1964. (London: SCM, 1969).
[64] (London: SCM, 1978), 236–72.   [65] (Maryknoll, NY: Orbis, 1987), 148–58.
[66] (Maryknoll, NY: Orbis, 1993), 43–4, 117–18, 124.

supported are among the means for revealing God and the divine plan of salvation; they constitute a major 'locus' for the crucified Christ's presence in history. But that same Christ is risen from the dead as a living promise for all, and as *the* liberating and joyful response to the human hunger for justice and freedom. Hence in the epilogue to *Jesus the Liberator* (pp. 272–3), Sobrino promises to deal with the resurrection in a forthcoming volume, a work that he reportedly expects to finish in 1996.

The 'practical' agenda connected with the resurrection must also feature the development of ethical systems based on Christ's resurrection and all that it entails. Main-line resurrection faith should surely produce systematic works which spell out the practice of Easter discipleship. The divine presence in the material world, initiated by creation and dramatically enhanced by the incarnation, is now being consummated by the resurrection and its universal promise. The destiny of all things in and through the risen Christ and his dynamic presence grounds moral values for justice, sexuality, the environment, and other major fields of human choice and activity. As an outsider to their discipline, I continue to be astonished that so many Christian ethicists—on the left, the right, and at the centre—continue to teach and write in ways that not only ignore the resurrection but also take little notice of Christ and what faith in him might entail for moral thought and living. Oliver O'Donovan's *Resurrection and the Moral Order. An Outline for Evangelical Ethics*[67] stands practically alone, a noble exception to the general neglect of the resurrection by Christian ethicists and moral theologians.[68] Even then, as his preface to the book's second edition in 1994 makes even clearer, he uses the resurrection to complement two traditional themes in evangelical ethics: the kingdom and creation.

(4) *Liturgical and Spiritual Questions*

Lastly, much Western theology, from the Middle Ages to the present, has proved non-symbolic, non-liturgical, and non-spiritual. However we interpret the causes of this neglect of symbolic,

---

[67] (Leicester: Inter-Varsity Press, 1986).

[68] See, however, S. S. Harakas, 'Resurrection and Ethics in Chrysostom', *Ex Auditu*, 9 (1993), 77–95. In his contribution to notes on moral theology for 1994, 'Jesus and Christian Ethics', *Theological Studies*, 56 (1995), 92–107, W. C. Spohn has nothing to report on the resurrection apart from a few passing remarks (pp. 98, 101, 104); interest is concentrated on the story of Jesus' ministry and death.

liturgical, and spiritual concerns, it has left the resurrection largely unexplored liturgically and spiritually. Theologians have rarely, if ever, thought of reflecting on the testimonies to Easter faith coming from liturgical texts, the spiritual writings of saints and mystics, works of religious art, and the great moments in sacred music that respond to the resurrection message.[69] Eastern Christianity, with its rich symbols, has kept alive much more effectively the sense that resurrection faith joyfully flourishes where it is performed liturgically and lived spiritually. What we lack is a fully deployed, up-to-date theology of the resurrection that is formed and fashioned in the key of liturgy.[70] A liturgically developed appropriation of the resurrection would, for instance, take its cue from the Eucharist and other liturgical actions which, in and for every new generation, witness to and 're-present' the redemptive revelation that is the Easter mystery. In all its richness the liturgy proves itself over and over again to be the great and convincing sign that the crucified and risen Christ is dynamically and ceaselessly present. Liturgy is not *about* Jesus' resurrection, but takes place *in* the spiritual world created by it.

This essay has taken me through various current issues and future proposals for resurrection studies. But Christian believers are always left with the haunting questions: what is it to know and live the resurrection? who knows and lives the resurrection 'best'? One thing is clear, however. Belief in the resurrection of Jesus has carried the Church for nearly twenty centuries. If Christians as a whole ever stop believing in, and living from, his resurrection, that will be when the Church stops being the Church of Jesus Christ.[71]

---

[69] See John Bowden, 'Resurrection in Music', in Barton and Stanton (eds.), *Resurrection*, 188–97; Winifried Kurzschenkel, *Die theologische Bestimmung der Musik* (Trier: Paulinus-Verlag, 1971); and an issue of Concilium, *Music and the Experience of God*, 202 (Apr. 1989).

[70] Before the Second Vatican Council (1962–5) the work of F. X. Durrwell, *The Resurrection* (New York: Sheed and Ward, 1960; French original 1954), widely helped to effect a liturgical and spiritual appreciation of the Easter mystery. His exegesis, however, needs substantial updating.

[71] For some valuable criticisms and comments I want to thank, in particular, Raymond Brown, Stephen Davis, Peter Carnley, Pheme Perkins, Francis Schüssler Fiorenza, Richard Swinburne, Frans Jozef van Beeck, Robert Wilken, and the members of a study circle that met at the Beda College in Rome.

Response by Peter F. Carnley

In this response to Gerald O'Collins's discussion of the current state of the questions relating to the theology of the resurrection, I wish to play the role of 'devil's advocate' by focusing on what he has to say concerning the proposals of John Hick.[1]

Hick avoids treating the Easter visions as encounters with the transcendent and surpassing mystery of the raised Christ as a religious object by explaining them as psychogenic projections, similar to visionary episodes that form part of near-death experiences, or visions that feature in the experiences of the recently bereaved. In this way, Hick allows the resurrection appearances of Jesus to be brought within a range of like historical occurrences that, given advances in medical techniques of resuscitation, are these days regularly reported, or that often feature in modern studies of bereavement. This makes the resurrection appearances understandable and manageable by accommodating them to a contemporary body of systematic knowledge.

In this way, the Easter event becomes something that happened within the self-contained experience of the disciples; nothing subsequent to his death is understood to have happened to Jesus. To this extent the revelatory content of the tradition has been reduced to dimensions that are humanly reasonable and understandable.

John Hick's proposals amount essentially to a new and revamped version of the so-called subjective vision hypothesis proposed by David Friedrich Strauss in 1835, which also involved reducing the Easter event to a set of purely psychological events experienced amongst the disciples. In Hick's treatment the suggestion is that the appearances may be compared with the experiences of people who, having been at the brink of death, are later resuscitated. These often involve reports of the vivid experience of 'seeing' into another world, sometimes featuring a heavenly light, and even involving the approach of a figure who is identified as 'Jesus'.

---

[1] J. Hick, *The Metaphor of God Incarnate* (London/Louisville, Ky.: SCM/Westminster, 1993), 24–6.

Gerald O'Collins's first objection to the drawing of this parallel is that such reports come from people 'who were revived after being clinically dead' (near to death?), but that 'being near to death' was not part of the experience of Peter, Paul, Mary Magdalene, and other Easter witnesses.[2]

To be scrupulously fair to John Hick, he does not really suggest this. His suggestion is that the visions or seeings of the raised Christ might be understood by us as being something like the seeings into another world reported in our day by people who have been near death, not that Peter, Paul, Magdalene, and others underwent experiences in which they themselves were near death.

In any event, the first comment I would like to make about this is that there may be more warrant in the tradition for making this kind of comparison than O'Collins is willing to allow. After all, in at least one of his reports of Paul's Damascus Road experience, Luke not only actually speaks of a vision (*optasia*), but has Paul say that, while praying in the Temple, 'I fell into a trance and I saw Jesus saying to me . . .' (Acts 22: 17-18). There is clearly a distinction to be made between being in a trance and being unconscious and near death, but the difference is immaterial with respect to the fact that Paul's experience of light, and the seeing of Christ associated with it, may be similar to, if not essentially the same as, what is reported by those who have been through near-death experiences, if we think in terms of a psychological cause. Also, the vision of Stephen in Acts 7: 55 might justifiably be understood as a kind of 'near-death' experience in which Stephen is severely psychologically stressed, if not unconscious. This involved a glimpse of the glory of God and the heavenly, exalted Christ sitting at God's right hand in the position of divine favour. On the other hand, the most detailed description of the raised Christ in the New Testament is that found in Revelation 1, where the author claims to have seen 'in the spirit' when he 'saw' the raised Christ.

I would have thought, also, that the kind of near-death experience following which a person reports having 'seen' a light and a person approaching the bedside, who is often actually identified as Jesus, could reasonably be compared also to the kind of experiences St Paul speaks of in 2 Corinthians 12 as 'visions and revelations of the Lord' in the context of his argument with the Corinthians about

---

[2] See above, pp. 11-12.

his own endowment with 'spiritual gifts'. Here Paul himself claims to have known a man fourteen years prior to writing (A.D. 40+) who claimed to have 'seen into the third heaven' and to have glimpsed the raised Christ there in glory.

In other words, whether in a trance, or caught up 'in the third heaven', or in the spirit, or in the context of the trauma of execution, the glimpse of the raised and heavenly Christ in the ambience of the glory of God does not seem to be presented as something radically unlike what is reported by those who have been near death. So, it seems to me on scriptural grounds not to be altogether out of court to suggest that the first Christians also had experiences which were similar to those described today by people who have been near death. The drawing of this comparison by John Hick seems reasonable enough. The really important question raised by Hick, however, is whether all the original Easter visions or appearances of Jesus may be thought of in this way, given the obviously legendary development of the stories to which modern redactional studies have alerted us.

It is usual for New Testament scholars to try to distinguish the kind of experience reported to Paul by the man who glimpsed the raised Christ when he was caught up in the third heaven and other 'visions and revelations of the Lord' from Paul's own primary experience of the Easter Jesus on the Damascus road.[3] If some kind of distinction or difference is to be sustained between the two kinds of experience, it may be, of course, just that the Damascus Road experience was temporally primary and life re-directing, while the later 'visions and revelations' of the Lord of which Paul speaks were secondary, the kind of experience that is confirmatory of faith, rather than originative. However, there also seem to be grounds for differentiating the actual quality of these respective experiences, in so far as the man to whom Paul refers in 2 Corinthians 12 [and whom many scholars take to be the apostle himself—eds.] was in some way transported into heaven and there glimpsed the raised Christ, whereas for Paul on the Damascus Road the raised Christ as it were 'comes from heaven to him': the one spoken of as a vertical going into heaven to glimpse Christ there, and the latter as a more horizontal coming of Christ from heaven, so to speak. Hick's

---

[3] See W. Pannenberg's discussion of this in *Jesus—God and Man* (London: SCM, 1968), 93–4. In the final analysis Pannenberg is unable to find criteria to distinguish objective from subjective visions.

comparison of the Easter appearances with the seeings reported by people who have come through near-death experiences seems to me to be a little more obviously appropriate in relation to the former than the latter.

However, I think we must admit that in either case it is clear enough that for Paul the raised Christ is a heavenly, glorified Christ, who either 'appears from' or is 'glimpsed in heaven', rather than one who walks around on the ground, and that the experience involved some phenomenon of light. Whether those travelling with Paul experienced all that Paul himself experienced is problematic, given that the traditions of Acts 9, 22, and 26 are confused about this. In any event, the quality of the experiences as mysterious and revelatory, with a sense of disclosure 'from heaven', is what cannot be eliminated from the Easter tradition as it relates to Paul, and this is the case both as Paul himself speaks of his own experience and, more theoretically, as he speaks of the 'spiritual body' of all believers, and of the raised Lord as the first-born of the new creation, and also as Luke reports Paul's experience in Acts.

This means that Hick's suggestion that all the reports and developed narratives of Easter appearances may arise out of primary experiences that were somehow like the experiences reported by those who have been near to death has at least to be taken seriously, perhaps more seriously than O'Collins has been prepared to allow.

When we turn to Hick's second suggestion, that the appearances can be understood by comparing them with the phenomenon of psychologically induced 'seeings' of deceased loved ones reported by recently bereaved people, we are clearly dealing with something closer to what was proposed by Strauss in his 'subjective vision hypothesis', since Strauss lived before the modern innovations in the medical resuscitation of those near death. The added complication for us today is that this kind of experience is now well attested in the literature on bereavement. Indeed, many of us may have heard such stories first hand in pastoral situations involving ministry to the bereaved, including really vivid descriptions of the apparently fleeting appearance or 'seeing' of a recently deceased loved one.

In relation to these experiences there is no suggestion of the subject's being in a trance or altered mental state or anything approximating the loss of consciousness that is a feature of reported near-death experiences. Frequently, the subjects of such experiences report that they were simply going about the business of trying to get on with life. And the question raised by John Hick's suggestion is: how is it possible to prove that the disciples' experiences after the trauma of Calvary were not experiences of this kind?

O'Collins's response at this point is that Hick generalizes the unique experience of the Easter Jesus by bringing it within a range of experiences that are said to be very common amongst bereaved people, but that in Jesus' death and resurrection we are dealing with something unique. But this is to assume what needs to be proved. If, as Hick suggests, it is a logical possibility (that is, if it is thinkable without self-contradiction) that the appearances could be understood in this way, to rule the suggestion out of court on the grounds that it generalizes what has a priori been deemed to be somehow unique simply begs the question.

Father O'Collins also argues that the (possible?) prior claims to divine authority of the historical Jesus and his humiliating death by public execution somehow separate the experience of his death from any experiences that bereaved people may normally have. I frankly do not see that this can amount to an answer to John Hick's proposal. Indeed, it can be argued that the intensity of the devotion to Jesus in the time before his crucifixion and the special (perhaps, divine) standing in which he was held by his disciples prior to his crucifixion followed by the horrendous end which befell him on the cross intensified the trauma of death in their case. If anything, this would make the post-mortem experience of bereavement even more likely to generate visions or appearances or seeings of a visionary kind than in the case of the normal experience of the death, let us say, of an aged parent after a long illness and the bereavement sequence that might follow it. I do not think that an a priori commitment to Jesus' uniqueness can be appealed to in order to head off the natural inclination amongst historians today to compare the visions experienced by the disciples with contemporary reports of psychologically induced visions of the departed amongst the bereaved. Indeed, perhaps historians have a responsibility to consider this possibility. What we need is evidence to rule out the possibility that the first experiences were similar to near-death experiences or the experiences of seeing loved ones of bereaved people in bereavement sequences. But what evidence could be appealed to in order to achieve this? What are the actual criteria for distinguishing the apostles' visions from the reported 'seeings' of the recently deceased by bereaved people?

Hick's ultimate misdemeanour in O'Collins's eyes is that he has assimilated the resurrection of Jesus to a general type of phenomenon, which therefore denies the resurrection's uniqueness. But surely this uniqueness is what we have to establish. We cannot begin with that as an a priori commitment. If, after a critical assessment of the evidence, we can somehow rule out the possibility that the appearances were psychologically induced visions, we may conclude that the resurrection of Jesus was not like the more general experience of the apparent 'seeing' of dead people in bereavement sequences. If we could prove that, we might then be able to assert the uniqueness of the Easter appearances as the objectively factual and historical ground of faith. We cannot legitimately argue, as O'Collins does, the other way around. We cannot start with an a priori commitment to the uniqueness of the resurrection, and then exclude the possible assimilation of the Easter appearance traditions to what happens in more general and common bereavement sequences.

On the other hand, Hick himself is careful to point out that his suggestion is merely a conjecture, which he offers as a possible explanation, and in fairness to him, he roundly affirms that 'we have to add that any unqualified assertions about what occurred in the days and weeks after Jesus' death, whether in terms of spiritual encounters or of physical miracles, can never be fully substantiated from an historical point of view'.[4] If this type of 'subjective vision hypothesis' based on contemporary findings of depth psychology is to be addressed, I think we have to take the strongest version of it, rather than what is offered just as a passing conjecture of the kind made by John Hick. We now have the far more aggressively and intensively argued thesis of Gerd Luedemann with which to contend.[5] At the very least, Luedemann makes out a prima-facie case for a psychogenic explanation of the visions to be taken seriously, by pointing to the likelihood of the antecedent operation of guilt in the mind of Paul the persecutor and of remorse in relation to Peter the betrayer. And the question is: how might it be possible at this distance and with the very fragmentary information at our

---

[4] Hick, *Metaphor of God Incarnate*, 25.
[5] G. Luedemann, *The Resurrection of Jesus* (Minneapolis: Fortress, 1994).

disposal to rule out this possibility? One can easily rule it out if one has first made an a priori dogmatic commitment to an 'objective vision hypothesis' in the manner of, say, Grass, or if one chooses to appeal to the idea of a divinely assisted or 'graced' seeing of an objective raised Jesus. However, if such a commitment is to be more than purely arbitrary, and if one is relying on the evidence of the appearances to provide the historical *ground* of faith, then, in strictly historical terms, where is the evidence to come from to rule out the possibility of psychologically induced visions as one explanation of the available evidence? Frankly, I do not see how, at this distance, and with the few fragments of evidence we have, and without the possibility of sitting down to do a *Larry King Live* with the witnesses so as to cross-examine them, we could ever come to a historical conclusion on this one. I note that even a reasonably conservative New Testament scholar such as James D. G. Dunn acknowledges that the 'subjective vision hypothesis' could be one explanation of the origin of the Easter appearances tradition, given the nature of the evidence we have.[6]

If we are prepared to allow that there is evidence in the New Testament of visions of an apparently subjective, psychologically conditioned nature, such as Stephen's vision in Acts 7: 55–6; Paul's heavenly vision as described by Luke in Acts 22 in terms of an element in a trance in the Temple; and the 'visions and revelations of the Lord' referred to by Paul himself in 2 Corinthians 12: 1, and concretely illustrated by reference to the person who was 'caught up into the third heaven', or as illustrated with more descriptive detail by John the Divine in Revelation 1, we are faced with a problem. If these experiences are to be distinguished from more fundamental encounters on which faith is allegedly to be based, we need to know what the criteria are for doing so.[7] I think, therefore, in the absence of evidence that would allow us to establish some kind of fundamental difference, we have no alternative than to admit defeat. We quite simply do not have the evidence to decide this matter historically, and I do not think, therefore that we can either dismiss Luedemann's hypothesis lightly or simply ignore it.[8]

---

[6] J. D. G. Dunn, *Jesus and the Spirit* (London: SCM, 1975), 133.

[7] See my discussion of Pannenberg and Grass on this point in *The Structure of Resurrection Belief* (Oxford: Clarendon, 1987), 68–72, 244–5.

[8] I notice that O'Collins has not engaged with Luedemann at all, save for a passing reference to his view that the empty tomb tradition is not a creation of Mark but a tradition he received. See above, pp. 16–17.

James Dunn's suggestion that the story of the empty tomb may be of assistance in securing the belief that the appearances were objective rather than subjective psychogenic visions depends, of course, on the degree of credence to be accorded to it. Unfortunately, the ambiguous nature of the evidence of the empty tomb, which gives rise to the current debate about whether it is to be regarded as historically accurate or factual or simply legendary, does not inspire a great deal of confidence at this point.

In relation to this issue O'Collins takes issue with Norman Perrin where the latter says: 'Scholars are coming increasingly to the conclusion that the empty tomb tradition is an interpretation of the event—a way of saying "Jesus is risen"—rather than a description of an aspect of the event itself.'[9] Similarly, Hans Küng argues that 'the majority of critical biblical exegetes . . . conclude that the stories about the tomb are legendary elaborations of the message of the resurrection'.[10] In response to these assertions, O'Collins cites some thirty scholars who believe in the historicity of the empty tomb. Unfortunately, he does not compile a similar list of those who support the contention of the legendary nature of the stories. I hesitate to do so myself, even if it could be done fairly easily,[11] because of serious methodological qualms about the propriety of so doing. After all, truth is not decided by democratic procedures. Such an approach smacks of the methods of the Jesus Seminar using coloured beads in bottles! What we need in order to resolve this kind of issue is not a poll of numbers of conflicting authorities on either side of the dispute, but convincing arguments. However, convincing arguments presuppose evidence, and I am afraid we do not have sufficient of it to decide the matter either way.

This does not mean that we can never be certain about historical matters, or that the word 'certain' can never be properly used in relation to the past. For we can be certain that there was a World War between 1914 and 1918. By claiming certainty in relation to such a matter, we mean to indicate that we have consulted sufficient evidence to come to the conclusion that no further assessment need be done, and that we can discount the possibility that further evidence might come to light which would disprove the occurrence

---

[9] Norman Perrin, *The Resurrection Narratives* (London: SCM, 1977), 82–3.

[10] Hans Küng, *Credo* (London/New York: SCM/Doubleday, 1993).

[11] Such a list might begin with Reimarus, Strauss, and Bultmann, and work through a range of modern post-Bultmannian scholars.

of the First World War. But in relation to the story of the empty tomb we simply do not have the kind of evidence that would allow us to ground a conclusion with that kind of certainty. Indeed, the very diversity of viewpoint amongst contemporary theologians on this point is a clear indication of the fact that nobody really knows with any certainty whether the empty tomb story is historically factual or legendary. Putting such a matter to democratic vote does not impress me. And if the wise person proportions his or her belief to the evidence, I think any responsible scholar must acknowledge today that this matter remains indeterminate. We cannot, therefore, follow James Dunn's suggestion that the empty tomb somehow resolves the question of the ambiguity of the appearances so as to decide with any degree of certainty whether they were objective or subjective visions.

It therefore seems to me that John Hick's suggestion that we can today account for the visions by appeal to similarities with experiences reported by those who have been near death and the natural operation on the psyche of the trauma of death and of the irreversible separation of the bereaved from a deceased loved one still poses one of the pressing questions facing the theology of the resurrection. The 'subjective vision theory' has been around in one form or another for the last two centuries. I do not think it is simply going to go away. I do not think it can simply be ignored. I do not think it has been adequately answered in Father O'Collins's essay. We can choose to ignore Gerd Luedemann and his thesis, John Hick's very similar but more tentative suggestion, and the views of anybody else who has run a similar line, stretching back to David Strauss in 1835, and we can shout louder about the alleged objectivity of the Easter appearances. But I am afraid that will not lay the 'subjective vision hypothesis' to rest.

Given this conclusion, I think we have to face the question of what difference it would actually make to faith if it were to be the case that there was a psychological cause of the Easter visions of Jesus. In other words, given that we do not have the historical evidence to rule out the possibility that the appearances may have been the product of psychological processes of bereavement amongst the disciples, what is our next move? If we are very unlikely ever to be able either to prove or to disprove the thesis that the appearances were psychologically induced 'subjective visions', rather than some kind of 'objective vision', where do we go from here?

Even Luedemann insists that a psychological explanation of the visions does not necessarily rule out the possibility that Jesus is alive with God (in some sense of 'is alive with God') as the exalted Christ. Though I suspect I have a different understanding from Luedemann of what is connoted by the words 'is alive', this is a point that I myself also made in passing in *The Structure of Resurrection Belief* nearly a decade ago.[12] There I referred to the purposive nature of psychic function: to explain a vision as the product of the 'subconscious' or 'personal unconscious' does not mean that it is somehow less than real or that it does not serve some positive purpose. At this point it is pertinent to note that Carl Jung himself once complained that: 'If, in physics, one seeks to explain the nature of light, nobody expects as a result that there will be no light. But in the case of psychology everybody believes that what it explains is explained away.'[13] Explaining the psychological cause of a vision does not explain it away. The experience of the vision remains as an actual experience rather than, let us say, a flight of creative imagination. But this still leaves the important question of the meaning of the vision: what is it to which it is pointing? Or what is it to which it is alerting a person? Indeed, the significance of phenomena of the human subconscious has to be interpreted; more often than not, such phenomena alert us to truths of which we should be more aware, but to which, for some reason, we are blind. If the 'subjective vision hypothesis' were to be proved, why could the visions not still point to the heavenly existence of the raised Christ?

I would argue that even if the appearances could be explained as psychogenic projections, that in any event does not necessarily inhibit belief in the heavenly existence of the raised Christ. It does mean, however, that we may have to look for another cognitive anchor for faith and hope. For, if it were to turn out to be accepted as the most satisfactory explanation of the available evidence, the 'subjective vision hypothesis' might not inhibit faith, but it almost certainly would not be sufficient to ground, and certainly not to sustain, the Church's continuing faith in the heavenly existence of the resurrected Christ.

---

[12] (Oxford: Clarendon Press, 1987), 245–6.

[13] C. G. Jung, 'Answer to Job', in *Psychology and Religion: West and East, Collected Works*, xi (New York: Pantheon Books, Inc., 1958), 463 n. Jung also says: 'I do not underestimate the psyche in any respect whatsoever, nor do I imagine for a moment that psychic happenings vanish into thin air by being explained' (ibid. 463).

It is at this point that I want to respond to O'Collins's comments in reference to my own view of the importance of the experience of the Spirit of Christ as the *Christus praesens* as I endeavoured to argue that in *The Structure of Resurrection Belief*. It is not true, as he says, that I argue that 'the experienced reality of Easter revelation and faith seems to have been and to remain largely confined to the experience of Christ's Spirit'.[14] I do not wish to *confine* the Easter event to an experience of the raised Christ as Spirit. Even if we are unable historically to resolve the question of the status to be assigned to the visions, and even if we acknowledge the legendary character of the redactional development of the appearance narratives, I think the reports of appearances as such are far too securely rooted in the tradition for us to be able to side-step their importance in the first coming to faith, or simply to devalue or ignore them. My point, however, is that the appearances tradition does not stand alone. In the earliest written stratum of the New Testament—that is to say, in the letters of St Paul—in addition to listing the appearances to the other disciples and to himself, St Paul speaks about, and indeed continually celebrates, the continuing *presence* of the raised Christ as Spirit, for 'The last Adam has become a life-giving Spirit' (1 Cor. 15: 45). What I argued in *The Structure of Resurrection Belief* was that this provides us with an additional datum in the cognitive nucleus of faith, an additional empirical anchor for faith, for which we urgently need an epistemology so as to explain how it is possible to identify and know the Spirit, not just as the 'Spirit of God' in some very general sense, but as the living Spirit of the remembered Jesus, the crucified one.

In other words, it is at this point that we can respond very aggressively and positively to the thesis of Sallie McFague, who reduces the Easter story to a paradigm of God's general presence and spiritual activity in the world at large. For her, the story of Jesus' resurrection becomes nothing more than a heuristic device to teach us something about God and the world. Curiously, Gerd Luedemann's final position comes down to essentially the same kind of thing. For them both, the decision of faith is a claim that is made not in response to the perceived presence of the raised Christ, but in response, as Luedemann says, to 'the historical Jesus, as he is presented to me by the texts and encounters me as a person through

---

[14] See above, p. 18.

historical reconstruction'.[15] Clearly, for Luedemann it is the man Jesus who, as the ground of faith, is 'the clue to God in our life', for 'notions of faith arise from the communion with God which is opened up as a result'. But this is communion with God understood in some very general sense, and if Christ enjoys a continuing life as the Exalted One, he is, according to Luedemann, 'hidden from us'; 'only God is manifest'. Without an epistemology of Easter faith which can account for the identification of the Spirit of the post-Easter community as not just the Spirit of God but also (in some sense of 'but also') the Spirit of Jesus, Luedemann has nowhere to go. He has no alternative than to fall back into a kind of pre-Trinitarian monotheistic monarchianism.[16]

O'Collins rightly urges in relation to McFague that Easter faith involves more than this, and the same could be said with respect to Luedemann. However, if it involves the claim that something happened to Jesus, and that faith, therefore, is in some sense a continuing engagement *with Jesus*, and not just with God understood in a monotheistic or unitarian sense, we need an epistemology that accounts for the claim to know the presence not just of the Spirit of God, but to know the Spirit as also (in some sense of 'as also') precisely the Spirit of the crucified Jesus.

The major part of *The Structure of Resurrection Belief* was devoted to providing an outline of such an epistemology, which I shall not attempt to repeat here. Suffice it to say that I still think the task of providing an epistemology that can account for the Christian claim to identify the presence of the raised Christ as a religious object in present experience, rather than just engage in what I think is a somewhat futile quest for the historical resurrected Jesus, is the most important challenge facing resurrection theology today. It might be said as well, of course, that this constitutes the most difficult challenge facing us today. It is understandable that it is the area that most theologians of the resurrection put into the too-hard basket. I think this is a pity.

---

[15] Luedemann, *Resurrection of Jesus*, 183.
[16] This retreat from the uncertainties of historical research to a kind of *sturmfreies Gebiet* grounded in the 'communion of God' derives from Wilhelm Herrmann, *The Communion of the Christian with God*, 4th German edn. 1903 (New York: Putnam, 1903).

3

Resurrection and the New Jerusalem

JANET MARTIN SOSKICE

Which would you rather be, a stone or a chip? Let us consider two stories about resurrection bodies.

The Stones

As you approach the town of Ely by train, travelling over the flat Fenlands, you may note amongst all the towers and spires on the horizon one particular jagged tower—from this distance it might be a farm building or an electricity pylon. As you draw closer, you notice that, though it seems to change position, this tower does not go away. In fact it gets larger. You see that it is definitely a church tower, maybe that of one of the little parish churches dotted about the countryside. But while those other churches appear and recede among the hedges and clumps of trees as the train moves past, this one remains, changing positions always, remaining in view. You may then see that there are actually two towers and realize that this is a much bigger building—a very big building indeed—sitting on a hill, on the only hill around.

This bigger building seems now to exercise some mysterious influence over the smaller ones—calling them up, as though the little churches were smaller fragments of its bulk. Not just church buildings but farm buildings, sheds, water-towers, little houses, all seem to be called up, elevated by that great stone structure that sits on the hill like a mother hen with her chicks attendant. And you realize that this is the cathedral, the New Jerusalem, the City of Zion; for medieval cathedrals like this one were deliberately built on hills as emblems, or types, of the New Jerusalem as described in the Book of Revelation, with its towers, gates, and dazzling walls.

When you get into Ely, the great building disappears temporarily from view. You could see it from six miles away, but now, only metres away, it is hidden by shops and offices and buses. But then you may round the corner, and there it is, straight up: the City of God, the angels, the saints, the nations. It is a female body—daughter of Zion, Mother Church. It is the male body of Christ, the dwelling of God with men and women.

Medieval rites of dedication for cathedrals made explicit the perceived connections between these buildings and the vision of the heavenly Jerusalem as given in the Book of Revelation. But the apocalyptic images of the book themselves, as Laurence Stookey remarks, have their 'roots in the Old Testament prophets who dream of the renewal of the Davidic kingdom'. Stookey continues:

Psalms and other poetic passages which referred originally to the earthly city of Jerusalem or Zion came to have an eschatological reference. Ezekiel's vision of the ideal temple is heavily dependent on the Temple of Solomon. The New Jerusalem of the Revelation is 'new' with reference to the historic city with which the writer was so familiar.[1]

In following this tradition of symbolic understandings, the Gothic architects were building not only in stone, but in images—a theological meditation in stone and glass.

Consecration liturgies, *circa* the tenth century, began with invocations of Psalm 24. In the translation from the Jerusalem Bible (which, I will, use throughout),

> Gates, raise your arches,
> rise, you ancient doors,
> let the king of glory in! (Ps. 24: 7)

Then followed reference to Jacob's establishment of a shrine at Bethel:

How awe-inspiring this place is! This is nothing less than a house of God; this is the gate of heaven! (Gen. 28: 17)

While these liturgical uses might at first blush seem to the modern reader to be little more than opportunistic invocation of biblical texts that speak reverently of sacred buildings, it would be wrong not to note that a developed theology of divine presence lay behind them. The antiphons speak of Jerusalem, the holy city, Zion, the place of God's tabernacling with the people. As Stookey points out,

---

[1] Laurence Hull Stookey, 'The Gothic Cathedral as the Heavenly Jerusalem: Liturgical and Theological Sources', *Gesta*, 8 (1969), 35.

the 'standard lesson in virtually all consecrations rites of this period' was from the Book of Revelation:

I saw the holy city, and the new Jerusalem, coming down from God out of heaven, as beautiful as a bride all dressed for her husband. Then I heard a loud voice call from the throne, 'You see this city? Here God lives among men. He will make his home among them; they shall be his people, and he will be their God.' (Rev. 21: 2–3)

As well as looking proleptically to the New Jerusalem, the Roman rite looks back to Solomon's dedication of the First Temple as a prototype (2 Chr. 7: 1–16). 'After this', notes Stookey, 'a portion of a sermon of St. Augustine is read, amplifying the awareness that the true temple of God is made not of inert rock, but of human hearts and spirits.'[2]

This is not, of course, an attempt to 'canonize' a particular kind of church architecture. It's an exercise in architectural and liturgical figuration, where the physical body of stone and glass and light becomes an emblem of the Temple, of the holy of holies, the dwelling of God, and also an emblem of the living Body of Christ in stone. The complexity of these structures reflects the complexity and specificity of the living Body of Christ—a Church made up of many distinct individuals who, not despite their individuality but because of it, can be brought through their Lord into a glorious architectonic whole.

I want to suggest to you the Temple as an image of the resurrection and of the resurrected body of Christ. It is not a usual image, perhaps because we think of the resurrected body as living and of stones as dead (yet ask any stonemason or sculptor if stones lack life!) Yet attention to the Temple imagery in the New Testament may go a long way towards prizing open for us what the resurrection of Jesus might have meant to the first Christians.

Jesus himself, we believe, said interesting and dangerous— indeed, possibly fatal things—about the Temple. Matthew has Jesus speak of the Temple during his appearance before the Sanhedrin. After several reportedly false witnesses, 'Eventually two stepped forward and made a statement, "This man said, 'I have power to

---

[2] Ibid. 37. The doors of the upper choir of Abbot Suger's St Denis bore an inscription that reminded those who might marvel at the workmanship that, bright though the work might be, above all the work, 'Should brighten the minds, so that they may travel through the true lights, To the True Light where Christ is the true door' (ibid. 39).

destroy the Temple of God and in three days build it up' " ' (Matt. 26: 60-1). Jesus does not deny this charge. It may be that this was another 'false' accusation. It may be that Jesus said some such thing. John's placing and elaboration of the 'temple destruction' saying might suggest this. There, pointedly after the cleansing of the Temple, Jesus is asked:

'What sign can you show us to justify what you have done?' Jesus answered, 'Destroy this sanctuary, and in three days I will raise it up'. The Jews replied, 'It has taken forty-six years to build this sanctuary: are you going to raise it up in three days?' But he was speaking of the sanctuary that was his body, and when Jesus rose from the dead, his disciples remembered that he had said this, and they believed the scripture and the words he had said. (John 2: 19-22)

Early Christians, it would seem, believed that Jesus had styled his own body as the Temple, or at least (*pace* John's Gospel) that Jesus' body could be styled as the Temple.[3] What might this mean for them? What did Temple mean for them? Paul is one of our earliest witnesses. The theme of the body as temple is one that he takes up and uses time and again in describing the mission and building of the Church. 'You are God's building', he tells the Corinthians,

By the grace God gave me, I succeeded as an architect and laid the foundations, on which someone else is doing the building. Everyone doing the building must work carefully. For the foundation, nobody can lay any other than the one which has already been laid, that is Jesus Christ. On this foundation you can build in gold, silver and jewels, or in wood, grass and straw, but whatever the material, the work of each builder is going to be clearly revealed when the day comes. (Cor. 3: 10-23)

A more specific identity for this 'building' is given a few verses later:

Didn't you realize that you were God's temple [*naos*, or 'sanctuary'] and that the Spirit of God was living among you? If anybody should destroy the temple of God, God will destroy him, because the temple of God is sacred; and you are that temple. (1 Cor. 3: 16-17)

Paul's string of metaphors seems to work in this way: Christ is the foundation, Paul the architect and builder, all Christians are

---

[3] I am aware of the gap between what Jesus might actually have said (possibly a straightforward reference to the Temple) and John's later theologizing. Either way, the association of the body of Jesus with the Temple is an interesting one—whether, that is, it was made by Jesus himself or by his early followers.

also builders and, at the same time, the building. This building is God's temple, or sanctuary, the place of God's dwelling.

I hope I have suggested that the 'cathedral as temple' is thus not a cold and lifeless image for resurrection, but lively and biblically resonant. As a theological figure, it has the further significant advantage of displaying the corporateness of the Christian conception of new life: the Christians are, each one, to be living stones, each one distinct but comprising together the great building whose foundation is Christ.

For Paul the image of the temple is, *au fond*, corporate, but with implications for the individual: each 'living stone' goes to make up the sanctuary, the place of God's dwelling. This, by the way, is an interesting key to Paul's moral teaching in First Corinthians:

> You know, surely, that your bodies are members making up the body of Christ; do you think I can take parts of Christ's body and join them to the body of a prostitute? Never! . . . Your body, you know, is a temple of the Holy Spirit, who is in you since you received him from God. (Cor. 6: 15–19)

While Christian moral teaching is often associated with the notion of the 'sanctity of life', the New Testament seems not particularly concerned with life *per se*. But Paul is *very* concerned with the sanctity of the *body*, for the body (corporate) of believers is the temple of the Holy Spirit. The individual parts of Christ's body (our bodies) cannot be joined to the body of a prostitute without defiling the whole. What might a renewed focus on the sanctity of the human body mean for Christian ethics? It would presumably no longer be possible to meet Christians adamant against abortion but bothered seemingly not at all by the sex trade or pornography. The same New Testament principles would seem to underline opposition to both— that is, the sanctity of the body as temple of the Holy Spirit.

So that is one story, the story of the stones and of the Temple as an image of the resurrection: Christ's risen body, the new Temple, is a New Jerusalem built of living stones. Each of the faithful goes to make up that glorious building and is, simultaneously, him or herself the temple of the Holy Spirit.

The Chips

For my second story, the story of the chips, I am indebted to Ted Peters's deft review of Frank Tipler's best-selling book *The Physics of*

Immortality, a book in which Tipler discusses the physical basis of 'immortal life'. Tipler is himself a scientist and self-confessed non-Christian. Though he himself rejects the claim that Jesus rose from the dead, behold, he shows us a better way. Let me refer you to Ted Peters's summary.

Tipler argues that if we live in a closed universe that will eventually double back on itself and collapse in a big crunch making all physical life as we know it impossible, the human race may still escape to a supra-physical dimension of reality in which conscious experiencing will go on forever. Tipler says there is a physical mechanism that leads to resurrection of living beings: it is computer simulation. By defining a living being as essentially an information processor, Tipler envisions an eschatological computing capacity in which all previously living beings will be simulated—reduplicated, replicated or living beings will be simulated—along with their respective environments to live in never ending subjective time. Objective time along with its physical cosmos may self-destruct; but the supra-physical society of resurrected emulations will live on eternally at what he calls 'Point Omega'.[4]

Ted Peters, reflecting on a funeral he has recently attended, asks himself, 'Is this where Ethel Mae is going . . . to await the simulation of her information processing pattern?' With Tipler we go beyond Feuerbach's modest claim that theology is anthropology. 'Theology is a branch of physics,' he (Tipler) exclaims; 'physicists can infer by calculation the existence of God and the likelihood of the resurrection of the dead to eternal life in exactly the same way as physicists calculate the properties of the electron.'[5] And, 'Science can now offer *precisely* the consolations in facing death that religion once offered. Religion is now a part of science.' *The Physics of Immortality* now appears as a new *Phaedo*, with the Socratic Tipler defending the immortality of the soul—or of a 'sort of' soul. Ted Peters continues:

Does Tipler believe in a human soul? Yes, sort of. He starts with his definition of a living being as 'any entity which codes information . . . and the human soul—is a very complex computer program'. This defines an individual person as a complex machine that processes information and enjoys some independence from the body. He can assume that life goes on forever if machines of some sort can continue to exist forever.[6]

---

[4] Ted Peters, 'The Physical Body of Immortality', *Center for Theology and the Natural Sciences Bulletin*, 15/2 (Spring 1995), 1.

[5] Ibid. 2.   [6] Ibid. 4.

Resurrection for Tipler is solely the result of a future evolutionary event in which life understood as information processing takes hold of its own destiny and creates a supra-physical environment for its existence just prior to the moment when the physical world self-destructs.[7]

Tipler, though not a Christian, believes his theory could explain Jesus' resurrection appearances, as a simulated person appearing and disappearing in different parts of the universe. But in the end, as Peters points out,

All Tipler is doing here is saying some interesting things about the Easter phenomenon. He sees no proleptic or redemptive powers in Jesus' resurrection that has any impact on the rest of us. In sum, for Tipler there is but a loose connection between Jesus' Easter body and our future resurrected forms.[8]

This is a very interesting observation. For Tipler the resurrection of Jesus has no immediate importance for the rest of us. In the story of the chips, then, Jesus appears as (only) the first 'virtual reality Adam', our pioneer in cyberspace. Jesus is the first individual to attain the information continuity to which all individuals may aspire.

Frank Tipler (as I would assume even he would admit) is no sure guide in matters of Christian theology. Yet it is not without interest that he should think that his remake of resurrection can offer 'precisely the consolations in facing death that religion once offered'.

Christian apologetics often suffers from its own successes, and a certain historic strand of evidentialist apologetics for the resurrection may, one has regretfully to conclude, explain Tipler. It can be argued, in any case, that following Locke's launch of the evidentialist challenge, the considerable energies spent on demonstrating the 'reasonableness' of belief in the resurrection (as a special case of miracle) has had the inadvertent effect of flattening popular Christian (and anti-Christian) understandings of what resurrection faith might be.[9]

---

[7] Ibid. 11.   [8] Ibid.

[9] Locke's own context, again, was rather different, and his insistence that religious beliefs must be held rationally was a challenge to fellow Christians, religious 'enthusiasts', not a criterion for debate between Christian and sceptic. On this, and on the way evidentialist strategies differ from earlier and different exercises in natural theology, see Nicholas Wolterstorff's elegant essay, 'The Migration of the Theistic Arguments: From Natural Theology to Evidentialist Apologetics', in Robert Audi and William J. Wainwright (eds.), *Rationality, Religious Belief and Moral Commitment: New Essays in the Philosophy of Religion* (Ithaca, NY: Cornell University Press, 1986), 38–81.

Let me make it clear that, in what follows, I do not wish to dissolve the resurrection into affect. I am perfectly happy to say that Jesus rose, even bodily, from the grave—an unrepentant empty tomber. But what I am less happy about is the way in which the empty tomb has come to be seen by many as almost the sum total of 'belief in the resurrection'. This is true of many who dismiss Christian belief in resurrection as a claim about things that go bump in the night, no more worthy of our attention than a claim to have sighted Elvis on the moon. It is sadly also true of not a few Christians.[10]

In this respect, then, we may be grateful to Frank Tipler, and his *etiolated orthodoxy* of the resurrection, for providing a straw man which, none the less, helps to demonstrate the points of strain in speaking to modern people about the resurrection.

What I mean by an *'etiolated orthodoxy* of the resurrection' would be largely subsumed by two basic assertions: first, that Jesus was raised (the tomb was empty), and second, that we too shall be raised. The 'goods' this delivers are similarly twofold: immortality is guaranteed, and personal identity is ensured—this last because a resurrection body side-steps some philosophical difficulties otherwise posed by the idea of the perdurance of a disembodied soul. These beliefs are all right—even highly commendable—as far as they go, but do they amount to resurrection faith? Is belief in a miraculously empty tomb, even conjoined with the belief that we too will rise, worth being martyred for? Is the hope that there is life after death, however important and moving, the hope that caused a group of Galilean peasants, persons with no worldly security, to drop everything and follow Jesus? Is this the 'faith' in the resurrection that caused his followers, last seen cowering in an upper room, to risk death and suffer death to preach? If so, would not Tipler be within his rights (if you accept his science) in saying that now science can offer 'precisely' the consolations in facing death that religion once offered?[11]

---

[10] I am not suggesting that any philosophers of religion involved in evidentialist apologetics themselves have taken this thin theological position, but only that in popular imagination, the attention paid (quite reasonably in its own terms) to defending the reasonableness of miracles and of the resurrection as an instance of miracle in Enlightenment apologetics has had this unintended effect. Those who contest my diagnosis may have had different experiences teaching and speaking to Christian (and non-Christian) groups than I have.

[11] Peters, 'Physical Body of Immortality', 2.

But let us assume that this is an etiolated version which, if necessary, is scarcely sufficient for what we might call 'full-blooded' resurrection faith. This last seemed to involve for the first Christians the belief that Jesus was the Christ, the promised one of Israel, who came to inaugurate a reign of justice and peace and to restore the world to its original created intent of wholeness and flourishing. The resurrection of Jesus, this conquest of death by the Lord's anointed, is the beginning of the restoration which will bring a new heaven and a new earth. To ask of contemporary Christians that they believe the resurrection of Jesus inaugurated a 'new creation' in which all our relationships one with another and with the world around us are changed is to ask a good deal more than that they believe that God has intervened in the 'natural' order. But talk of a new creation is figurative, and some would say even florid, language. Let us see what sense we might make of it.

New Testament scholars often say that we do not know enough from the Gospels to take a stand on the resurrection of Jesus. There is not enough evidence. It seems impossible to doubt, however, that some of the New Testament writers themselves believed in Jesus' resurrection—Luke and John in a bodily resurrection.[12] Paul's writings are more ambiguous on the precise nature of resurrection, but that resurrection is of vital importance to his theology is clear. Indeed, he thwacks the Corinthians over the head with resurrection belief in 1 Corinthians 15:

Brothers, I want to remind you of the gospel I preached to you . . . that Jesus died for our sins, in accordance with scriptures—and that he was raised to life on the third day in accordance with the scriptures. Now if Christ raised from the dead is what has been preached, how can some of you be saying that there is no resurrection of the dead? (1 Cor. 15: 1, 3–4, 12)

If Christ is not raised, he says, then he is a perjurer, and all our hopes perish. Paul certainly did not think that the main significance of the resurrection of Jesus was that it proved God exists, or that God could intervene in what we call the 'causal order'—of this, presumably, Paul had no doubt. Paul's understanding of the resurrection, like his understanding of atonement, pervades his letters, and

---

[12] Matthew may suggest bodily resurrection, but Mark has no resurrection appearances at all. I am grateful to Dr Marcus Bockmuehl for help on this point, and others, in this essay.

is not readily reducible to a few points. We might find some interesting traces, however, by considering the way in which Paul and some other New Testament writers mobilize imagery of the Temple.

I have already mentioned that the builders of medieval cathedrals placed themselves within a long and complex tradition of use of temple symbolism going back to the texts of the Hebrew Bible itself. In the New Testament the Temple is symbolically associated with the Church, with the body (especially that of Christ, but also that of the individual Christian), with Zion/Jerusalem, with the holy of holies, and with perfect sacrifice. This does not mean that these topics can be substituted one for the other; rather, images overlap, variously contrasting with and informing other usages. Such imagery has been described as 'kaleidoscopic'[13] (since the images merge into one another), but the comparison with a kaleidoscope does not quite elicit the simultaneity of the figuration—the way in which each image may simultaneously enrich and be enriched by the others in joins. The Temple images, through the Jewish and Christian texts, move over each other like a series of maps on transparencies, all of the same physical site, but all bearing different information—this one of political history, another of contemporary nation-states, another of natural mineral resources, and so on.

Let us begin with the city of Jerusalem. Jerusalem, through the texts of the Hebrew Bible, gets a mixed press: not originally a Jewish city, it becomes David's capital, and, most important, David brings the Ark to it. The holy of holies, once housed in a tent or tabernacle, is brought to rest in the city. Second Chronicles described how Solomon, son of David, builds the Temple in Jerusalem, and at the same time makes an important ascription of place; 'Solomon then began to build the house of Yahweh on Mount Moriah where David his father had a vision' (2 Chr. 3: 1). The site of Solomon's Temple (Jerusalem/Mount Zion) is thus identified in 2 Chronicles with the place of Abraham's near-sacrifice of Isaac.[14]

Abraham, we recall, had been promised that he would become a great nation through whom all the nations of the world would be

---

[13] John Sweet (following Paul Minear), 'A House Not Made With Hands', William Horbury (ed.), *Templum Amicitiae: Essays on the Second Temple Presented to Ernst Bammel*, JSOTSS 48 (Sheffield: JSOT Press, 1991), 374.

[14] Chronicles is a book of the Second Temple period, which suggests a theological purpose at work in the identification.

blessed (Gen. 18: 1 ff.). Yet in Genesis 22 Abraham is told, 'take your son, your favoured one, and go to the land of Moriah and offer him as a burnt offering'. Isaac (not his eldest son, but his favoured one and the one through whom he understands his succession will take place) he is told to sacrifice. (Christian readers may perhaps be struck here by recollection of the 'beloved son' motif as it appears in Matthew 3: 17 when God speaks from the heavens at the time of Jesus' baptism, 'This is my Son, the Beloved, my favour rests on him'.[15]) When 2 Chronicles identifies the site of Solomon's Temple with Moriah, Jerusalem is identified as the site where Abraham showed himself willing to sacrifice his 'promise' and descent, his 'immortality', at God's behest. It is the place of supreme sacrifice.

Solomon's Temple grew in importance. As housing the Ark, it symbolized Yahweh's election of the city as God's dwelling; thus the Deuteronomist, 'Yahweh causes his name to dwell there' (Deut. 12: 11). Jesus lived in the time of Herod's Temple, a time when the Temple appears to have been, for many Jews, a glorious but ambiguous symbol. The Essences eschewed what they regarded as the corruption of the Jerusalem Temple and had their own counter-Temple movement wherein their own community was styled as the Temple.[16] Yet the Temple, even for those critical of its contemporary management, remained the unquestionable sign of God's presence with Israel. Powers to create and redeem hung significantly about the figure of the Temple. As Paula Frederickson points out, the Hebrew Bible begins with the creation of the universe and ends with the call, following the Exile, to rebuild the Temple. 'These two narrative poles of the Bible establish the typological field of later Jewish eschatology. Put plainly: when final redemption comes, it will come as a renovation of creation, and a new Temple and new Jerusalem figure prominently.'[17] Return from exile implies rebuilding. Creation is fulfilled in redemption.

This brings us to the extremely interesting question of Jesus'

---

[15] For an exploration of this motif in Jewish and Christian texts see Jon D. Levenson, *The Death and Resurrection of the Beloved Son* (New Haven: Yale University Press, 1993).

[16] See Tom Wright's very interesting article 'Jerusalem in the New Testament', in P. W. L. Walker (ed.), *Jerusalem: Past and Present in the Purposes of God* (Cambridge: Tyndale House, 1992), 56.

[17] Paula Frederickson, 'Vile Bodies: Paul and Augustine on the Resurrection of the Flesh', in Mark S. Burrows and Paul Rorem, (eds.), *Biblical Hermeneutics in Historical Perspective* (Grand Rapids, Mich.: Eerdmans, 1991), 77.

Temple sayings. At various places in the Gospels Jesus is credited
with saying he would destroy the Temple (Mark 14: 58; 15: 29).
At one time these sayings were thought by New Testament scholars to be retrojections, later theological additions following the
destruction of the Jerusalem Temple. Consensus now seems to be
growing in another direction. There are good reasons to believe that
Jesus did speak of a forthcoming destruction of the Temple, a charge
levelled against him in the crucifixion narratives. Nor would Jesus
have been alone in predicting the fall of Jerusalem and its Temple.
The corruption of the ruling classes in Jerusalem and disaffection
amongst northerners (such as were Galilean peasants) with the perceived privileges and decadence of the south and Jerusalem were
commonplace.[18]

Many New Testament scholars now think that Jesus' teaching,
preaching, and actions need to be placed within the context of then
current Jewish restoration eschatology. Amongst its elements were
anticipation of an imminent divine intervention whereby God would
impose his rule (kingdom), the re-gathering of the twelve tribes,
renewal of true worship and sacrifice in Jerusalem and its Temple,
and the ingathering of the Gentiles. Ideas of resurrection, especially
of those who had died as martyrs to their faith, were gaining
ground. Jesus, it has been argued, shared the common perceptions
of Jews of the Second Temple period in seeing the Temple as the
place of God's presence and certain salvation; but he also perceived
God to be doing something new. If, indeed, we can credit Jesus with
the Temple sayings in the Gospels and with the association made
explicit by John of his own body with the Temple, then Jesus
appears to be saying that he himself is the locus for this new work.
'We heard him say', say his accusers, ' "I will pull down this
Temple that is made with hands and in three days I will build up
another, not made with hands" ' (Mark 14: 58, cf. Matt. 26: 61;
John 2: 19).

Other New Testament imagery associated with Jesus also elicits
the Temple—for instance, that of 'living' or running water. The
prophets, looking forward to the coming of the righteous king, often
used metaphors of running water: 'when that day comes, running
waters will issue from Jerusalem' (Zech. 14: 8). Isaiah, in another
passage well known to Christians through its use in hymns, says in

---

[18] Wright, 'Jerusalem in the New Testament', 59–63.

a vision of the New Jerusalem, 'Come everyone that thirsts, come to the water. Though you are poor, come, buy and eat.' The Essenes, as mentioned, in their counter-Temple movement styled their own community as the new temple, cherishing Ezekiel's vision of the rebuilt Temple, pure and holy, from which living water would run.[19] It is not surprising, then, that in John's Gospel we find Jesus during the Feast of Tabernacles, the Jewish harvest festival and one especially associated with imagery of water and promised fruitfulness, standing in the Temple and crying out, 'If any man is thirsty, let him come to me! Let the man come and drink who believes in me!' The evangelist glosses: 'As scripture says: From his breast shall flow fountains of living water' (John 7: 37–8). Some of those listening, John tells us, said 'He is the Christ'; others, 'Would the Christ be from Galilee?'; but once again we have eschatological actions, Messianic claims, and Temple precincts.

Tom Wright is one of those who credits Jesus himself with the explicit association of his own body and the Temple. Wright goes so far as to say that 'Though people say that Israel had no idea of incarnation, this is clearly a mistake: the temple itself, and by extension Jerusalem, was seen as the dwelling place of the living God. Thus it was the temple that Jesus took as his model, and against whose claims he advanced his own.'[20] If, indeed, Jesus styled his own body as counter-Temple, then his Temple sayings take their place in an acting out of one of Israel's oldest goals: she was to be 'a light for the nations' (Isa. 42: 6); God's house in Jerusalem was meant to be a 'place of prayer for all the nations' (Isa. 56: 7; Mark 11: 17). But God would now achieve this through the new Temple, which was Jesus himself and his people.[21] Jesus himself would 'act as the replacement of the temple, which was of course the dwelling-place of the Shekinah, the tabernacling of Israel's God with his people'.[22]

With some of this Temple imagery in the (later) Gospels in mind, let us return to (the earlier) Paul. Paul as one 'late born' and, in his

---

[19] Ibid. 56.   [20] Ibid. 62.   [21] Ibid.

[22] Ibid. 58. Wright's position is not uncontroversial. It is not clear, as suggested earlier, that Jesus (in contradistinction to his followers and the NT writers) associated his body with the Temple. Nor is it clear that 'replacement', with its supersessionist overtones, is the most felicitous term to use here. On this see Marcus Bockmuehl, *This Jesus* (Edinburgh: T. & T. Clark, 1994), 60–76. For my purposes it is not necessary to insist, as Wright seems to, on Jesus' self-understanding in terms of the Temple.

own understanding, apostle to the Gentiles, feels the resurrection message with particular urgency. In Romans 11 Paul invokes the Zion tradition in speaking of the promise to the Jews:

have the Jews fallen for ever, or have they just stumbled? Obviously they have not fallen for ever: their fall, though, has saved the pagans in a way the Jews might now emulate. Think of the extent to which the world, the pagan world, has benefited from their fall and defection—then think how much more it will benefit from the conversion of them all. Let me tell you pagans this: I have been sent to the pagans as their apostle, and I am proud of being sent, but the purpose of it is to make my own people envious of you, and in this way to save some of them. Since their rejection meant the reconciliation of the world, do you know what their admission will mean? Nothing less than a resurrection from the dead! (Rom. 11: 11–15)

And then:

One section of Israel has become blind, but this will last only until the whole pagan world has entered, and then after this the rest of Israel will be saved as well. As scripture says: *The liberator will come from Zion, he will banish godlessness from Jacob. And this is the covenant I will make with them when I take their sins away.* (Rom. 11: 25–7)

Zion/Israel will be a source of blessing to the world. According to Wright, Paul is not anticipating some Platonizing of Jerusalem. The 'new Jerusalem' is not a place of non-material reality, but the place of God's present and future reality. This new Zion, like the old, would be (figuratively at least) the place of the Temple.

With this image of the new Zion in mind, we can approach Paul's use of the figure of the Temple. In Paul's writings, as mentioned earlier, both the corporate body of believers (the Church) and the individual Christian are spoken of as 'temple'. While to the contemporary reader this image may conjure up no more than a certain architectural splendour (I once heard a comedian say that his own body was not so much a 'temple' as a 'Methodist meeting-house of the Holy Spirit'), Wright argues that Paul's use of this image, within twenty-five years of the crucifixion and with the Temple still standing, must be seen as strong, provocative, and theologically resonant. John Sweet argues that Paul knew of the Jesus' Temple sayings, and probably also believed that Jesus had made Cephas/Peter the 'rock' or foundation stone for the new Temple. 1 Corinthians 3 reads, in this light, as an extended literary conceit on the question of edification, moving between metaphors of feeding, gardening, and building. Paul had already in the opening sentences of his letter chided the Corinthians for their factionalism and slogans; 'I am for Paul', 'I am for Apollos', 'I am for Cephas' (1 Cor. 1: 12).

Then he continues:

What I fed you with was milk, not solid food, for you were not ready for it . . . Isn't that obvious from all the jealousy and wrangling that there is among you . . . What could be more unspiritual than your slogans, 'I am for Paul' and 'I am for Apollos'? After all, what is Apollos and what is Paul? . . . I did the planting, Apollos did the watering, but God made things grow . . . We are fellow workers with God; you are God's farm, God's building.

And then the passage already cited:

By the grace God gave me, I succeeded as an architect and laid the foundations of which someone else is doing the building . . . For the foundation . . . is Jesus Christ. . . . Didn't you realise that you were God's temple and that the Spirit of God was living among you . . . the temple of God is sacred; and you are that temple. (1 Cor. 3: 2–17)

The body of the Christian individual, as well as the 'body' of Christians together, is the Temple—the pre-eminent dwelling-place of God with men and women—and this dwelling-place is the body of Christ.

Christopher Rowland insists that resurrection belief is not only belief about something that happened 'just then', but was always, even for the first disciples, about what this means now and what we do now.[23] In the context of Second Temple Judaism the conviction amongst his followers that Jesus had been raised must have been a conviction that an eschatological event such as had been promised had already occurred, and that they could look forward to the realization of God's kingdom on *earth*. The Book of Revelation looks forward to that kingdom on earth—indeed, to a time when the division of heaven and earth is to disappear. It is worth noting that in Revelation the New Jerusalem contains no temple, 'since the Lord God Almighty and the Lamb themselves were the temple' (Rev. 21: 22). God's throne is in the New Jerusalem, and living waters, promised by the prophets and possibly by Jesus himself, stream from this throne.

---

[23] Christopher Rowland, 'Interpreting the Resurrection', in P. Avis (ed.), *The Resurrection of Jesus Christ* (London: Darton, Longman & Todd, 1993), 70.

Rowland argues that the language of bodily resurrection in the Gospels must be taken very seriously. The Gospel writers had other repertoires of exaltation language at their disposal: they knew the legends of Enoch, Elijah, and Moses; but, says Rowland, for the Gospel writers,

Jesus' post-mortem existence was not just an example of an apotheosis; he was the Messiah. The contours of what it was appropriate to say about him needed the language of eschatology to make sense of who he had been. . . . A wedge should not be driven between the testimony of 1 Corinthians 15 and the Resurrection narratives in the Gospels. The centrality of resurrection in Paul's thought should give us pause before we attempt to argue for the secondary character of the narratives in the Gospels. The particular choice of discourse used of the fate of the crucified Jesus is related to the eschatological convictions of the earliest disciples.[24]

Rowland points out that the focus of resurrection faith is not for Paul or for these early followers the empty tomb, but the 'present dimension of the risen life of Christ in his followers . . . where he may be met *now*, for that is a matter of eternal importance (Matt. 25: 45)'.[25] The conquest of death and bodily resurrection are important to God's promise of a new creation. None the less, as Rowland concedes, the exaltation imagery of the New Testament was certainly susceptible to a reading which put the weight on our sharing communion with Christ in the next life. The result would be an exaltation tradition detached from eschatological hope which could then be used as a means of positing a better, post-mortal world over and against this one. 'Heaven could then be a haven where the beleaguered soul could ascend where Christ had gone before.'[26] Such an accommodation does seem to have taken place in the early Church, to cope, perhaps, with the delay in the Lord's coming. Once privatized and married to Greek ideas of immortality, the significance of Jesus' risen and bodily life becomes simply the way in which it anticipates our own private and individual risen destinies—personal identity ensured. Rowland suggests that however 'traditional' such a theology might be, it can only be wrested from the New Testament by selective use, and

at the expense of evacuating the language of the Resurrection of its theological power. God has ceased to be God of the universe in travail when it

---

[24] *The Resurrection of Jesus Christ*, 78.   [25] Ibid.   [26] Ibid. 82.

is abandoned to its steady demise as the elect merely have to pursue the way of the heavenly pioneer into the holy place. The ecclesia becomes the outpost of that holy place above whither the souls of the elect are bound for eternity.[27]

What is lost is the central affirmation of Christian hope for the transformation of the universe, such as we find in Romans 8.

Rowland seems at times dismissive altogether of the hope of life after death, preferring commitment to work for the coming of the kingdom; but the two are surely not incompatible. Anyone who has lost someone they love will know that depth of longing one has to meet that person again. Especially when lives end tragically and pointlessly, it is both natural and Christian to hope for God's creative restoration of that life.[28] But the New Testament hope seems at times not less, but more, than this hope for the continuity of those we love; it is a hope for the restoration of life itself and of the world itself. If a resurrection faith becomes too exclusively a hope for the next life for humans (an etiolated orthodoxy of which Tipler's would be a crude caricature), there is no hope of the triumph of God's justice on earth, no point in praying that God's kingdom will come and will be done *on earth* as it is in heaven, and no salvation for non-human creation (trees that 'clap their hands' and hills that 'rejoice'). Trees and valleys, and even all the animals, are indeed no more than the great 'stage set' on which the drama of the saving of souls is acted out. (I have always considered the phrase 'the vale of soul making' to be worryingly Gnostic.)

There is nothing 'wrong' with the hope of heaven. Indeed, it is of the essence of Christian faith; but so too is the hope for the new creation and for the coming of the kingdom 'on earth, as it is in heaven', however little, this side of the eschaton, we may understand what this might mean. It may well be, however, that many centuries of focus too exclusively on matters of personal destiny has led to a situation in which the modern Christian reader of the Bible is blind to the profoundly social and ethical aspects of Paul's resurrection faith. You, and I, and we, Paul argues, are the temple of the Holy Spirit, the Body of Christ, the place where God dwells with

---

[27] Ibid. 79.

[28] Which is not to say that this cannot be an authentically Jewish hope as well. Indeed, as Alan Segal's chapter in this volume argues, it was very likely tragic death of the young which fuelled the growth of Jewish belief in the resurrection of the body, a belief which Christianity inherited.

women and men—now and for ever, and what we do now is of utmost importance.

A modestly etiolated orthodoxy of the resurrection—Christ is risen, God does miracles, we will rise—makes relatively little demand on us, other than for our cerebral assent. The resurrection of Jesus on this reading guarantees our personal continuity, in a way Tipler might approve, but has no implications for our work for justice in the world, nor for environmental concerns. Curiously, considering what is at issue is the resurrection of the *body*, it has little implication for our understanding of our intrinsic sociality: that is, for our embodiedness as one body, first with other believers, then with all peoples. But wouldn't this, especially in the Tipler variant, all be a little boring—lonely, even? And would St Paul even recognize in this Tipleresque vision a resurrection faith for which he was willing to give his life?

How much more robust is Zechariah's vision of the coming of the kingdom, one surely known to the Gospel writers, to Jesus and to Paul, and echoed in John's account of Jesus' final entry into Jerusalem;

> Rejoice heart and soul, daughter of Zion!
> Shout with gladness, daughter of Jerusalem!
> See now, your king comes to you;
> he is victorious, he is triumphant,
> humble and riding on a donkey
> on a colt, the foal of a donkey.
> He will banish chariots from Ephraim
> and horses from Jerusalem;
> the bow of war will be banished.
> He will proclaim peace for the nations.
> His empire shall stretch from sea to sea,
> from the River to the ends of the earth. (Zech. 9: 9–10)

In that day the earth shall be filled with the glory of God as the waters cover the sea.

4

Resurrection as Glory: Divine Presence and Christian Origins

CAREY C. NEWMAN

Christianity's break with Judaism still baffles those who study it. Metaphors abound in the attempt to grapple with the relationship's complexity: was it one of rival siblings, a parent and child, parting friends, or related strangers?[1] Despite the ability of such metaphors to match the plurality and ambiguity of both Jewish and Christian communities in the first two centuries of the common era, the major questions still persist: when did the break occur, and for what reason(s)?

There are two interpretive camps on this issue.[2] On the one hand are those who argue that the seed of discord was a 'high' Christology which was sown quite 'early' (that is, by the middle of the first century, if not sooner). Those giving this explanation point to the scandalous redefinition of monotheism enacted by Jesus and his followers. Simply stated, to Jews, to worship Jesus alongside Yahweh was nothing short of heresy, and it is this 'Christ devotion', in all its variegated forms, which caused the rift.[3] On the other hand are those who argue that the split was 'late' (middle second century) and gradual, and that the points of dispute included a whole

---

[1] Alan F. Segal, *Rebecca's Children: Judaism and Christianity in the Roman World* (Cambridge, Mass.: Harvard University Press, 1977); Claudia Setzer, *Jewish Responses to Early Christians: History and Polemics, 30-150 C.E.* (Minneapolis: Fortress, 1994), 189; James D. G. Dunn, *The Partings of the Ways* (London/Philadelphia; SCM/Trinity, 1991); Stephen G. Wilson, *Related Strangers: Jews and Christians 70-170 C.E.* (Minneapolis: Fortress, 1995).

[2] Cf. the differing estimations contained within James D. G. Dunn (ed.), *Jews and Christians: The Parting of the Ways A.D. 70 to 135*, WUNT 1/66 (Tübingen: Mohr-Siebeck, 1992).

[3] Larry W. Hurtado, *One God, One Lord: Early Christian Devotion and Ancient Jewish Monotheism* (Philadelphia: Fortress, 1988), and Martin Hengel, 'Christology and New Testament Chronology', in *Between Jesus and Paul: Studies in the Earliest History of Christianity* (Philadelphia: Fortress, 1983), 30-47.

range of sociological issues. Nothing in the honorific titles ascribed to Jesus, nothing in the elevated way in which his life is described— not even his resurrection!—and nothing in the liturgical practices of earliest Christianity would have offended Jewish sensibilities. The relationship between Christians and Jews, even if it is to be explained much later in Christological terms, is best analysed in its earliest days by communal differences over Temple, Halachah, and circumcision.[4]

In this essay I address the large and vexing questions of Christian origins and Jewish–Christian relations by investigating the logic behind and the implications of the New Testament's identification of Jesus as Glory. Specifically, I ask if there was anything within the New Testament's use of Glory language which would cause a Jew (i) to regard it as heresy and thus (ii) to separate. Or, to put the questions from the Christian side, is there anything within the New Testament's use of Glory language which would mandate the creation of a new community, distinct from Judaism(s) of the period, with its own symbolic world, identity markers, and boundary lines?

To accomplish this, I briefly outline the different ways Glory signs the visible, movable divine presence within the Hebrew Bible. I then plot how Glory came to sign *eschatological* divine presence within (i) the prophets, (ii) the throne visions of Second Temple Jewish apocalypses, (iii) Jesus' own vision of the future, and (iv) early Christianity. Next, I isolate the resurrection as the narrative, historical, and theological trigger for the confessional equation 'Jesus is the Glory of Yahweh'. Finally, I sketch some of the profound sociological implications inherent in such a confession.

GLORY AS DIVINE PRESENCE IN THE HEBREW BIBLE

While the כבד word group appears about 400 times in the Hebrew Bible (depending on textual readings), and possesses a noto-

---

[4] Dunn, *Partings of the Ways*, esp. chs. 10 and 11; Jack T. Sanders, *Schismatics, Sectarians, Dissidents, Deviants: The First One Hundred Years of Jewish–Christian Relations* (Valley Forge, Pa.: Trinity, 1993), 82-98; but see Wayne Meeks, 'Breaking Away: Three New Testament Pictures of Christianity's Separation from Jewish Communities', in Jacob Neusner and Ernest S. Frerichs (eds.), *'To See Ourselves as Others See Us': Christians, Jews, 'Others' in Late Antiquity*, SPSH (Chico, Calif.: Scholars, 1985), 93-116; Claudia Setzer, ' "You Invent a Christ!" Christological Claims as Points of Jewish–Christian Dispute', *USQR* 44 (1991), 315-28.

riously wide range of meaning,[5] this study focuses upon just a small slice of the כבד's semantic range: namely, those places where כבד (both denotatively and connotatively) signs divine presence. The phrase 'Glory of Yahweh' (כבד יהוה) appears thirty-six times in the Hebrew Bible,[6] and these can be divided into two mutually exclusive semantic profiles: constructions which employ 'movement' terminology and constructions which employ 'appearance'/'sight' terminology.[7]

In the first profile the Glory of Yahweh is said to 'fill'/'settle', 'rise'/'go up', 'come'/'arrive', 'enter'/'depart', or merely 'stand still'/'be over'. This movement relates Glory to various spaces where Yahweh is thought to be (visibly) present—Mount Sinai, the tabernacle, the Temple, objects associated with the Temple, the court of the Temple, the city which houses the Temple (that is Jerusalem), and even the whole earth. Movement also associates Glory with special people closely associated with Yahweh's presence—for example, Moses, the priests, King Solomon, and the prophets (especially Isaiah and Ezekiel). The closely circumscribed group of people function as 'sacred mediators' because of their intimate contact with Yahweh's Glory.

In the second profile, the Glory of Yahweh is said to 'appear'. Glory 'appears' in and at places where Yahweh's presence is

---

[5] On the כבד's semantic range, consult the following: Francis Brown, S. R. Driver, and C. A. Briggs, *A Hebrew and English Lexicon of the Old Testament* (Oxford: Clarendon, 1952), 457-9; Claus Westermann, 'כבד', in E. Jenni and C. Westermann (eds.), *Theologisches Handwörterbuch zum Alten Testament . . .* (2 vols.; Munich/Zurich: Chr. Kaiser/Theologischer, 1984), i. 794-812; Jan de Waard and Eugene A. Nida, *From One Language to Another: Functional Equivalence in Bible Translating* (Nashville: Thomas Nelson, 1986), 163-4. Here, and in the section which follows, I draw freely upon my *Paul's Glory-Christology: Tradition and Rhetoric*, NovTSupp, 69 (Leiden: Brill, 1992), 17-104.

[6] Exod. 16: 7, 10; 24: 16, 17; 40: 34, 35; Lev. 9: 6, 23; Num. 14: 10, 21; 16: 19, 42 [17: 7]; 20: 6; 1 Kgs. 8: 11; 2 Chr. 5: 14; 7: 1, 2, 3; Pss. 104: 31; 138: 5; Isa. 35: 2; 40: 5; 58: 8; 60: 1; Ezek. 1: 28; 3: 12, 23; 8: 4; 10: 4 (twice); 10: 18; 11: 23; 43: 4, 5; 44: 4. Additionally, seven times כבוד is collocated with names for God other than יהוה, six times with אל (Pss. 19: 2 and 29: 3; Ezek. 9: 3; 10: 19; 11: 22; 43: 2), and once with אלהם (Prov. 25: 2). The contexts indicate that כבוד אל possesses the same semantic value as כבד יהוה (cf. Ezek. 10: 18 with 10: 19 and Ezek. 11: 22 with 11: 13—though it is doubtful that the same could be said for כבוד אלהים, where the meaning of כבוד is 'advantage' or 'benefit').

[7] Though customarily associated with a closely circumscribed set of words (i.e. movement-sight-space-person terminology), a few times כבד יהוה is associated with other syntagma. Even here, however, movement and/or sight implications are not totally absent. Cf. Exod. 24: 17; Ps. 19: 2; Isa. 58: 8; Ezek. 1: 28.

expected—in a cloud, on top of Mount Sinai, at the door of the Tent of Meeting, and over the Temple—and 'appears' to the whole assembly or congregation, all the children of Israel, to others outside Israel, or, more generally, to all flesh.

Because the Glory of Yahweh is associated with either 'movement' or 'appearance' terminology, it does not denote an attribute of Yahweh's character (like mercy or love, which cannot be 'seen' and does not 'move'). Neither is the meaning of the Glory of Yahweh exhausted by 'fire' or 'brightness', terms used to describe its appearance. Rather, *in the Hebrew Bible the Glory of Yahweh signs the visible, movable divine presence.*[8] To see or experience Yahweh's Glory is to see or experience Yahweh.[9] A few examples will help map the referential domain of Glory as divine presence.

(1) The theophany to Moses on Mount Sinai (Exod. 24: 15–25b) functions paradigmatically for the Priestly tradition's very technical use of the Glory of Yahweh. The passage can be divided into three major strophes. In the first, the 'Coming' or 'Arrival', 24: 15b–16a ('the cloud covered the mountain'; 'the glory of the Lord settled on Mount Sinai') is parallel to 24: 18a ('and Moses entered the cloud'; 'and went up on the mountain'). In the second strophe, the 'Remaining' or 'Abiding', 24: 16a ('and the cloud covered it [the mountain] six days') is parallel to 24: 18b ('and Moses was on the mountain forty days and forty nights'). In the third strophe, the

---

[8] The semantic antonym for כבוד יהוה would thus be its 'absence', 'departure', or 'disappearance' (e.g. 1 Sam. 4: 21–2; Ezek. 9: 3; 10: 4, 18, 19; 11: 22, 23; Hos. 9: 11–12; 10: 5–6).

[9] Other linguistic formulations have similar semantic behaviour to Glory of Yahweh. The pronominal and nominal constructions employing כבד,, when Yahweh is the referent, are also associated with movement and visibility terminology (Exod. 33: 8, 22; Num. 114: 22; Deut. 5: 24; 1 Sam. 4: 22; Pss. 26: 8; 29: 9; 9; 57: 6, 12; 63: 3; 72: 19; 97: 6; 102: 17; 108: 6; 113: 4; Isa. 4: 5; 6: 3; 60: 2; 66: 18, 19; Ezek. 3: 23; 39: 21; 43: 2). Since the pronominal and nominal constructions employ a wider range of verbs, they must be considered less technical. The כבוד יהוה should also be compared with other formulations which employ יהוה in a construct relationship. In the Hebrew Bible, יהוה is collocated with 100 or more different words. The attributes of Yahweh (e.g. anger, dread, love, wrath, indignation, goodness, vengeance, righteousness, terror, zeal, joy, power) are not associated with 'movement' or 'appearance' terminology. Even symbols of 'divine presence' which are associated with 'movement' and 'appearance' terminology behave significantly differently from 'Glory of Yahweh' (see Thomas W. Mann, *Divine Presence and Guidance in Israelite Traditions: The Typology of Exaltation* (Baltimore: Johns Hopkins University Press, 1977), 252–61). Simply stated, Glory signs Yahweh's presence in ways that other linguistic formulations do not.

'Call' or 'Word', 24: 16b ('and on the seventh day he called to Moses out of the midst of the cloud') is parallel to 25: 1 ('the Lord spoke to Moses').[10]

While the narrative goal is to build the tabernacle, the place for Yahweh's Glory to dwell, the theophany *legitimized* Moses, and him alone, as *the* sacred mediator. Only Moses is allowed to experience Yahweh's divine presence, his Glory. Yet, the parenthetical description of Glory as a devouring fire limits Yahweh's approachability, even for a legitimized mediator like Moses. Glory is to be feared and respected.

The inclusions to Exodus 24 are found in Exodus 40 and Leviticus 9. In Exodus 40 the Glory of Yahweh exchanges the mountain top for the newly completed tabernacle, and thereby 'a sign of legitimacy and approval' is granted to the new place of worship.[11] Leviticus 9 gives the same special approval to the tabernacle as a place of sacrifice, and the group of legitimized mediators widens to include Aaron and his sons. Glory in Exodus 24 and 40 and Leviticus 9 establishes sacred office, time, mediator, and order.[12]

(2) The hallmark of a royal theology is the kingship of Yahweh. Yahweh was celebrated as the sustainer king of ancient Israel, the one who blesses and prospers his people.[13] A second, and closely related, theme is that the human king of Israel is Yahweh's vice-regent on earth. To the king, the divinely elected representative, Yahweh promised protection, and through the king Yahweh mediated blessing. It is not surprising, then, to find Glory connected with both Yahweh as king and the human king as the representative.

Psalm 24 extols the enthroned Yahweh as the world's 'King of Glory',[14] and may have celebrated the movement of the Ark to

---

[10] Claus Westermann, 'Die Herrlichkeit Gottes in der Priestershrift', in H. Stoebe (ed.), *Wort-Gebot-Glaube: Festschrift für W. Eichrodt zum 80. Geburtstag*, BzTAT 59 (Zurich: Zwingli, 1970), 231.

[11] Martin Noth, *Exodus: A Commentary*, OTL (Nashville: Westminster, 1962), 283.

[12] Westermann, 'Herrlichkeit', 237.

[13] Walter Brueggemann, 'Trajectories in Old Testament Literature and the Sociology of Ancient Israel', *JBL* 98 (1979), 180. The royal trajectory '(1) prefers to speak in myths of unity; (2) speaks a language of fertility (creation) and continuity (royal institutions); (3) preferred mode of perception is that of universal comprehensiveness; (4) tends to be socially conserving with a primary valuing of stability; [and] (5) focuses on the glory and holiness of God's person and institutions geared to that holiness'.

[14] H.-J. Kraus, *Psalms 1–59: A Commentary* (Minneapolis: Augsburg, 1988), 315.

Jerusalem and the establishment of the sanctuary.[15] The high point
of the procession is the theophany of Yahweh's Glory. The
antiphonal cries for the Temple doors and gates to open is so that
Yahweh may appear.[16] After a triad of requests, Yahweh Sabbaoth
(the warrior) is identified as the 'King of Glory'.[17]

The royal hymns on creation (Pss. 8, 19, 29, 104) also speak
pointedly about Yahweh's Glory. Whether or not one views the 'son
of man' in Psalm 8 as a primal/archetypal human (cf. Gen. 1: 26),
there is no denying that royal theology pervades the psalm. Thus
Yahweh's crowning of a 'human' with Glory as the high point of creation mirrors Yahweh's special relationship with the king. The regular enjoyment of Yahweh's divine presence, his Glory, forms a central
part of Temple liturgy, and democratizes the unqualified blessing of
God upon king, Temple, nation, and the world. Glory in a royal context assures of Yahweh's rightful and benevolent control over all.

(3) Divine presence can also connote judgement. The penalty for
squandering the gift of Yahweh's Glory can be detected in the
prophets. Jeremiah indicates that Yahweh will punish his people for
their infidelity. The rhetorical question (Jer. 2: 11a), 'Has a nation
changed its gods, even though they are no gods?', frames the issue
around monotheism. Jeremiah then reports Yahweh's charge: the
nation has committed an unparalleled capitulation: they 'have
changed their glory[18] for that which does not profit' (Jer. 2: 11b).
By paralleling the exchange of Glory (v. 11) with forsaking Yahweh
(the 'me' of v. 13), Jeremiah clearly identifies Glory as the divine
presence. Jeremiah thus sets Judah's appalling abandonment of
Yahweh in a blessing/cursing context. By deserting Glory, the
nation has not only lost the nourishment of life provided by the 'living waters', but has fruitlessly hewn cisterns which 'can hold no
water' (v. 13). By alluding to the capture of the Ark by the
Philistines (2 Sam. 4), Hosea foresees that Yahweh's Glory will
again be 'exiled'. When this 'deportation' occurs, the creative

---

[15] Erhard S. Gerstenberger, *Psalms*, FOTL 14 (Grand Rapids, Mich.: Eerdmans,
1988), 119.

[16] Artur Weiser, *Psalms: A Commentary*, OTL (Philadelphia: Westminster, 1962),
234–5.

[17] Cf. Tryggve N. D. Mettinger, *The Dethronement of Sabaoth: Studies in the Shem
and Kabod Theologies* (Lund: C. W. K. Gleerup, 1982), 24–5.

[18] The MT of v. 11b reads 'its glory', and is (probably) a scribal correction of 'my
glory' or 'their glory'. In either case, the referent is Yahweh.

processes of life cease. 'Ephraim's glory shall fly away like a bird—no birth, no pregnancy, no conception! Even if they bring up children, I will bereave them till none is left. Woe to them, when I depart from them' (Hos. 9: 11-12)! Like a 'miscarrying womb' and 'dry breasts' (v. 14), the absence of Yahweh's Glory signifies infertility—'no birth, no pregnancy, no conception'. Glory, the symbol of Yahweh's life-giving presence among his chosen people in a royal theology, shall 'fly away like a bird' (v. 11a).

To sum up: As a symbol of divine presence, Glory could (i) legitimize sacred mediators, (ii) connote the unqualified blessing of Yahweh, and (iii) signify, through its absence, the judgement of Yahweh.

GLORY AS AN ESCHATOLOGICAL SIGN

In all likelihood, standing behind—an archetypally uniting—Glory as divine presence, in all its ramified uses, is an old theophanic tradition that associated Glory with the appearance of a storm god, an echo of which can still be heard in Psalm 29: 3: 'Glory thunders upon the waters.' Here Glory defeats the powers of chaos and subdues enemies. Whether associated with Sinai, monarchy, or a prophetic judgement oracle, Glory never lost its theophanic power to sign Yahweh's presence. That the prophets adopted the theophanic tradition as a strategic subgenre insured that Glory was destined to become a sign of *eschatological* divine presence.

1. *The prophetic hope trajectory.* The Exile forced Jews to rethink their tradition and what they understood about their God. While the formation and shape of much of the Hebrew Bible can be read as an attempt by Jews to grapple with this historical and theological crisis, it is the prophets who most explicitly addressed the issues stemming from exile. Here Yahweh's judgement dominates the prophetic horizon. Exile equals punishment—even if it is pedagogical. But the texts do look through, and beyond, judgement for a day of forgiveness, deliverance, restoration, and even eschatological transformation.[19] The historical catastrophes, though certainly still

[19] Ronald E. Clements, 'Patterns in the Prophetic Canon', in G. W. Coats and B. O. Long (eds.), *Canon and Authority: Essays in Old Testament Religion and Theology* (Philadelphia: Fortress, 1977), 42-55.

regarded as terrifying dialogues with Yahweh, began to point to a re-created and transformed future.[20] Thus the prophets portray the first-fruits of an apocalyptic world-view.[21] Glory plays a key role in this view of the end: it signs the transforming eschatological presence of Yahweh.

Second Isaiah opens with a vision which mixes Sinai, exodus, and royal motifs (Isa. 40: 3–5).[22] The appearance[23] and subsequent royal parade of Glory in the plain sight of 'all flesh' not only secures release, but telegraphs the news of Yahweh's solidarity with his people. Filled valleys, levelled mountains, and a universal theophany all unite to elevate this scene to eschatological restoration.

To evoke eschatological finality, Isaiah also employs imagery of creation's renewal and unprecedented abundance (Isa. 35: 1–2). No doubt a pun on כבד as 'wealth' and 'fame', the oppressor nations shall have their 'glory' and 'majesty' given away. By contrast, the revelation of Glory (as the visible presence of Yahweh) enacts a joyful return for the 'ransomed of the Lord' (v. 10).

The prophetic hope for the future often centres on the symbol of Jerusalem/Zion. Through one of his 'visions' Zechariah paints an eschatological picture of Jerusalem (Zech. 2: 1–5). The transformed city will be unmeasurable, possess no walls, and experience abundance. Yahweh, the great warrior, will protect the city with fire and Glory.[24]

Isaiah 4: 2–6 echoes the same theme. The arrival of Yahweh not only restores what once was—the glories of a Davidic kingdom— but eschatologically amplifies what will be. Mixing Sinai with royal imagery, the prophet speaks of a day when the Lord will once again 'tabernacle' in Zion.[25] This time, however, Yahweh will 'create' a new (and permanent) place for his Glory to rest. From 'Mount Zion

---

[20] Mircea Eliade, *The Myth of the Eternal Return*, Bollingen Series, 46 (New York: Pantheon, 1954), 102–10.

[21] Paul Hanson, *The Dawn of Apocalyptic* (Philadelphia: Fortress, 1975).

[22] J. Kenneth Kuntz, *The Self-Revelation of God* (Philadelphia: Westminster, 1967), 166–8; Carroll Stuhlmueller, *Creative Redemption in Deutero-Isaiah*, AnBib, 43 (Rome: Biblical Institute, 1970), 97.

[23] C. Van Leeuwen, 'De Openbaring van de Kebod YHWH in Jesaja 40: 5', in H. H. Grosheide (ed.), *De Knecht: Studies rondom Deutero-Jesaja* (Kampen: J. H. Kok, 1978), 100.

[24] Susan Niditch, *The Symbolic Visions in Biblical Tradition*, HSM 30 (Chico, Calif.: Scholars, 1980), 172.

[25] Hans Wildberger, *Jesaja*, BK 10 (Neukirchen-Vluyn: Neukirchener, 1980), i. 161.

and in Jerusalem' the Lord will reign, and there Yahweh again will 'manifest his Glory' (Isa. 24: 23).

Although the 'Kingdom of God' is not prominent in the Hebrew Bible, it is connected to the traditions of Zion/Jerusalem—and thus to Glory. God's works tell of 'the glory of the kingdom'. God's kingdom is an 'everlasting kingdom' which endures throughout all generations (Ps. 145: 10–13). Yahweh as 'King' (of the world) could be used as a shorthand expression for summing up prophetic assurances about the future.[26] Psalm 145: 10–13 fits squarely within this eschatological tradition.[27] Yahweh's future rule of the whole world is so certain that it can be celebrated as a present blessing. Yahweh proves his sovereignty through his deeds, and his deeds, in turn, announce the presence of his kingdom. The eschatological kingdom is one characterized by Glory—Yahweh's presence.

The eschatological enthronement of Yahweh in Zion inaugurates a new age for Israel, and initiates the conversion of the nations. In numerous passages, all of which are saturated with exodus, Sinai, and royal images,[28] Isaiah describes a new day (Isa. 60: 1–3, 10–11; 66: 19). Isaiah 60 describes a grand theophany, a revelation Glory, with two, coterminous consequences: the transformation of Zion so that she becomes the (unique) bearer of Yahweh's Glory ('Glory shall be seen upon you') and the ingathering of the nations ('all the nations shall come to your light'). In Isaiah 62 and 66, Zion is not only the bearer of Glory, but the instrument by/through which the nations will enjoy Yahweh's presence. Glory begins to function as an archetype of eschatological conversion, and forms the leading edge of Glory's participation in Second Temple Judaism's traditions of transformational mysticism.

To sum up: By moving beyond a simple deconstruction of a royal theology, the prophets reinvest Glory with eschatology to proclaim a new world. Yahweh will one day manifest his Glory and reconfigure the existence of (all) his people. Glory thus participates in a complex web of images (i) to signify the eschatological reversal of Israel's historical fortunes, (ii) to define Zion as eschatological centre

---

[26] N. T. Wright, *The New Testament and the People of God* (Minneapolis: Fortress, 1992), 303.

[27] Walter Eichrodt, *Theology of the Old Testament*, OTL 2 vols.; (Philadelphia: Westminster, 1961, 1967), i. 199.

[28] Bernhard W. Anderson, 'Exodus Typology in Second Isaiah', in B. W. Anderson and W. Harrelson (eds.), *Israel's Prophetic Heritage: Essays in Honor of James Muilenburg* (New York: Harper & Brothers, 1962), 177–95.

of Yahweh's transforming deeds, (iii) to announce Yahweh's rule over the whole world, and (iv) to effect the conversion of nations.

2. *The throne vision trajectory.* Glory also formed part of the characteristic field of signifiers used in 'throne visions' of Second Temple Jewish apocalypses.[29] A throne vision can be defined as a seer's vision of God seated on a throne, often surrounded by angels. Such throne visions commonly entailed graphic descriptions of God, a description of the heavenly hosts who oftentimes are engaged in the worship of God, and the highlighting of one, special angelic mediator who is either beside God or is seated upon a throne.[30] Throne visions are indebted, in both content and form, to visionary material in the Hebrew Bible, particularly the inaugural call of Ezekiel 1 and the vision of Daniel 7.

Glory in Ezekiel 1: 26-8 forms part of the confrontation between the prophet Ezekiel and Yahweh.[31] Here Ezekiel describes Yahweh as having a human-shaped form and seated upon a throne-chariot. The text then identifies this human-shaped form as Glory: 'such as the appearance of the likeness of the glory of the Lord'. This remarkable anthropomorphic depiction of Yahweh's presence wielded a powerful influence upon other visions of God and, most interestingly, the throne visionary characterization of a/the chief mediator figure who often does God's eschatological bidding.[32]

The throne vision of 1 Enoch 14 displays the influence of Ezekiel 1 (and to a lesser extent Isa. 6). Both visions make reference to wheels (Ezek. 1: 16; 1 Enoch 14: 18), a throne (Ezek. 1: 26; 1 Enoch 14: 18; cf. Isa. 6: 1), God's garment (Isa. 6: 1; 1 Enoch 14: 20), and cherubim (Isa. 6: 2; 1 Enoch 14: 11, 18). Further, the visionary depiction of Yahweh in human shape of Ezekiel 1: 26-8 explains the anthropomorphic description of God in 1 Enoch 14. God wears a garment (v. 20); and no one qualifies to enter the house 'or to look at his face[!]'. Why? Because 'the face' excels in

---

[29] Klaus Koch, *The Rediscovery of Apocalyptic*, SBT 2/22 (London: SCM, 1972), 32.

[30] John J. Collins, *Daniel, with an Introduction to Apocalyptic Literature*, FOTL 22 (Grand Rapids, Mich.: Eerdmans, 1984), 2-24; Martha Himmelfarb, *Ascent to Heaven in Jewish and Christian Apocalypses* (Oxford: Oxford University Press, 1993).

[31] Norman Habel, 'The Form and Significance of Call Narratives', *ZAW* 77 (1965), 313.

[32] Christopher Rowland, *The Open Heaven: A Study of Apocalyptic in Judaism and Early Christianity* (New York: Crossroad, 1982).

'splendor and glory'.[33] Christopher Rowland concludes that 'there is no doubt that the author of 1 Enoch 14 sees a human figure on the throne, though the precise outlines of the figure are left unexpressed'.[34] Most importantly, 1 Enoch 14's entitling this human-shaped God as the 'Great Glory' can best be explained by the influence of the dramatic vision contained in Ezekiel 1.[35] The enthroned 'Great Glory' should be read as a pure and unmediated manifestation of God himself.

Daniel 7 also possesses ties with Ezekiel 1. D. S. Russell has detailed some of the more obvious connections:

In each case there appears a throne set on wheels and aflame with fire (Ezek. 1: 4, 15 f., 21, 26, and Dan. 7: 9 f.) on which sits God himself in appearance like a man (Ezek. 1: 26 f.) or one Ancient of Days (Dan. 7: 9 f.); this chariot-throne is accompanied by a great cloud (Ezek. 1: 4) and the Son of Man comes with the clouds of heaven (Dan. 7: 13); in each case there appear four great beasts (Ezek. 1: 5 ff., and Dan. 7: 3 ff.) which, though their appearance and functions are different, emphasize as in Ps. 8: 4 f. the distinction between man and the animal creation.[36]

Whereas in Ezekiel 1 there is but *one* heavenly, human-shaped figure (understood to be the Glory of Yahweh), Daniel 7: 13-14 adds a *second* heavenly figure—the one like a Son of Man. The addition of a second figure caused no small amount of confusion, especially from the Jewish perspective. Surely the 'Ancient of Days' should be understood to be Yahweh; but who is the Son of Man?[37]

Although the context in the book of Daniel narratively identifies the Son of Man with the 'saints of the most high', when the vision is considered on the grounds purely of form and tradition, the text borders dangerously on ditheism, since the second figure acquires the anthropomorphic description used of Yahweh in Ezekiel 1: 28.[38]

---

[33] Following the reading of Matthew Black, *The Book of Enoch or 1 Enoch: A New English Edition with Commentary and Textual Notes*, SVTP 7 (Leiden: Brill, 1985), 150.

[34] Rowland, *Open Heaven*, 22.

[35] Mary Dean-Otting, *Heavenly Journeys: A Study of the Motif in Hellenistic Jewish Literature*, Judentum und Umwelt, 8 (Frankfurt-on-Main: Peter Lang, 1984), 54-5.

[36] D. S. Russell, *The Method and Message of Jewish Apocalyptic 200 BC-100 AD*, OTL (Philadelphia: Westminster, 1964), 341.

[37] See Alan F. Segal, *Two Powers in Heaven: Early Rabbinic Reports about Christianity and Gnosticism*, SJLA 15 (Leiden: Brill, 1977), for the controversial role Dan. 7 played in the Rabbinic debates with both Christians and Gnostics.

[38] Matthew Black, 'Throne-Theophany Prophetic Commission and the "Son of Man": A Study in Tradition-History', in R. Hamerton-Kelly (ed.), *Jews, Greeks and Christians: Religious Cultures in Late Antiquity. Essays in Honor of William David Davies*,

Daniel 7 thus effects also both a semiotic shift and a semantic rein-
vestment of Glory. Glory thus becomes a symbol of divine investiture which demonstrates the exalted position of the Son of Man.

The same sort of shift can be detected in the Similitudes of Enoch
(1 Enoch 37–71), another area in which the influence of Ezekiel 1
can be detected. In several passages (e.g. 1 Enoch 45: 1–3c; 55:
3–4; 61: 1–6, 8; 69: 29) Glory forms part of the 'divine equipment'
which the Son of Man possesses.[39] The placement of the Elect
One/Son of Man upon the 'throne of Glory' is for the sole purpose
of eschatological judgement—something traditionally reserved for
God. Further, to 'sit' on a 'throne of glory' characterizes the Son of
Man in anthropomorphic terms, and, depending on how one construes the phrase (possessively?/objectively?), this anthropomorphic
figure is close to being divinized. By installing the Elect One/Son of
Man on the 'throne of Glory', the Lord of the Spirits confers an
exalted status upon the angelic figure, second only to the deity,
since the throne belongs to God.[40]

Glory is thus a regular part of visionary texts. That is, when a
seer peers into the heavens, he or she sees Glory. In the throne
visions of Jewish apocalypses (i) Glory signs the anthropomorphi-
cally described presence of God and (ii) defines the Son of Man as
God's special agent—a characterization that borders on diviniza-
tion. This provocative use of Glory in throne visions owes itself to
the tradition dependent upon Ezekiel 1.

3. *Jesus and the coming Son of Man in/with Glory sayings.* When we
turn to the New Testament and ask, 'Did Jesus employ Glory language in any substantive way?', we are driven to the rocky coast
of the Son of Man tradition. The sixty-nine (thirty-nine excluding
parallels) synoptic Son of Man sayings have been most often divided
into three categories: sayings concerning the present earthly activity of the Son of Man; sayings which refer to the suffering, death,

SKLA 21 (Leiden: Brill, 1976), 60–3; Horst Robert, *Methodische Probleme der
Neutestamentlichen Christologie*, WMANT 25 (Neukirchen-Vluyn: Neukirchener,
1967), 80–3; Rowland, *Open Heaven*, 95–8. Cf. Maurice Casey, *Son of Man: The
Interpretation and Influence of Daniel 7* (London: SPCK, 1979), 32–3.

[39] Sigmund Mowinckel, *He That Cometh* (Oxford: Blackwell, 1956), 372–4;
387–8, 409.

[40] Cf. 1 Enoch 9: 4; 25: 3; Jub. 31: 20; T. Job 32: 2–3; T. Abr. 13: 4; Apoc.
Abr. 25: 3; Hans Bietenhard, *Die himmlische Welt im Urchristentum und Spätjudentum*,
WUNT 1/2 (Tübingen: Mohr-Siebeck, 1951), 53–100.

and resurrection of the Son of Man; and sayings which refer to the future coming and forensic activity of the Son of Man.[41] Of particular interest are sayings within the last group which depict the Son of Man coming 'in glory' or 'on the clouds with Glory' to occupy the 'throne of glory'.

For whoever is ashamed of me and of my words in this adulterous and sinful generation, of him will the Son of man also be ashamed, when he comes in the glory of his Father with the holy angels. (Mark 8: 38; parallels: Matt. 16: 27; Luke 9: 26)

Jesus said to them, 'Truly, I say to you, in the new world, when the Son of man shall sit on his glorious throne, you who have followed me will also sit on twelve thrones, judging the twelve tribes of Israel.' (Matt. 19: 28)

'And then they will see the Son of man coming in clouds with great power and glory.' (Mark 13: 26; parallels: Matt. 24: 30; Luke 21: 27)

'When the Son of man comes in his glory, and all the angels with him, then he will sit on his glorious throne.' (Matt. 25: 31)

Despite the linguistic, literary, and theological questions which perpetually swirl around these Son of Man sayings, several things can be said.

First, as a general principle of criticism, the fact that the phrase 'Son of Man' is found almost exclusively on the lips of Jesus argues strongly for its authenticity. Otherwise, what we are asked to believe is 'that the one person who is said to have used the phrase is the one person who cannot have used the phrase'.[42] While it is difficult to see why the early Church would make this phrase Jesus' self-designation of choice, especially when it clearly preferred other titles (as the confessional/hymnic material demonstrates), a good case can be made for the opposite: the reason the early Church kept the phrase, even though it was not central to its preaching of Jesus, is out of respect for the tradition.[43] Thus, at least in principle, the phrase (from all three categories) can and should be traced to Jesus himself.

---

[41] Chrys C. Caragounis, *The Son of Man: Vision and Interpretation*, WUNT 1/38 (Tübingen: Mohr-Siebeck, 1986), 146 and n. 11.

[42] I. Howard Marshall, *The Origins of New Testament Christology*, 2nd edn. (Downers Grove, Ill.: Inter-Varsity Press, 1990), 72.

[43] However, Seyoon Kim, 'The "Son of Man"' as the Son of God, WUNT 1/30 (Tübingen: Mohr-Siebeck, 1983), demonstrates the essential structural and theological affinity between the Son of Man sayings in the Gospels and the preaching of the Son of God in the early Church.

Second, this line of reasoning is all the more convincing with regard to Jesus' use of the third person to refer to himself in an eschatological context. A saying like Mark 8: 38 (and parallels), at first blush, appears to refer to two persons—Jesus and an expected Son of Man. In large measure, this is the strongest argument for authenticity, for the early Church would have been hard pressed to introduce such ambiguity if it was its desire to identify Jesus clearly as the Son of Man. Thus even Bultmann accepts Mark 8: 38 as authentic, but only on the grounds that Jesus is referring to someone other than himself.[44] However, there is absolutely no evidence that Jesus ever expected any other eschatological figure. As Oscar Cullmann says, such a theory 'raises more problems than it solves'.[45] Further, on closer inspection, Jesus is not referring to someone else, but, with reticence characteristic of apocalypses,[46] is using the third person to refer to himself. The 'me' of verse 38 is none other than the Son of Man.[47] Such a curious procedure fits with other aspects of Jesus' self-revelation—he tends to conceal, hide, and obscure.

Third, in these Son of Man in Glory texts Jesus intentionally echoes Daniel 7, and thereby places these Son of Man sayings squarely within the throne vision tradition stemming from Ezekiel 1. Notwithstanding the linguistic arguments to the contrary, the most obvious textual connection between Daniel 7 and these texts is the phrase itself, 'Son of Man'. Other textual connections reverberate as well. Both Daniel 7 and the sayings listed above employ visionary language and refer to the Son of Man's coming, to thrones, clouds, and angels.[48] Thus, in these sayings Jesus provocatively identifies himself with Yahweh's heavenly agent of Daniel 7.

Fourth, Jesus depicts his own future advent/return as the Son of

---

[44] Rudolf Bultmann, *History of Synoptic Tradition*, rev. edn. (New York: Harper & Row, 1963), 151-2; H. E. Tödt, *The Son of Man in the Synoptic Tradition*, NTL (London: SCM, 1965), 40.

[45] Oscar Cullmann, *The Christology of the New Testament*, rev. edn. (Philadelphia: Westminster, 1963), 156 and n. 4.

[46] Alan F. Segal, *Paul the Convert: The Apostolate and Apostasy of Saul the Pharisee* (New Haven: Yale University Press, 1990), 58-9. Jesus' use of the third person may well be analogous to Paul's in 2 Cor. 12.

[47] Morna Hooker, *The Gospel According to Saint Mark*, BNTC (Peabody, Mass.: Hendrickson, 1991), 210-22, and idem, *The Son of Man in Mark* (Montreal: McGill University Press, 1967), 116-22.

[48] See the table of parallels in Caragounis, *Son of Man*, 172.

Man in the language of an eschatological theophany.[49] All the texts employ ἔρχομαι as a technical term for a theophany.[50]

Fifth, at this eschatological apocalypse the Son of Man will sit upon the 'throne of glory'. The phrase 'throne of Glory' comes directly out of the throne vision tradition, and could depend directly on the Similitudes of Enoch.[51] The Son of Man's sitting upon the throne of Glory is for the purpose of eschatological judgement, and thus signals the functional transference of the duties of Yahweh to himself.

Sixth, in his eschatological theophany, Jesus, as the Son of Man, will come 'in Glory' (ἐν . . . δόξῃ) and 'with Glory' (μετὰ . . . δόξης). Both phrases refer to the divine presence which will accompany the Son of Man at his 'coming'.[52] That is, both phrases specify the *circumstances associated with* the coming: Jesus will come shrouded, draped, and encompassed by Yahweh's presence, his Glory.[53] These astounding statements, by asserting that Jesus will participate in Yahweh's eschatological presence, boldly and scandalously move beyond any imaging of a divine agent within Second Temple Judaism. *Jesus' Son of Man in/with Glory sayings not only defined his own future role as God's chief, singular agent (that is, the one who will do Yahweh's eschatological bidding), but also so closely identified him with Yahweh's Glory that the two can no longer be separated.* These sayings effectively open a breach in the wall of Jewish monotheism, and may well have been a/the contributing reason for his execution.[54]

---

[49] G. R. Beasley Murray, *Jesus and the Kingdom of God* (Grand Rapids, Mich.: Eerdmans, 1986), 3–10, 26–35; T. Francis Glasson, 'Theophany and Parousia', *NTS* 34 (1988), 259–70.

[50] i.e. ἔλθῃ, Mark 8: 38 = Luke 9: 26 (cf. Matt. 16: 27, ἔρχεσθαι); Matt. 25: 31; ἐρχόμενον, Mark 13: 26 = Matt. 24: 30 = Luke 21: 27; J. Schneider, ἔρχομαι, in *TDNT* ii. 670.

[51] Caragounis, *Son of Man*, 171 and nn. 177, 178.

[52] Construing both the dative and genitive as referring to attendant circumstances, see James H. Moulton, W. F. Howard, and Nigel Turner, *A Grammar of New Testament Greek* (4 vols.; Edinburgh: T. & T. Clark, 1963), iii. 257.

[53] While at Mark 8: 38 and Matt. 16: 27 the Glory belongs to the 'Father', in the parallel at Luke 9: 26 (cf. Matt. 25: 31) the Son of Man shares his Glory with the Father and the angels. I. Howard Marshall, *The Gospel of Luke*, NIGTC (Grand Rapids, Mich.: Eerdmans, 1979), 376–7, sees this as Luke's attempt to heighten the Christology. But could it be the other way around?—i.e. that Luke was trying to tone down a statement in his tradition which was too heady.

[54] Cf. Mark 14: 62 and parallels where the coming of the Son of Man sitting at the right hand of Power (a near homologation for the right hand of Glory) earns Jesus the charge of blasphemy. This charge reflects more than just laying claim to

4. *Early Christianity.* The last bit of evidence for Glory as an eschatological sign comes from early Christian texts. These texts can be divided into two profiles: (i) the continued use of Glory to sign eschatological divine presence (that is, Glory as what is expected or hoped for at the end); and (ii) the use of Glory to sign the eschatological divine presence *in the future parousia of the resurrected Jesus.*

All the texts in the first profile contrast the present suffering experienced by believers with the Glory of the eschatological future. In Romans 5 present suffering (v. 3) stands in direct contrast to the 'hope of the glory of God' (ἐλπίδι τῆς δόξης τοῦ θεοῦ, v. 2). The afflictions associated with 'this age' (τοῦ νῦν καιροῦ) pale in comparison with the apocalypse of Glory (τὴν μέλλουσαν δόξαν ἀποκαλυφθῆναι) which awaits as at the parousia (Rom. 8: 18). The warranting basis for Peter's exhortation is that he has participated in the sufferings of Christ (ὁ συμπρεσβύτερος καὶ μάρτυς τῶν τοῦ Χριστοῦ παθημάτων), as well as the eschatological Glory (ὁ καὶ τῆς μελλούσης ἀποκαλύπτεσθαι δόξης κοινωνός, 1 Pet. 5: 1).[55]

These texts demonstrate that Christians, like the prophets, continued to hope for an age ushered in and defined by Yahweh's Glory. Significantly, however, at this grand theophany, Christians expected to be transformed into Glory: the eschatological goal of Christian experience is participation in the divine presence. The present suffering/future Glory structure of these passages may well reflect the cross/resurrection shape of early Christian preaching and the Jesus tradition—an observation which points to how Glory, divine presence, resurrection, and parousia are all linked together in a fundamental way.

---

be a/the Messiah (so C. E. B. Cranfield, *The Gospel According to St. Mark*, CGTC (Cambridge: Cambridge University Press, 1959), 445). It is claiming to be equal with God, and thus the ironic charge. Dunn, *Partings of the Ways*, 52, 168, 174, misses the point entirely: by making the issue of the trial Jesus' attack on the Temple, by making Jesus reluctant to own up to his Messianic deeds, and by draining the Son of Man sayings as non-inflammatory to Jewish ears, Dunn is able to side-step completely the provocative character of Jesus' statements.

[55] Is Peter saying that he is currently sharing in the expected Glory? Most interpret ὁ καί τῆς μελλούσης ἀποκαλύπτεσθαι δόξης κοινωνός in a future sense: 'I will share in the Glory when it is revealed.' Still others see the phrase as a reference to the transfiguration (so E. G. Selwyn, *The First Epistle of St. Peter*, 2nd edn. (London: Macmillan and Company, 1947), 228). On this latter interpretation, then, the transfiguration would be a proleptic experience of the final parousia. Still, the parousia, whether anticipated or experienced in the transfiguration, is an apocalypse of Glory. Cf. Luke 9: 31-2; 2 Pet. 1: 17.

A second set of texts also employ Glory to sign the end, but do so in a way that reflects a profound and controversial referential shift. No longer is the eschatological age simply defined as the apocalypse of Yahweh's Glory; it is the advent of Jesus and his Glory. Five texts help establish this point.

(i) Colossians 1: 27 asserts that the previously hidden mystery of Gentile inclusion in the saving purposes of Yahweh is confirmed by Christ's mystical union with the believer: 'To them God chose to make known how great among the Gentiles are the riches of the glory of this mystery, which is Christ in you' (ὅ ἐστιν Χριστὸς ἐν ὑμῖν). The author then glosses this phrase as 'the hope of glory' (ἡ ἐλπὶς τῆς δόξης). Glory is still the object of Christian hope, but Christ is now its defining centre. 'Christ (in you) is the hope of Glory.' (ii) Colossians 3: 4 works from the other direction. 'When Christ who is our life appears, then you also will appear with him in glory' (τότε καὶ ὑμεῖς σὺν αὐτῷ φανερωθήσεσθε ἐν δόξῃ). The text envisions that Jesus' apocalypse in/with Glory will transform believers into the likeness of his divine presence. (iii) Titus 2: 13 exhorts believers to sobriety and patience in light of 'the appearing of the glory of our great God and Saviour Jesus Christ' (ἐπιφάνειαν τῆς δόξης τοῦ μεγάλου θεοῦ καὶ σωτῆρος ἡμῶν Ἰησοῦ Χριστοῦ). Despite vigorous debate over how to construe the Greek of this verse, one can say that Jesus, who is both God and Saviour, will bear the eschatological divine presence (that is, Glory) at his parousia.[56] (iv) Peter encourages believers in their sharing of Christ's sufferings so that they 'may also rejoice and be glad when his glory is revealed' (1 Pet. 4: 13). The particular point of interest here is the phrase ἐη τῇ ἀποκαλύψει τῆς δόξης αὐτοῦ. The future apocalypse[57] is not defined by the revelation of the Father's Glory; nor does Jesus share it with the Father; δόξα belongs to Jesus alone. (v) The way in which Jesus substitutes for Yahweh and the way in which Glory,

---

[56] I understand θεοῦ and σωτῆρος as dependent on δόξης and as referring to one person. Further, Ἰησοῦ Χριστοῦ stands in apposition to θεοῦ and σωτῆρος (so RSV, NASB, NRSV). Thus I read the passage as affirming that Jesus Christ is both God and Saviour and that his appearance will be an appearance of Glory. For support of this reading, as well as detailed criticism of other options, see Murray J. Harris, *Jesus as God: The New Testament Use of Theos in Reference to Jesus* (Grand Rapids, Mich.: Baker, 1992), 173-85, esp. 85 n. 53, and Raymond Brown, *An Introduction to New Testament Christology* (Mahwah, NJ: Paulist, 1994), 181-2.

[57] The phrase ἐν τῇ ἀποκαλύψει should be interpreted temporally: it points to a particular event at a particular time.

as a sign of Yahweh's presence, is applied to Jesus in eschatological settings can best be seen in the second letter to the Thessalonians.

> This is evidence of the righteous judgement of God, that you may be made worthy of the kingdom of God, for which you are suffering—since indeed God deems it just to repay with affliction those who afflict you, and to grant rest with us to you who are afflicted, when the Lord Jesus is revealed from heaven with his mighty angels in flaming fire, inflicting vengeance upon those who do not know God and upon those who do not obey the gospel of our Lord Jesus. They shall suffer the punishment of eternal destruction and exclusion from the presence of the Lord and from the glory of his might, when he comes on that day to be gloried in his saints, and to be marveled at in all whose have believed. (2 Thess. 1: 5-10a)

The phrases ἀπ᾽ οὐρανοῦ and μετ᾽ ἀγγπελων echo Daniel 7 generally and the Gospel Son of Man tradition in particular.[58] Κυρίου Ἰησοῦ then substitutes for the Son of Man. The 'Lord' of verse 9 must therefore be the 'Lord Jesus' of verse 7, who, at his parousia, shall render judgement upon the unruly and exclude them from 'presence of the Lord and the glory of his might'. This is almost a verbatim quote of Isaiah 2: 10 (LXX), the only linguistic difference being the deletion of φόβου.[59]

Isa. 2: 10 ἀκὸ προσώπου τοῦ φόβου κυρίου καὶ ἀπὸ τῆς δόξης ἰσχθύος αὐτοῦ

2 Thess. 1: 9 ἀπὸ προσώπου τοῦ   κυρίου καὶ ἀπὸ τῆς δόξης ἰσχύος αὐτοῦ

This text, therefore, effects a controversial referential transference: quoting an Old Testament passage emphasizing the eschatological 'Day of the Lord', the juridical functions reserved for Yahweh are now said to be executed by Jesus.[60] Further, the referent of the title κύριος shifts from Yahweh to Jesus,[61] a shift all the more scandalous since Isaiah 2: 11 is a strongly monotheistic passage. This clear referential shift from Yahweh to Jesus reflects early Christianity's redefinition of the Godhead via an eschatological Christology (or a Christocentric eschatology). And it is precisely

---

[58] Matt. 16: 27; 25: 31. Cf. John A. T. Robinson, *Jesus and his Coming* (Philadelphia: Westminster, 1957), 107 and 109 n. 1.

[59] Cf. Isa. 2: 19, 21 (LXX).

[60] L. Joseph Kreitzer, *Jesus and God in Paul's Eschatology*, JSNTSS 19 (Sheffield: JSOT Press, 1987), 120-1.

[61] David L. Capes, *Old Testament Yahweh Texts in Paul's Christology*, WUNT 2/47 (Tübingen: Mohr-Siebeck, 1992), 153-4.

here, in an eschatological context,[62] that δόξα stands for Jesus when he stands for Yahweh.

Thus in early Christianity Jesus' parousia is depicted as an eschatological theophany of Glory, Yahweh's divine presence. The question then is: how and why did early Christianity begin to make this provocative referential shift? In what follows the resurrection of Jesus will be singled out as the trigger for substituting Jesus for Yahweh's eschatological, divine presence, his Glory.

THE RESURRECTION OF JESUS AS THE INAUGURATION OF ESCHATOLOGICAL GLORY

We now turn to passages where the resurrection of Jesus is brought into close association with divine presence, Glory.

I. *Hebrews 2: 9*. The expositional material of Hebrews 1: 5–2: 18 presents a sustained contrast of the Son with angelic figures. Through a catena of Old Testament quotations the author asserts the Son's relational, functional, and ontological superiority (1: 5–9), even though he or she must embarrassingly concede the Son's death (2: 10–18). In 2: 5–9 the author effects a crucial textual and theological transition.[63]

For it was not to angels that God subjected the world to come, of which we are speaking. It has been testified somewhere,

'What is man that thou are mindful of him,
or the son of man, that thou carest for him?
Thou didst make him for a little while lower than the angels,
thou hast crowned him with glory and honour,
putting everything in subjection under his feet.

. . . But we see Jesus, who for a little while was made lower than the angels, crowned with glory and honour because of the suffering of death, so that by the grace of God he might taste death for every one.

(Heb. 2: 5–9)

---

[62] v. 7 describes Jesus' eschatological appearance as an apocalypse (ἐν ἀποκαλύψει τοῦ κυρίου Ἰησοῦ); see n. 56 above.

[63] George H. Guthrie, *The Structure of Hebrews: A Text-Linguistic Analysis*, NovTSupp, 72 (Leiden: Brill, 1994), 199, 144.

The quotation (vv. 6b–8a) and exposition (vv. 8b–9) of Psalm 8: 5–7 (LXX) provides the key textual hinge, while the theological transition occurs through repeated references to the life of Jesus— his incarnation (ἠλατωμένον, v. 9), death (τὸ πάθημα τοῦ θανάτου, v. 9), and resurrection (ὑπέταξαν, v. 5; ὑπέταξας, v. 8a; ὑποτάξαι, v. 8b; ἀνυπότακτον, v. 8c; ὑποτεταγμένα, v. 8d), all set in an eschatological context (τὴν οἰκουμένην μέλλουσαν, v. 5; τὸν βραχύ, v. 9). The narrative architecture of this passage defines 'crowned with glory and honour' (δόξῃ καὶ τιμῇ ἐστεφανωμένον, v. 9) as a reference to Jesus' resurrection, and therefore a homologation for ὑποτάσσω. To be 'crowned with Glory' is to be raised from the dead, an act which commences eschatological subjection.[64]

The author not only applies this psalm to Jesus (making this a psalm celebrating Jesus), but retrofits the psalm in light of the crucial events of Jesus' life. In its original context the phrase 'to be made a little lower' paralleled 'to be crowned with glory and honour'. When read through the lens of Jesus' life, 'to be made lower' refers to his incarnation, while his crowning with glory refers to the resurrection/exaltation. Such a Midrashic rereading sounds very much like an early Christian sermon.[65] The liturgical character of the passage confirms such a suspicion.[66] The 'crowning with glory and honour' parallels the twofold 'glory and honour' in the hymnic fragment of Revelation 5: 12–13 and the 'receiving of the name above every name' (that is, the name κύριος, the Lord, Yahweh) in the hymn of Philippians 2: 5–11. This passage, therefore, is a window on to what the earliest Christians were believing and thinking: that Jesus' resurrection was an investiture of eschatological Glory.

2. *Philippians 3: 21.* Paul's warning to the Philippians concerning false teachers and teaching (Phil. 3: 1–19) reaches a rhetorical climax in his dogged affirmation of Christian hope (Phil. 3: 20–1).

But our commonwealth is in heaven, and from it we await (ἀπεκδεχόμεθα) a Saviour, the Lord Jesus Christ, who will change (μετασχηματίσει) our

[64] So F. F. Bruce, *The Epistle to the Hebrews*, NICNT (Grand Rapids, Mich.: Eerdmans, 1964), 37–9.

[65] E. Earle Ellis, 'Midrash, Targum and New Testament Quotations', in *Prophecy and Hermeneutic in Early Christianity*, WUNT 1/18 (Tübingen: Mohr-Siebeck, 1978), 193.

[66] Martin Hengel, 'Hymns and Christology', in *Between Jesus and Paul: Studies in the Earliest History of Christianity* (Philadelphia: Fortress, 1983), 78–96, at 85.

lowly body to be like his body of glory (σύμμορφον τῷ σώματι τῆς δόξης αὐτοῦ), by the power which enables him even to subject all things to himself (κατὰ τὴν ἐνέργειαν τοῦ δύνασθαι αὐτὸν καὶ ὑποτάξαι αὐτῷ τὰ πάντα).

Αὐτοῦ should be construed possessively (that is, it is the body which belongs to Jesus), δόξης objectively (that is, Jesus' body is a body characterized by Glory, the eschatological divine presence).[67] The resurrected Jesus, therefore, already possesses a body of Glory, an eschatological, transformed body. Believers, too, will undergo a final act of transformation into conformity with this eschatological Glory of Jesus. This metamorphosis will occur at the parousia, which early Christianity depicted as an apocalypse of Glory.

The striking new piece of information is the *means* by which Jesus obtained this eschatological transformed body of divine presence. The phrase κατὰ τὴν ἐνέργειαν τοῦ δύνασθαι αὐτὸν καὶ ὑποτάξαι αὐτῷ τὰ πάντα recalls Psalm 8: 7 (LXX) and its common use in earliest Christianity.[68] In fact, the parallels with Ephesians 1: 20 are so striking that it is hard not to conclude that a confessional fragment stands behind both passages.[69]

Phil. 3: 21 κατὰ τὴν ἐνέργειαν τοῦ δύνασθαι αὐτὸν καὶ ὑποτάξαι αὐτῷ τὰ πάντα

Eph. 1: 20, 22 ἣν ἐνέργειαν ἐν τῷ Χριστῷ ἐγείρας αὐτὸν ἐκ νεκρῶν καὶ καθίσας ἐν δεξιᾷ αὐτοῦ ἐν τοῖς ἐπουρανίοις . . . καὶ πάντα ὑπέταξεν ὑπὸ τοὺς πόδας αὐτοῦ.

Both Philippians 3: 21 and Ephesians 1: 20, 22 isolate the resurrection of Jesus as an apocalyptic power unleashed to subdue all enemies. The resurrection of Jesus, then, is the in-breaking of eschatological Glory—a prolepsis of the final apocalypse of Glory which will transform all those who share in Christ and finish the process of cosmic subjection.[70]

---

[67] Gerald F. Hawthorne, *Philippians*, WBC 43 (Waco, Tex.: Word, 1983), 173; Marvin R. Vincent, *The Epistles to the Philippians and to Philemon*, ICC (Edinburgh: T. & T. Clark, 1897), 121.

[68] Cf. 1 Cor. 15: 25; Eph. 1: 22-3; Heb. 2: 5-9; 1 Pet. 2: 22; Barnabas Lindars, *New Testament Apologetic: The Doctrinal Significance of the Old Testament Quotations* (Philadelphia: Westminster, 1961), 50, 168.

[69] Hawthorne, *Philippians*, 169; A. T. Lincoln, *The Epistle to the Ephesians*, WBC 42 (Dallas: Word, 1992), 51.

[70] Cf. James D. G. Dunn, *Christology in the Making: An Inquiry into the Origins of the Doctrine of the Incarnation* (London: SCM, 1980), 109-10, who reads the passage—as he does nearly all the Glory texts!—through the lens of an Adam theology.

3. *I Peter 1: 21.* Yet another confessional passage textually and theologically juxtaposes δόξα and resurrection: 'Through him you have confidence in God, who raised him from the dead and gave him glory (θεὸν τὸν ἐγείραντα αὐτὸν ἐκ νεκρῶν καὶ δόξαν αὐτῷ δόντα), so that your faith and hope are in God' (1 Pet. 1: 21). There can be no doubt that ἐγείραντα αὐτὸν ἐκ νεκρῶν formed part of early Christianity's confession of faith.[71] Καὶ δόξαν αὐτῷ δόντα could be (i) part of the earliest confessional formula (which does not appear elsewhere) or (ii) Peter's own addition. In either case, the phrase structurally parallels δόξῃ καὶ τιμῇ ἐστεφανωμένον of Psalm 8: (LXX) and Hebrews 2: 9, and isolates the resurrection as the moment of Jesus' investiture with eschatological Glory. Notably, then, Jesus as a bearer of eschatological divine presence is tied to believers' faith and hope. It is not just that God raised Jesus (as crucial for Christian theology as that is!), but that, in his resurrection, the divine character of Jesus, his Glory, becomes an essential confessional element. '[T]o believe in Christ's glory is to believe in God, who gave it to him.'[72]

4. *Romans 6: 4.* This possesses both a liturgical and a confessional prehistory. When Paul writes 'We were buried therefore with him by baptism into death, so that as Christ was raised from the dead by the glory of the Father (ὥσπερ ἠγέρθη Χριστὸς ἐκ νεκρῶν διὰ τῆς δόξης τοῦ πατρός) we too might walk in the newness of life', he witnesses to the early Christian practice of baptism and to the homologia that 'Christ was raised from the dead'.

The activity of the Father and the passivity of the Son were common features of resurrection formulas employing ἐγείρω.[73] These formulas sometimes included a reference to the means by which the raising of Jesus took place—for example, the 'Spirit' (Rom. 8: 11), 'power' (1 Cor. 6: 14), 'strength' (Eph. 1: 19), or divine 'energy' (Col. 2: 12). Romans 6: 4 points to Yahweh's Glory as the *means* of

---

[71] Acts 3: 15; 4: 10; 5: 30; 13: 30; Rom. 4: 24; 8: 11; 10: 9; 1 Cor. 6: 14; 15: 4, 14; 2 Cor. 1: 9; 4: 14; Gal. 1: 1; Eph. 1: 20; Col. 2: 12; 1 Thess. 1: 10; 1 Pet. 1: 21. See further Peter Stuhlmacher, 'Auferweckung Jesu und Biblische Theologie', *ZTK* 70 (1973), 367–405.

[72] David M. Hay, *Glory at the Right Hand: Psalm 110 in Early Christianity*, SBLMS 18 (Nashville: Abingdon, 1973), 77.

[73] R. B. Gaffin, *The Centrality of the Resurrection: A Study in Paul's Soteriology*, BBM (Grand Rapids, Mich.: Baker, 1978), 62–6, and n. 71 above.

Jesus' resurrection.[74] Cranfield, Käsemann, and Bruce are all surely correct to understand δόξα here as God's resurrection and life-giving power.[75] Along with Spirit, Glory thus becomes one of the apocalyptic symbols which announces the eschatological triumph of God in the resurrection of Jesus.[76] 'When Paul says that Christ was raised from the dead "through the glory of the Father" he means that the resurrection was an eschatological event, ushering in the time of the fulfillment of God's purpose.'[77]

5. *1 Timothy 3: 16.* The last passage which connects Glory and resurrection is also a New Testament confession/hymn celebrating Jesus.

> Great indeed, we confess, is the mystery of our religion:
> He was manifested in the flesh,
> vindicated in the Spirit,
> appeared to angels,
> preached among the nations,
> believed on in the world,
> taken up in glory.

Into whatever strophic arrangement one may wish to divide this passage, the last line 'taken up in glory' (ἀνελήμφθη ἐν δόξῃ) must refer to the resurrection/exaltation/enthronement of Jesus, and is thus comparable to similar affirmations in other preformed confessional/hymnic texts:

... and designated Son of God in power ... by the resurrection of the dead (Rom. 1: 4)
... who was raised from the dead, who is at the right hand of God ... (Rom. 8: 34)
... highly exalted him and bestowed upon him the name which is above every name (Phil. 2: 9)

---

[74] James D. G. Dunn, *Romans 1-8*, WBC 38A (Dallas: Word, 1988), 315; cf. Matthew Black, *Romans*, NCBC, 2nd end. (Grand Rapids, Mich.: Eerdmans, 1989), 88, who construes the dative as attendant circumstances and not as means.
[75] C. E. B. Cranfield, *The Epistle to the Romans*, ICC (2 vols., Edinburgh: T. & T. Clark, 1973), i. 304; Ernst Käsemann, *Commentary on Romans* (Grand Rapids, Mich.: Eerdmans, 1980), 166; F. F. Bruce, *Romans*, TNTC (Grand Rapids, Mich.: Eerdmans, 1963), 138.
[76] J. Christiaan Beker, *Paul the Apostle: The Triumph of God in Life and Thought*, 2nd edn. (Philadelphia: Fortress, 1984), 278-83.
[77] C. K. Barrett, *The Epistle to the Romans*, H/BNTC (New York: Harper & Row, 1957), 123.

... he sat down at the right hand of the Majesty on high ... (Heb. 1: 3)
... who has gone into heaven and is at the right hand of God ... (1 Pet.
3: 22)

Despite the linguistic differences, the phrases should be read as
structural parallels seeking to work out the significance of the resurrection of Jesus. These hymnic fragments thus form the paradigmatic field for understanding ἀνελήμφθη ἐν δόξῃ.[78] It, too, refers to
the resurrection of Jesus.[79]

To sum up: (i) I submit that early Christianity's interpretation of
Jesus' resurrection as a prolepsis of eschatological Glory best
explains the referential shift from Yahweh to Jesus in eschatological
texts depicting the parousia of Jesus as an apocalypse of Glory.
Surely the narrative-theological horizon generated by the Jewish
Scriptures (and the traditions dependent upon them) permitted and,
at some points, even encouraged such a strategic redeployment of
Glory; but it was the resurrection of Jesus which became the critical, historical moment for Jesus' investiture with eschatological
divine presence. (ii) That the interpretation of Jesus' resurrection as
an in-breaking of eschatological Glory occurs in various literary traditions (Hebrews, Petrine, Pauline, post-Pauline) and does so in passages reflecting the earliest liturgical (baptism, singing of hymns),
exegetical (Midrash on psalm 8), and credal (the formulas employing ἐγείρω) practices of the Church means that this interpretation
occurred very early in the life of the Church. The earliest practices
of the earliest Christians reflecting their earliest beliefs all, with one
voice, isolate and emphasize the resurrection as the inauguration of
eschatological Glory. One last task remains: to moor Glory language
in a specific social context and chart the communal implications of
its use.

TOWARDS A SOCIOLOGY OF GLORY LANGUAGE

In this section I advance two theses: (i) the identification of Jesus
with the Glory of Yahweh creates and reinforces the boundary lines

---

[78] Reinhard Deichgräber, *Gotteshymnus und Christushymnus in der frühen
Christenheit: Untersuchungen zu Form. Sprache und Stil der frühchristlichen Hymnen*,
SUNT 5 (Göttingen: Vandenhoeck & Ruprecht, 1967), 136 n. 2. The resurrection,
ascension, and exaltation to God's right hand cannot be separated into distinct
events.
[79] Cf. 1 Cor. 15: 43: ἐγείρεται ἐν δόξῃ.

between Judaism and Christianity; and (ii) the use of Glory to map a believer's progress toward final eschatological transformation builds cohesion and stability *within* the Christian community.

1. *Creating boundaries: Jesus is the Glory of Yahweh.* Many of the texts examined thus far have implicitly identified Jesus as the Glory of Yahweh. We now turn to some texts which make this identification explicit, and measure the social force such an identification effects.

Jewish monotheism was especially important in a missionary context. It certainly helped sort out differences between Christians and the larger Hellenistic world.[80] Paul's congratulations to the Thessalonian Christians for having 'turned to God from idols, to serve a living and real God' (1 Thess. 1: 9; cf. Gal. 1: 6) isolated monotheism as a key theological and communal component of their new identity. To the Corinthians Paul could say: 'we know that an idol has no real existence, and that "there is no God but one",' even if paganism offered many idols and lords (1 Cor. 8: 4–5). The recitation of the creed 'there is one God, the Father, from whom are all things and for whom we exist, and one Lord, Jesus Christ, through whom are all things and through whom we exist' (1 Cor. 8: 6) socially located the Christian: the conversion from many gods to one god mirrored the communal shift from paganism to Christianity.

Glory language also helps to sort out communal distinctions between the larger Hellenistic world and the fledgling Christian Church.

Yet among the mature we do impart wisdom, although it is not a wisdom of this age or of the rulers of this age, who are doomed to pass away. But we impart a secret and hidden wisdom of God, which God decreed before the ages for our glorification. None of the rulers of this age understood this; for if they had, they would not have crucified the Lord of glory. (1 Cor. 2: 6–8)

The special revelation made known only to believers—that is, the true identity of the Lord of Glory—formed part of Church's 'language of belonging'. As Meeks states: 'Certainly a group that possesses information to which no one else has access is a group

---

[80] Robert M. Grant, *Gods and the One God*, LEC 1 (Philadelphia: Westminster, 1986), 45–53.

strongly conscious of the boundaries between itself and the non-members.'[81] The boundary lines are further reinforced in this passage by the use of 'insider/outsider' imagery. By assigning the 'rulers of this age' the responsibility for Jesus' death, the text demonstrates a negative view of the society at large. As widespread and influential as pagan worship was, the redefinition of Jewish monotheism undertaken by Christians related, first and foremost, to a struggle between *Jews and Christians*. Paul is again very specific at this point.

In discussing the relationship between Judaism and his own Christian community, Paul says that a veil remains over the face of the Jewish ways of reading the sacred texts (2 Cor. 3: 15). The emphasis upon ignorance underscores the distance of his congregation from Judaism(s). But when a Jew 'turns to the Lord' (ἐπιστρέψῃ πρὸς κύριον, 2 Cor. 3: 16)—that is, discovers Jesus *as* the Lord—the veil of ignorance is removed. Paul identifies this moment of conversion, this movement from a Jewish community to a Christian one, as encountering the 'glory of the Lord' (τὴν δόξαν κυρίου κατοπτριζόμενοι,[82] 2 Cor. 3: 18) or discovering 'the light of knowledge of the glory of God in the face of Jesus Christ' (φωτισμὸν τῆς γνώσεως τῆς δόξης τοῦ θεοῦ ἐν προσώπῳ [Ἰησοῦ] Χριστοῦ, 2 Cor. 4: 6). In a text which has in view Jewish-Christian relations, Paul defines the community identity in terms of a high, Glory Christology—Jesus is the very presence of Yahweh. As Alan Segal notes, such a christological construal opens up a 'giant social fissure' between Paul and his Jewish opponents.[83]

Paul is not the only one self-consciously to use a Glory Christology to mark boundary lines between Jews and Christians. The hymnic fragment preserved at Hebrews 1: 1-4 identifies Jesus as Yahweh's Glory and the exact representation of Yahweh's nature (ὃς ὢν ἀπαύγασμα τῆς δόξης χαρακτὴρ τῆς ὑποστάσεως αὐτοῦ, Heb. 1: 3). Two observations are in order. (i) The hymn formed part of the author's strategy to distinguish between Jesus and angels. The catena of Old Testament texts and the sustained Midrash on these texts which follows in Hebrews 1: 5-2: 18 proves the point.[84]

---

[81] Wayne Meeks, *The First Urban Christians: The Social World of the Apostle Paul* (New Haven: Yale University Press, 1983), 91-2.

[82] I tend to construe this oft-debated participle as 'behold' (in the Gospel) rather than 'reflect' (in Paul's apostolic ministry).

[83] Segal, *Paul the Convert*, 155.   [84] Hengel, *Between Jesus and Paul*, 84.

The confusion between Jesus and angelic figures—especially Jesus' ontological superiority—may well imply some Jewish apocalyptic-mystical group who refused to venerate Jesus and considered him as just an angelic figure. This explains the binary shape of the hymn: it focused upon Jesus and God and Jesus *as* God. (ii) the performative force of singing this hymn (or reciting, if a confession) was to reinforce community boundaries. No less powerful than, say, the Lord's Supper or baptism, the ritual of confessing 'Jesus as the Glory of Yahweh' created and reinforced the boundary lines between Christianity and Judaism.[85] Thus, the ontological identification of Jesus with Yahweh via Glory language marked boundary lines between Jews and Christians.

2. *Creating cohesion: transformation into Glory.* Conversion only began the process of communal commitments. Christian congregations needed to stress differences between themselves and the outside world, be it Jewish or pagan, but also needed to produce cohesiveness within the community. Biographical reconstruction became one of the many ways in which Christians built cohesive communities. By telling and retelling both their own particular stories and the story of the founder figure, Christians were able to emphasize the *sociomorphic* demands of conversion (the necessity of resocialization) and the *physiomorphic* implications of transformation (the necessity of character re-formation).

Sociomorphic language portrays salvation in terms of social relations—those of master/slave, father/son, judge/accused, friend/enemy—whereas physiomorphic language portrays salvation by means of organic images—growth/decay, life/death, division/union, change in shapes (often involving mirrors or reflected vision).[86] Whereas the sociomorphic register most often relates to conversion (and thus helps to mark boundary lines between Christians and outsiders), the physiomorphic register more often relates to the process of spiritual transformation (and thus helps build unity and cohesiveness within).

---

[85] The distinction often made, that this is a hymn *about* Christ rather than *to* him, is irrelevant. The confession/hymn was liturgy which celebrated the saviour figure, Jesus. I don't think anyone would argue that an OT psalm about Yahweh's deeds was somehow less honorific than a psalm directed to him.

[86] Meeks, *First Urban Christians*, 164-92, esp. 182-9. Meeks here draws upon the work of Gerd Theissen, 'Soteriologische Symbolik in den paulinischen Schriften: Ein strukturalistischer Beitrag', *KD* 20 (1974), 282-304.

While any of the texts which describe the believer's final destiny as sharing in the eschatological divine presence of Jesus may fairly be considered as reflecting physiomorphic transformation, there are two texts in particular which indicate that metamorphosis into Glory has *already* begun within the context of the Christian community.

Beloved, do not be surprised at the fiery ordeal which comes upon you to prove you, as though something strange were happening to you. But rejoice in so far as you share Christ's suffering, that you may also rejoice and be glad when his glory is revealed. If you are reproached for the name of Christ, you are blessed, because the spirit of glory and of God rests upon you. (1 Pet. 4: 12–14)

At first glance this text appears to deal with community boundaries. By calling attention to persecution, Peter looks as if he is distinguishing between those on the inside (Christians) and those on the outside (the persecutors). A closer reading, however, demonstrates the physiomorphic character of this passage.

The difficulties which may come are said to occur *within* (ἐν ὑμῖν, v. 12a), and occur for the maturation of Christians (πρὸς πειρασμὸν ὑμῖν γινομένῃ, v. 12b). Peter has already alluded to how internal biographic transformation mirrors external difficulties (1: 6–7).[87] Participation in Christ's sufferings (κοινωνεῖτε τοῖς τοῦ Χριστοῦ παθήμαιν) is the legitimate ground for both present and future joy. This clearly indicates that physiomorphic transformation is what is in view: the community/Christian should joyfully embody the sufferings of their founder figure. Christians are 'blessed' (μακάριοι), even if charged with blasphemy, for holding to the 'name of Christ'.[88] Because, Peter assures, 'the spirit of glory and of God rests upon you' (τὸ τῆς δόξης καὶ τὸ τοῦ θεοῦ πνεῦμα ἐφ᾽ ὑμᾶς ἀναπαύεται). Having just made reference to the apocalypse of Glory awaiting all believers, Peter affirms that believers are even now participating in that Glory through the Spirit. Transformation into eschatological Glory thus becomes an important warranting basis for endurance and continued progress. Despite the difficulties, the community should persist in well-doing.

---

[87] Cf. Jas. 1: 2–3; Rom. 5: 3–5.
[88] The charge of blasphemy indicates that Glory is again tied to a breach of (Jewish) monotheism; this text is about the way in which monotheistic claims, Jesus' identity, and community cohesiveness work together.

In 2 Corinthians 3: 18 Paul characterizes the process of transformation into the resurrection likeness/image of Christ as a metamorphosis into Glory (μεταμορφούμεθα ἀπὸ δόξης εἰς δόξαν). This verse permits insight into Paul's understanding of transformation. Ἐικών and δόξα partake of the same paradigmatic field: by beholding the resurrected Glory of God in Christ (in the preaching of the gospel), one is transformed into the image of Christ. That is, the revelation of Christ as Glory (ἀπὸ δόξης) inaugurates a process of transformation which ultimately resolves into a final transformation in the Glory of Christ (εἰς δόξαν). God enables and sustains transformational progress by the Glory of Christ.[89]

1 Peter 4: 14 and 2 Corinthians 3: 18 suggest that biographical metamorphosis is ongoing in the life of the believer/community. Transformation into Glory is transformation into the eschatological divine presence, the resurrected Jesus, and transformation into each other—a key aspect of millenarian groups. Unity within the community is achieved through this metamorphosis: everyone can and must be changed. Christianity replaced Jewish Halachah with a pattern of transformational mysticism, and thereby changed the way to build community cohesiveness.[90]

CONCLUSION

In this chapter I have defended the thesis that the resurrection of Jesus, as depicted in early Christian creeds, confessions, and hymns, was interpreted as his investiture with, and inauguration of, eschatological divine presence—that is, the Glory of Yahweh. Further, I argued that identification of the resurrected Jesus as the Glory of Yahweh carried profound sociological implications—the creation and maintenance of a new community. These conclusions depend upon several other observations: (i) that the phrase 'Glory of Yahweh' signed Yahweh's divine presence; (ii) that in the prophets

---

[89] In several other texts Paul states that spiritual enablement comes from resurrection Glory: Eph. 3: 16: ἵνα δῷ ὑμῖν κατὰ τὸ πλοῦτος τῆς δόξης αὐτοῦ δυνάμει κραταιωθῆναι διὰ τοῦ πνεύματος αὐτοῦ εἰς τὸν ἔσω ἄνθρωπον; Phil. 4: 19: ὁ δὲ θεός μου πληρώσει πᾶσιν χρείαν ὑμῶν κατὰ τὸ πλοῦτος αὐτοῦ ἐν δόξῃ ἐν Χριστῷ Ἰησοῦ; Col. 1: 11: ἐν πάσῃ δυνάμει δυναμούμενοι κατὰ τὸ κράτος τῆς δόξης αὐτοῦ. In all three cases, κατά introduces the ground of divine enablement.

[90] This has been most clearly seen and substantiated by Segal, *Paul the Convert*, 150–83.

Glory became a sign of eschatological divine presence; (iii) that Glory could sign anthropomorphic depictions of Yahweh in apocalyptic visions; (iv) that Glory became a regular feature of God's chief agent in Jewish apocalypses; (v) that Jesus employed Glory to define his own future role as the Son of Man; (vi) that earliest Christianity took over the hope for a future age defined by eschatological Glory, and (vii) effected a profound referential shift by replacing the expectation for an apocalypse of Yahweh's Glory with Jesus *with and as* the Glory of Yahweh.

I now wish to turn my attention, briefly, to some implications of this research, specifically as it relates to the resurrection of Jesus. First, while it is commonly recognized that the story of Jesus must be nested within a larger narrative framework—that is, the story of Jesus must be construed against the narrative expectations generated by the Hebrew Bible—an equally true correlate is not always recognized: words, phrases, titles, and images applied to Jesus also have a *narrative* context: namely, the crucial events of his life. Therefore, resurrection, as the inauguration of the future, becomes the best way to understand Glory—and not the other way around.[91]

Second, if Glory signed the eschatological divine presence (which I think on balance it did), and if Christians were convinced that Jesus was the divine presence—that is, that Jesus was the embodiment of the Glory of Yahweh (which, again, I think they were)—then Christians could/would/should engage in religious devotion to/with/through Jesus (as I think the New Testament confirms). The real question, then, is: how did Christians become convinced that Jesus was in fact the Glory of Yahweh, the embodiment of Yahweh's presence? The short answer is the resurrection, for it was there, as the Christian texts indicate, that Jesus' divinity became fully evident.

Thus, third, the resurrection is crucial for Christian origins. The resurrection generated a Christology, and a Christology generated a new community. The rupture between Jews and Christians came early, and it came as a consequence of the resurrection. Since the resurrection meant that God had been redefined, Jewish monotheism as it had been traditionally understood was in the dock. The

---

[91] Leander E. Keck, 'Toward the Renewal of New Testament Christology', in M. C. de Boer (ed.), *From Jesus to John: Essays on Jesus and New Testament Christology in Honour of Marinus de Jonge*, JSNTSS 84 (Sheffield: JSOT Press, 1993), 321-40.

new community which gathered and in eschatological jubilation celebrated Jesus the Lord has stepped outside the bounds of Jewish monotheism. And, I believe, this is why Paul was on the road to Damascus—not because Christian Jews (or Jewish Christians) had abandoned Halachah (as surely many other Jews had). It was not because this new Jewish group had threatened the Temple. Paul persecuted Christians because these Jews had compromised Jewish monotheism by worshiping Jesus as the Lord, the Glory—something he was destined to do as well when he, with an unveiled face, discovered that the resurrected Jesus was Yahweh's divine presence.

5

Life After Death: The Social Sources

ALAN F. SEGAL

In spite of the Gallup poll's pervasive and helpful interest in American attitudes towards religion, it usually skirts over some crucial aspects of American religious life. According to the poll, the numbers of Americans who believe in life after death is amazingly high: seven Americans out of ten believe in life after death, practically identical with the figures of half a century ago, a figure which seems to dispute any notion that Americans are losing their faith or that our society is secularizing.[1]

We do not have equivalently detailed data about belief in resurrection. Indeed, the failure of the pollsters to ask detailed questions about this critical doctrine may hide where the secularization has taken place. Anecdotal evidence from pastors, as well as my own observations of both contemporary Jews and Christians, leads me to think that the congregants of liberal and main-line churches, like the equivalent synagogues, have very ambivalent ideas about the doctrine of resurrection, both as applied to Jesus and as anticipated for the righteous and faithful; while conservative and fundamentalist groups put not just life after death but *resurrection* at the centre of their beliefs. Indeed, Reform Judaism, in order to show itself to be a rational religion based on the revealed law of the Jews, has removed all references to resurrection, or תחית המתים, in the liturgy. Conversely, Moses Mendelssohn considered the concept of the immortality of the soul to be a significant part of rational religion.

This is a very strange state of affairs in American life, because both Christianity and Rabbinic Judaism put belief in the resurrection, not just life after death, at the centre of their beliefs and creeds. Christianity required the notion of resurrection once it experienced

---

[1] See George Gallup, jun., and Jim Castelli, *The People's Religion: American Faith in the 90's* (New York: Macmillan, 1989), 58-9.

the first Easter. 'How can one not believe in resurrection if Christ is already raised?', asked Paul (1 Cor. 15), though I paraphrase, and indeed resurrection is at the centre of every Christian creed. The rabbis, for their part, took time off from their ethical deliberations to say that resurrection was absolutely central to their faith. If you don't believe in it, you won't get it (Sanhedrin, 10). Again, I paraphrase. But later we shall have an opportunity to look at Paul and the rabbis more closely. On the other hand, virtually all scholars of the Hellenistic period see the notion of the immortality of the soul as a valuable foreign importation from Greek, and particularly Platonic, thought.

THE BIBLE ON LIFE AFTER DEATH

Interestingly, the earliest parts of the Bible do not concern any life after death worth having; at times the Bible even seems deliberately to avoid talking about it. Resurrection is totally unknown in the Bible until much later. Indeed, the advice of the Bible is very practical:

The days of our life are seventy years, or perhaps eighty, if we are strong; even then their span is only toil and trouble; they are soon gone and we fly away. Who considers the power of your anger? Your wrath is as great as the fear that is due you. So teach us to count our days that we may gain a wise heart. (Ps. 90: 10–12; NRSV (and throughout))

Of course, the metaphor of 'flying' leaves the text open enough to accommodate later notions of soul flight. But a fair reader will see that the whole force of the passage is to counsel the Israelite to treat this life as seriously as possible, for death is the known end. Any reader who systematically surveys the oldest sections of the biblical text becomes impressed with how the Bible studiously avoids the concept of life after death. The reasons for this silence must be conjectured, and cannot be demonstrated; but one sensible guess would be the Hebrew text's enmity towards foreign cults. We know well that the Bible normally turns the objects of veneration in other, neighbouring countries into the material objects of God's creation. Thus the heavens of Hebrew life are not gods, but the handiwork of God. At the same time, we have clear evidence that the Israelite populace did venerate these objects, and were opposed by prophet and priest.

In the same way, we find no extended discussion of the notion of life after death or the realm of the dead in biblical thought, not because it did not exist in popular Israelite thought probably, but because the Bible is reticent about opening the door to what it calls idolatry or the Canaanite veneration of spirits or ghosts. There is much less evidence of this particular likelihood, but any quick survey of the world's notions of life after death shows that the belief in ghosts and spirits at least is almost universal in human experience, where it serves a myriad of different social purposes, perhaps the most important being retribution or the protection and respectful burial of the dead. But divination and ancestor worship must also be mentioned as often supported by the notion that something of the dead personality has survived death. Indeed, the notion of spirits is probably older than the human race itself, since we find gravegoods in Musterian and Neanderthal burial sites, and they are a separate species from our own.

This almost universal human background can be seen protruding in some narratives. For instance, take the famous story of Saul and the witch of Endor (1 Sam. 28: 6–17). We see here something of what the Bible studiously avoids. Samuel is just as reticent as the medium to engage in this behaviour. As in other cultures, there was in Israel an abode of the dead, usually called Sheol, but sometimes called by other names suggesting a pit or waste. It was not a place of reward or punishment. Very like the Greek Hades, all the dead go there. There is no reward or punishment in this depiction. But, unlike Hades, the dead (or at least Samuel) do not have to wait for word from above to know about human events. Samuel already knows the future. And it is this quality of ancient Near Eastern mythology which disturbs the writers most, perhaps. Because of his supernatural powers, the ghost Samuel is called an *Elohim*, a *god* emerging from the ground. On the other hand, the plural verb may imply several 'gods' or 'supernatural judges' appearing, of which Samuel is one.

The most poignant part of this story is the way in which Saul must convince the woman to perform the ritual, which he has specifically forbidden and which she does not want to perform. Samuel, though dead, is still a prophet, and knows the outcome of the forthcoming battle. Perhaps all the dead do, or all the dead whose advice can be sought. He tells Saul the most horrible news possible. Saul had suspected the worst anyway, ever since he had stopped receiving prophetic dreams. God has truly abandoned him.

(How different this is from our world. We would, of course, be very upset if God started talking to us by any means. But Saul had become used to hearing from him often. The intimacy between God and man here suggests to me that this story is literary rather than historical, by the way. It is the intimacy of the relationship between God and the patriarchs that most tips us off to its highly imaginative character.)

But, literary or historical, for Saul to have called upon the witch of Endor is clearly the last, most sinful act of a very desperate man in the eyes of the later narrator. The woman in an act of kindness slaughters a calf for the abandoned king, Saul, who has not eaten all day, a detail which suggests actual rites for a prophetic seance.

So far as this passage of biblical narrative is concerned, then, the dead can be recalled, but it is sinful to do so, probably because to do so suggests that they are divine beings, breaching the canons of monotheism (a slightly anachronistic way to express it).

In simpler form, the issue must be the relationship to foreign cults. As Deuteronomy (18: 9–14) says, one is not to imitate the practices of those nations, which are further specified as infant sacrifice and magic. In this version, the rules are clearly influenced by Judahite experience with Assyrian religion as well.[2] The word 'witch' (מכשפה) used to describe the enchantress in 1 Samuel is the same word used to describe the last of the enchanters in Deuteronomy (מכשף), except that the gender is common (masculine) in Deuteronomy. The reason given for the prohibition is that monotheism is violated when the children of Israel are allowed to practise religiously like those who preceded them and were dispossessed by the Lord for their sinfulness—passing their sons and daughters through fire. What we might call the Hebrew impulse to monotheism, then, was consistent with Hebrew suspicion of foreign cults and what seems to be a deliberate failure to spell out notions of life after death, lest it define powers in opposition to God or areas where his rule does not extend.

And, of course, though the psalms were written over a vast period of time, some possibly even in periods when the notion of life

---

[2] Brian B. Schmidt, *Israel's Beneficent Dead: Ancestor Cult and Necromancy in Ancient Israelite Religion and Tradition*, Forschungen zum Alten Testament, 11 (Tübingen: Mohr–Siebeck, 1994).

after death had been encouraged by Hellenistic culture, most of them do not colour the abode of Sheol morally, although there are some moralizing tendencies in statements like 'the good will praise you' while the evil will be lost. Most of the psalms use Sheol as a way to convince God not to kill the psalmist in his distress: 'For you do not give me up to Sheol, / or let your faithful one see the pit' (Ps. 16: 10). This is roughly equivalent to the remarks of Isaiah 38: 18–19:

> For Sheol cannot thank you,
>   death cannot praise you;
> those who go down to the pit cannot hope
>   for your faithfulness.
> The living, the living, they thank you,
>   as I do this day;
> fathers make known to children
>   your faithfulness.

Psalm 49 states that there will be a moral reckoning in the grave which the rich cannot bribe their way through. But it does not specify what that reckoning will be. Though throughout the Bible there are some notions that the good remain with God, since God would not suffer his righteous to perish,[3] the general scepticism of the biblical writers continues even once Greek influence is felt in the land.

The book of Ecclesiastes, whose date is controversial, but which is now almost entirely thought to evince Greek, and especially Stoic, influence, does not see any necessity of invoking the Platonic notion of immortality of the soul (Eccles. 9: 3–10). In this passage, Qoheleth accepts Sheol with its lack of moral rewards.

---

[3] Note places where Psalms uses the term 'forever' or 'length of days' with exaggeration: Pss. 21: 4; 22: 26; 25: 1; 31: 5; 36: 9; 37: 18. For instance, 'may your hearts live forever' in Ps. 22: 26 probably does not imply anything more than a wish. Nor does the following imply anything more than Sheol, together with the hope that God will continue to guard the psalmist there: 'Into your hand I commit my spirit; you have redeemed me, O Lord, faithful God' (Ps. 31: 5). The 'forever' at the end of Ps. 23: 6 ('I shall dwell in the house of the Lord forever') is a tendentious translation of 'length of days' in Hebrew: לְאֹרֶךְ יָמִים . Nor does the motto of Columbia University from Ps. 36: 9: *In Lumine Videbimus Lumen* 'In your light we will see light' Ps. 37: 18, often quoted in support of life after death, seems to me to imply the opposite: 'The Lord knows the days of the blameless, and their heritage will abide forever.' Pss. 86: 11 and 145: 1 suggest that the faithful will glorify God's name for ever, which may perhaps imply a moral reward after the grave. But it scarcely articulates anything resembling a 'beatific' view of life after death.

There is a brief notion of judgement earlier, but it appears ironic:

Moreover I saw under the sun that in the place of justice, wickedness was there, and in the place of righteousness, wickedness was there as well. I said in my heart, God will judge the righteous and the wicked, for he has appointed a time for every matter, and for every work. I said in my heart with regard to human beings that God is testing them to show that they are but animals. For the fate of humans and the fate of animals is the same; as one dies, so dies the other. They all have the same breath, and humans have no advantage over the animals; for all is vanity. All go to one place; all are from the dust, and all turn to dust again. Who knows whether the human spirit goes upward and the spirit of animals goes downward to the earth? (Eccles. 3: 16–21)

All reward is evanescent or in this life. Qoheleth's reaction to this knowledge is Stoic in form—not despair, but ἀπάθεια, courageous indifference. It is not much different from the famous Stoic epitaph, which is so common in the Hellenistic period: 'I was not, I was, I am not, I don't care' (*non eram, eram, non sum, non curo*). And this is part of the heroic facing of death in the ancient world which Freud admired so much. Like Sidduri in the Old Babylonian version of the Gilgamesh epic, Qoheleth suggests a *carpe diem* theme. Enjoy life. Eat and drink with enjoyment; let your family give you pleasure; dress well. This life is all that we can know. Don't count on anything more (and this is Job's answer as well).

There is no doubt in my mind that this attitude is continuous with previous Hebrew notions, as we see in the Bible's understanding of Sheol. Though the book seems deeply influenced by Stoicism, the basic notion of Sheol in place of life after death is part of Hebrew thought. Indeed, the notions found in Ecclesiastes could have been written by an ancient Near Eastern Wisdom writer in Israel, Egypt, or Babylonia. The Stoicism can be seen in the more personal voice and the interest in personal observation, the style of communication more than the specific notions found within the book. It will remain the dominant notion of the Israelite aristocracy through to the destruction of the Temple.

Even in the later, much more pious apocryphon *The Wisdom of Jesus Ben Sira*, we find similar notions which ignore life after death. All rewards and punishments are considered to be part of this life. Adversity is a test of one's faith: 'Opt not for the success of pride; remember it will not reach death unpunished' (9: 12). Even more important is Ben Sira's famous discussion of death:

> Give, take, and treat yourself well,
>> for in the netherworld there are no joys to seek.
> All flesh grows old, like a garment;
>> the age-old law is: all must die. (Sir. 14: 16-17)

There are two ways, principally, in which a person outlasts death in Ben Sira's estimation. The first is through children (30: 4-5), who represent their parents after death. The other is by means of a lasting good reputation (41: 11-13).

This approach to life, which Freud characterized as facing death heroically without illusion, continues in Hebrew though principally amongst the Sadducees. They are aristocratic by birth, not talent, and they continue the most ancient traditions.

But there is evidence of the gradual imposition of the idea of life after death in the later prophets and psalms. One of the most famous passages is Ezekiel 37: 1-14, although the context suggests that it is meant to be the vehicle of a vision, not an actual happening. The other passage which is often invoked in demonstration of ancient views of life after death in Israelite thought is in Isaiah 24-7, the Isaianic apocalypse. Here is the famous, well-known passage:

> Like a woman with child,
>> who writhes and cries out in her pangs
>> when she is near her time,
> so were we because of you, O Lord;
>> we were with child, we writhed,
>> but we gave birth only to wind.
> We have won no victories on earth,
>> and no one is born to inhabit the world.
> Your dead shall live, their corpses[4] shall rise.
> O dwellers in the dust, awake and sing for joy!
> For your dew is a radiant dew,
>> and the earth will give birth to those long dead.[5]

>> (Isa. 26: 17-19)

It is the people who are the subject of the passage. The prophet points out the previous failures of the people. They have tried already to return to the Lord. But, as in Ezekiel 37, their endeavours were in vain. It seems to me that this passage, like the Ezekiel one, is meant to be a prophetic vision, not an actual scene.

---

[4] Correction. Compare Syr Targum: Heb. 'my corpse'.
[5] Heb. 'to the shades'.

The first clear reference to life after death can be defined exactly, with regard to both its date and the specific circumstances that produced it:

At that time Michael, the great prince, the protector of your people, shall arise. There shall be a time of anguish, such as has never occurred since nations first came into existence. But at that time your people shall be delivered, everyone who is found written in the book. Many of those who sleep in the dust of the earth[6] shall awake, some to everlasting life, and some to shame and everlasting contempt. Those who are wise shall shine like the brightness of the sky,[7] and those who lead many to righteousness, like the stars forever and ever. (Dan. 12: 1-3)

Here is the first explicit reference to resurrection in the Hebrew Bible. And we can fix its arrival. The date is 168 BCE, or thereabouts. The sign of the resurrection is the arrival of Michael. It is a time of unprecedented, terrible tribulation. But the people whose names are written in the book shall be rescued. The book has never been mentioned before in Hebrew thought, though it quickly becomes part of standard Jewish lore (e.g. Ascension of Isaiah 9: 21-2), providing the central image for the liturgy of Rosh Hashanah (See M. Rosh Hashanah 1: 1).

The writer is aware of the previous writing on the subject. The language of Daniel 12: 1-3 is taken directly from Isaiah 26: 19. The writer of Daniel has certainly taken the ambiguous prophecy of Isaiah in a literal sense, saying that the sleepers in the dust will literally rise. But he has not taken the writing literally in every respect, because he has some definite notions about the identity of the resurrected. He goes on to say that the righteous will not be resurrected alone. Some of those whose behaviour has been reprehensible will also be resurrected, for eternal contempt and shame. Later discussions of resurrection will confine themselves to providing a reward for the righteous. This particular passage, the earliest *undoubted* reference to resurrection in the Hebrew Bible, suggests that both the righteous and the very evil need to be resurrected for the purpose of giving them their well-deserved rewards. This hope no doubt comes from the observation that some of the good have been suffering, not for forgetting God's word and law, but precisely because they have observed it. The converse for the greatly evil. The

---

[6] Or 'the land of dust'.   [7] Or 'dome'.

context for this observation must surely be persecution and martyrdom, as we shall see.

Besides the general resurrection and punishment, a very interesting special reward is promised to those who make others wise (המשכילים). They shall shine like the brightness of the heavens (כזהר הרקיע), those who lead the many to righteousness like the stars for ever (ככוכבים לעולם ועד). They shall be luminous beings, shining as stars, like the angels, for stars and angels had been identified since earliest times (e.g. Judg. 5: 20 and also Job 38: 7).

This vision serves as the basis for the doctrine of resurrection even in Rabbinic Judaism. In the much later Jewish prayer for the dead, *El Malay Rahamim* (אל מלא רהמים), it is directly quoted. In that prayer, a regular part of Jewish interment and memorial services, the dead are said to be in heaven, shining with the brightness of the heavens, 'under the wings of the Shekinah'. The term for brightness or splendour is Zohar (זהר), and this is probably the basis for the title of the most famous book of Jewish mysticism, *The Zohar*, written in the High Middle Ages. So there is no question that this passage is important to later tradition.

Now there is no scriptural basis for this heavenly reward. Though Scripture can be adduced retrospectively in support of the imagery of sleep and wakening, we do not get a rational explication of the preceding scripture. Instead, the passage is framed as a prophetic dream. This innovation in Hebrew thought is decided not by exegesis but by the arrival of revelation. For me this clarifies the social position by which the previous Scriptures were re-understood as a specific prophecy of resurrection. The innovation was authored by revelatory dreams of prophets who beforehand must have been contemplating the meaning of the precedents in Isaiah and Ezekiel, but were only able to make this interpretation when a revelation was received to make it acceptable.

Revelation in Judaism is also specific to historical circumstances. We think we know the specific events that produced the revelation of resurrection in Daniel. It was not written during the Persian period, as it purports to be, but during the persecution surrounding the Maccabean War. During this period, Jews were martyred for their faith (2 Macc. 6: 18–31). Note here that Eleazar refuses to eat pork, or even to eat acceptable food when the crowd has been told it is pork. So the old man Eleazar dies a martyr's death, even though he is offered a merciful and respectable way out, because in his last remaining years, he does not want to make a mockery of the rules by which he has lived his entire life.

Soon the seven brothers and the mother are put to the same torture. Very few scholars would actually date this passage to the time of the evil edicts of Antiochus. Second Maccabees was seemingly written in Greek, and after some decades had passed since the events. On the other hand, the passages in 2 Maccabees 6 and 7 could easily come from a separate source which was inserted into the text by the editors of 2 Maccabees, giving it possibly an earlier provenance.

This gruesome story differs in several important ways from the story that came before (2 Macc. 7). Although the children are as valiant as the old man, their reasons for allowing themselves to be martyred are quite different. Several of the children make brave statements about a reward for martyrs in the world to come:

'You accursed wretch, you dismiss us from this present life, but the King of the universe will raise us up to an everlasting renewal of life, because we have died for his laws'. (v. 96)

[A]nd said nobly, 'I got these from Heaven, and because of his laws I disdain them, and from him I hope to get them back again'. (v. 11)

When he was near death, he said, 'One cannot but choose to die at the hands of mortals and to cherish the hope God gives of being raised again by him. But for you there will be no resurrection to life!' (v. 14)

All of this seems to be a way of spelling out what the first brother says: 'The Lord God is watching over us and in truth has compassion on us, as Moses declared in his song that bore witness against the people to their faces, when he said, "And he will have compassion on his servants" ' (2 Macc. 7: 6).

And, of course, the compassion of God, which makes the whole notion of resurrection necessary in the case of martyrdom, is a way of spelling out the prophecy that we have already seen in Daniel 12. Resurrection shows God's continuing mercy in vindicating those who suffer martyrdom. The resurrection will be bodily—in fact, very bodily, as the third son's remarks make clear. The effect of this extreme attention to the body in the restoration of this world shows that the tradition of resurrection is not at all obligated to Platonic thought or even Greek thought, although 2 Maccabees is certainly a book that was written first in Greek and uses Greek cultural norms in a variety of ways. The palpability of the bodily resurrection, wherever it comes from, has become a quintessentially nationalist, Hebrew idea, organizing national liberation from the Syrian Greeks. It is the remedy given by God to the Jews because of the cruelty and oppression of foreign domination, a notion which will carry on directly into the Roman period. And it is easy to see why it is stressed at this particular moment. The persecutors have destroyed the bodies of the martyrs. But God's mercy guarantees that they will have them back and have the pleasures of their bodily existence again when God raises them. In the epitomist's comments in 2 Maccabees 12: 43 f., we also see a similar interest in resurrection: 'In doing this he acted very well and honourably, taking account of the resurrection (ἀνάστασις). For if he were not expecting that those who had fallen would rise again (ἀνάστῆναι), it would have been superfluous and foolish to pray for the dead'. (2 Macc. 12: 43).[8] Note here how the Greek words for resurrection, the very ones that become so important in the New Testament, are here outlined.

In such proclamations of earthly compensation for the pleasures foregone by martyrdom, one other important aspect of the tradition is often overlooked. The mother encourages her martyr sons in several ways, but nowhere more importantly than when she exalts God's creative powers:

'I do not know how you came into being in my womb. It was not I who gave you life and breath, nor I who set in order the elements within each of you. Therefore the Creator of the world, who shaped the beginning of humankind and devised the origin of all things, will in his mercy give life and breath back to you again, since you now forget yourselves for the sake of his laws.' (2 Macc. 7: 22–3)

And even more clearly in 2 Maccabees 7: 28:

'I beseech you, my child, to look at the heaven and the earth and see everything that is in them, and recognize that God did not make them out of things that existed. Thus also mankind comes into being'. (ἀξίω σε, τέκνον, ἀναβλέψαντα εἰς τὸν οὐρανὸν καὶ τὴν γῆν καὶ τὰ ἐν αὐτοῖς πάντα ἰδόντα γνῶναι ὅτι οὐκ ἐξ ὄντων ἐποίησεν αὐτὰ ὁ θεός, καὶ τὸ τῶν ἀνθρώπων γένος οὕτω γίνεται.)

This is, in most estimations, the first clear statement of *creatio ex nihilo*, the first time God is clearly praised as creator from nothing (Sir. 24: 8 also suggests this, but is normally dated a bit later). In

---

[8] See also 2 Macc. 7: 9, 14, and also 12: 38–46.

Genesis, of course, God does not actually create everything—darkness (חוֹשֶׁךְ) and the deep (תהום) precede creation. The writers of the great prologue in heaven of Genesis 1 were not sensitive to the theological principles which we have inherited from Aristotelianism. Even Isaiah 45: 7 praises God as the creator only of light and darkness. One normally thinks that Aristotelian principles suggest the necessity that God create out of nothing, lest anything that is conterminous with God be also thought of as coequal with him. But this passage in 2 Maccabees shows that the motivation for stressing creation from nothing is actually the growing notion of bodily resurrection. God needs the power not just to preserve the souls of the righteous alive. He needs the power to create their bodies again from nothing. In the previous examples where resurrection is discussed, a bodily residuum remains: the dry bones knit together in Ezekiel, and the corpses of those who rest in the dust become the basis of the awakened and resurrected saints in Daniel. Here the text seems impelled to stress that God can create as he will, because in this power rests his promise to the martyrs. The martyrs will be resurrected from nothing, just as all humans come from nothing. It is not the creation of the world which is stressed here, but the mysterious creation of each individual. The result of this assertion is reassurance that God can certainly resurrect the righteous from dust, and even from nothing if nothing remains. There is no gainsaying the absolute innovations which the sudden importation of ideas of life after death found in Hebrew thought. Evidently the Roman occupation radicalized many different parts of the population.

It is doubtful that this idea was accepted universally in Jewish life. After all, we have good evidence that the Sadducees and Pharisees differed radically on the issue in the first century. Nor is it the only idea of God's mercy that circulated in Hebrew culture. In Jubilees we have the notion that the lives of the righteous at the end will be extended to the spans experienced by the primeval heroes. Only the Sadducees are not affected by it in some way.

The texts found at Qumran show that this sectarian group also believed in resurrection and life after death, perhaps even as angels, as Josephus implies. Yet, although it is clear that these promises of resurrection, ascension, and heavenly immortality as angels come from a sectarian background, the ideas were so attractive to the culture as a whole that they spread out far more widely than the sectarian conventicles of first-century Judaism. They appear among the Pharisees, who were hardly a millenarian sect, though they apparently did have a distinct group identity.

IMMORTALITY OF THE SOUL AND RESURRECTION OF THE BODY

In back of this seeming anomaly lies the ambiguity of the existence of a second doctrine of life after death which entered Judaism. The idea of the immortality of the soul was entering Jewish life from the other end of the social spectrum, through absorption of Greek philosophical ideas—in particular, Platonic notions of the immortal soul. Judaism did adopt these notions, but during this period the classes which adopted them were not those which adopted notions of resurrection. Indeed, they were in some ways the polar opposite. Resurrection was the preserve of the disenfranchised classes of people who could not abide foreign domination. By contrast, immortality of the soul was adopted mainly by classes of people who learned Greek culture and benefited from it. They were deeply involved in Greek intellectual ideas, or were attempting to combine Judaism with the intellectual currents of their day. They would include Philo, Josephus, several other Jewish philosophical writers, and, finally, the Pharisees, or more precisely, the rabbis, as they gave up their sectarian status and became the ruling body in Jewish life. In doing so the Pharisees synthesized the notion of an immortal soul with the notion of bodily resurrection.

But let us concentrate first on the clear-cut contrasts before we discuss the mixture of the two concepts. It seems clear that while the young martyred men expect a return of the physical body which was denied them by their martyrdom, a fitting reward which returns their youth and strength to them, immortality of the soul, both in Greece and in its Jewish versions, stresses the ideals of a more aged intellectual class—continuity of consciousness. Sacrificing youth may want complete restoration of their lives, but the wise aged look for the continuity of the wise consciousness that they have so assiduously developed. In so doing, they may actually have discovered, and certainly valorized, the notion of self-conscious reflection, of which the immortality of the soul is a natural extension.

While Philo and Josephus operated explicitly out of educated

Greek notions of life after death, other elements in Jewish life absorbed the notions without the philosophical proofs and demonstrations. The Wisdom of Solomon uses a Greek notion of immortality in describing the more traditionally Jewish notion of resurrection for martyrs:

> But the souls of the righteous are in the hand of God, and no torment will ever touch them. In the eyes of the foolish they seemed to have died, and their departure was thought to be a disaster, and their going from us to be their destruction; but they are at peace. For though in the sight of men they were punished, their hope is full of immortality. (Wisd. 3: 1–4)

The occasion of the discussion is the death of the righteous, and, in keeping with the apocalyptic sensibility, the writer of Wisdom claims that they are immortal, with God. Yet, here, unlike the apocalyptic works, there is no obvious end of time with a judgement. There is no remedy for death, in that no one returns from it. Rather, their souls are in the hand of God, an idea which, ultimately, is quite similar to the notion in Psalms of the righteous preserved by God from Sheol. This passage, while it extols the martyrs, offers a quite different kind of notion from the apocalyptic formula for compensation of the righteous. Collins writes that the claim of the last verse 'introduces a dichotomy between appearance and reality which is foreign to the wisdom tradition'.[9] That may be so. In any event, both of us feel the influence of Greek thought behind these verses, though I see them as a natural extension of more native, nationalist, Jewish notions as well, this time reflected by classes of people who are open to cultural mixing. They do not necessarily see Greek culture as a problem, though they are proud of the sacrifice of the Jewish martyrs.

Even more important is the social context of these ideas, which place them squarely in the higher echelons of Jewish society, among those who have seen fit to articulate the inchoate notion of an afterlife in the Bible with the help of Greek philosophy. The millenarian notion of afterlife is, in these places, quite different from this Hellenized, Wisdom tradition. Once the tradition has ramified in

---

[9] J. J. Collins, 'The Root of Immortality: Death in the Context of Jewish Wisdom', *Harvard Theological Review*, 71 (1981), 177–92, esp. 190–1. See also Martinus de Boer, *The Defeat of Death: Apocalyptic Eschatology in 1 Corinthians 15 and Romans 5*, JSNTSS 22 (Sheffield: JSOT Press, 1988), 61. I agree with de Boer over against Collins in his statement that the narrator comes perilously close to denying death. However, I suspect that Collins meant his statement in quite a different way.

various ways, many more complicated combinations become possible, but at the beginning different origins for the different notions of life after death existed in Jewish thought.

Similarly, the trend which is foremost in the Maccabean literature includes interest in immortality, as we have seen. But by the time of the writing of 4 Maccabees, it is clear that the fashion in which immortality will be sought will be in a synthesis of Greek and First Temple Israelite thought:

Although the ligaments joining his bones were already severed, the courageous youth, worthy of Abraham, did not groan, but as though transformed by fire into immortality he nobly endured the rackings.

(4 Macc. 9: 21-2)

[B]ut all of them, as though running the course toward immortality, hastened to death by torture. (4 Macc. 14: 5)

[B]ut, as though having a mind like adamant and giving rebirth for immortality to the whole number of her sons, she implored them and urged them on to death for the sake of religion. (4 Macc. 16: 13)

[F]or on that day virtue gave the awards and tested them for their endurance. The prize was immortality in endless life. (4 Macc. 17: 12)

By contrast with the corresponding passage in 2 Maccabees, there is no elaborate discussion of resurrection here, and no corresponding cosmological argument that God made everything, hence can re-create from nothing those who are dead. Instead, there is a clear relationship between martyrdom and immortality, but astral immortality, even with fire serving as the element cleansing mortality from the martyrs. It is not enough to say that resurrection is a native Jewish notion while immortality of the soul is a Greek notion. These ideas enter Jewish society in different ways, and begin to underscore the social fragmentation that is exacerbated by the Greek conquest in the fourth century BCE. By the first century we have clearly differentiated social circumstances, which also show up in the various understandings of life after death.

Thus, the second notion of immortality to enter Jewish thought in the first century is that of the immortal soul. It can be used in relation to martyrdom, but it is not organically related to martyrdom in the same way that bodily resurrection is. As opposed to the young men and women who died for their faith and for whom the return of the body constituted an adequate notion of God's justice, the notion of life after death for an immortal soul is a product of intellectual development, primarily among intellectuals who have been deeply affected by Greek culture. These include Philo and Josephus and the writers of 4 Maccabees, but not the traditional Sadducees, who merely continued in the intellectual life of Israelite culture that preceded them.

The social structure of first-century Judea is described primarily by Josephus, who mentions that there are Sadducees, Pharisees, and Essenes (*Jewish War* 2. 119; *Antiquities* 18. 11-12). The Sadducees appear to be the traditional aristocracy, priestly in nature. On the other hand, their philosophy, which denies life after death, does not appeal to many, according to Josephus (*Jewish War* 2. 164-5). So they are not merely a social and political grouping; they have clear religious views as well; or, their social position implies a certain position with regard to life after death. 'The Sadducees hold that the soul perishes along with body' (*Antiquities* 18. 16). The Sadducees do not believe in fate, feeling that God is distant from human beings and that we must take responsibility for what we will: 'All things lie within our own power so that we ourselves are responsible for our well-being, while we suffer misfortune through our own thoughtlessness' (ibid. 13. 173). Finally, Josephus says that the Sadducees do not look forward to any other rewards and punishments after death. People are to be compensated for their deeds in this world. In Josephus' organization of the issues, belief in life after death and the issue of justice in this world are intimately connected. Furthermore, Josephus' portrayal of Sadducees is paralleled in the Gospels, where Jesus and the Sadducees argue over the existence of resurrection (Matt. 22: 23-33; Mark 12: 18-17; Luke 20: 27-40). In the Matthean version Jesus argues for the concept of resurrection with an argument reminiscent of that of the Pharisees.

Jesus demonstrates the concept of resurrection by quoting two different scriptures and assuming that there can be no seeming contradiction between them. Since Scripture says that YHWH is God of Abraham, Isaac, and Jacob and he is also called 'the living God' (actually, God of the living), then the patriarchs must still be alive. This is not only an effective argument in the first century; the Gospels are much impressed with it. It is so effective that it makes the Pharisees, who also believe in resurrection, jealous.

Indeed, Rabbinic literature also criticizes the Sadducees for not believing in resurrection. They are, in Rabbinic eyes, obtusely literal in understanding the scripture. But that only underlines what we can see from the historical development of the concepts of resurrection and afterlife in Judaism. There is no easy way to derive resurrection from any biblical text before Daniel. Obviously, the Sadducean Bible would not have contained the visions in Daniel. Although we have no identifiably Sadducean text—that is, no writing that we can identify as specifically Sadducean in a sectarian sense—it is quite likely that many biblical and intertestamental books actually reflect their perspective. The Wisdom of Jesus ben Sirach—Ecclesiasticus as it is called in Greek—which was written by a Wisdom teacher in the earlier Greek period and which, as we have already seen, does not contain any concept of life after death, could easily have been highly prized among them.

There is an easy and clear parallel between the social position of the aristocrats and their explicit theology. As lords of the land, they have a relatively privileged life. They appear to need no other rewards than those they receive in this world. But, of course, this is not an inevitable correlation. One could easily imagine exactly the opposite—where the aristocrats take for themselves the rewards of the next world, just as they take the rewards of this one. Such was the case in the Egypt of the Pharaohs, for instance. Indeed, the great aristocratic Jewish philosopher of Alexandria, Philo Judaeus, adopts a very Platonic notion of the immortality of the soul. Logic alone does not make this social history inevitable. What explain the particular correlation found in Hebrew thought are the traditional concerns of Israelite culture—its abhorrence of notions of an afterlife, probably because of its relationship to idolatry, and the virtual lack of the notion in the Hebrew Bible. This puts the Sadducees in rather close association with the Epicureans and Stoics of the early Hellenistic period. Because of this traditional value, the aristocrats were more easily impressed by one of the high philosophies of Greek life—Stoicism. Like the aristocratic Stoics of Greek culture, the highest-class rulers of Hellenistic Israel felt that life could be faced in bravest and most steadfast terms without reference to any afterlife.

The Pharisees had a social position which is harder to understand from their religious life. The Sadducees had to share power with the Pharisees, who were apparently a skilled class of scribes and craftsmen who studied the Law in detail. Not only did Josephus describe them as the most accurate interpreters of the Law; he did so in language suggesting that they already possessed the 'oral law' which was characteristic of the rabbis. Josephus describes their product as *nomima* ('legal enactments'; *Life* 191), and says in several places that they handed down (*paredosan*) regulations not recorded in the Torah of Moses (*Antiquities* 13. 297; 17. 41). The Greek terminology suggests oral transmission, as does the sentence structure, which contrasts the Pharisaic enterprise with the written law. Josephus describes the Pharisees as more abstemious in their personal habits than the patrician Sadducees. 'They simplify their standard of living' (ibid. 18. 12). He says that they are not impressed by luxury or seek it in this world. Rather, they are respectful and deferential to elders and keep their word (ibid. 18. 12). The Pharisees are affectionate to each other, and cultivate harmonious relationships within the community (*Jewish War* 2. 166).

The Pharisees, who are expert at understanding the Law, believe that there are rewards and punishments, as well as life after death. They are educated men, helpful in running the state. Though Josephus is from a priestly family himself, and so heir to the Sadducee position, should he desire it, in his autobiography he states that he learned to govern his life according to the styles of the Pharisees, since he wanted a career in public life (*Life* 10–12). However, this is not to be interpreted as Josephus' conversion to the Pharisees.[10] Josephus often appears not to like Pharisees much, especially in his public career as a general during the war, when they were constantly trying to have him removed from office. Evidently, his background made him suspect, and his attempt to live as a Pharisee was less than entirely convincing. In his later writings Josephus suggests that they are the class of people which Rome can best trust to govern the land after the destruction of the Temple. But that is many years after the war. On the other hand, more religious persons found the Pharisees' piety impressive. Jesus says that unless one's 'righteousness surpasses even that of the Pharisees, a person will certainly not enter the kingdom of heaven' (Matt. 5: 20). Jesus' admiration had limits, however, because, according to Mark, they could be criticized as setting aside the commands of God in order to observe their own traditions (Mark 7: 9).

Again, Josephus loads notions of reward, punishment, and providence on to their concept of life after death. He says that the Pharisees attribute everything to fate and to God at the same time

---

[10] See Steve Mason, *Flavius Josephus on the Pharisees* (Leiden: Brill, 1991).

(*Jewish War* 2. 162). Logically, this is hard to imagine, so Josephus continues by saying that we all have individual choice, but that fate co-operates in each action (ibid. 2. 163). Indeed, the Rabbinic movement, which rests on the traditions transmitted by the Pharisees, maintains that 'everything is foreseen, yet free will is also given'. Or, the rabbis say, 'everything is in the hands of heaven except the fear of heaven', meaning that God has control over everything, although a person has the power and ability to deny God. As Josephus says: 'Though they postulate that everything is brought about by fate, still they do not deprive the human will of the pursuit of what is in human power, since it was God's good pleasure that there should be a fusion and that the will of humanity with its virtue and vice should be admitted to the council-chamber of fate' (*Antiquities* 18. 13-14).

Of course, Josephus does not neglect the Pharisees' view of resurrection. He says: 'Every soul, they maintain, is imperishable, but the soul of the good alone passes into another body, while the souls of the wicked suffer eternal punishment' (*Jewish War* 2. 163). This does not mean that Josephus believed in metempsychosis or reincarnation. Rather, it appears to mean that Josephus envisioned another, different kind of body for imperishable souls. The body which we have in this life is corruptible; therefore, like Paul, he sees a new incorruptible flesh to be the reward of the good. It may well be that this is identical with, or close to, the notions which we find in Enoch.

What is interesting about this party system in first-century Judaea is that it was a combination of political and religious differences which apparently separated the two groups. And resurrection was one of the subjects that distinguished them. This means that in the century and a half to two centuries between the Maccabean War and the appearance of the dream visions of Daniel, and the writings of Josephus and the New Testament the notion of life after death had become very popular in Israel. This is most dramatically confirmed by a story told by Luke about Paul. It is not mentioned in Paul's letters, so it may be an apocryphal story that grew up in the generation between Paul and his biographer. But it illustrates that the issue of life after death was still being fiercely fought in first-century Judaea (Acts 23: 6-10).

Shortly after the events narrated in Luke's early history of the Church, and probably written about the same time and place,

Josephus' *Jewish War* also discusses the issue of life after death amongst the inhabitants of Judaea. We have already seen how he figures the issues of resurrection for his Roman audience. When he discusses the act of martyrdom which ended the First War against Rome, Josephus is at his most articulate. The speech of Eleazar ben Yair, one of the leaders of the defenders of Masada against the Roman siege, is clearly the work of Josephus himself. He describes the hopeless situation, and then writes an appropriately heroic speech for the leader of the defence.

The first appeal is to heroism. Clearly, God has determined that they should all die, since the Romans are close to vanquishing them, although they have had the best position possible and an enormous cache of supplies and weapons. On the other hand, God has graced them with information which many of their compatriots do not have—the knowledge of their imminent capture. He therefore urges a noble death in liberty (ἐλευθέρια δ᾽ ἡ τοῦ γενναίου θανάτου; *Jewish War* 7. 326) rather than slavery and dishonour.

Though many are convinced by this appeal, others are more compassionate for their wives and children. For this reason, Eleazar proceeds to a discussion of the immortality of the soul (περὶ ψυχῆς ἀθανασίας; ibid. 7. 341). Josephus reports that 'Death truly gives liberty to the soul and permits it to depart to its own pure abode, there to be free of all calamity' (οὗτος μὲν γὰρ ἐλευθερίαν διδοὺς ψυχαῖς εἰς τον οἰκεῖον καὶ καθαρὸν ἀφίησι τόπον ἀπαλλάσσεσθαι, πάσης σύμφορᾶς ἀπαθεῖς ἐσομένας; ibid. 7. 344).

Josephus continues by positing that the soul is the principle of life in the world—whatever it inhabits is alive, and whatever it abandons dies immediately. He then tries to demonstrate that the soul is independent of the body in sleep, and will be all the more so after death.

This is pure Platonic thinking, which may have impressed Josephus' readers deeply. But it is unlikely to be anything like the ideas of immortality that the desperate defenders of Masada might have embraced. They, like all other Jewish sectarian groups of the day, were probably more attracted by the notion that they would be resurrected in their bodies, to enjoy the rest of the life which had been denied them by faith. We have noted that all the nativist groups of the first century, Christianity included, embraced notions of a bodily resurrection, not the immortality of the soul. It is, in fact, Josephus' use of Greek notions of immortality to describe the

Hebrew notion of resurrection that has totally confused scholarship on the different social backgrounds of the two ideas. Once we see where the two different notions come from, it is easy to disentangle the opposing notions and see Josephus, rather, as the first of many to try to bring the two concepts together. But this was not easy.

Paul is apparently engaging in the same kind of hermeneutical enterprise when he answers the question of the nature of resurrection in 1 Corinthians 15: 35-45. There is an interesting double vision in Paul's attempt to talk about spiritual bodies. This seems to be a way of mediating between Greek notions of soul or spirit and the Jewish apocalyptic notion that the body of the martyr is to be resurrected. In any event, it is Paul's own insight that is clearest here. The Gospels, which are not so concerned with the issue of being understood as a preacher in this way, come out much more strongly in favour of the more traditional, apocalyptic Jewish notion of resurrection of the body:

That same hour they got up and returned to Jerusalem; and they found the eleven and their companions gathered together. They were saying, 'The Lord has risen indeed, and he has appeared to Simon!' Then they told what had happened on the road, and how he had been made known to them in the breaking of the bread.

While they were talking about this, Jesus himself stood among them and said to them, 'Peace be with you.'[11] They were startled and terrified, and thought that they were seeing a ghost. He said to them, 'Why are you frightened, and why do doubts arise in your hearts? Look at my hands and my feet; see that it is I myself. Touch me and see; for a ghost does not have flesh and bones as you see that I have.' And when he had said this, he showed them his hands and his feet.[12] While in their joy they were disbelieving and still wondering, he said to them, 'Have you anything here to eat'? They gave him a piece of broiled fish, and he took it and ate in their presence. Then he said to them, 'These are my words that I spoke to you while I was still with you—that everything written about me in the law of Moses, the prophets, and the psalms must be fulfilled.' (Luke 24: 33–44)

Here, uniquely in the Gospels, Jesus' resurrection is separated from his ascension. During the interim the risen Jesus clarifies many of the issues that appear to have troubled his followers. Jesus appears physically to the disciples, and clarifies that he has not appeared as a spirit. Rather, it is his physical body that appears. He

---

[11] Other ancient authorities lack 'and said to them, "Peace be with you" '.
[12] Other ancient authorities lack v. 40.

celebrates the Lord's Supper, eating bread and drinking wine, and, lastly, even showing that he can eat a piece of fish. Only after he has clarified this point above and beyond the point of the Eucharist does he ascend to heaven.

In the Gospel of John, the physicality of the resurrection is even more clearly outlined.

But Thomas (who was called the Twin[13]), one of the twelve, was not with them when Jesus came. So the other disciples told him, 'We have seen the Lord.' But he said to them, 'Unless I see the mark of the nails in his hands, and put my finger in the mark of the nails and my hand in his side, I will not believe.'

A week later his disciples were again in the house, and Thomas was with them. Although the doors were shut, Jesus came and stood among them and said, 'Peace be with you.' Then he said to Thomas, 'Put your finger here and see my hands. Reach out your hand and put it in my side. Do not doubt but believe.' Thomas answered him, 'My Lord and my God!' Jesus said to him, 'Have you believed because you have seen me? Blessed are those who have not seen and yet have come to believe.' (John 20: 14b–29)

Here, doubting Thomas must touch the wounds of Jesus before he believes in the physicality of the resurrection. The Church is clearly involving itself in important ways in a dialogue between more apocalyptic Jewish Christians and more Hellenized Christians of all kinds on the nature of Jesus' post-resurrection existence. If he is purely a spirit, the argument seems to run, then there is nothing unique about Jesus' post-mortem life. Like all spirits or immortal souls, Jesus merely appears on earth in his 'shade' or 'ghostly' form. But these stories clearly say that the resurrection was corporeal and very real. It was unique; it was bodily; it was apocalyptic; and it was God's merciful response to Jesus' willing martyrdom. The result is that Jesus is the first of those to rise bodily from the dead at the end of time. The intellectualist notion of the immortal soul is entirely ignored. Even the story of the resurrection of Lazarus (John II: 17–44) is portrayed in this way, though it basically has the form of a miracle in the Johannine narrative.

But the Church cannot ignore the concept of immortality of the soul for long. Indeed, Christianity found it to be the hardest of all the ideas of natural theology, and resisted the combination for two

---

[13] Greek: *Didymus.*

centuries.[14] Simply, this is why the claims of Christianity make most sense in a context in which the resurrection of the body can be claimed. In this context, Jesus' own martyr's sacrifice makes sense. His own resurrection is the first of the dawning age, in which all the righteous who follow him will be resurrected as well. But what can Jesus' sacrifice mean in a world that has, in principle, accepted the notion of the immortality of the soul as a purely natural process. Since every soul is immortal, what is the special salvation which Jesus' sacrifice brings? None. Christianity's claim regarding Jesus' death makes perfect sense in Jewish sectarian environment, but it can seem almost meaningless in a Platonic environment. Thus, Christians, unlike the upper classes of Judaea, must be very careful how they appropriate Greek philosophical thinking. This is a nagging subterranean question which follows Christianity across the boundary between Hebrew eschatology and Greek psychology. The steps necessary to demonstrate the final Christian absorption of the concept of the immortal soul cannot be outlined here. Suffice it to say that the Christian community began to separate the immediate reward of the dead—immortality of the soul—and the ultimate *telos* of history—the resurrection of the body. In so doing, it was, in effect, using the notion of the immortality of the soul to defuse its apocalypticism. For once the immortality of the soul is put into the equation, appropriately baptized for Christian use, then God's mercy can be preserved without any necessity of insisting on the imminent end of the world. It was partly through this process that Christianity, almost uniquely in world history, turned itself from a marginal Jewish apocalyptic cult into a world religion, yet managed to preserve the uniqueness of Jesus' message in a Greek environment.

The rabbis have an entirely different problem. They have no problem making these two notions go together or adopting any number of florid and imaginative additions to the doctrine. But Christianity made the whole notion of apocalyptic ends suspect. When one looks at the Rabbinic discussions of resurrection in the Talmud, one sees what appears to be an enormous scepticism setting in. The rabbis fight to show that none of the specific descriptions in Scripture are to be generalized, and that some are not to be believed as proofs of

---

[14] See Jaroslav Pelikan, *Christianity and Classical Culture: The Metamorphosis of Natural Theology in the Christian Encounter with Hellenism* (New Haven: Yale University Press, 1993), esp. ch. 20, 'Life in the Aeon to Come', 311-26.

resurrection at all. Their scepticism is a way of defusing the tremendous revolutionary potential which is inherent in the original doctrine of resurrection.

THE MISHNAH AND THE TALMUDS

The earliest identifiable book of Rabbinic Judaism is the Mishnah. It is a communal book of law, of multiple authorship, recording the many discussions of the earlier rabbis, and redacted by the year 220 CE. It is based on Israelite law of the First Temple period, 922–587 BCE, and many centuries of legal discussion. It undoubtedly contains much earlier material, possibly even some material going back to the men of the great assembly, a quasi-historical and ill-understood institution of the Persian period. But the particular formulation of the laws probably comes almost entirely from the Tannaim, the early rabbis of the first two centuries. Having traced its legal material to Ezra, Nehemiah, and the men of the great assembly, the Mishnah can confidently claim that it contains the word of God from Sinai, because it assumes that before Ezra the process of transmission back to Moses was organic and whole, through Joshua, the elders, and the prophets: 'Moses received the Law from Sinai and committed it to Joshua, and Joshua to the elders, and the elders to the prophets; and the prophets committed it to the men of the Great Assembly. They said three things; Be deliberate in judgment, raise up many disciples, and make a fence around the Torah' (Avoth 1. 1).

This document maintains that it was they—not the priests—who were the loyal transmitters of these ancient traditions, even though we know that in previous centuries the priests were indeed one of the great sources of legal enactments. They make no secret of their impatience with priestly expertise in their own time, ceding priests roles as functionaries in the Temple, which was destroyed in 70 CE. By 220 CE no one could have realistically expected its rebuilding soon. On the other hand, the Mishnah mentions as great preservers of tradition several Pharisaic leaders or family names whose identities are confirmed by Josephus and the New Testament. Although it would be incorrect to say that the rabbis and especially the Tannaim, those who are mentioned in the Mishnah, are the same as the Pharisees, there is an organic development between them.

Just as we cannot automatically identify the Pharisees and the rabbis, because they lived in different times, so we must also guard against automatically assuming that the traditions of the Tannaim are identical with those of the Pharisees, even though this is precisely what the Tannaim maintain. On the other hand, when we investigate the issue of life after death, we discover that the traditions of the Tannaim are very close to what the New Testament and Josephus say about the Pharisees. The Rabbinic doctrine appears deeply connected to its first-century Pharisaic background. Here is one place where Josephus and the New Testament can show us that the traditions of the rabbis, which we first see in the third century, were undoubtedly in existence by the first. On the other hand, the particular formulation of the doctrine, as we have it in the Mishnah, at the beginning of the third century, is different from anything we might have expected from our first-century witnesses. This does not necessarily argue that the language of the doctrine was formulated late, because we have discovered many surprising contrasts between the way Josephus describes the sects of the first century and the documents that we have recovered; it merely suggests that Josephus' figuration of the Pharisees may have been equally skewed by his political and social agenda.

The Mishnaic notion of life after death is discussed extensively in the tractate Sanhedrin, chapter 10, which deals with the laws of the Sanhedrin and especially with capital punishment:

Mishnah 1: All Israelites have a share in the world to come, for it is written, *Thy people also shall be all righteous, they shall inherit the land for ever; the branch of my planting, the work of my hands that I may be glorified* (Isa. 60: 21). And these are they that have no share in the world to come: he that says that there is no resurrection of the dead prescribed in the Torah, and [he that says] that the Torah is not from Heaven, and an Epicurean. R. Akiba says: Also he that reads the books of the 'outsiders', or that utters charms over a wound and says, *I will put none of the diseases upon thee which I have put upon the Egyptians; for I am the Lord that heals you* (Exod. 15: 28). Abba Saul says: also he that pronounces the Name with its proper letters.

Having defined the doctrines and rituals which exclude one from the world to come, the rabbis continue for some time, discussing which of the biblical villains are also excluded and which are not even to be judged, topics which we shall need to rehearse in a moment. It is worthwhile noting that the rabbis begin from the assumption that all Israelites receive a share in the world to come.

The proof for this is really a pretext, as we discovered, because there are no accurate discussions of life after death before the book of Daniel. But they took Isaiah 60, which talks about inheriting the land for ever, as a particular kind of shorthand. It would have to be a pretext because the earlier passages do not seem to have resurrection in mind. The passage says only that the Israelites will inherit the land for ever. Of course, that is precisely what has been called into question by the destruction of the land and its demotion to a Roman province. The passage has been reinterpreted, therefore, to mean something more spiritual, even though it does not clarify the kind of eternal life in talking about 'the world to come'. Such a concept was unknown in the earlier periods, but here it functions both to guarantee life after death in the Bible and to safeguard the Scripture from obvious falsification.

On the other hand, they quickly turn to the legal connotations of the discussion, and not necessarily the most obvious one—namely, who is to be excluded from this promise. They don't mind indulging in what can only be their private ironic humour: If you don't believe in the world to come, you don't get it. Moreover—and this is the most important section from the point of view of later discussion in the Talmud—you must believe that resurrection of the dead (תחית המתים, literally, the vivification of the dead) is mentioned in the Torah itself. We come suddenly on what will be the technical term for resurrection amongst the rabbis, showing that the doctrine is already quite well formulated, even in this somewhat unsystematic discussion. Yet, what occupies rabbinic attention in the subsequent commentary is not the precise meaning of the term 'resurrection', as one might expect, but where the doctrine is evidenced in the Torah. The word 'Torah' can mean a variety of things. In this context, it is taken in its narrowest sense, to mean the first five books of Moses.

Furthermore, the quotation from Isaiah, which in its original context, was surely not about eternal life or resurrection, suggests that, for the purposes of this part of the Rabbinic discussion, 'the world to come' may mean something as simple as living on this earth eternally in roughly the same conditions as we do now. The only difference is that the Jews (or the righteous Jews, as will be clarified somewhat below) will live for ever in their own land. This may, in fact, be partly understandable as a further exegesis of Daniel 12: 2, where some of those who sleep in the earth will be resurrected. The interpretation of Daniel 12: 2 implicit in this passage would then be that all the Israelites are included in the 'some of those who sleep in the dust'. This in turn suggests where the otherwise difficult references to judgement come in the next paragraphs of the Rabbinic discussion. The Daniel 12 passage can be understood to mean that judgement will follow for some, but not for all humans who have ever lived. The specific identification of those groups occupies a significant part of the following discussion, as we shall see.

What is immediately striking about this assertion is that it does not indulge itself in any of a variety of discussions which we have already seen in other Jewish sects and in the various philosophical discussions of the ancient world. In the Mishnah, which is often held up as a quintessential literature of casuistry, a literature that discusses subtly what right and wrong are and what the various punishments are for infractions of justice, there is no major discussion of which heinous crimes will cause Israelites to be permanently stricken from the rolls of those who will be resurrected. Instead, the passage begins to describe which of those biblical villains, members of the Israelites or not, will not be resurrected or judged:

Mishnah 2: Three kings and four commoners have no share in the world to come. The three kings are Jeroboam and Ahab and Manasseh. R. Judah says: Manasseh has a share in the world to come, for it is written, *And he prayed unto him, and he was intreated of him and heard his supplication and brought him again to Jerusalem into his kingdom* (2 Chr. 33: 13). They said to him: He brought him again to his kingdom, but he did not bring him to the life of the world to come. The four commoners are Balaam and Doeg and Ahitophel and Gehazi.

The first question which appears to occupy the Mishnah is whether all Israelites are really entitled to life in the world to come. It picks what are clearly meant to be the most heinous of all Israelite sinners in the Bible and asks whether they have a share. The answer is no—except for Manasseh, about whom there is slight evidence that he repented: 2 Chronicles is interpreted to mean that, although it is certainly far-fetched. From this we learn two things: there are some Israelites who are so evil that they are denied a place in the world to come. But repentance can annul the decree even for the most vicious of all sinners of all time.

Mishnah 3: The generation of the Flood have no share in the world to come, nor shall they stand in the judgement, for it is written, *My spirit shall not judge with man for ever* (Gen. 6: 3). [Thus they have] neither judgement nor spirit. The generation of the dispersion have no share in the world to come, for it is written, *So the Lord scattered them abroad from thence upon the face of all the earth* (Gen. 11: 8); so the Lord scattered them abroad—in this world; and the Lord then scattered them from thence—in the world to come. The men of Sodom have no share in the world to come, for it is written, *Now the men of Sodom were wicked and sinners against the Lord exceedingly*; wicked in this world, *and sinners* in the world to come. But they shall stand in the judgement. R. Nehemiah says: Neither of them shall stand in the judgement, for it is written: *Therefore the wicked shall not stand in the judgement nor sinners in the congregation of the righteous* (Ps. 1: 8). Therefore the wicked shall not stand in the judgement—this is the generation of the flood; nor sinners in the congregation of the righteous—these are the men of Sodom. They said to him: They shall not stand in the congregation of the righteous, but they shall stand in the congregation of the ungodly. The spies have no share in the world to come, for it is written, *Even those men that did bring up an evil report of the land died by the plague before the Lord* (Num. 14) died—in this world; by the plague—in the world to come. The generation of the wilderness have no share in the world to come, nor shall they stand in the judgement, for it is written, *In this wilderness they shall be consumed and there they shall die* (Num. 14: 35). So R. Akiba. But R. Eliezer says: It says of them also, *Gather my saints together unto me, those that have made a covenant with me by sacrifice* (Ps. 50: 5). The company of Korah shall not rise up again, for it is written, *And the earth closed upon them* in this world, *and they perished from among the assembly*, in the world to come. So R. Akiba. But R. Eliezer says: It says of them also, *The Lord kills and makes alive, he brings down to Sheol and brings up* (1 Sam. 2: 6). The Ten Tribes shall not return again, for it is written, *And he cast them into another land like this day*. Like as this day goes and returns not, so do they go and return not. So R. Akiba. But R. Eliezer says: Like as the day grows dark and then grows light, so also after darkness is fallen upon the Ten Tribes shall light hereafter shine upon them.

Readers who have never before encountered Rabbinic discussion may have trouble at first with the connections made and the arguments between the discussants even in this rudimentary discussion. Notice that various rabbis often appear to disagree with each other, and that the disagreements are in some way created by the texts themselves, since the rabbis may come from different places and different times. Clearly people remembered the positions of various sages on particular texts and issues, and the Mishnah was a way of sorting out the issues by subject-matter. The Mishnah, in fact, is organized according to a principle of the subject-matter of various laws, not as a commentary on the Bible.

This particular passage makes this clear. It is Daniel 12 that mentions both resurrection and judgement. Even though Daniel 12 is the backbone of the passage, this is not actually stated. After some examples of which Israelites are saved and which condemned, the reader learns something that is never stated—namely, that repentance annuls a decree of no resurrection. We now learn something else. The topic of discussion switches to various biblical non-Israelites and how they will fare in the last judgement. The precedents are not good. Certainly the great sinners of the generation of the flood are lost, and they will not even be resurrected in time of judgement. It is assumed that anyone taking part in the discussions will already know all the biblical quotations relevant, and will only need to discover the best arguments for uncovering the truth. The repetitions in Scripture are used to show that they will neither live in this world nor be resurrected in the world to come. Thus, the principle that the Bible provides us with guidance is taken quite literally. All the precedents for the argument depend on biblical quotations, interpreted by various rabbis. And the rabbis can disagree. For instance, with regard to the generation of Sodom, some rabbis thought that it would be resurrected for judgement but not attain the world to come. But R. Nehemiah finds the right combination of scriptural passages to show that this is not possible. As with the previous question, it appears that the rabbis are using not just their considerable expertise to answer questions about the final disposition of biblical characters but some interesting principles about how divine justice is dispensed. As with many Rabbinic discussions, the principles themselves are left wholly or partly unarticulated.

It is suggested that the generation of the wilderness, who are Israelites, will not benefit from the world to come. But R. Eliezer again finds a precedent for saying that even though they sinned they will be part of the world to come, showing that God has mercy even on the stiff-necked, rebellious generation of Moses. The same is true of the followers of Korah, who rebelled against Moses and were swallowed by the earth. There are certainly grounds for thinking them condemned. Yet again, the final word appears to be that God has separated them. The scriptural grounds for this conclusion may seem forced. And it is never wholly clear to modern readers whether the rabbis are seriously discussing these issues or using them as examples for their very finely honed talents—*tours de force* for their own mutual appreciation and demonstration of their greatly rarefied talents. But, in any case, no matter how much gamesmanship and virtuosity is contained in these writings, the conclusions are serious, because they demonstrate that God desires mercy and contrition, and forgives even heinous crimes. Yet a certain degree of freedom with the text is already evident, a freedom that undoes the original intention of the biblical passages—which was certainly to report a terrible death by earthquake of the party of Korah. Once the issue of life after death has seriously entered the Rabbinic purview, a whole new set of agendas must be addressed, and the rabbis are, in some sense, writing their brief on those subjects. They must answer, or at least address, the issue of the relationship between punishment after death and punishment in this life: here they do exactly that, implying that earthly punishment does not prevent future reward. They must also deal with questions of inclusion and exclusion; they must settle questions of justice and mercy; they may even want to describe the process of meting out justice, as the apocalypticists or, less floridly, the Christians do.

But they settle the issues as they emerge. The text then goes on to answer questions of what will happen to the most heinous idolaters—especially, idolaters amongst the Israelites who apostatize. The whole issue of the final disposition of most Gentiles is left somewhat ambiguous, as is the final disposition of most ordinary Israelites. The answer to the question of whether Gentiles will be saved, or have a part in the world to come, is that they will be rewarded on the basis of righteousness. Those who are righteous will be rewarded in exactly the same way as Israelites. Those who are not will perish as idolaters. But the answer is not treated here. It is left for another section of Mishnah and Tosefta, and is debated sharply. It will necessarily involve a great deal more technical reading of various texts, and take us far afield. So let us first finish the section in front of us.

Another question which might be answered here, but apparently is not, is how the issue of reward and punishment interacts with the notion of the world to come. There is no mention of hell for malefactors or permanent punishment of any sort. Indeed, Rabbinic Judaism is extremely reticent to discuss hell—as if the benevolence of the eternal God would not allow most souls to be permanently condemned. Only in later Jewish folklore do we find any concept of hell, and there not often.

This particular almost seems to limit the question deliberately.

There is undoubtedly a parochialism in this exercise. But the rabbis lived in a world in which each ethnic group was responsible for itself primarily. The greater issue of the disposition of all humanity is not ignored in rabbinic thought. But it is not worked out here. The rabbis attempt to spell out whether Israel in general will be resurrected, stand for judgement, or deserve the world to come. The categories apparently come from Daniel, but their application to biblical history is what demonstrates their actuality. The abject are discussed, because this helps actualize the categories of Daniel. Ordinary people's sins are not addressed. A number of different approaches have been taken in an attempt to understand the relationship between the last judgement and individual reward and punishment. The section may be assuming that ordinary sins are punished in this world, as is certainly the case in the Hebrew Bible and is frequently assumed in Rabbinic Judaism. At the very least, one might assume that a person's death might atone for most sins. This is the opinion of several rabbis. Then again, some commentators have made reference to a later notion of limbo or hell, to be dwelt in until the sin is finally repaid. Then the Israelite can be resurrected. The concept is never raised here, but it occupies later commentators because of its absence.

The story becomes even more interesting when the Talmudic discussion is added to this interesting third-century Mishnah. (Of course, the issues may be earlier, since they are well attested by non-Rabbinic sources.) The Talmud is comprised of the Mishnah plus a commentary, called the *gemara*, from either Babylonia or Palestine. The Palestinian Gemara and the Mishnah form the Palestinian Talmud, which is shorter and less authoritative than the Babylonian Talmud, which is the standard compendium of law for classical Rabbinic Judaism. The Babylonian Talmud is a composite document that stretches from the third to the seventh century. Both Talmuds are divided into six orders, and, in turn, into sixty-three tractates. The Mishnah is the size of a large desk dictionary. Each of the Talmuds, with its various commentaries, is the size of an ample, multi-volume encyclopaedia.

The Babylonian Talmud's discussion of this Mishnah begins on folio 90a, with a quotation of the Mishnah. The first question which the Gemara asks is why the Mishnah rules with such severity? In other words, why does it insist that the punishment for those denying life after death is not to receive it? This is an interesting question, since the Mishnah itself never seemed terribly cruel to start with. But the Amoraim were concerned that denying someone life after death for not believing in it seemed harsh, especially as the Mishnah had admitted all Israel, even those who sinned, to the world to come. One supposes that subsequent generations of rabbis were sensitive to the possibility that the punishment of losing eternal life was arbitrary and severe, considering that murderers who confess and pay the ultimate penalty are still in principle possible candidates for the world to come. The question, however, is substantively answered by reference to equity, or 'measure for measure'. That is, denial of the world to come is the appropriate and equitable punishment for someone who denies life after death, even though it seems harsh. Obviously, as above, anyone who recants heresy is automatically admitted. It is interesting that the rabbis are puzzled by a punishment that stands merely on a belief, not an action, while it is precisely belief that makes for salvation or damnation in Christianity, for instance.

After this, the Gemara raises the issue which will dominate its discussion of life after death: how is resurrection derived from the Torah? Here it is clear that the term 'Torah' means only the first five books of Moses. Since we know from historical analysis that the first sure reference to life after death is in the book of Daniel, and that even the first hints of it are as late as the prophets, it seems a foolish task to try to derive it from the Torah. But, of course, the rabbis didn't have modern historical criticism. They are clearly aware of the problem, however; but this serves as a challenge to their exegetical skills. The first candidate is Numbers 18: 28: 'And you shall give the Lord's offering to Aaron the priest.' The rabbis are implicitly pointing out that the commandment contains no time limitation; but Aaron did not live for ever on earth, so, since Scripture must be true and never proved false, Aaron must be still 'alive', and will be resurrected. Immediately, the school of Rabbi Ishmael, which is credited with the rather modern notion that the language of the Torah is human language, suggests what most modern interpreters would think first: that perhaps 'to Aaron' really means 'to one like Aaron': namely, his priestly descendants in the Aaronide line. The effect of this discussion is thus to put the passage in question as a proof of life after death. This is a quite astonishing moment. It is the first time within a community accepting life after death that the demonstration of it is brought into question. But it is characteristic of Rabbinic exegesis. No one can say that the Amoraic rabbis denied the doctrine which Josephus claimed was central to the Pharisees. But we are clearly in different times in the Gemara. Even the most sacred assumptions are in principle subject to the same scrutiny as issues concerning contested ownership and marriage and divorce. This issue becomes a constant refrain between the intervening digressions. Passages which are presented as possibly demonstrating life after death follow (the asterisk signifies that the passage is allowed to stand as a proof): Exodus 6: 4, *Deuteronomy 31: 16, Isaiah 26: 19, Song 7: 9, Deuteronomy 11: 21, *Deuteronomy 4: 4, *Numbers 15: 31, Psalm 72, Isaiah 35, Isaiah 25: 9, Isaiah 65: 20, Deuteronomy 32: 39, *Exodus 15: 3, *Joshua 8: 30, *Psalm 34: 5, Isaiah 52: 8, *Deuteronomy 33: 6, *Daniel 12: 2, *Daniel 12: 13, *Ezekiel 37. Several of the passages are from later books of the Bible, adduced at first in conjunction with books from the first five and then later in earnest in their own right.

Many of the proofs are subjected to rigorous scrutiny of the sort we have seen above:

Sectarians asked Rabbin Gamaliel: Whence do we know that the Holy One, blessed be He, will resurrect the dead? He answered them from the Torah, the Prophets, and the Hagiographa, yet they did not accept it [as conclusive proof]: From the Torah, for it is written *And the Lord said unto Moses, Behold thou shalt sleep with thy fathers and rise up* [again]. But perhaps, said they to him [the verse reads], *and the people will rise up?*

Indeed, the rabbis assume that we all understand the passage well enough to know that the next word in the sentence after rise up is 'the people'. The normal word order in narrative Hebrew prose is exactly 'and rise up the people', meaning the people shall arise. So the normal understanding of the passage would be that Moses will die and the people shall rise up. The rabbis' proof depends on making the full stop one word into the next sentence. Thus, the objection of the heretics seems valid to us, as it probably did even to the rabbis. Only Deuteronomy 11: 21 or 4: 4 is said to please them:

Thus he did not satisfy them until he quoted this verse, *which the Lord swore unto your fathers to give* . . . (Deut. 11: 21) to them; not to you, but *to them* is said: hence resurrection is derived from the Torah. Others say that he proved it from this verse. But ye that did cleave unto the Lord your God are alive every one of you this day (Deut. 4: 4).

On the other hand, there are places where the great inventiveness of the rabbis is accepted and even admired:

> Our rabbis taught: *I kill and I make alive* (Deut. 32: 39); I might interpret, I kill one person and give life to another, as the world goes on. Therefore the Bible says: *I wound and I heal.* Just as the wounding and healing refer to the same person, so putting to death and bringing to life refer to the same person. This refutes those who maintain that resurrection is not intimated in the Torah.

This is an exquisite argument, depending on the notion that one must first be wounded in order then to be healed. On the other hand, we moderns can never overcome the suspicion that the objections are more persuasive than the proofs. Indeed, there is nothing to prevent us from thinking that the original poetry in Deuteronomy meant that God healed and struck down different people, just as he can quicken and kill. Such is the force of the Rabbinic method. Once one has learned it from the paradigm of the rabbis, one can use it even to deny the very doctrine which they seek to defend. It is almost a parade example of deconstructionism. Because of this method of scrutinizing every doctrine in this way, some modern Jews would certainly deny that Judaism depends on the notion of resurrection in any literal way. And they might even turn to this passage to show how all doctrine must be made subject to our own rational scrutiny.

Of course, this irony of deconstruction is peculiarly our own modern perspective, not theirs, for the rabbis refused to take the method that far. In fact, a quick look at the liturgy reveals that life after death is repeatedly valorized in daily prayers. For instance:

> You are mighty, eternally, O Lord.
> You bring the dead to life, mighty to save.
> You sustain the living with loving kindness
> With great mercy you bring the dead to life again.
> You support the fallen, heal the sick, free the captives;
> You keep faith with those who sleep in the dust.
> Who can compare with Your might, O Lord and King?
> You are Master of life, and death, and deliverance.

This is the second paragraph of the Amidah, the prayer recited at every Jewish service. It is but one of innumerable references to the resurrection which dot the prayer-book. Evidently, then, the lessons learned through careful scrutiny of doctrine were meant to have natural limits.

The prayer for the dead is not the Kaddish prayer, which is a doxology. The Jewish prayer for the dead chanted at memorial services and at the graveside does mention life after death. It says: 'God, full of mercy, who dwells on high, let the holy and pure find perfect rest under the wings of your Shechinah in the heights, let them shine as the brightness of the heavens, the souls of all those dear ones who are remembered today for a blessing.' This is not the entire prayer. But it does reproduce that part which is taken from Daniel 12. The dead are to shine with the brightness of the heavens, just as Daniel 12 suggests. Thus, even in the later Rabbinic period, Daniel 12 continued to be prominent in Jewish life under Rabbinic aegis. Indeed, Rambam, in systematizing the Rabbinic notion, cannot give up the idea; yet, in his philosophical writing he scarcely gives personal immortality any space at all, preferring instead the philosophical and very aristocratic notion of the immortality of the ideas of the mind.

At the beginning I noted that Americans seem deeply divided on the notion of resurrection, although we subscribe to the notion of life after death by a wide majority. The liberal and main-line churches and synagogues are very dubious about the notion of bodily resurrection, while affirming life after death as a soul or spirit. The fundamentalist and charismatic churches and the most conservative members of the Jewish community not only like notions of life after death, but put them at the centre of their beliefs. We now see that this pattern was in some ways characteristic of Jewish religious life in the first centuries as well. It would be hard to identify fundamentalism with apocalypticism. They are not the same phenomenon at all. But fundamentalism does share with first-century apocalypticism a sense of being beset by a philosophical system which is seen as hostile to faith and hence threatening.

Nothing calls the truth of religious doctrine more into question than noticing that the doctrine has a history, especially if the doctrine changes radically over time. Part of responsibly explaining that history is to search out the social and political reasons why certain concepts and doctrines appeal to religious persons at specific times and why they cease to appeal at other times. Such considerations tend to teach us to be sceptical of the eternal claims of dogma; for one period's claims of eternal truth seem but expressions of specific class interests and desires. But they do not totally discredit the human effort to express the importance of transcending our material and existential circumstances. In the case of notions of life after death, that history is fascinating, because it shows time and again that the particular ways in which God chooses to be merciful and just depend thoroughly on contemporary appraisals of divine justice and mercy. And to a very great extent, the same issues of justice and mercy are very much part of our notions of existential finitude today.

6

'Seeing' the Risen Jesus

STEPHEN T. DAVIS

I

The New Testament claims that certain people—Mary Magdalene, Peter, Thomas, Paul, and others—saw the risen Jesus. 'Have I not seen Jesus our Lord?,' Paul asks (1 Cor. 9: 1). Through the three women at the tomb, the disciples receive the promise: 'he is going ahead of you to Galilee; there you will see him' (Mark 16: 7). And the other disciples say to Thomas (John 20: 25), 'We have seen the Lord.'[1]

Suppose we assume that Jesus really was raised from the dead and really did appear to certain people—that is, that the whole story of his post-resurrection appearances to individuals and to groups was not simply a legend or a case of fraud or a mistake of some sort. Suppose, that is, that the witnesses to the resurrection did, as claimed, see the risen Jesus.

What kind of 'seeing' was this? Was it normal or abnormal seeing? Was the thing that they saw—that is, Jesus' risen body—a material object like a tree or a house or another human body? Were the perceptual processes that were at work in seeing Jesus normal; that is, were they working in the same way as they worked when Mary Magdalene saw a tree or a house or another human body? This is what I aim to discuss in the present chapter. What *kind* of seeing was involved in those experiences described by such words as 'We have seen the Lord'?

Let me distinguish among three different ways of seeing or visualizing something. The first is *normal vision*. In such cases, something like this happens: photons of light are disturbed—that is, are

---

[1] Note the fact that the claim to have seen Jesus alive after his death runs from the earliest NT witness (Paul) through Mark to one of the later books in the NT (John).

either scattered, deflected, or absorbed by interacting with an external object; some of those disturbed photons are absorbed by the retina of the eye; they contain information—that is, the specific wavelength of the light, as well as its intensity and distribution on the retina, determine our interpretation of what we see; from the eye, electrical-chemical messages are sent to the brain, which interprets those signals and recognizes the shape, location, colour, and so on of the external object. I shall assume that normal vision entails both (1) that the perceptual processes work as they regularly do, and (2) that the object seen is a material object.

At the other extreme is what I will call *subjective vision*. This is a situation where someone sincerely claims to see something, no one else can see it, and the reason that no one else can see it is because the item purportedly seen is not real, is not objectively there to be seen. (I will say little about this category—usually called a hallucination—in the present essay.)

The third category fits between the first two and is important for present purposes. Let us call an *objective vision* a situation where someone sincerely claims to see something, no one else can see it, and the reason that no one else can see it is because it is not the sort of thing that can be seen by normal vision. That is, the person who has the objective vision has been enabled by God to see the real and objective presence of the thing; the see-er has an ability to see it that others lack.[2]

Thus the issue that I will discuss—what sort of seeing was involved in seeing the risen Jesus—is, so to speak, an intramural debate among people who believe that Jesus really was raised from the dead and really was seen. People who hold that Jesus was *bodily* raised from the dead[3] can also engage in the debate,

[2] I choose to refer to this category as 'objective vision' because that term is already in use in the theological literature of resurrection. (See e.g. W. Pannenberg, *Jesus—God and Man*, 2nd edn. (Philadelphia: Westminster, 1977), 93–9.) 'Grace-assisted seeing' or even 'graced seeing' might otherwise have been better terms. It should be noted that the distinction between objective and subjective vision is sometimes understood in a different way; an objective vision is a situation where God intentionally and perhaps telepathically grants Jones a vision of something despite the fact that the thing visualized is not objectively there in external reality, and a subjective vision is a situation where Smith's vision of something is in some sense self-induced.

[3] As I do in my *Risen Indeed: Making Sense of the Resurrection* (Grand Rapids, Mich.: Eerdmans, 1993), 43–61. It should be noted that several assumptions and arguments of the present essay presuppose conclusions reached in *Risen Indeed*, and probably do not stand very well apart from it.

because it is still open to question what sort of body we are talking about.

Given the assumption that Jesus really was raised and, accordingly, that the appearances were not subjective visions, the two possibilities with which we must concern ourselves are normal vision and objective visions. The first possibility is, as noted, that the seeing of Jesus by the witnesses to the resurrection was fully normal in every or virtually every sense. Mary Magdalene's seeing Jesus was like my seeing a colleague walking down the corridor in Pitzer Hall. Mary's eyes and brain were working normally, and what she saw was a material object—that is, a body that took up space, occupied a certain location, deflected photons, and so forth. (This does not entail, incidentally, that Jesus' resurrection was a mere resuscitation; as I will argue later, his raised body might well have been both a transformed 'glorified' body and a material object.) Anybody who had been there beside Mary Magdalene could also have seen the risen Jesus. A camera could have taken a snapshot of the risen Jesus.

The second possibility, as also noted, is that what Mary visualized (Jesus' raised body) was so abnormal (a 'spiritual body' from heaven) that it could only have been seen by her with special assistance from God. It was not the sort of object that human eyes, working normally and unaided by God, can see (just as there are sounds that we cannot hear). Her 'seeing' of Jesus was enhanced, graced seeing, seeing illuminated by the Holy Spirit, an objective vision. No one else who was there, unaided by God, would have perceived or recognized Jesus. A camera would have detected nothing, or at least nothing recognizable.

Let us call these two perceptual experiences 'seeing' and 'visualizing', respectively. (These are technical definitions; I do not claim that they reflect ordinary usage.) Seeing is the first possibility, where Mary's perception of Jesus was entirely or basically like normal sight, and visualizing is the second possibility, where Mary's perception of Jesus was assisted by God, an objective vision. I will use the words 'perceive' and 'encounter' as neutral between seeing and visualizing; that is, when I say that someone perceived or encountered the risen Jesus, I am leaving the question open whether it was normal sight or an objective vision.

My own view, for which I will argue here, is that seeing is much preferable to visualizing.[4] That is, contrary to the tendency of many of the twentieth-century theologians who hold that Jesus truly was resurrected from the dead (and of course some twentieth-century theologians do not allow as much), the witnesses who encountered Jesus in the resurrection appearances saw him.[5]

II

There is no denying that a quick and pre-critical reading of the appearance stories in the New Testament (together with some brief claims to have encountered the risen Jesus—e.g. Luke 24: 34; 1 Cor. 9: 1; 15: 8) would naturally lead one to hold that the witnesses to the resurrection saw, rather than visualized, him. The natural impression that we get from these stories—their plain sense—is that normal vision was involved.[6]

Perhaps the history of Christian art depicting the resurrection has had an unconscious effect on the way we read the stories—in countless paintings, drawings, and frescos, the resurrected Jesus is

---

[4] In my book *Risen Indeed* I expressed the opinion that the witnesses to the resurrection saw the risen Jesus in a normal sense of the word 'see', but I did not argue for that position. When it came time to plan the present book, co-editor Gerald O'Collins, who does not hold this view, suggested that I use the opportunity to make a case for normal seeing. At first, I was not enthusiastic. I felt that when I wrote *Risen Indeed* I had pretty much exhausted what I knew about the resurrection. Moreover (as I pointed out in that book), I am not a biblical scholar. Furthermore, I knew that the friends of 'graced seeing' rarely produce arguments on behalf of that theory, so that if I were to write the suggested essay, I would have to supply the missing arguments so that I could then try to answer them. But despite these three considerations, Gerald's judgement (as is now obvious) prevailed.

[5] There is an important question that is related to the one that I am discussing: viz. whether the resurrection appearances recorded in the NT were of a unique and limited sort, in principle unavailable to later Christians. Despite the arguments of Wilhelm Michaelis and others (see his article 'Horao', in *TDNT* v. 315–82), I will assume that the answer is yes. The point has been conclusively made by Daniel Kendall, SJ, and Gerald O'Collins, SJ, in their article, 'The Uniqueness of the Easter Appearances', *CBQ* 54/2 (Apr. 1992), 287–307. Seeing Jesus, they say, 'was an experience restricted to the first generation of disciples, above all to the apostolic eye-witnesses of that generation. Other and later Christians relate personally to Jesus (through faith and love), but they do not see him' (p. 299).

[6] I do not oppose the attempt of Scripture scholars to arrive at sensible conclusions about the dating and early forms of existing biblical texts (in this case, the resurrection accounts), but my view is that Christian theology ought to be done on the basis of those texts that the Church has taken as canonical, not on the basis of their hypothesized literary ancestors. I will so argue in the present chapter.

depicted as being just as solid and perceivable and made of flesh and bone as the others in the pictures.[7] With the possible exception of a halo, his body looks like everybody else's.

But how might a more critical and theologically sophisticated reader of the New Testament argue that the witnesses saw (rather than visualized) the risen Jesus? Primarily by attending to the biblical descriptions of the appearances, as summarized by Luke: 'After his suffering he presented himself alive to them by many convincing proofs, appearing to them during forty days and speaking about the kingdom of God' (Acts 1: 3). Taking a synoptic view of all the stories and brief claims, Jesus is said *to have been seen* (or to have appeared or to have shown himself) (Matt. 28: 17; Luke 24: 34, 39–46 ('Look at my hands and feet'); John 20: 14, 18 ('I have seen the Lord'), 21; I Cor. 15: 5–8), *to have spoken* (Matt. 28: 9, 18–20; Luke 24: 17–30, 36–49; John 20: 15–17, 19–23, 26–9; 21: 5–23; Acts 1: 4–8), *to have walked* (Luke 24: 13–28), *to have distributed food* (Luke 24: 30; John 21: 13), *to have eaten* (Luke 24: 41–3; Acts 1: 4; 10: 41), *to have performed 'signs'* (John 20: 30), *to have given a blessing with his hands* (Luke 24: 50), *to have shown his hands and side* (John 20: 20), and *to have been touched* (Matt. 28: 9; Luke 24: 39; John 20: 17, 27 (only the first of these three texts specifically states that Jesus' body was touched; the other two imply it)).

My point is not that all this physical detail in the appearance stories settles the question of seeing versus visualizing. Thus far my only claim is that the natural way to read these stories—prior, that is, to approaching them critically or with certain theological convictions in place—is in terms of seeing. In the absence of convincing reasons to the contrary (and we will momentarily explore some such purported reasons), it seems sensible to understand the perception of the risen Jesus in the appearance stories in terms of normal sight. (I will return to this point in Section VI.)

III

Nevertheless, many contemporary exegetes and theologians opt for visualizing as opposed to seeing, and we need to consider the

---

[7] This plausible suggestion has been made by Gerald O'Collins, SJ, in his *What Are They Saying About the Resurrection?* (New York: Paulist, 1978), 47–8.

reasons for this. As Gerald O'Collins points out, 'Most New Testament scholars would be reluctant to assert that the risen Christ became present in such a way that neutral (or even hostile) spectators could have observed him in an ordinary "physical" fashion.'[8] Unfortunately, arguments for this position are rarely given; so I have endeavoured to supply a few. There seem to be six arguments that can be given in favour of the resurrection appearances being instances of enhanced perception. Let me discuss them in turn.

1. *The raised Jesus appeared only to believers.* If this claim were true, it might constitute a powerful argument for the conclusion that perceptual abilities enhanced by God were necessary to perceive the risen Jesus, for it might make sense to hold that only those who believed were blessed by God with the requisite enhanced perceptual abilities.

But of course the main claim being made here is not true, and it is altogether surprising that so many scholars make it. Let me mention three people who were unbelievers at the time of their encounter with the risen Jesus. (1) Thomas was hardly represented as a believer in Jesus as the risen Lord when he encountered Jesus in the house with the doors shut (although immediately on perceiving Jesus he became a believer in him as 'My Lord and my God' (John 20: 28)). (2) It seems quite possible that James the brother of Jesus was not a believer when the risen Jesus appeared to him (1 Cor. 15: 7). Apparently a non-believer during Jesus' earthly ministry (Mark 3: 21, 31–5; 6: 3; John 7: 5), it can plausibly be argued that he came to believe because the risen Jesus appeared to him. Note that James is listed among the 120 disciples who were together in Jerusalem after Jesus' ascension (Acts 1: 13–15; cf. also 15: 3; Gal. 2: 1 f.).[9] (3) The apostle Paul is another obvious example, but

---

[8] See his *The Resurrection of Jesus Christ* (Valley Forge, Pa.: Judson Press, 1973), 59.

[9] The difficulty here is that of identifying which James, among the three or so mentioned in the NT, Paul was referring to in 1 Cor. 15: 7. It seems probable that he had in mind James the Lord's brother, the one who became a 'pillar' of the early Church (Gal. 2: 9). Note that Cephas and James are mentioned by name in both 1 Cor. 15: 5–8 and Paul's own account of his first post-conversion visit to Jerusalem (Gal. 1: 18–19). Indeed, Reginald Fuller says: 'If there were no record of an appearance to James the Lord's brother in the New Testament we would have to invent one in order to account for his post-resurrection conversion and rapid advance' *The Formation of the Resurrection Narratives* (Philadelphia: Fortress, 1971), 37.

I will postpone until later a discussion of the issues surrounding his conversion and the appearance of the risen Jesus to him. The only claim in the neighbourhood of which we can be sure is that the raised Jesus made no great and grandiose appearances to the general public—that is, to friend and foe alike. There is no record of any appearance to Pontius Pilate or to Caiaphas or to the crowd that had so recently called for his execution. As Luke has Peter openly admit, Jesus appeared not to 'all the people but to us who were chosen by God as witnesses' (Acts 10: 39–40). The testimony in favour of the resurrection of Jesus in the New Testament all comes from insiders in the Christian movement, not from neutral or antagonistic observers.

But it is obvious that this rather thin fact is a frail reed with which to buttress a claim that the resurrection appearances were episodes of visualizing rather than seeing. As noted, some who were *not* believers (and thus were probably not ideal candidates for graced perception) encountered the risen Jesus.

2. *The resurrection of Jesus was not a resuscitation.* This claim has long puzzled me. Let me explain why. Suppose we define the term 'resuscitation' as the restoration of clinically dead or nearly clinically dead human beings to their previous lives. Resuscitations occasionally occur in hospitals these days, and there were several apparent resuscitations in the Bible too—for example, Jesus' raising of Lazarus. One key criterion for a raising from the dead being a resuscitation (as opposed to a resurrection) is that the resuscitant must inevitably die a second time at some later point, and at that time death would presumably be permanent.

What puzzles me is not the claim itself—it is obviously and unremarkably true. The New Testament's witness is that Jesus was not merely restored to his previous life, but rather was transformed to a new and glorious life fit for the kingdom of God. What I find odd is the vehemence with which it is argued. Especially those scholars who set out to argue that the resurrection of Jesus did not genuinely occur, or occurred only in some 'spiritual' sense, invariably begin with a robust attack on resuscitation. One almost gets the impression that there are defenders of resuscitation hiding behind every tree, and that everything depends on their being refuted.

Indeed, *I* got this impression about ten years ago, when, as an interloper from another discipline, I started reading the theological literature on resurrection. I kept waiting to encounter the books or articles or those (obviously sightly obtuse) resuscitation theorists. It took me a while to realize that there are no such people. Perhaps some unlettered Christian folk, if asked what they believe about resurrection, would come up with an inchoate version of resuscitation, but I am aware of no scholars who defend such a view.

Nevertheless, as noted, the New Testament certainly teaches that Jesus was resurrected rather than resuscitated, and some scholars take this to be an argument for visualizing as opposed to seeing. But there appears to be confusion here. It is true that the resurrected body of Jesus possessed strange new properties. With an apparent ability to appear and disappear at will, it seemed to be free of certain of the natural laws that we must obey. Note the way John depicts Jesus as appearing in a room despite its locked door in John 20: 19, 26, the way he suddenly disappeared from the sight of the Emmaus disciples in Luke 24: 31, and the way he ascended out of the disciples' sight in Luke 24: 51 and Acts 1: 9. Some interpret this to mean (and I agree with them) that the appearances were not encounters with a resuscitated Jesus, but rather were 'eschatological disclosures "from heaven" of an already exalted One'.[10]

But my point is that it does not follow from any of this that Jesus' raised body was not a material object (although it certainly was an unusual one), something that took up space, occupied a certain location, *and could be seen.* Perhaps the following fallacious argument has had a certain influence here:

(1) A resuscitated body can be seen.
(2) Jesus' body was not a resuscitated body.
(3) Therefore, Jesus' body could not be seen.

Notice further that nobody takes the sudden transportation of Philip from the desert road near Gaza (where he had been speaking with the Ethiopian eunuch) to Azotus (Acts 8: 39–40) as evidence that he had no physical body.[11]

Paul Badham has argued[12] that there is a contradiction involved

---

[10] O'Collins, *What Are They saying About the Resurrection?*, 11.

[11] I owe this last point to Robert H. Gundry, 'The Essential Physicality of Jesus' Resurrection According to the New Testament', in Joel B. Green and Max Turner (eds.), *Jesus of Nazareth, Lord and Christ: Essays on the Historical Jesus and New Testament Christology* (Grand Rapids, Mich.: Eerdmans, 1994), 214.

[12] Paul Badham, 'The Meaning of the Resurrection of Jesus', in P. Avis (ed.), *The Resurrection of Jesus Christ* (London: Darton, Longman & Todd, 1993), 28–9.

in Jesus' resurrection body being both sufficiently spiritual to pass through walls and sufficiently physical to be seen and touched. But not only is there no logical contradiction here—there is not even much in the way of a difficulty. The only sort of thing that logically *can* appear and take up space in a room, locked doors or not, is a physical object. Immaterial objects like, say, the number six, failing as they do to possess physical location, never take up space in a room (or anywhere else). If the raised Jesus appeared in a room, the raised Jesus' body was a material object, and so presumably could be seen and touched.

But perhaps Badham's deepest concern is to understand how a physical body can, as he says, pass through walls. But where does the New Testament say that Jesus 'passed through the walls' of the room? I would have thought the idea was that Jesus simply appeared or materialized in the room. It is of course not part of our normal experience that physical objects simply appear in a given place—that is, without having traversed the intervening places between the place where they were and the place where they are. Still, I see no logical or conceptual difficulty here. It seems that an omnipotent being would have it well within its power to make a human body materialize in a room.

3. *The meaning of* ophthe. *Ophthe* is the aorist passive form of the Greek verb *horao* (I see). The word is used nine times in the New Testament in relation to the raised Jesus (Luke 24: 34; Acts 9: 17; 13: 31; 26: 16a; 1 Cor. 15: 5–8 (four times); and 1 Tim. 3: 16). When used with the dative, it is usually translated 'He appeared', and as such emphasizes the revelatory initiative of the one who appears. 'He let himself be seen' is almost the sense (as opposed to something like 'he was seen').

Some scholars who favour objective visions rather than ordinary seeing argue that this conclusion is entailed by the New Testament's use of *ophthe*. Thus Badham says: 'most New Testament scholars believe that the word *ophthe* . . . refers to spiritual vision rather than to ocular seeing'.[13] The argument is that the religious use of *ophthe* is technical, marks a clear difference from

---

[13] Paul Badham, 'The Meaning of the Resurrection of Jesus', in P. Avis (ed.), *The Resurrection of Jesus Christ*, 31. Michaelis (in his article cited in n. 5) is probably the most influential recent scholar who holds that the appearances were revelatory encounters with Jesus that primarily involved hearing rather than sight.

ordinary visual perception of physical objects, and entails some sort of spiritual appearance, vision-like experience, or apprehension of a divine revelation.

But other scholars have pointed out that *ophthe* can also be used (and is so used in both the New Testament and the Septuagint) for ordinary visual apprehension of a human being or a material object (e.g. Acts 7: 26). That is, it can be used both for ordinary seeing of material objects and for the visualizing of supernatural beings. Indeed, there are other Greek words (*horama* and *optasia*) that are normally used for what we would call visions, especially of things that are normally invisible like God or angels (see Matt. 17: 9; Acts 9: 10; 16: 19).

It is true that the use of *ophthe* does not *require* that the sense be that of normal vision, but normal vision is not ruled out either. Indeed, the word covers a whole range of visual phenomena. When Paul says that the risen Jesus 'appeared to me,' the notion of normal vision of a material object is neither required nor ruled out. However, for non-linguistic reasons, the appearance that Paul cites to 'more than five hundred' (1 Cor. 15: 6) must surely refer to seeing rather than visualizing. Raymond Brown rightly ridicules the very idea of more than 500 people having the same objective vision as 'synchronized ecstasy'.[14]

But the simple point is that *ophthe* does not require the sense of visualizing as opposed to seeing, and in view of examples like Acts 7: 26 the argument that it does collapses. We must decide what is meant in each instance of its use by analysis of the context (among other things), not simply by lexical fiat. It is not possible to decide the nature of Jesus' resurrection appearances on the basis of a linguistic analysis of one verb.[15]

4. *Doubt and failure of recognition.* An argument in favour of visualizing as opposed to seeing concerns the common motifs in the appearance stories of (1) failure at first to recognize Jesus (Luke 24: 16, 31, 37; John 20: 14-15; 21: 4; cf. also the appendix to Mark:

---

[14] Raymond E. Brown, SS, *The Virginal Conception and Bodily Resurrection of Jesus* (New York: Paulist, 1973), 91. No doubt an omnipotent being could achieve such a thing as a vision shared by over 500 people, but in the light of all the evidence it strains credulity to think that God actually did so in this case.

[15] See Hans Grass, *Ostergeschehen und Osterberichte*, 4th rev. edn. (Göttingen: Vandenhoeck & Ruprecht, 1970), 186-9.

'He appeared in another form of two of them' (16: 21)), and (2) doubt that it is Jesus (Matt. 28: 17; Luke 24: 11; John 20: 24–5). The argument would be that those who were not blessed with enhanced perception—that is, who were not recipients of the objective vision of the risen Jesus—either did not recognize Jesus (until with God's help they *were* able to visualize him) or else doubted.

This is certainly a possible interpretation of the appearance stories. But one item that might be taken in support of it seems to me actually to argue against it: namely, the explicit statements in the Emmaus story (Luke 24: 13–35) that Cleopas and his unnamed companion failed to recognize Jesus because 'their eyes were kept from recognizing him' (24: 16) and that later they did recognize him because 'their eyes were opened' (24: 31). This point seems to me to cut the other way: it suggests that the two Emmaus disciples *would quite normally have recognized Jesus* had their eyes not been supernaturally kept from recognizing him. The literal sense seems to be that their eyes were restrained or held back, and that later their eyes were opened by God.[16] In other words, it sounds in this case as if a special act of God was necessary to *prevent* recognition until the appropriate moment.[17] Perhaps, then, *anybody* who had been there on the road to Emmaus could have seen and recognized Jesus (apart from such a special divine act). Perhaps a camera could have taken a picture of him.

Are there other, more sensible ways of explaining the twin motifs of doubt and failure to recognize than to posit objective visions? Yes, I believe there are. For one thing, we need to remind ourselves that the disciples were convinced that Jesus had truly died. And contrary to the claims of some twentieth-century theologians (who make it sound as if first-century folk were almost pantingly eager to believe in resurrection and other miracles, and would do so at the drop of a hat), they were as convinced as we are that dead people stay dead. They were definitely not expecting to encounter Jesus.

Accordingly, it ought not to be surprising that initial encounters

---

[16] See Joseph A. Fitzmyer, SJ, *The Gospel According to Luke (X–XXIV)* (Garden City, NY: Doubleday, 1985), 1563, 1568. Fitzmyer calls the usage in v. 31 ('their eyes were opened') the theological passive, which suggests that it was an act of God.

[17] Some interpret the blindness of Cleopas and his companion in entirely natural terms, simply as continuing Luke's theme of spiritual blindness (Luke 9: 45; 18: 34; 19: 42). See e.g. Grant Osborne, *The Resurrection Narratives: A Redactional Study* (Grand Rapids, Mich.: Baker, 1984), 238. I do not read the Emmaus pericope this way, however.

with the raised Jesus might have produced lack of recognition and even doubt. It should not surprise us that in some cases Jesus was recognized only after he spoke, or after he blessed and broke bread, or after he encouraged observation of the pre-mortem wounds, or after he suggested fishing on the right side of the boat. The disciples first had to deal with their own incredulity before they could accept the resurrection. Later they surely recognized what the Church came to call their own 'slowness of heart to believe' (Luke 24: 25).

Secondly, there may be several layers of explanation for the two motifs. As noted, on at least one occasion failure to recognize was said (as I interpret the text) to be due to divine initiative (Luke 24: 13–33). In other cases, there were perhaps more natural explanations, like distance (John 21: 4), a combination of confusion and lack of light (John 20: 14–15), or the suddenness of Jesus' appearing (Luke 24: 36–7). It also seems possible that Jesus' countenance had been altered somewhat (thus the comment in the Marcan appendix, 'He appeared in another form' (Mark 16: 12)). But the main point on which I want to insist is that in every case of doubt and/or failure of recognition, the overriding factors were: (1) the fact that the disciples were in shock, dealing with their own anguish over losing Jesus and their fears for their own safety, and (2) the fact that seeing Jesus alive again was the last thing they expected.[18]

5. *Paul's conversion.* The story of Paul's conversion on the road to Damascus (told three times in the book of Acts, at 9: 1–22; 22: 6–16; 25: 12–18) seems to have influenced the way some scholars read the accounts of Jesus' resurrection appearances. For that story does seem to describe something like an objective vision, since the experience was intelligible to Paul (as an encounter with Jesus), but not to his companions. In the first account, the others who were with Paul 'heard the voice but saw no one' (Acts 9: 7), and in the second account, they 'saw the light but did not hear the voice of the one who was speaking' (Acts 22: 9).

I am not interested here in trying to harmonize these two apparently discrepant accounts. My point is that some people may think that the resurrection appearances of Jesus were like Paul's Damascus Road experience in being unseeable by, or unintelligible to, other people; that is, they were objective visions—this especially

---

[18] See Murray Harris, *Raised Immortal* (Grand Rapids, Mich.: Eerdmans, 1983), 56.

since in his own writings Paul insists that he has seen the risen Jesus (1 Cor. 9: 1; 15: 8; Gal. 1: 12, 16), which most scholars read as references to his Damascus Road conversion experience.

Interestingly, Luke seems to limit resurrection appearances of Jesus to the period between his crucifixion and some forty days later (see Acts 1: 3). This must mean that he holds that subsequent encounters with Jesus that involve any sort of visualization are to be classified either as visions or as resurrection appearances of a different sort from the earlier ones. And this is the Church's traditional interpretation of Luke's words: after the ascension, there were no more resurrection appearances of the paradigmatic sort.[19] This must mean that, according to Luke's scheme, Paul's encounters with Jesus, however many there were, of whatever sort they were, were appearances that were in at least some important sense different from the earlier ones to Mary Magdalene and the others. (This would also apparently include the appearances to Stephen (Acts 7: 53-6) and to John of Patmos (Rev. 1: 12-18).)

And Paul himself may have recognized something like this distinction when he introduced a reference to his own encounter with Jesus with the words, 'last of all, as to one untimely born, he appeared also to me' (1 Cor. 15: 8).[20] Luke also represents Paul as referring to his conversion experience as 'a heavenly vision (*optasia*)' (Acts 26: 19). Note also that in 2 Corinthians 12: 1-7 (where Paul was almost certainly not referring to his conversion experience),[21] he seems to be distinguishing between two sorts of ecstatic or revelatory experiences, those 'in the body' and those 'out of the body'. Perhaps the first sort includes real experiences and the second sort includes visions.

---

[19] Theologically this seems a wise decision. Otherwise, the Church throughout its history would have had to contend with, and reach judgements about, all sorts of purported resurrection appearances with all sorts of purportedly authoritative new revelations from the Risen One.

[20] Here I disagree with Brown, *Virginal Conception*, 53 n., who says: '[Paul] regards the appearance to himself on the same level as the appearance to the others, even if it is the last.' At one level, of course, Brown is correct—Paul surely considered his encounter an important part of what validated his status as an apostle, and he held that he was second to none of the other apostles in this regard. My question is whether Paul considered his encounter with the risen Jesus as being on an epistemic par with the earlier appearances to the others. The evidence cited in the present paragraph makes me doubt it.

[21] The phrase 'fourteen years ago' points to a date in the early 40s rather than to the conversion experience in the 30s.

If this is the case, then Paul's Damascus Road experience (at least as it is described by Luke) is not a proper model for interpreting the resurrection appearances of Jesus, for deciding whether the witnesses saw or visualized Jesus. The point is this: there is no good reason to interpret the resurrection appearances recounted in the Gospels and listed in I Corinthians 15: 5–7 as experiences that were like Paul's conversion experience. Indeed, there is every reason to deny this 'Damascus Road' interpretation of them, because it requires complete rejection (perhaps as legendary accretions) of all the physical detail of the appearance stories. And even if Paul's conversion experience does (contrary to what it seems that Luke is saying) count as a resurrection appearance in the fullest sense, this does not mean that it can be used as a grid to be imposed on the other appearance accounts. As I have been arguing, they simply do not fit it very well.

6. *The Pauline notion of 'spiritual body'.* Some theologians argue that in I Corinthians 15 Paul is talking about a resurrection body that is normally invisible to humans on earth, and that therefore all perceptions of the risen Jesus are objective visions. In responding to this line of argument, I am forced to skim lightly over points that were made in detail in *Risen Indeed*.[22] In that book I argued: (1) that Paul's notion of a spiritual body involves corporeality—that is, that Paul was talking about a material object; (2) that Paul's notion of a spiritual body reconciles what otherwise might look like discrepancies between the heavily physical motifs in the appearance stories in the Gospels (eating, being touched, etc.) and the more ethereal or numinous motifs in those same stories (appearing in a room despite locked doors, etc.); (3) that the New Testament accordingly offers a unified view of the resurrection of Jesus; (4) that all redactional attempts to argue that the physical motifs are late and unreliable and that they emerged through a long and quasi-evolutionary process from earlier 'spiritual' appearance traditions have failed;[23] and (5) accordingly, that the notion of bodily resurrection (but not resuscitation) is the best way for Christians to understand and preach the Easter message.

[22] See esp. 43–84.
[23] In my opinion, no one has convincingly argued that there was ever a period in the history of the Church, let alone a document, in which the resurrection of Jesus was understood in non-physical terms. Note that 1 Cor. 15: 3–7, probably the oldest datable Easter tradition in the NT, speaks of resurrection rather than exaltation.

Although he does not specifically mention seeing, Willi Marxsen perhaps implies that a spiritual body cannot be seen but only visualized. He says: 'And of course a spiritual body in the Pauline sense cannot eat or be touched.'[24] Even my friend and conference co-host Gerald O'Collins (normally highly reliable on all matters resurrectional) seems to me to lose his way at this point by referring to 'glorious (normally invisible?) matter'.[25] (But perhaps he redeems himself with the inserted question mark.)

My question is: where did Marxsen learn that a Pauline spiritual body cannot eat or be touched? What made O'Collins even questioningly suggest that a Pauline glorified body cannot be seen? It seems perfectly possible to accept everything that Paul says in 1 Corinthians 15 about resurrection bodies and still hold that they are material objects that can be seen. Paul does insist that 'flesh and blood cannot inherit the kingdom of God' (1 Cor. 15: 50). But this means that the old, earthly body cannot enter the kingdom of God as it is (this is one of the powerful theological arguments against resuscitation), that it must first be transformed into a glorified body (Phil. 3: 32). But a glorified body (*soma*) is still a body—that is, still a material object that can be seen.[26]

IV

We have been discussing six arguments that might be given in favour of the claim that the appearances of the resurrected Jesus to Mary Magdalene and the others were objective visions rather than instances of ordinary seeing. Some of the arguments are stronger than others, but as we have seen, serious objections can be raised against all six of them.

The central claim of the first argument—that the raised Jesus appeared only to believers—is simply false, no matter how many times it is repeated. The second argument—the one that concerns

---

[24] Willi Marxsen, *The Resurrection of Jesus of Nazareth* (Philadelphia: Fortress, 1970), 70.

[25] Gerald O'Collins, *What Are They Saying About the Resurrection?*, 46.

[26] This point is compellingly argued by Robert Gundry, *Soma in Biblical Theology: With Emphasis on Pauline Anthropology* (Cambridge: Cambridge University Press, 1976), 159 ff. See also William L. Craig, *Assessing the New Testament Evidence for the Historicity of the Resurrection of Jesus* (Lewiston, NY: Mellen, 1989), 120-6, 133-7, 158.

resuscitation—is irrelevant to the matter at hand once it is granted (as it must be) that a glorified (and not just resuscitated) raised body can be a material object. The third argument—about *ophthe*—is a serious one, but as we saw, the frequent use of this word in connection with Jesus' resurrection appearances does not by itself settle the question of seeing versus visualizing. The fourth argument—which concerns the motifs of doubt and failure to recognize Jesus in the appearance stories—is also an important consideration, but I argued that these motifs can be adequately explained even if the raised Jesus was seen rather than visualized. About the fifth argument—which concerns the influence of Paul's conversion story in Acts on the 'objective vision' interpretation of the appearance stories—I argued that there should be no such influence. In response to the sixth argument—about Paul's notion of a 'spiritual body'—I argued that there is no good reason to think of it as something that is normally invisible or unobservable.

The strongest argument in the opposite direction—that is, in favour of seeing (as opposed to visualizing)—is the massive physical detail of the appearance stories. Suppose the risen Jesus really did (as the stories claim) appear (in various settings, at various times of day, for various lengths of time, to various people and groups of people), walk, talk, distribute food, perform signs, and allow himself to be touched. If so, it seems sensible to interpret the stories in the way that the Church and Christian artists have traditionally understood them: namely, that the risen Jesus was physically present in a way that could, in a perfectly normal sense, be observed.[27]

It is sometimes said that the physical detail of the appearance stories in Luke and John was to convince the disciples not that Jesus was physical but that he was real. But those who make this claim never seem to go on to answer the question: a real *what*?[28] Perhaps this omission is so prevalent because those who fail to answer the question recognize that any answer to it that did not involve a physical body would inevitably lead to a thoroughly non-biblical view of

---

[27] Here again I disagree with O'Collins, who argues that the physical detail of the stories is designed to highlight '(a) the reality of the resurrection, (b) the continuity between the risen Lord and the earthly Jesus, and (c) the disciples' status as witnesses'. He adds: 'The graphic, physical touches of the Easter stories in Luke and John serve to express these points and no more' (*What Are They Saying About the Resurrection?*, 49–50). I can affirm everything here except the crucial last three words.

[28] See Gundry, 'The Essential Physicality', 210.

survival of death—for example, to the Platonic notion of the immortality of the soul. I have no problem with the claim that the physical detail of the stories was designed to prove the physical and thus personal continuity of the risen Lord with the Jesus who had been crucified. But I am arguing that the primary reason for the physical detail is that in its canonical writings, the early Church was correctly remembering the actual nature of the appearances themselves.

The status of the evidence at our disposal (so it seems to me) is such that it is much preferable to hold that the risen Jesus was seen rather than visualized. But why is this view so commonly rejected? One sometimes gets the impression from the friends of objective visions that the notion of a physically present resurrected Jesus is somehow uncouth or *outré*.[29] I do not share such feelings; I feel no sense of embarrassment whatsoever in holding that a camera could have taken a snapshot of the raised Jesus, say, feeding the seven disciples beside the Sea of Tiberius (John 21: 1-14).

V

I have been arguing that the biblical stories of the resurrection appearances of Jesus are to be understood in terms of ordinary vision. Thus far my argument has been based entirely on historical-critical grounds, and I want to rest the claims of the present essay primarily on those grounds. However, it seems to me possible to argue for the same conclusion in two other ways. Let me now briefly do so.

1. *The early Church interpreted the resurrection appearances in terms of ordinary vision.* I will not try to establish this point in detail, especially since the modern concept of an objective vision was apparently not used by early Christian thinkers. Still, it is clear that orthodox treatments of the resurrection in the second century all

---

[29] Brown echoes the feeling of many theologians and Scripture scholars when he says: 'The partial ambiguity of our sources about the nature of "seeing" makes incredible some of the modern speculation as to whether the risen Jesus could have been photographed or televised, and whether he could have been seen by non-believers. This type of question does not show any appreciation for the transformation involved in the Resurrection' (*Virginal Conception*, 91 fn.).

took it for granted that Jesus was seen by the witnesses in an ordinary sense of the word 'see'.

One extreme example, where it was made explicit that nonbelievers saw the risen Jesus, is the remarkable resurrection scene in the *Gospel of Peter*. In that account, the guards at the tomb actually observed the risen Jesus leaving the tomb supported by two angels. 'The heads of the two reached to heaven,' it says, 'but the one whom they bore with their hands reached beyond the heavens.' Explaining the events at the tomb to Pontius Pilate, the guards declared, 'Truly he was a son of God.'[30]

Turning to the Church Fathers, Ignatius of Antioch (*c*.30-107) is a good place to begin. He cited and stressed the biblical accounts of Jesus encouraging the disciples to touch his resurrection body and to examine the pre-mortem wounds. Jesus rose from the dead, Ignatius said, not just 'in appearance' but 'in the body'. 'He both ate and drank with [the disciples] during forty entire days.' Ignatius concluded: 'And I know he was possessed of a body not only in his being born and crucified, but I also know that He was so after His resurrection, and believe that He is so now.'[31]

Like Ignatius, Justin Martyr (fl. *c*.150) was critical of those who maintained that 'Jesus himself appeared only as spiritual, and not in flesh, but presented merely the appearance of flesh'.[32] Against Docetic tendencies in the Church, Justin emphasized the resurrection of the body. He argued that it was to confirm his bodily resurrection that Jesus appeared in physical form, allowed the disciples to examine the pre-mortem wounds, and ate with them. Justin went on to say: 'And when he had thus shown them that there is truly a resurrection of the flesh [and] that it is not impossible for flesh to ascend into heaven . . ., "He was taken up into heaven while they beheld", as he was in the flesh.'[33]

Doubtless with some of the same heresies in mind, Irenaeus (d. *c*.200) also stressed the 'fleshiness' of the resurrection and the biblical accounts that underscore that notion. He said, 'In the same manner, therefore, as Christ did rise in the substance of the flesh, and pointed out to his disciples the mark of the nails and the open-

---

[30] See David R. Cartlidge and David L. Dungan (eds.), *Documents for the Study of the Gospels* (Philadelphia: Fortress, 1980), 85. The quotations are from v. 40 and 45.

[31] Alexander Roberts and James Donaldson (eds.), ANF i. (Grand Rapids, Mich.: Eerdmans, 1989), 85 (*The Epistle of St. Ignatius to the Smyrnaeans*, III).

[32] Ibid. 295 (*Fragments of the Lost Work of Justin on the Resurrection*, II).

[33] Ibid. 298 (*Fragments*, IX).

ing in his side (now these are the tokens of that flesh which rose from the dead), so "shall he also", it is said, "raise us up by His own power".'[34]

There are, of course, limitations on how far this first argument can take us. For one thing, some people do not particularly care what the Fathers had to say. For another, some might argue that the opinions of the Fathers on this topic are suspect because they wrote before the advent of the historical-critical method in scriptural studies. For a third, some might try to relativize the views of the second-century Fathers by arguing that their emphasis on the physicality of the resurrection merely reflects their theological context, one in which orthodoxy was endangered by Docetic and Gnostic tendencies.

But for those who want to take Christian tradition seriously and who think (as I do) that any theological opinion which all or virtually all the Fathers held is at least prima facie probable, the argument to the effect that the second-century Fathers all appeared to hold that the resurrected Jesus was seen in an ordinary sense is certainly worth noting.

2. *The theological significance of appearances amenable to ordinary vision.* As noted, my primary argument in this chapter is the historical one that Jesus' resurrection appearances were actually seen rather than visualized. But this does not preclude theological or even apologetic significance. I reject the notion, implicit in some New Testament scholarship, that finding a theological purpose behind a certain scriptural account is inconsistent with that account being a true account of what actually occurred.

Well then, what theological difference does it make (if I am correct) that the risen Jesus was seen rather than visualized, that anybody (believer or not) who had been in the right place at the right time could have seen him, that no special or extraordinary divine assistance was needed? There are several points that could be made, but I will focus on two, the first a brief point about Christian doctrine, the second a more detailed apologetic point.

The doctrinal item is this: the claim that the witnesses saw, rather than visualized, Jesus underscores the Christian notion of

---

[34] Alexander Roberts and James Donaldson (eds.), ANF i. (Grand Rapids, Mich.: Eerdmans, 1989), 532 (*Irenaeus Against Heresies*, V, VII, 1).

incarnation, the claim that God became a human being in Jesus Christ.[35] As Aquinas says in a slightly different context (he was discussing the question of why the angel of annunciation was seen by the Virgin Mary via normal sight), the angel was seen by Mary because 'he came to announce the Incarnation of the invisible God. Wherefore it is becoming that, in order to make this known, an invisible creature should assume a form in which to appear visibly.'[36] In other words, incarnation rules out all Gnostic-like denigration of bodily existence and the bodily senses. The claim that God became flesh means that sight and the other senses are not to be belittled or abhorred. Of course I am not saying that the friends of graced seeing deny or even consistently should deny incarnation. But the claim that the risen Jesus was seen rather than visualized is a strong way to underscore the notion that God took on a human body, and that the human body cannot, accordingly, be all bad. The body was not only created by God and is thus good; the body is the vehicle through which we come to know God. Those like Mary Magdalene who saw Jesus saw God made visible.

Let me now turn to the apologetic point. As everyone recognizes, the claim that Jesus was raised from the dead was at the centre of the message that the earliest Christians preached. They were very much interested in trying to convince people to believe as they did. Now imagine the following situation. One of the witnesses to the resurrection (say, Mary Magdalene) is speaking to a non-believing friend. She says: 'Yes, I saw him; that's why I believe he was raised from the dead; that's why I'm so sure. Sorry, but *you* wouldn't have seen him even if you had been there beside me. Only those who were especially blessed by God with enhanced vision could have seen him. The most you would have seen was possibly a bright light. But I was one of the lucky ones; I saw him.'

One suspects—to put it mildly—that such an argument would lead the non-believing friend to be suspicious. Even if it were obvious that Mary was sincere—that is, was not involved in a lie or fraud—the thought would strongly occur to the friend that Mary had been deluded. There would be every reason to hold that her

---

[35] I owe this point to Janet Martin Soskice. See her essay, 'Sight and Vision in Medieval Christian Thought', in Martin Jay and Teresa Brennan (eds.), *Vision* (London: Routledge, 1996), 29–43.

[36] *ST* 3a. 30. 3.

purported 'especially blessed vision' was not veridical. Of course, this same suspicion could be raised—and doubtless *was* raised— even if Mary had claimed to see rather than visualize the risen Jesus. Still, it is clear that there is far more room for doubt on the 'visualization' account than on the 'ordinary sight' account. On the second account, Mary's claims at least *could have been* empirically verified in a respectable public sense. On the first account, they could not have been. Accordingly, the apologetic task faced by the witnesses to the resurrection was slightly easier because they could say (if I am right in my central claim here), 'I saw Jesus.'

That Jesus was seen rather than visualized by the witnesses to the resurrection accordingly has this theological implication: what they saw was Jesus, not an impostor or a hallucination or a mass of ectoplasm or a sort of interactive hologram. And the fact that it was Jesus could have been verified in a quite ordinary sense—in a similar way to how I might verify a claim that a colleague of mine is walking down the hall—that is, simply by looking. In other words, convincing evidence for the resurrection of Jesus was present for anyone to have seen. It was not held in reserve for the benefit of a few initiates. The evidence for the resurrection of Jesus was not arcane and psychological, but public and empirical.

VI

Let me explain what I take to be the logic of my central argument in this essay. As I argued earlier, any sensible attempt to arrive at the plain sense of the scriptural accounts of the resurrection appearances of Jesus—whether that reading is done in the second century or the twentieth—would entail that the risen Jesus was seen rather than visualized. That is, the risen Jesus was a physical body that was objectively present to the witnesses in space and time, and he was accordingly seen in a normal sense of that word. Now that reading of the stories, like any reading of any text, can be overturned in favour of another reading by convincing reasons. We have examined six arguments that can be used to overturn the traditional reading. We have found them all unconvincing and, in some cases, rather easy to defeat. In my view, then, we are left with the Church's traditional reading of the resurrection texts. Jesus was seen.[37]

Suppose I am right in my main claim: that it was seeing rather than visualizing; anybody who had been there with Mary Magdalene could similarly have seen Jesus; a camera could have taken a picture of him. Does anything of interest follow about the nature of resurrection faith?

Here it would be helpful to distinguish (as Brown does[38]) between *sight* and *insight*. Anybody who had been there (I hold) could have seen Jesus. It would even have been possible (I suggest) for an unbeliever—one, let's say, who happened to have known Jesus—to have recognized him. 'This is Jesus of Nazareth,' such a person could have said. But apart from the illumination of the Holy Spirit, such a person would lack insight. 'What on earth happened? I thought he had died,' such a person might have reflected. Or: 'I have no idea why he seems to be here, but there must be some rational explanation.'

Were enhanced powers of perception—powers that were granted to some and denied to others—necessary to have seen the risen Christ? I am arguing that the answer to that question is no. But was a special grace necessary to see the risen Christ in such a way as to recognize him as Lord and to grasp what he was calling one to be and do? Of course.

In other words, only the person to whom God has given the gift of faith will have the insight to be able to say: 'He is here alive because God raised him from the dead.' Or even: 'He is Lord.'[39] A person who makes such a confession, whether that person was a member of the first generation of Christians or lives today, is a witness to the resurrection.[40]

---

[37] Or, as Sherlock Holmes says (near the end of 'The Beryl Coronet'), 'It is an old maxim of mine that when you have excluded the impossible, whatever remains, however improbable, must be the truth.'

[38] *Virginal Conception*, 112–13.

[39] Indeed, 'We have seen the Lord' seems to be the normal testimony of the witnesses to the resurrection (1 Cor. 9: 1; Luke 24: 34; John 20: 18, 25; 21: 7), rather than 'We have seen Jesus'. (The one exception is Matthew—see 28: 5, 9, 10, 16. 18.)

[40] I would like to thank Professors Gerald O'Collins, SJ, William L. Craig, Carey Newman, and Pheme Perkins for their helpful comments on earlier drafts of this essay.

7

Biblical Criticism and the Resurrection

WILLIAM P. ALSTON

I

The general topic of this paper is the historical (in)accuracy of the Gospel accounts of appearances of the risen Jesus. More specifically, I will be concerned with the bearing of contemporary Gospel criticism on that issue. A number of studies have reached largely negative conclusions as to what we can learn from these accounts about what happened in the alleged encounters of the disciples with their risen Lord. My central concern here will be to assess the arguments that are brought forward to support such conclusions. By way of preview, that assessment will itself be largely negative. In my view those arguments often fall far short of adequately supporting their conclusions.

Thus the discussion will be confined to the historical questions. What can we learn from the Gospels about what actually happened on and just after the first Easter? In enforcing this restriction I by no means suggest that there are not other, and at least equally important, issues concerning the resurrection. It is far from my intention to denigrate the role of faith or the relevance of the resurrection to Christian life; and I fully recognize that it is more important to enter into an appropriate *relationship* with the risen Christ than it is to figure out exactly what happened in Palestine at that time, or to enter into the minutiae of historical investigation.[1] Nevertheless, since it is crucial to the Christian faith and the Christian life to recognize that Jesus *was* restored to life after the crucifixion and has continued an (exalted and glorified) life ever since, whereby he is in effective touch with us, it is certainly not irrelevant to Christian concerns to do the best we can to determine what

---

[1] See G. O'Collins, *Jesus Risen* (New York: Paulist, 1987) for a salutary emphasis on these other matters.

we can reasonably believe about Jesus' return to life after his death and burial.

However, my approach to the historical questions is somewhat different from more usual ones. It is often supposed by biblical scholars that questions as to what happened at a certain time and place are to be answered, if at all, by the standard procedures of (secular) historical investigation. If these procedures fail to yield an answer or, worse, indicate that the balance of probability lies with the negation of certain historical reports in the Gospels, then we cannot be rationally justified in accepting those reports. Unless we embrace an irrational faith, we must reject them and, if we continue as Christians, find some other basis for Easter faith.

This approach obviously presupposes that we have no access to the facts of salvation history other than the standard procedures of historical investigation. If so, we must accept the results of such investigation or go without. But that is not the position of many committed Christians. They do not approach historical questions about the resurrection out of the blue, with nothing to go on at the outset. On the contrary, they think, believe, and *live* within a context that is partly defined by the acceptance, in a response of faith, of (more or less all of) what the Church delivers to them concerning what God is like and what He has done and plans to do, especially *vis-à-vis* us.[2] From that starting-point, what is, or should be, a Christian's concern with contemporary biblical historical scholarship? Something like this (and here is where the distinctive character of my approach comes out most clearly). Since she is already working within certain views on the matter, her mind is far from being completely open at the outset. She does not take historical research to be the sole determiner of what to believe about these matters. But if, as I suppose, she recognizes such research to be relevant to what she should believe, in what way is it relevant? By having a confirming or disconfirming bearing on the belief system she already has. Obviously, it could be confirmatory at some points and disconfirmatory at others.[3] The historical results thus serve to

---

[2] The details depend, of course, on which branch of the Church and which segment of the branch is involved.

[3] And while I am prescribing an attitude for the committed Christian, I will add that just as in science there are no conclusive experiments, as philosophers of science and scientists have been increasingly recognizing, so it is here. Just as a scientific theory can be adhered to in the face of any experimental results whatever by making appropriate adjustments to the theory, so no results of historical research

shore up or weaken parts of the Christian belief system, without being allowed the presumption of completely determining even the historical parts thereof by themselves. And I hold, without being able to give an adequate defence of the position here, that this is a rational position for her to take.[4]

It is from this perspective that I consider negative conclusions of historical scholarship concerning Gospel accounts of appearances of the risen Jesus. I am interested in them as possibly having a dis-confirmatory force *vis-à-vis* certain items in a Christian belief sys-tem. I am concerned to assess the strength of the arguments for these conclusions so that I can assess the degree to which they pose a serious problem for that system. One important difference between this approach and the one with which I contrasted it has to do with what it is proper to expect, or need, in the way of historical 'proof' or evidence for historical components of Christian belief, such as the belief that Jesus is alive and appeared to his disciples after his death and burial. My idealized Christian believer neither expects nor feels any urgent need of such a proof. She accepts all this initially as part of 'signing on' with the Church, as part of her faith response to the Church's proclamation.[5] Thus she, and I, are undisturbed by the frequent statements of historical biblical scholars that historical investigation cannot establish this or that item of Christian belief—for example, that the post-resurrection events were as depicted in one or another Gospel, or that 'he rose again from the dead and ascended into heaven'. But, being an intelligent, reflective, and rational person, she wants to know what has been discovered by historians that has any bearing on beliefs like those. When and if she becomes convinced that such results are forthcoming, she will

can definitively and conclusively overthrow a religious doctrine. (That is not to say, of course, that it will always be reasonable to hang on to a system in the face of cer-tain results of investigation.) But this additional complexity will play no role here.

[4] In this essay I cannot develop an epistemology of Christian belief. Hence I will have to leave it largely inexplicit what properly goes into the basis of Christian belief other than results of historical investigation. I have just spoken of a faith response to the proclamation of the gospel by the Church, but that is by no means the whole story. For more of the story see W. Alston, *Perceiving God: The Epistemology of Religious Experience* (Ithaca, NY: Cornell University Press, 1991), esp. ch. 8.

[5] I concentrate here on the cognitive aspect of this faith response. But please do not take this to reflect a view as to what is most important in faith. I have no incli-nation to think that faith is mostly a matter of propositional belief, or that this is what is most important about it. I only think that it is *an* important component and is intimately related to the rest.

take account of them in her continuing reflection on, and possible modifications of, her belief system.[6]

So I will scrutinize claims by historical scholars to have established conclusions that have a negative bearing on Gospel accounts of resurrection appearances. But how will I select from the legion of such claims? First, I locate the discussion within the context of certain agreements. I will confine myself to scholars who accept some kind of continuance of life on the part of Jesus after death and burial (not necessarily life as an embodied human being) and who agree that in this post-resurrection period Jesus in some way 'appeared' or 'manifested' himself to his disciples. That restricts the territory to those who agree not only that after the crucifixion something momentous happened to the disciples but also that something momentous happened to Jesus. Moreover, it restricts the discussion to those who take resurrection 'appearances' to involve some kind of awareness of a real presence of a living Jesus, as contrasted with a view according to which the 'appearances' were merely 'subjective visions', states of consciousness that were wholly within the mind of the disciples and that involved no cognitive contact with Jesus as a distinct living person.[7] Hence I will not spend time on such views as that the whole resurrection business was deliberately fabricated by the disciples or the early Church, or that the disciples were subject to some mass hallucination or delusion, or that Jesus rose from the dead only in the sense that the movement he initiated lived on after him or in the sense that the memory of his life, work, and personality was so strong that it was as if he was still actually present to his followers, or . . .[8]

Within the territory so delimited I will focus on recent studies that seriously address themselves to the historical accuracy of the Gospel accounts, treatments that employ such techniques as form criticism,

[6] Even though my approach to the problem is in terms of the assumptions just laid out, I do not think that my conclusions are relevant only against that background. If I am right in the criticisms I develop in this paper, it follows that certain negative conclusions of certain biblical scholars are inadequately supported. And that conclusion would stand whether or not I am right about what hangs on the results of historical research.

[7] Note that a thinker could pass my first requirement for admission but not the second: i.e. he could believe that Jesus became alive again after death and burial but deny that the 'appearances' to the disciples involved any genuine interaction with Jesus. I don't mean to suggest that this would be a reasonable combination.

[8] Needless to say, all this would have to be considered in a comprehensive discussion of the topic.

redaction criticism, and attempts to reconstruct the history of the
tradition behind a certain Gospel passage. Further, my targets will
be taken from what I consider the best and strongest examples that
meet these conditions.

There is still the question of how much of the Gospel accounts a
writer must reject in order to be eligible for consideration here. It
will not be enough to deny that the Gospel accounts are accurate
in every detail; that is obvious from the important discrepancies
between them. On the other hand, I do not want to restrict myself
to those who reject the accounts completely. I could just say that I
will consider accounts that deny *important* or *fundamental* features
of the accounts, leaving it unspecified just what that amounts to.
But I will give the essay a more specific focus by concentrating on
the question of a *bodily* resurrection. The Gospels that contain
appearance narratives, at least Luke and John,[9] are insistent that
Jesus appeared in a human body that was visible and tangible, even
though not in all respects like a normal human body. Since this is
such a prominent theme in those Gospels, and since there are excellent studies that deny the historicity of this feature, I will make this
a unifying thread for the discussion. Do the considerations adduced
by my authors suffice to show that Jesus did not appear to the disciples in bodily form, or at least that this is very unlikely, or that it
is unreasonable to suppose this to have been the case?

In embarking on this task, I presuppose that the evangelists, in
their narratives, intend to be providing factually accurate information, which is something that scholars often *seem* to deny. In some
cases they actually do so. For example, it is alleged by some that the
evangelists made no distinction between what was said or done by
the historical Jesus and what was spoken or done in his name by
inspired prophets in the early Church.[10] Again, it is held that their
narratives were simply *expressions* of their faith, or the faith of the
Church, rather than factual claims.[11] But more often scholars make
other points that are mistakenly taken by themselves or others to
imply the denial of my presupposition. Thus it is often said (1) that
the *ultimate* aim of the Gospels is to induce faith in Jesus as Christ

---

[9] I will briefly consider below where Matthew stands on this.

[10] See e.g. N. Perrin, *Rediscovering the Teaching of Jesus* (New York: Harper & Row,
1967), 26–7.

[11] See e.g. W. Marxsen, *The Resurrection of Jesus of Nazareth* (Philadelphia:
Fortress, 1970).

or Lord; (2) that the evangelists did not approach their task with the modern historian's critical attitude toward evidence; (3) that they were not bothered by minor discrepancies in details, either within a single Gospel or between their work and other Gospels, with which, presumably, they were acquainted; (4) that some of the differences between the Gospels indicate that each author was shaping the account in terms of his own theological perspective [and also with a view to the community for whom they were writing—eds.], and (5) that in reported speech there is no attempt to give the exact words but only the sense of what was said. But none of these implies that the evangelists were not concerned to provide accounts that, at least in the main, were factually accurate. As for (1), it is certainly a distinct possibility (I would say, an overwhelming probability) that they sought to induce faith by, *inter alia*, telling people about certain things that actually happened. As for (2), one obviously doesn't have to possess the sophisticated methodology of the modern historian to have as one's aim an accurate narration of events. As for (3), one can be more or less careless with details and still attempt to give an account that is correct in the main. As for (4), one can give a certain theological 'spin' to one's version without abandoning the aim at faithfulness to the facts as to what was done, undergone, or said. And as for (5), one can aim for accuracy as to *what was said*, rather than as to *the words in which it was said*.

The foregoing undoubtedly gives the impression that I will now proceed to discuss several studies that meet my conditions. And that is the aim of a larger work for which this is a pilot project. But, rather than either inflating this chapter intolerably or giving superficial treatment to several authors, I will, here and now, concentrate on one book, Reginald Fuller's *The Formation of the Resurrection Narratives*, with some side comments on other works. I pick Fuller because his book is the richest in detail. He brings a greater variety of considerations to bear on the problems than any other important treatment with which I am familiar. Furthermore, he is an admirably clear writer. One can (usually) tell exactly what he is suggesting and just what his reasons are for the positions he takes.

It may be a useful propaedeutic to issue a few animadversions on some currently popular convictions and attitudes that are relevant to the issues I will be discussing.

First, the resurrection is not a 'historical' event because it is 'eschatological' and therefore comes at the 'end of history'.[12] And because of the latter, it cannot strictly be dated, whether on the 'third day' or otherwise; it is not in time.[13] I can recognize several senses in which the resurrection is eschatological: it involves transforming Jesus into a different sphere or mode of existence; it constitutes in some sense the realization of eschatological expectations; and so on. But in whatever sense it is eschatological, that sense had better be compatible with Jesus still existing and acting *in time*, doing things at particular times. Unless we are to dispense with appearances altogether, these took place at particular times on particular 'datable' days. Just to mention the most heavily documented one, Jesus appeared to Paul during a journey Paul was making on a particular day. Again, the resurrection itself—the transition of Jesus from death to new life—is not described in any of the canonical Gospels. But that is not because it is intrinsically undatable. If Jesus was dead on Good Friday afternoon and alive at some time later, there must have been some moment at which the transition took place.

Second, intimately related to this talk of the 'transcendence of history' is the view that there is no literal, straightforward way of describing the risen Lord and his appearances because he has transcended the categories of space and time. As a result, we are forced to use metaphorical, symbolic language, and we cannot form any clear notion of the subject-matter.[14] But, in the first place, the claim of transcendence of space begs the question against the evangelists who report corporeal visible appearances. If one has succeeded in discrediting those reports, one may opt for a non-spatial mode of being for the Risen One, but it won't do to assume this *before* assessing the appearance accounts in Luke and John. And as for transcendence of time, the above remarks apply here as well.[15]

Third, historical research can take us only to the earliest records or earliest stage of tradition. It cannot tell us anything about what

[12] Reginald Fuller, *The Formation of the Resurrection Narratives*, (New York: Macmillan, 1971), 22.

[13] Ibid. 23.

[14] See e.g. R. Brown, *The Virginal Conception and Bodily Resurrection of Jesus* (New York: Paulist, 1973), 73, 89, 92, 106, 125.

[15] I, of course, do not deny that the resurrection and the risen Christ, like everything else, are often spoken of metaphorically. I only deny that they can only be spoken of metaphorically *because* of the lack of location in space or time. For that matter, if I were to go into this matter thoroughly, I would argue that we are not restricted to metaphor in speaking of what transcends space and time.

lies behind that, what 'actually happened', whether the earliest records were correct.[16] The historian can discover only what certain persons believed about what happened to Jesus after his death, not what did happen to him.[17] I can't see that there is much to be said for this. First, there is the question of whether the judgement is supposed to apply to history generally or only to those situations where there is a paucity of evidence.[18] The former alternative, besides being absurd on the face of it, runs strongly counter to the practice of historians, who regularly purport to inform us as to what happened at particular times and places. Surely we know, by reasonable standards for knowledge, that Napoleon was defeated at the Battle of Waterloo, not just that many people at various times believed that he was. The weaker claim that where evidence is very scanty we can't check our sources well enough to draw solidly grounded conclusions as to what in fact happened is much more reasonable. But that leaves us with the question of whether we are in that situation with respect to this or that report in the Gospels. And that has to be determined by detailed investigation of the relevant details, not by sweeping statements as to what is in principle possible for historical research.

II

I now turn to the parts of Fuller's book that bear on my chosen theme. It will be useful to have before us at the outset a statement of his position. Fortunately Fuller provides a summary at the end of the book. It is too long to reproduce in full, but here is a summary of the summary:

At the earliest stage of the tradition the appearances were not *narrated*; rather, the resurrection was *proclaimed* in the language of Jewish apocalyptic. To this Paul added in 1 Corinthians 15: 3–8 a list of persons and groups to whom the risen Jesus had appeared, including, at the end of the list, himself. Since the appearance to Paul is the only one of which we have a first-hand report, since Paul considers it as the same general sort of thing

---

[16] This view is so widespread as to need no specific documentation. For statements by two authors discussed in this paper see Fuller, *Formation of Resurrection Narratives*, 7, and Marxsen, *Resurrection of Jesus of Nazareth*, 115–17.

[17] See e.g. Marxsen, *Resurrection of Jesus of Nazareth*, 119.

[18] Marxsen, e.g. says things that make it sound like a generalized comment on the limits of history.

as the others, and since his was an experience of light and/or the hearing of a voice, rather than an encounter with a humanly embodied person, we can assume that the other appearances were of this same general sort. Paul says nothing of an empty tomb, but since he was thinking of the resurrection as a transformation of Jesus' body into a new mode of existence, this would be incompatible with that body decaying in the tomb. The empty tomb story goes back a long way in the tradition, and, though variously redacted in the Gospels, it presumably has a factually correct core.

The appearance narratives would seem to be a late development, expanding the Pauline list by attaching stories to them, and, in the process, 'materializing' the risen Jesus, endowing him with an abnormal but visible and tangible human body. There is no reason to accept these details as factually accurate, but we can see various significant features of the disciples' interactions with the risen One peeping through these narratives. Finally, there is no reason to suppose that the resurrection and the ascension were separated temporally, as Luke would have it. It fits the evidence better to suppose that the resurrection involved a direct translation of Jesus from the grave to an exalted and glorified existence, which he continues to enjoy to this day and for ever.[19]

Thus Fuller is a long way from those who would reject the objectivity and 'historicity' of the resurrection. He accepts and defends the conviction that Jesus was restored to life from the grave, that this is of fundamental importance to the Christian life and human destiny, and that Jesus thereby enjoyed the kind of exalted and transformed life that is expressed by saying 'He is sitting at the right hand of the Father'. On the other hand, he forthrightly rejects the picture presented by Luke and John of a visible, tangible, *humanly* (though atypically) *corporeal* risen Jesus. (And that rejection includes anything like literal speech of the Risen One to the disciples and apostles.) It is this rejection on which I wish to concentrate.[20] I will look at what Fuller does to support the rejection of a corporeal resurrection and determine how strong that support is. Since his argument is long, complex, and multi-faceted, I will not be able to discuss everything, but will comment on what I take to be his most important points.

I will discuss three subdivisions of Fuller's overall argument: (1) the relation of the Pauline 'tradition' reported in 1 Corinthians 15 to the Gospel appearance narratives, (2) the idea that the post-

---

[19] Summary of Fuller, *Formation of Resurrection Narratives*, 168–82.

[20] A longer treatment would bring in the empty tomb stories as well, but I will have to forgo that here.

resurrection Jesus enjoyed an 'exalted' status from ground zero and hence was not even quasi-humanly embodied, and (3) the analysis of details of the Gospel narratives.

III

1 Corinthians 15: 3–8 may be taken as our earliest surviving testimony to the resurrection, assuming that it was written around 53–4.[21]

[3]For I delivered to you as of first importance what I in turn had received; that Christ died for our sins in accordance with the scriptures, [4]that he was buried, that he was raised on the third day in accordance with scriptures, [5]and that he appeared to Cephas, then to the twelve. [6]Then he appeared to more than five hundred brethren at one time, most of whom are still alive, though some have fallen asleep. [7]Then he appeared to James, then to all the apostles. [8]Last of all, as to one untimely born, he appeared also to me.[22]

Fuller subjects this passage to minute analysis, entering into a variety of issues. Suffice it to say that he provides good reason for supposing that 3b–6a and 7 constitute very early tradition that Paul had received. What concern me are the implications Fuller draws from this passage, in the context of the rest of the Pauline material, for the assessment of the appearance narratives in the Gospels.

1. On Fuller's analysis of the Pauline texts concerning the resurrected state, particularly 1 Corinthians 15: 35–54, 2 Corinthians 5: 1–5, and Philippians 3: 21, Paul thought of the resurrection body as continuous with the body of this life, not a replacement, but also not just the same but rather the original body transformed into a new and more glorious mode of existence (pp. 17–22). Fuller, like many others, belabours the view that Jesus' resurrection was a mere 'resuscitation of a corpse', restoring it to the same kind of life it previously enjoyed, as in the raising of Lazarus.[23] The bearing of

---

[21] In this essay I will accept the most commonly received dating of NT writings, which is assumed by Fuller, even though I do not consider the matter to be definitively settled with respect to the Gospels, and even though it is still a topic of lively controversy.

[22] Biblical quotations are from the RSV.

[23] Davis, in his chapter in this volume, says that he has been unable to find any proponent of a pure resuscitation view. Since I have been similarly unsuccessful, I will join him in ignoring that issue.

this on the Gospel narratives depends on further details about this 'glorified, exalted body' and what implications this has for *corporeality, visibility,* and *tangibility.* I will go into that later.

2. Fuller wrests a great deal from the list of appearances. He takes the appearances to Cephas and the twelve as 'church founding appearances', the foundation of the 'eschatological community' (p. 35).[24] The appearance to 500 brethren is construed as the 'first-fruits of the church-founding function of Peter and the twelve' (p. 36). Fuller then makes the not unreasonable assumption that the disciples fled back to Galilee after the crucifixion. He cites in this connection the message to the women at the empty tomb from the 'young man' in Mark 16: 7 (taken by Fuller to be the next oldest text after the Pauline epistles), 'But go, tell his disciples and Peter that he is going before you to Galilee; there you will see him, as he told you.' On this basis Fuller takes these 'church founding' appearances to have occurred in Galilee, and the actual carrying out of the commission to begin after a return to Jerusalem. As for the appearances to James and all the 'apostles', Fuller picks up certain hints in Galatians and Acts concerning Paul's second visit to Jerusalem for the so-called apostolic conference, hints to the effect that James took the lead in launching wider missionary activities. Thus Fuller takes these appearances to be 'mission inaugurating' and to have occurred in Jerusalem.

Later we will see how Fuller uses these suppositions in his analysis of the Gospel accounts. My present point is that they rest on the slenderest of evidence. It is arbitrary in the extreme to derive conclusions as to the content and significance of these appearances from such indications as those just cited. If these hypotheses came into conflict with Gospel narratives, as they do with Luke and John placing the 'church founding' appearances in Jerusalem, that does not give us much reason to oppose the evangelists' testimony.[25]

---

[24] One point he relies on here is the relation of 'twelve' (remember that according to the Gospels there were only eleven of the original twelve disciples available at this point) to the twelve tribes of Israel and words in Matt. 19: 28: 'You will also sit on twelve thrones, judging the twelve tribes of Israel.'

[25] Marxsen (*Resurrection of Jesus of Nazareth*) reads even more into the Pauline data. He advances the startling hypothesis that the resurrection faith (faith that Jesus is still alive and active) of all the disciples (and by extension of all Christians) stems from Peter's faith, which in turn, we are told, stemmed from an 'appearance' of the risen Jesus to Peter. (For Marxsen the faith of the early Church is the basic

3. How did Paul understand 'appeared' in this passage? Was he thinking of it as an appearance in bodily form to the senses, as in Luke and John? And if not, then what? The Greek word here, *ophthe*, can have various meanings; but Fuller connects these occurrences with its use in the Septuagint to report divine revelatory manifestations, frequently involving verbal communication.

[T]he questions as to how they [the human recipients] see, whether with the physical eye or with the eye of the mind or the spirit, is left entirely undetermined and unemphasized. . . . What is seen and heard can only be described as 'revelation'. These are disclosures not of something which is visible or discernible within this world or age by ordinary sight or insight. . . . It is in such a context that we must place the *ophthe* of 1 Corinthians

resurrection datum for the historian.) This leaves him free to take the following approach. Rather than try to find historically sound answers to questions about the other appearances Paul mentions (as Fuller and many other scholars do), he turns instead to the question of why all these people and groups were mentioned in this connection (p. 91). His answer is that the point of doing so is to drive home the point that the faith of all these persons and groups in the Church was based on the first appearance to Peter! (p. 92). He is careful to disavow any intention to deny that there were further appearances beyond that to Peter, though he takes it to be quite uncertain whether there were. But he holds that the intention of the formula we find in Paul 'is to trace back the later functions and the later faith of the church, as well as the later leadership of James to the one single root' (p. 95): viz. the appearance to Peter and his consequent faith. If we ask what evidence he has for this astounding thesis, it boils down to Luke's report that those returning from the Emmaus journey were told 'The Lord has risen indeed, and has appeared to Simon' (24: 34). Marxsen takes this to indicate that the rest of the disciples believed that Jesus was alive just on the testimony of Peter without Jesus' having appeared to them. The only other reason he gives is that it is inconceivable that Peter did not tell the others of the initial appearance to him (p. 89), but then he has to appeal to Luke again for evidence that this was enough to lead them to faith. It seems extraordinary to me that Marxsen would base such a wild hypothesis on such slender evidence. He thinks that we can set aside the clear testimony of Paul (and his sources) that there were all these appearances, not to mention the Gospel accounts, on the basis of this tenuous argument. It is also paradoxical that the argument depends heavily on the account of Luke, although in other connections Marxsen gives scant credit to that account. (It is true that at one point in this very discussion he says: 'All we can say about Luke 24: 34 is that *according to Luke's Gospel itself* the disciples believed before Jesus had appeared to them. Whether this was actually the case we are not yet in a position to say.' But since he never gives any further reason for his hypothesis, without trusting Luke on this point, his argument that we can explain all the data on the basis of one appearance to Peter collapses.) Here is a historical scholar who is in the forefront of those who are leery in crediting the Gospel accounts with historical accuracy, uncritically taking one bit of testimony from such an account and using it to reject (or call into question) what is, by common consent, the most solid testimony we have of appearances of the risen Jesus. (I should add that this aspect of Marxsen's book is not typical of the whole, which contains much fascinating and much sound discussion.)

15: 5–7 (cf. Luke 24: 34; Acts 13: 31, 9: 17; 26: 16). They designated not necessarily physical seeing . . . but a revelatory self-disclosure or disclosure by God of the eschatologically resurrected Christos. (pp. 30–1)

On this reading, as the last sentence indicates, *ophthe* does not rule out physical seeing, but it is not restricted to it. Fuller tries to be more definite by taking Paul's experience, as narrated by himself in Galatians and by Luke at three points in Acts, as a model for understanding the appearances generally. 'Here we have a first-hand statement by one who himself was a recipient of an appearance, deliberately placed by him in the series of appearances. What we know of Paul's appearances . . . can be applied . . . to the interpretation of the earlier appearances' (p. 43).[26] This approach is rendered less straightforward than it would be otherwise by the differences in the accounts in Galatians and Acts. But Fuller, reasonably enough, suggests that 'All three accounts [in Acts], therefore agree that in the Damascus road encounter there was a visionary element and an auditory element, and that the inner meaning of the encounter was apprehended by Paul alone. It would be safe to infer that these three common elements are pre-Lukan, not redactional' (p. 46). He then proceeds to generalize to all the appearances:

Such appearances, we may conclude, involved visionary experiences of light, combined with a communication of meaning. They were not in their innermost essence incidents open to neutral observance or verification, but revelatory events in which the eschatological and christological significance of Jesus was disclosed, and in which the recipient was called to a particular function in salvation history. (p. 48)

If all the appearances were like Paul's Damascus Road experience in these respects, then the Gospel stories of encounters with a risen Jesus who possesses a visible and tangible quasi-human body are seriously misleading. But, in my judgement, Fuller's argument for this generalization of the Pauline pattern is extremely weak. Why suppose that Paul's putting his own experience in the same *list* as the others indicates that he took their experiences to be similar in

---

[26] Peter Carnley (*The Structure of Resurrection Belief* (Oxford: Clarendon, 1987), 238–9), along with various scholars, also asserts that Paul's placing the appearance to him in the same list with the others implies that the other appearances were very much like his. O'Collins (*Resurrection of Jesus Christ* (Valley Forge, Pa.: Judson Press, 1973)), on the other hand, dissents (p. 35), as does Davis in his chapter in this volume.

these respects to his?[27] Why isn't it at least as reasonable to think that he was prepared to recognize that the appearances took a variety of forms?[28] After all, his was much later. It would not be unreasonable for him to think it natural that corporeal appearances were limited to the immediate post-resurrection period, whereas at his late date the risen Christ would naturally appear in a different mode, since his situation was different. At least Fuller has given us no reason to prefer his supposition to that one.[29]

4. Finally, Fuller infers from the absence of any appearance narratives in Paul's report of the tradition, that there were no narratives current at that time. He makes a similar inference from the absence of such narratives in Mark (and in Matthew, assuming that Matthew pre-dates Luke and John). Speaking of the various attempts to account for the mysterious way in which Mark's Gospel breaks off (taking 16: 9-20 to be a later addition), Fuller writes:

All these hypotheses assume that Mark had appearance stories at his disposal. . . . It is this assumption that ought to be questioned . . . the earliest church did not narrate resurrection appearances, but proclaimed the resurrection. Paul adds to this proclamation a list of appearances. . . . But there is nothing to indicate at the time of the origin of these primitive formulae that appearances *stories* were actually in circulation. . . . (p. 66)

Since the earlier strata of the New Testament have no narratives of appearances, it does not seem necessary for Christian faith to believe in the literal veracity of any of these particular accounts [in Luke and John]. (p. 178)

This is a massive *argumentum ex silentio*. There are no resurrection narratives in Pauline letters. Therefore, there were no such narratives in circulation at that time. But why suppose that Paul includes everything that was currently in the Church tradition in his extant letters (or in all his letters for that matter)? The letters were written

---

[27] There is also the question of whether Paul was correct in doing so. But since Paul was certainly in contact with some of the recipients of the appearances, and perhaps with most, he was in a position to know something about the matter.

[28] Carnley, *Structure of Resurrection Belief*, 240-1, dismisses the idea that the appearances to the disciples and apostles might have taken quite different forms, but he gives no reason for this judgement.

[29] Fuller might also say that Paul gives no indication that he takes the appearances to be of fundamentally different types. But he gives no indication of the contrary either. As I shall have repeated occasion to point out, the argument from silence is a very frail one, especially when applied to letters dealing with specific current problems. In that context Paul had no time to go into many questions that interest later historical scholars.

to address specific problems of the churches to which they were addressed. Admittedly this leads Paul into quite a bit of theological development, but it does not lead him into story-telling about *any* phase of Jesus' life, death, *or* post-resurrection doings. It is a familiar crux of New Testament study that Paul virtually never has anything to say about details of Jesus' life and ministry, the most notable exception being the Last Supper (1 Cor. 11: 23–5). Are we to infer from this that there were no stories of Jesus' life, ministry, and passion in circulation at the time? Why, then, single out appearance narratives for special treatment? The absence of such narrations in the Pauline letters is easily explained on other grounds. Paul was writing to people who presumably were well acquainted with such stories about Jesus as were in circulation. Why should he weigh down his letters by repeating all this, especially since his purpose was to respond to particular problems faced by his addressees. We can infer nothing about the presence or absence of appearance narratives in the earliest tradition from their absence in the Pauline corpus.[30]

Mark is a different matter. We can hardly claim that Mark was not in the business of narration! Therefore, it is not wholly unreasonable for Fuller to take the lack of appearance narratives there to indicate their unavailability. But still the matter is hardly clear. I find it extremely difficult to believe that the author intended to end his Gospel at 16: 8. In my view, this is no way to end a story. The young man in the empty tomb enjoins the women to tell his disciples that he is going before them to Galilee where they will see him. But they said nothing to anyone, for they were afraid. That's it! If we came across a secular story from, say, the Middle Ages, our oldest manuscripts of which ended like that, we would feel sure that the ending had been lost somehow or that the author had died before finishing it, like Puccini with *Turandot*, or for some reason had abandoned it or been prevented from finishing it. In addition,

---

[30] It is interesting to elaborate imaginary analogues of this line of argument. Suppose that some future historian is interested in the doings of the Marquis de Sade. He has various accounts, the earliest of which date from forty years after Sade's death. He also has ten letters of a French nobleman from the early nineteenth century, letters that make no mention of Sade. Can he infer from this that no stories of Sade's notorious doings were current in the nineteenth century? That would be a most precarious inference unless we can assume that whenever anyone wrote a letter (or at least ten letters), it would be likely that he or she would mention Sade if Sade were known to him or her.

the last sentence ends with the conjunction *gar* ('for'), and as I understand from Fuller (p. 65), there is no other example of a book ending with 'gar'. There are various ingenious attempts to explain why Mark would deliberately end the book this way, such as Perrin's suggestion that Mark was simply continuing this theme of the utter failure of the disciples to keep the faith![31] But it seems clear to me that the most reasonable hypothesis is that either Mark was prevented from finishing the book or that the end has been lost. In any event, the attractiveness of that explanation prevents us from taking the absence of appearance narratives to show that none were in the tradition at that time.

A similar point is to be made about Fuller's treatment of the final scene in Matthew, which he denies is an 'appearance narrative'.

Nothing is said of the form in which the Lord appeared, nothing is said of his disappearance in the end. There are no *theios aner* (divine man) traits. The scene is an artificial theologoumenon, constructed on the basis of the primitive statement that the disciples 'saw' the Lord. Matthew has no *narrative* of this appearance at his disposal, presumably because at this time no such narrative existed. (p. 91)

True it's not much of a narrative. It's not a strong candidate for a Pulitzer prize. But it certainly goes significantly beyond just saying 'he appeared to them'. They worshiped him, but some doubted. We are told what the physical setting was (a mountain in Galilee) and what Jesus said to them. But even if it isn't a full-fledged narrative, once again we cannot infer from this that no such narratives were available. Why suppose that each evangelist made use of everything available to him? If, as is usually supposed, Matthew and Luke made use of Mark, they didn't use everything that was available to them from that source. Why suppose they made use of everything available to them from other sources?

IV

A second component of Fuller's argument involves the claim that there is an incompatibility between the resurrected Jesus' 'exalted',

---

[31] N. Perrin, *The Resurrection According to Matthew, Mark, and Luke* (Philadelphia: Fortress, 1977), 30–1.

'glorified', 'transcendent', 'eschatological', or 'heavenly' status, and his appearances in bodily form. Here is a summary statement:

Actual narratives of the appearances are found only in the later Gospel strata. They are just beginning in Matthew and one is found in a still some-what early form in John 20: 15 ff. The appearances on the mountain in Galilee in Matthew 28 and by the lakeside in John 21 still depict a revela-tion of One risen and exalted into a transcendental mode for existence. . . . In the latest strata, Luke 24 and John 20, the narratives had developed from revelatory encounters with the transcendent Risen One into appear-ances of the Risen One in the early form of a divine man. At this stage, traits of the more supernaturalized presentations of the earthly Jesus in the later Hellenized Gospel tradition are transferred to the resurrection narra-tives. . . . But something of the earlier sense that the Risen One appears as a transcendent being still remains.

In the light of this history of the tradition, what is essential for Christian faith in the resurrection to believe today? . . . The Christian cannot be required to believe that the Risen One literally walked on earth in an earthly form as in the Emmaus story, or that he physically ate fish as in the Lukan appearance to the disciples at Jerusalem, or that he invited phys-ical touch as in the Thomas story. There are two reasons why this should be so. First, not only do the earlier accounts know nothing of these features, but the resurrection faith of the earliest community, conceived in apoca-lyptic terms as a transformation into an entirely new (eschatological) mode of existence, directly contradicts it. Second, the Evangelists are here taking up popular stories, forged in the milieu of the 'divine man' concept, and using them for purposes of their own. What the believer must listen to is therefore the purpose and intention of the Evangelists in using these stor-ies. They used them not simply to relate past events (though they doubtless assumed that the reports were historically correct), but in order to assert, e.g. the identity-in-transformation between the earthly and the Risen Jesus. (pp. 171-3)

Leaving aside questions as to what Christians are required to believe, the argument here goes as follows:

(1) The earliest community construed the resurrection in terms of a trans-formation into a transcendent, eschatological mode of existence.
(2) The appearance narratives in Luke and John, in terms of a risen Jesus in human form, contradict this.
(3) We can explain these later versions in ways that give these features of them no historical value.

I will deal with the third point in the next section when I look at aspects of Fuller's detailed treatment of these narratives. I have no wish to dispute the first. So my criticism will be directed to the second.[32]

In order to discuss the question of incompatibility, we must be more specific both as to what an 'exalted' or 'heavenly' mode of existence involves, and as to how to understand the Lucan and Johannine 'bodily' representations of the risen Jesus.

As for the former, the first thing to note is that these concepts of exaltation and glorification will differ depending on the Christology (and theology) of the user. They will mean something different to John with his pre-existent Logos Christology than to those with a more adoptionist outlook. But that is a large subject, and I will try to say something useful without getting into it. New Testament writers would seem to take at least the following as marks of exaltation: (a) Divine authority (whether derived or inherent). Thus Fuller writes that since Jesus says in the final scene of Matthew that all authority has been given to him, he is speaking as the Exalted One. The same point is involved in John's report that he endowed the disciples with the Holy Spirit by breathing on them (20: 22) and that he authorized them to forgive sins (20: 23). And the evangelical commission reported by Luke (24: 47) could be construed as presupposing such an authority. (b) A presence that seems transcendent, numinous, or full of mystery. This is evidenced by the

---

[32] Fuller's assumption of this incompatibility comes out clearly in his treatment of the final scene in Matthew. He says that Jesus' speech in the final scene 'is here placed in the mouth of the Exalted One, not of the earthly Jesus' (p. 90). It is certainly reasonable to say that Jesus appears as the 'Exalted One', since he says 'All authority in heaven and on earth has been given to me'. But what about the contrast with 'the earthly Jesus'? The saying is not represented as coming from the pre-crucifixion Jesus, if that is what is meant by the 'earthly Jesus'. But, clearly, what Fuller intends by that phrase is a 'corporeal' Jesus. And it is not clear that Matthew didn't intend this. We are properly cautioned not to read Matthew here in the light of the appearance narratives of Luke and John, where the Risen One is clearly represented as embodied in a human way. But, sticking to the Matthean text, why suppose that Matthew means to represent Jesus as incorporeal? I would say that the passage is non-committal on this, and can be interpreted either way. I can only conclude that Fuller reads the appearance as incorporeal because of his assumption that a corporeal appearance would be incompatible with exaltation. For other allegations of such an incompatibility see Pheme Perkins, *Resurrection: New Testament Witness and Contemporary Reflection* (Garden City, NY: Doubleday, 1984), 20–1 and elsewhere; Carnley, *Structure of Resurrection Belief*, 72–81; O'Collins, *Resurrection of Jesus Christ*, 83–4. Brown, on the other hand, points out that one could hold that there was 'a corporeal resurrection in which the risen body is transformed to the eschatological sphere' (*Virginal Conception*, 85). See also Stephen Davis's chapter in this volume, pp. 132–4, 139–40, 141–4.

reactions of awe, fear, and trembling that his presence evokes (Luke 24: 37; Matt. 28: 10, John 21: 12). This feature is particularly evident in the appearance to Paul on the Damascus Road.

Before continuing with the discussion of the incompatibility thesis, point 2 above, let me say a bit about my indisposition to quarrel with point 1. The marks of exalted status I have just sketched are clearly present in the Gospel pictures of the immediate post-resurrection Jesus. I don't see that anything in Fuller's book shows that the very earliest tradition thinks of the resurrection in this way; but there are indications of this that other writers mention. There are various passages, some of them with a presumably early provenance, that speak of an exaltation or glorification of Jesus. Here is one from Paul's letter to the Philippians, a passage usually supposed to be from an early Christian hymn.

[H]e humbled himself and became obedient unto death, even death on a cross. Therefore God has highly exalted him and bestowed on him the name which is above every name, that at the name of Jesus every knee should bow, in heaven and on earth and under the earth, and every tongue confess that Jesus Christ is Lord, to the glory of God the Father. (2: 8–11)

Another supposed hymn fragment comes from 1 Timothy 3: 16:

> He was manifested in the flesh,
> vindicated in the Spirit,
>   seen by angels,
> preached among the nations,
> believed on in the world,
>   taken up in glory.[33]

This is, indeed, evidence for an early construal of resurrection in terms of heavenly exaltation. But these passages have also been used to support Fuller's claim that a conception of bodily resurrection was absent in the earliest tradition. And here the argument creaks. Let us suppose that the quoted bits from Philippians and 1 Timothy are indeed fragments of early Christian hymns. Then the argument is that the fact that these passages make no mention of a bodily appearance of the risen Jesus indicates that the earliest tradition contained no such belief. But this is another extremely shaky

---

[33] Marxsen mentions these passages (*Resurrection of Jesus of Nazareth*, 144–7), though for a different purpose—to show that in the NT 'being risen' is not the only way to 'express' the faith that Jesus is still alive and active.

argumentum ex silentio. For one thing, we should not forget that we have, at most, only a bit of each hymn. But even if we had the whole of both of them, why should we suppose that the author(s) included in their hymns everything that was currently believed about Jesus' post-resurrection career? It is hardly common practice for hymn writers to 'tell all'. The Christmas hymn, 'Of the Father's Love Begotten' says nothing of Bethlehem, or the manger, or the shepherds. Can we infer from this that the author, Marcus Aurelius Clemens Prudentius, had never heard of these things, that he had never read the Gospel of Luke? And so it is with hymns generally.

To return to the main line of the argument, how should we understand the appearances' 'incorporated form' in the Gospels of Luke and John. In both Gospels Jesus makes a point of insisting that he is not a 'spirit', that he 'has hands and feet', 'flesh and bones' (Luke 24: 39–40). He eats fish before them (Luke 24: 42).[34] John 20 has him show the disciples his hands and his side and, in the second appearance, he invites Thomas to put his hand in his (Jesus') side. Clearly the corporeality is not represented as an optical (and tangible) illusion, an hallucination that Jesus produces to reassure the disciples. The body is represented as *his* body. Luke has him say 'See my hands and my feet, that *it is I myself*' (24: 39; my emphasis). So as Luke and John represent the matter, Jesus *at that stage* exists in a humanly embodied form. To be sure, this is no ordinary human body. He mysteriously disappears from sight after the meal with the travellers to Emmaus (Luke 24: 31). He appears out of thin air (Luke 24: 36) as well as disappearing into it (Luke 24: 31). He suddenly appears among them in a locked room (John 20: 19). Even at this stage, on these accounts, his body has at least been transformed in certain respects.

With this background I am ready to tackle Fuller's claim of incompatibility. Why should we suppose that an exalted, heavenly Jesus would not (could not?) appear to his disciples in corporeal form? Luke and John obviously don't think so, since, as I have already pointed out, they both, and especially John, combine an emphasis on corporeality with an emphasis on divine authority and numinosity. Indeed, these features of exaltation are also present in the Gospel accounts of Jesus' earthly ministry when he is obviously

---

[34] Although in John 21 he is not explicitly reported as eating, the impression is that he ate breakfast with the disciples.

embodied.[35] For example, Jesus is not infrequently depicted as presuming to forgive sins; the reaction to this clearly shows that it is
taken by some of his auditors to involve a claim to exalted status.
The Gospel of John is loaded with claims to speak the words of the
Father, to be in or with the Father, to have come from the Father,
and so on.[36] But, leaving aside the way the evangelists think about
the matter, let us consider the question on its own merits and decide
what we should think about the relationship. Is an exalted status
compatible with being (at least temporarily[37]) embodied in the ways
Luke and John depict. Well, why not? What is there about exaltation that rules this out? No doubt, it seems more congenial to think
of divine authority and transcendence as attaching to a being that
is not even pro tem in such a lowly form as a quasi-human body.
To think otherwise would seem to accord too much dignity to ourselves. At least, that is the way it seems if we do not take the doctrine of the incarnation seriously. But if we do take it seriously, that
entails a radical revision of our thought on these matters. It is a
major theme of the incarnation that, strange as it may seem, it is
not incompatible with the highest possible divine status to take on
embodied human form. Indeed, it is a familiar theme of Christian
theology (more familiar in the East than in the West) that God
greatly raised humanity in status (exalted it? glorified it?) by deign-
ing to become a human being in all respects except sin. 'For he was
made man that we might be made God' (Athanasius).[38] Statements
like this presuppose a continuing influence of God on us that we
might realize this possibility. That influence is provided by the Holy
Spirit. Aquinas speaks of the 'light of grace' as 'a participation in
the divine nature'.[39] Or, as 2 Peter has it, 'His divine power has

---

[35] Fuller would reject this consideration since, as we have already seen, he takes
features of the Gospel accounts of the pre-crucifixion ministry that are similar to the
post-resurrection appearances in Luke and John to themselves stem from the 'later
Hellenized Gospel tradition', and hence to have no historical value as accounts of the
pre-crucifixion period.

[36] To be sure, as far as John is concerned, the scholarly consensus is that much
of this is read into the record by the evangelist, rather than being a historically faithful portrait of the earthly ministry of Jesus. But my present point is only that Luke
and John do not take a heavenly authority and status to be incompatible with
human embodiment.

[37] If Jesus was quasi-humanly embodied immediately after the resurrection, must
we suppose that he continues in this state through all succeeding time (or in eternity)? I will have a bit to say about that question in a moment.

[38] *De Incarnatione*, 54, NPNF, 2nd ser., 4, 65.   [39] *ST* Ia. 2ae. 110. 3.

granted to us all things that pertain to life and godliness, through the knowledge of him who called us to his own glory and excellence, by which he has granted to us his previous and very great promises, that through these you may escape from the corruption that is in the world because of passion, and become partakers of the divine nature' (1: 3–4). Another expression of this is the notion of being 'born again', which is often understood not merely as adoption by God, but as an actual sharing in the divine nature. As Aquinas wrote, 'Adoptive sonship is really a shared likeness of the eternal sonship of the Word.'[40] Though this quasi-divinization of human nature through the incarnation is a not unfamiliar theme in Christian theology, New Testament scholars seem to forget it when they assume that it would be unworthy, unfitting, or otherwise inappropriate for an exalted Jesus to appear to his disciples in human form.

Here is another perspective on this matter from Christian theology. The corporeality of the risen Christ is not confined to the immediate post-resurrection encounters with the disciples. From St Paul on, the Church, the community of believers, has been construed as the 'body of Christ'. And, at least according to Catholic Christianity, Christ has been thought of as corporeally present in the consecrated bread and wine of the Eucharist. If it is not incompatible with divine dignity and status to encounter us in these corporeal forms, how could that charge be levelled against an exalted Jesus encountering his disciples in something like the form in which he existed during his earthly ministry? Thus it would seem that those who consider the exalted and glorified status of the risen Lord to rule out encountering the disciples in a partially human bodily form are seriously off base, for theological reasons.

To be sure, there are theological problems with a quasi-human embodiment of the risen Jesus. In particular, what happens to this body in the ensuing heavenly rule of Jesus at the right hand of God? Both evangelists leave this 'up in the air', John figuratively and Luke literally—well, perhaps not quite literally, but Luke does represent Jesus as being lifted up into a cloud (Acts 1: 9). I think we have to say that there is no satisfactory answer to this question in the New Testament.[41] But this is only one of the numerous loose

---

[40] *ST* 3a. 3. 8.
[41] To be sure, this problem disappears if we take the embodiment to be an illusion perpetrated by Jesus for the sake of a more personal encounter with the

ends left by biblical accounts. We cannot toss out everything that doesn't answer all the questions we would like answered.

V

The third prong of Fuller's argument involves an attempt to discredit Luke's and John's accounts more directly by an analysis of them. The analysis is quite detailed, proceeding line by line for the most part. I cannot discuss all of this here. I will concentrate on those portions that are especially important for the question of the corporeality of the risen Jesus, devoting most attention to Luke. But first let me stress that I do not by any means reject all of Fuller's treatment. At many points he is, in my judgement, clearly in the right. Here are some examples.

Fuller, like many other scholars, points out differences between the Gospel accounts that make a coherent harmonization impossible. Sticking to the appearances, and in addition to points of fine detail, there are the following important discrepancies.

1. *Location.* Matthew, after a brief encounter of Jesus with the women, sets the major appearance and commission to mission on a mountain in Galilee. Luke, on the other hand, locates all the appearances in and around Jerusalem. John includes both Jerusalem and Galilean appearances. The difficulty is not that it would be impossible, or even unlikely, that Jesus should appear to disciples in both regions.[42] The serious problem is dual. (a) What looks to all the world like different versions of the same appearance is located in different places. Thus, whereas Matthew has Jesus giving his evangelistic commission to the disciples in Galilee, both John and Luke locate it in Jerusalem. (b) Though Luke does not say explicitly, 'There were no appearances outside the Jerusalem area', he narrates several there, all on Easter day and evening, and then, at least in his Gospel, has Jesus departing from the disciples that evening.

disciples. He really existed in some way, but he made it appear, for the moment, that he was in a quasi-humanly embodied form. But, in addition to flirting with Docetism, this suggestion would involve rejecting the Lucan and Johannine accounts as drastically as Fuller does. For these evangelists represent Jesus as bending over backwards to insist that his corporeality is genuine.

[42] In Fuller's filling out of Paul's list of appearances he locates some in Galilee and some in Jerusalem.

2. *Time.* As just indicated, Luke compresses the appearances into one 24-hour day.[43] While neither Matthew nor John give such precise timing, the impression is that the appearances are spread out over more than a day. In both cases the disciples would have had to make their way from Jerusalem to Galilee between appearances.

3. *The Holy Spirit.* John has Jesus bestow the Spirit on the disciples on Easter evening, whereas Luke has Jesus tell them, just before the ascension, to wait in Jerusalem until they receive the promised Holy Spirit—looking forward to Pentecost. I agree that we cannot suppose all these accounts to be completely accurate as they stand.

While in this irenic mood, I should also mention that Fuller is far from rejecting the Gospel appearance narratives *in toto*. On the contrary, he takes them to be *versions* of genuine appearances the memory of which was preserved in the tradition, but shaped and modified in various ways by the evangelists and/or their sources, ways that prevent them from being literally accurate in all their details. Thus the final scene of Matthew, the bestowal of the Holy Spirit and the commission to the disciples on Easter evening in John, and the similar Easter evening scene in Luke (without the bestowal of the Holy Spirit) he takes to be different versions of the appearance to 'the twelve' recorded by Paul. And the appearance in the last chapter of John he takes to be a (much altered and elaborated) version of the initial appearance to Peter. More specifically:

> The Johannine resurrection appearance to the disciples at Jerusalem is unique in associating the Christophany with the gift of the Spirit. It may well be that John has here preserved an authentic insight from earlier tradition. (p. 174)

> Turning now to the appearance narratives of the intermediate stratum we find several themes in the verbalizations of Matthew 28: 18-20. First, there is an emphasis on the authority of the Risen One (v. 8). This theme has been prominent in the Easter faith almost from the beginning. (p. 77).

> We come now to the *Pasce oves* scene (John 21: 15-19). This appears to be an attempt to express in narrative form the theological significance of the appearance to Peter as it occurs in the primitive lists. (p. 177)

And so on.

Enough of this reconciliation. I now turn to features of Fuller's analysis of the narratives that he takes to discredit their depiction

---

[43] Though at the beginning of Acts he says that they continued for forty days!

of the risen Jesus as embodied in (more or less) human form. First, Fuller argues that all narratives of appearances are late.

> The Christophany of Matthew 28: 11–17 is the first instance we have of a materialization of the appearances. This materialization seems to originate here, not from any anti-Docetic motive such as we find in the later tradition (see especially Luke 24: 13), but from the exigencies of narrations. So long as the appearances were merely listed (1 Cor. 15: 5 f.; Mark 16: 7), their spiritual character could be preserved intact. But they could be narrated as external events only by modelling them on the stories of encounters with Jesus during his earthly ministry. It is particularly significant that it is precisely those later traits in the narrative tradition of the earthly Jesus' ministry which represent him as a 'divine man' (*theios aner*) that are taken into the resurrection narratives. Thus the women 'touch' his feet (cf. Mark 5: 22) and they 'worship' him (cf. Mark 5: 6). This is the strongest argument against the primitive character of the appearance *narratives*. (p. 79)

What Fuller is presumably referring to as 'the strongest argument' is the similarity of the appearance narratives to certain stories in the Gospels which he and other scholars assign to the Hellenistic phase of the development of the tradition. As such, neither the pre-crucifixion stories in question nor their post-crucifixion analogues can lay claim to a historical basis, at least in their 'divine man' features. But I find this argument extremely weak; if it really is Fuller's ace card, he is in big trouble. I am unable here to go into the question of whether the alleged pre-crucifixion models really did originate in the Hellenistic phase of the tradition and hence cannot represent memories of specific incidents in the ministry of Jesus;[44] but even if Fuller is right about that, the mere fact of similarity is not much of a reason for thinking that the appearance stories were deliberately composed on the model of such Hellenistic material. Why shouldn't the risen Jesus act and speak in ways that bear some similarity to Hellenistic portrayals of him in his earthly ministry? Or, to put this in terms of the tradition, why shouldn't there have been very early,

---

[44] See also Fuller, *Formation of the Resurrection Narratives*, 106: 'There are grounds for thinking that Luke drew his special material from Syrian tradition. . . . It was here, in circles which loved to tell stories and operated with a *theios aner* (divine man) interpretation of the earthly Jesus, that the late resurrection narratives may well have originated. In them the Risen One is portrayed on the one hand precisely [sic] as if he were still the earthly Jesus: he walks with his disciples, he accepts an invitation to supper in their home, and he breaks the bread before them as he had done during his earthly ministry. All these data are reproduced from the tradition of the earthly Jesus in the Gospels.'

fact-based traditions of such encounters with the Risen One that exhibit these similarities. It is only if we have some other reason for denying that early provenance that we are forced to look around for some other source for the stories, in which case Fuller's hypothesis would gain some credibility. And, as we have seen, Fuller is thinking in terms of such reasons. This passage makes it explicit that he supposes the early tradition contained only *lists* of appearances and construed them in 'spiritual' terms. But we have also seen the weakness of his arguments for this, arguments which suppose that the absence of narratives and references to corporeality in the Pauline letters and Mark are a strong indication that there was no such material early on. I have already said what I have to say about that reasoning.

The same point is to be made of his claim that the Emmaus story (and presumably he would say the same of the other narratives in Luke and John) 'looks like the product of story-telling proclivities of the community' (p. 106). It is only if we can dismiss an early, fact-based provenance on other grounds that we are warranted in appealing to a hypothetical 'story-telling proclivity'.

Another general feature of Fuller's treatment of these narratives is that he more than once charges them with conflating or mixing up the different appearances listed by Paul. This stems from what I noted earlier to be a speculative hypothesis that the appearances to Peter and 'the twelve' were 'church founding' in nature and located in Galilee, whereas the appearances to James and 'all the apostles' were 'mission inaugurating' and located in Jerusalem. With this background, Fuller takes both Luke and John, in their accounts of the missionary charges to the disciples, to have misaddressed them to the disciples rather than to 'all the apostles' (pp. 117, 139). But given the tenuous character of Fuller's argument for his interpretation of Paul's list of appearances, I am inclined to repose at least as much trust in the evangelists to get these matters straight. After all, for all Fuller has to tell us, it may be that they were working with traditions that stemmed from the original disciples.

I now turn to other points Fuller makes about the narratives in Luke. The Emmaus story, because of its careful 'literary' form, is a favourite hunting-ground for discerners of different strata of tradition, redactional contributions, interpolations, and tensions between different components. I find even the best historical critics to have much too low a threshold for conflict in Gospel accounts, and too great a readiness to attribute 'contradiction'. These tendencies are not lacking in Fuller's discussion of the Emmaus story. Thus he says that the flashback to the primary appearance to Simon after the main characters have returned to the eleven in Jerusalem 'stands in contradiction to the Emmaus story, which seems to regard the appearance to Cleopas and his companion as the first of the appearances, for the earlier flashback [the two travellers relating to Jesus the discovery of the empty tomb] contains no reference to appearances' (p. 105). But that earlier flashback contained no reference to appearances because, according to the story, Cleopas and his companion only learned of the appearance to Simon *after* returning to Jerusalem. Hence there is no contradiction. Again, Fuller judges that '¹⁹a prophet mighty in deed and word before God and all the people, ²⁰and now our chief priests and rulers delivered him up to be condemned to death, and crucified him' are 'preformed kerygmatic materials inserted by the Evangelist into his narrative source' (p. 105). But why shouldn't such characters as Cleopas and his companion in that sort of situation say something like this? And hence, why shouldn't the earliest source of the story contain something like this? A similarity to kerygmatic speeches in Acts shows, at most, that these were common themes in the early Christian community. Finally, consider verses 25–7: '²⁵And he said to them, "O foolish men, and slow of heart to believe all that the prophets have spoken! ²⁶Was it not necessary that the Christ should suffer these things and enter into his glory?" ²⁷And beginning with Moses and all the prophets, he interpreted to them in all the scriptures the things concerning himself.' Fuller says that they 'are typical expressions of Lukan theology' (p. 106). This is undoubtedly *some* basis for ascribing them to Lucan redaction, but it still amounts to no more than a live possibility. Further reasons would have to be given for regarding this as more likely than the supposition that the risen Jesus said something of the sort to some followers. Indeed, we would also have to exclude the possibility that Luke incorporated these ideas into his theology because of his acquaintance with (possibly reliable) traditions as to what Jesus said here and elsewhere. This, of course, gets us into the whole question of what can be attributed to Jesus by way of views on Old Testament prophecy of his status and career, something I cannot deal with here. My present point is only that highlighting the similarity to Lucan convictions is not enough to support the attribution to redaction.

Here is Fuller's summary statement of his dissection of the Emmaus story:

It may contain a basic nucleus of historical fact, if it can be identified with one of the appearances included among the appearances 'to all the apostles' and especially if the name Cleopas warrants some connection with James. A primitive *statement* of such an appearance, if it is historical, was later thrown into the form of a *narrative* with the kind of legendary elements one might expect in such an environment as Syria—still fairly Semitic in outlook, but with overtones of the *theios aner* (divine man) Christology. This stage contributes such elements as: Jesus as the Risen One traveling as an earthly figure yet mysteriously incognito, the earthly form of the conversation, the meal (though, as we have seen, this may belong to earlier and perhaps even historical tradition), the recognition. . . .

Lastly, there comes the Lukan redaction. Drawing upon other traditional materials (the synoptic predictions, Palestinian and Hellenistic forms of the Christological kerygma, the primitive motif of the resurrection 'in accordance with the scriptures') and adding the corrective reference to the first appearance to Peter, Luke refabricates this story. (p. 113)

Well, it may be so. But, as we have seen with certain points, Fuller falls far short of showing that it must be so, or even that it is more likely to have this history than any of innumerable others. In particular, he has failed to rule out the possibility that all the main elements of the story derive from early memories of an incident that, in fact, involved many of those elements.

Turning to the appearance to the eleven on Easter evening (Luke 24: 36–49), after relating it to the Pauline appearances to the twelve and to 'all the apostles', Fuller has this to say:

But the character of this appearance has received a highly apologetic coloring not merely absent from 1 Corinthians 15: 5, but quite contrary to it. The motif of doubt . . . has been redirected to provide the occasion for a massively physical demonstration. The Risen One invites his disciples to touch him so that they can see for themselves that he is not a 'spirit' or 'ghost', but a figure of flesh and blood. This new interpretation of the mode of the resurrection (resuscitation of the earthly body) is quite contrary to the apocalyptic framework of the earliest kerygma of 1 Corinthians 15: 5, to Paul's concept of the *pneumatikon soma* . . . and to the presentation in Mark 16: 1–8 and in Matthew 28: 16–20. But it was made inevitable by the development of appearance narratives. . . . For appearances could be narrated only by borrowing the traits of the earthly Jesus—he must walk, talk, eat, etc., as he had done in his earthly life. These features . . . are now drawn out and emphasized in the interests of apologetic. (p. 115)

Here we find some familiar themes—attributing a spiritual conception of resurrection to Paul and the earliest tradition, identifying a bodily resurrection with mere 'resuscitation', the incompatibility of exaltation and bodily appearance, and the explanation of 'materialization' as needed for narrative. The new element is the suggestion that the insistence on corporeality is introduced also for apologetic reasons, directed to those who would reject a resurrection of the body.[45] This is a special case of another favourite device of Gospel critics—taking any feature of a speech or narrative that is in line with interests, needs, or convictions of the early Church to have been inserted by the early Church, and hence not to be an accurate account of the deeds or words of Jesus. This is one more instance of the 'it could have happened this way, and so it did' principle. Some scholars not only argue in this way, but erect it into a principle. Here, for example, is Perrin setting out what he calls the 'criterion of dissimilarity', which he says to be the 'fundamental criterion for authenticity upon which all reconstructions of the teaching of Jesus must be built'.[46] '[T]he earliest form of a saying we can reach may be regarded as authentic if it can be shown to be dissimilar to characteristic emphases both of ancient Judaism and of the early Church' (p. 39).

Perrin credits Bultmann with originating this criterion: 'We can count on possessing a genuine similitude of Jesus where, on the one hand, expression is given to the contrast between Jewish morality and piety and the distinctive eschatological temper which characterized the preaching of Jesus, and where on the other hand we find no specifically Christian features' (p. 205).[47]

We can see the untenability of this methodology if we consider how it might be applied by some historian of the far distant future to the alleged utterances of Martin Luther King, jun. The historian would reject as inauthentic everything King allegedly said that was in accordance either with the civil rights movement of his time or with the movement as it developed after his death. In doing so, he would not be left with much, and he would be rejecting an enor-

---

[45] A similar suggestion is found in many authors, including Perkins, *Resurrection*, 87; Perrin, *Resurrection According to Matthew, Mark, and Luke*, 67; Carnley, *Structure of Resurrection Belief*, 67–8.

[46] Perrin, *Rediscovering the Teaching of Jesus*, 39.

[47] In the section of his book from which the above formulation is taken, Perrin refers to formulations and uses of the criterion by Jeremias, Käsemann, and Conzelmann.

mous mass of discourse actually produced by King. Of course, some of the Gospel material deemed unhistorical on this basis may well have been inserted in the early church period. But it is going far beyond reasonable procedure to suppose that the mere parallel of the material with early Church interests and convictions is sufficient to show that this was its provenance.

Though my main concern has been to combat Fuller's arguments against the supposition that the risen Jesus appeared in a (more or less) human bodily form, I will also say a word about his dismissal of some of what the risen Jesus is alleged to have said to the disciples. In opposing certain of Fuller's claims about this, I have no wish to maintain that the Gospels give us verbatim transcriptions of Jesus' words in these appearances, any more than they do in their accounts of his ministry. At best, we have a faithful summary of the content of what he said. And it is Fuller's rejection of that at certain points to which I shall take exception. We must also remember that one's attitude toward the accounts of corporeal appearances affect this issue. If one takes seriously a bodily appearance, one can think in terms of speech in a much more literal sense than if one does not. Nevertheless, the issue of how close the accounts come to a faithful reflection of the message Jesus was conveying, however that was done, arises in both perspectives.

Here I will confine myself almost entirely to Fuller's treatment of Jesus' 'great commission' in the final scene of Matthew. Some of his negative points are well taken. We cannot suppose that Jesus gave, as this point, a command to 'make disciples of all nations'. If he had, the mission to the Gentiles would not have been such a problem for the Jerusalem Church (p. 84). Nor does what we know about baptism in the early Church allow us to suppose that the risen Lord enjoined the Trinitarian formula for baptism (pp. 86–8). However, I can't go as far as Fuller in taking the speech to be a rewrite. We find the 'attribute to redaction wherever possible' principle at work when he ascribes the command to 'teach them to observe all that I have commanded you' to Matthew's view of Gospel as the new Torah and his associated special interest in teaching the rules (pp. 88–9). Fuller rightly observes in this connection that a commission to teach is found only in Matthew. But there are other possible explanations of this. It is a familiar point that accounts of many incidents differ among the Gospels, and not all of these are plausibly attributed to theologically motivated redaction. Surely they are sometimes due to the facts that (a) witnesses don't always see and report things the same way, and (b) details get altered in the course of transmission without anyone deliberately doing this. Thus, so far as I can see, it is at least as likely that Jesus did issue such a commission, which was preserved in one tradition but omitted in others. Again, Fuller opines that the combination of the three sayings in the scene—the declaration of authority, the missionary charge, and the promise of the abiding presence—was due to Matthew, on the grounds of the large number of Mattheanisms that the verses contain (pp. 90–1). But this could just as well be due to Matthew's way of formulating a combination he found in the tradition.

Finally, the 'I am with you always, to the close of the age' Fuller takes to be, in its original form, 'a creation of Christian prophecy, circulated as a logion of the Exalted Christ, declaring the presence of the Exalted One in the assemblies of the faithful' (p. 90). He ascribes the 'If you forgive the sins of any, they are forgiven; if you retain the sins of any, they are retained' of John 20: 23 to a similar source (p. 141). But this would seems to be another 'it could be that way, so it is that way' inference.

VI

Let me review what I have said and have not set out to do in this essay. Though my topic is the historical accuracy of the Gospel accounts of resurrection appearances, and although I am, in a way, defending a positive attitude, I have not even sought to establish *some* degree of accuracy of these accounts. Instead, I have examined a representative attempt by a New Testament scholar, Reginald Fuller, to show, or at least show it to be very likely, that for the most part these accounts have very little historical value; and I have contended that his arguments for that conclusion are very weak. To be sure, the conflict between Fuller and myself is less stark than it might have been because each side is far from being as radical as possible. Fuller, as I noted, does not deny that the accounts contain at least germs of historical truth. I, for my part, do not deny that they cannot be taken as accurate in every detail. Hence, to sharpen the issue, I focused on a question on which Fuller and I are in flat disagreement, whether Gospel portrayals of the risen Jesus as existing in a (more or less) human body can be shown to be without historical value. I examined several aspects of Fuller's defence of an affirmative answer to this question and argued, in each case, that the considerations he adduces are much too weak to support his conclusions. Even though I have not attempted to mount an argument *for* the thesis that Jesus did in fact appear after his death and burial in this form, I believe that my critique of Fuller does have an important bearing on what it is reasonable to believe about this matter. For, as I suppose, the fact that the Church proclaims a message that includes such appearances is, for the Christian at least, a prima-facie reason to suppose that such appearances did occur. Hence, if one can knock down attempts to show that they did not occur (or that it is not reasonable to suppose that they did), that will, for the Christian, leave Church doctrine on this point in possession of the field.

Let me emphasize once again the modesty of my claims. I do not assert that the accounts of Matthew, Luke, and John are accurate in every respect. Indeed, I have agreed that they cannot be correct in every detail. My claim is only that it is reasonable for a Christian to believe that there were appearances to the disciples that were of the general character reported by the evangelists. I have left it pretty much open just how much of the Gospel accounts it is reasonable to accept, except for saying that we cannot accept all the placing and dating they give us, and that we can accept that Jesus appeared to them in human bodily form. Of course, what I have actually argued for here is much less than a full claim formulated two sentences back about what it is reasonable for a Christian to believe. I have supported only one aspect of that claim: namely, that New Testament criticism has not shown that it is not reasonable to believe this. (And even there my argument supports this only on the assumption that the arguments against Fuller can be generalized to other critics who draw similar conclusions.) To fully support the claim, I would have to move on to the positive side of the coin, indicate what grounds there are for accepting the accounts (for the most part), and show that they are sufficient for rational acceptance. Other than just suggesting that Church proclamation provides some basis, I have not attempted that here. It is a major task in itself. So what I claim to have done here is to have shown that one representative attempt to discredit belief in a humanly corporeal resurrection of Jesus fails.[48]

I should mention one other relevant task that I have not undertaken. Fuller, like other recent Gospel critics, undertakes a reconstruction of the emergence of Gospel materials from the earliest stages of the tradition. We have seen that he takes this development to be such as to leave the appearance accounts in Luke and John with little credibility as factual reports. It is natural to expect one who rejects Fuller's treatment to suggest some alternative story of the formation of these accounts as at least equally well supported by the evidence. I do not agree that one cannot support a claim to the rationality of accepting the Gospel accounts without succeeding at this task. Nevertheless, it obviously would be desirable to have in hand a 'history of the tradition', or at least some suggestions thereto, that would be consonant with a more positive attitude toward the historical value of the appearance narratives in Luke and John. I could not provide this even if I had space to do so, for I lack the necessary expertise. I will have to content myself with pointing out that there is a wealth of possibilities here, all falling under the following general rubric.

Let us say that Jesus really did exist in a (highly unusual) human body of the sort depicted in Luke and John, one that rendered him visible and tangible, but that also made his identity only sometimes recognizable and that enabled him to appear and disappear in an instant. Naturally, stories of such appearances would circulate in the very early Church, and they would undergo modification, elaboration, displacement, corruption, and all the rest, in accordance with well-known tendencies of oral tradition. By the time the three Gospels containing such narratives came to be written, these stories existed in versions not wholly consonant with one another in terms of places and times as well as in more minor respects. And, of course, some appearances will have been preserved in some tra-

---

[48] My concentration here on the issue of whether the risen Jesus existed in a (more or less) human bodily form may give the impression that I suppose that it is crucial for the Christian faith to believe this. But that would be a mistake. As I see it, what is crucial in this matter is that Jesus of Nazareth was alive shortly after his crucifixion and death, and that he continues to live and be active in the world. Compared with that, the question of just what form this continued life takes, in the immediate post-crucifixion period or otherwise, is of secondary importance. Nevertheless, it is of some interest whether the accounts of his appearances in Luke and John can, in the main, be relied on.

ditions and not in others. Finally, each evangelist put his own theological 'spin' on his version. Yet certain basic facts come through. After his death and burial Jesus appeared more than once to one or more disciples in quasi-human form, spoke to them and gave them commissions, and assured them that he was alive and would continue to be alive and active in the mission he assigned them. It is something like this that I have been arguing that treatments like Fuller have not eliminated from rational acceptance.

Though my criticism has been restricted to one scholar's treatment of one bit of the Gospels, I believe that some of my points have much more general application. I take myself to have identified certain failings that are prominent in much New Testament criticism. Here are a few of these.

(1) There is the line of argument I have encapsulated in the slogan, '*It is possible that it happened this way, therefore it did*'. Forms of this include:
(a) Taking any material that reflects interests, needs, or convictions of the early Church to have been added to the tradition because of that, rather than being based on actual happenings at the period the narrative concerns.
(b) Any material that is in line with an evangelist's theological perspective must have been due to his reconstrual of the matter.
(c) If stories could have originated because of a 'story-telling proclivity', then we will assume that they did.
(d) If certain alleged words of Jesus could have originated with a Christian prophet in the early Church, then we will suppose that they did.
(2) *The argument from silence that we saw to be so pervasive in Fuller.* If our (admittedly extremely scanty) sources do not contain a certain kind of material, it must not have been available when those sources were composed.
(3) *Extremely speculative suggestions that are allowed to play a major role in an argument.* An example from the above would be Fuller's supposition that the appearance to Paul was typical of all the appearances of the risen Jesus.
(4) *A low threshold for conflict.* See, for example, the contradiction Fuller purports to find in the Emmaus story.

Behind these defects, and others, I find some general tendencies. Perhaps the most pernicious of these is the attempt to extract too much from too little. Recent Gospel critics seem driven to achieve definite results at any cost, despite the thinness of the data at their disposal. In particular, inspired by the path-breaking work of Bultmann and Dibelius, they strive to reconstruct the history of the pre-Marcan Gospel tradition, in spite of lacking sufficient basis to do so. They are thus led into such extravagances as excessive reliance on the *argumentum ex silentio* and the confusion of free speculation with historical fact. As I have already made explicit, I do not, by any means, deny all value to the Gospel researches of this century. Quite the contrary. They have made contributions of great value to our understanding of the documents, their settings, their background, and the different historical values of their components. But, at the same time, they have, if Fuller's book is any indication, produced much chaff along with this wheat. It is high time that some interested and qualified parties, who are able to take a discriminating look at this literature without opposing the whole enterprise, set out to separate the wheat from the chaff, so that the fruits of contemporary Gospel scholarship may be properly appreciated.

To return to Fuller, when one finds that the arguments against corporeal appearances are so weak, one is naturally led to look for a hidden agenda that is at least partially responsible for the conclusions. Here is a speculative suggestion, which I throw out for your consideration.

There are Gospel critics who reject, on principle, any reports of divine intervention in the affairs of the world, anything that God is reported to have brought about other than what would have happened had only natural, this-worldly influences been involved. Bultmann is only the most famous of these, and he has had many followers. Fuller is not of this company; nor is anyone else who recognizes that Jesus of Nazareth, that very individual person, resumed his life after his death and burial and continues to live and be active in the Church and in the lives of his followers. Surely that involves innumerable happenings in this world that are other than what they would have been had only natural causes been involved. Every interaction of this risen Jesus with human beings is a signal case in point. But though Fuller, and other scholars who fall within the limits I set out in this essay, do not reject the miraculous in general, they are inclined, I would suggest, to look askance at forms of it that they find crude, sensational, melodramatic, or blatant. I strongly suspect that this antipathy to the crudely obvious is behind a reluctance to take seriously the possibility that the risen Lord existed in a human bodily form and interacted with his disciples in this guise. If some such attitude is behind the scenes, that would help to explain how otherwise brilliant and acute scholars would reject the

Lucan and Johannine accounts of the resurrection appearances on the basis of such arguments as I have been examining. But such an attitude is far from a respectable reason for the position. Surely it is the height of folly to try to second-guess God. If God should, in his infinite wisdom, see fit to raise Jesus in human bodily form, having earlier seen fit to become incarnate in that form, who are we to cry 'How gauche!'?

Response by Sarah Coakley

I should first say (which may prove disappointing for those anticipating a showdown between an analytic philosopher and a feminist
theologian) that I do not have any fundamental objections to the
main thrust of Alston's essay. Indeed, I think he has established
very elegantly and convincingly that New Testament scholarship of
this generation (Fuller being a good case in point, if now somewhat
dated) is often unnecessarily coy—or downright repressive—about
supernatural events in general and bodily resurrection in particular. This leads to a persistent intensifying of sceptical presumptions
against credulity where the Gospel resurrection narratives are concerned, as Alston's argument demonstrates with persistent clarity.

There are, it is true, aspects of Alston's New Testament exegesis
which I find doubtful. His interest in salvaging 'historical' material
from the Gospel accounts leads to a resistance to the insights of
redaction criticism, a position which I find intrinsically unconvincing and perhaps even a distraction from the strength of his main thesis. In particular, his treatment of the Lucan resurrection narratives
(see e.g. p. 175 on Luke 24: 36–49) rejects out of hand the possibility that Luke has massaged his sources a little to emphasize the
straightforward corporeality of the risen Jesus. This is done by means
of a broad-stroke critique of the 'criterion of dissimilarity' principle
(p. 176), a critique that in any case succeeds only by an element of
caricature (since New Testament scholars—even Perrin—do not
accept material about Jesus to be authentic *only* 'if it can be shown
to be dissimilar to . . . emphases both of ancient Judaism and of the
early church'). Be that as it may, what Alston diverts our attention
from here is the clear *tension* between the Gospel accounts on the
nature of the resurrected body. In Luke Jesus' body has this 'hard'
quality of physicality which is, not coincidentally, also connected in
the same Gospel writer with the ascension narratives: a body like
this has to (literally) go away somewhere else if it is no longer to

continue to be seen on earth. Moreover, Luke confronts the possible
(or actual) suspicion that the risen Jesus was nothing but a 'ghost'
(Luke 24: 37). All this displays somewhat different interpretative
'interests' from the other Gospel writers. To admit this is not, however, to reject all Luke's material as inherently inauthentic, or *merely*
'apologetic' (as Fuller appears to argue). But it does pose the problem of deciding which strands of the Gospel accounts to attribute to
interpretive restructuring, either by the Gospel writer or by the bear-
ers of oral tradition; and Alston's unwillingness to confront this
hermeneutical complexity, or the actual contradictions between the
Gospel accounts, renders his central argument (against the dogmatic
New Testament sceptics) less powerful and nuanced than it might
otherwise be.

Similarly, I would want to quibble over some other finer-tuning
details in Alston's treatment of the New Testament texts. This is the
failure to underscore, on pp. 160-1, that Paul seemingly *did* sense
a difference between the Christic 'appearance' to him and the earlier ones (see 1 Cor. 15: 8 ff.), and was defensive about his status as
'apostle' in relation to this (the underlining of this point would actually help Alston's thesis here). Since, however, I am prepared to
accept the major conclusions of Alston's essay as read, I will not
here extend the list of debating points that a New Testament scholar
undoubtedly would want to pursue. This is because I think that
there are other, more interesting theological and philosophical matters that call for discussion.

What concerns me is that in Alston's effort to counter the ill-
founded scepticism of New Testament scholarship, he glosses over a
number of more subtle dimensions of the resurrection narratives
that call for nuanced reflection (and which he is peculiarly well
placed to illuminate, granted his earlier distinguished work on religious language and epistemology). I would therefore like to press
him on these issues, and see if they can help to point a way beyond
the divide between 'liberal' theology and analytic philosophy of religion evident in the papers presented here. I have five questions (or
clusters of questions): which I will pose thus:

1. *The 'insider/outsider' issue.* At the start of his essay Alston indicates what he takes to be the methodological distinctiveness of his
approach (pp. 149-50). He stresses that he is operating from the
perspective of an already committed Christian, not that of

'(secular) historical investigation' (p. 148). And this tilts the weighing of probabilities throughout: he is inclined to *trust* the biblical
narrative rather than distrust it. (It is elsewhere, in his *Perceiving
God*,[1] that he explains what cumulative factors would constitute a
rational 'grounding' of the Christian faith in the first place.) So far,
so good. But what seems odd is that the language of 'outsider' (secular?) historical research still obtrudes itself into the discussion at
various points. Thus he starts by asking 'What can we learn from
the Gospels as to *what actually happened?*' (p. 148). This Rankean
phrase ('wie es eigentlich gewesen') is most naturally read as implying some position of objective historical truth *prescinding* from
Christian evaluation or interpretation. Likewise, he speaks on
p. 152 of 'factually accurate information' and whether the evangelists intended to supply it; and he insists that they *were* interested
in the 'historical Jesus'. (It is worth noting that the latter is a slip-
pery term, since it glosses the difference between what I would call
the 'earthly Jesus' and the scientifically established 'historian's Jesus'
of the post-Enlightenment period. Alston *seems* here to be reading
back the concerns of the latter into the Gospel writers' interest in the
former.) Even though he clarifies that 'historical' information of this
sort could only *disconfirm* items of belief (pp. 149–50), the credence
he grants to the status of this dispassionate (?) 'historical scholarship' (p. 149) is in prima-facie tension with his stated intention of
adopting an intra-Christian perspective throughout. Does he, or
does he not, believe that secular historians enjoy some capacity to
probe 'what actually happened' in a mode abstracting from (all?)
hermeneutical colouring? If so, is this sharp separation of epistemology and ontology convincing?

This ambiguity, incidentally, is reminiscent of—though clearly
not the same as—a parallel tension I find in the argument of
Alston's *Perceiving God*. In chapter 1 he insists on the possibility of
a form of 'direct awareness' that is 'distinguishable from *any* elements of conceptualization . . . or "interpretation" ' (p. 27), and
to which perception of God may be compared; whereas the second
half of the book adopts the 'doxastic practice' approach founded in
socially established mechanism and interpretative *beliefs*. Which, I
wonder, is more important to Alston? And is the former—the supposed capacity for non-conceptual, non-interpretative apprehen-

---

[1] (Ithaca, NY: Cornell University Press, 1991), ch. 8.

sion—convincing at all? As in this strand of argument in *Perceiving God*, so (rather differently) in this essay on the resurrection, Alston clings to the hope that there might be areas of human knowing—perceptual or (here) historical-critical—that somehow *abstract* from the interpretative or hermeneutical lens. But can this really be so, and how would one establish it? Further, and incidentally, would Alston want to claim that any of the resurrection appearances qualify as 'directly' perceived in the sense discussed in *Perceiving God*? (I presume not, but the question is at least worth raising.)

2. *Who or what is the risen Christ?* This point can be addressed much more succinctly. Alston is concerned, rightly in my view, to defend the Gospel accounts of the physicality of Jesus' risen body. But he is coy about spelling out the implications of the 'atypical' (p. 180) nature of this corporeality, except to say that the 'body has at least been transformed in certain respects' (p. 167). His final footnote seems to be rather defensive and unclear on this point: does he really *not* think it 'crucial' to believe in this '(more or less) human bodily form'? Certainly, the identity of the risen Christ is *continuous* with 'Jesus of Nazareth', but does he take the changes to be insignificant? I find this theologically very puzzling. It re-summons the positivist spectre of 'bare facts' minus 'interpretation' (see point 1); and it apparently gives no room to the hugely rich and important Pauline doctrine of the 'body of Christ' as *both* an extension of the life of Jesus *and* a transformative (and omnipresent) corporate reality (though I note the relevant remarks on p. 169). Perhaps this is where analytic philosophy of religion meets its Waterloo on resurrection matters. It has the hugest difficulty in conceiving of *corporate* identity in Christ: the hold of a certain form of individualism on it is too tenacious. It wants 'facts' about 'Jesus of Nazareth's' afterlife (and so tends to be drawn to the 'literal' physicality of Luke's account: see Stephen Davis's chapter in this volume); but it backs off explication of what life 'in Christ' means, in all its symbolic density. Perhaps I can press the point thus: if Alston takes the biblical narrative as seriously as he says he does, *why* is the 'form' of Christ's continuing presence 'of secondary importance'? Does not the biblical narrative precisely call into question some of analytic philosophy of religion's most cherished presumptions about the nature of the (individual) self?

3. *Resurrection and religious language.* This leads us immediately to the connected point about language. At several moments in the essay Alston bats away the suggestion that Jesus' resurrection should be discussed in metaphorical terms at the expense of 'literal' speech (see pp. 154, 157, 177). This is apparently on the presumption that commitment to a *bodily* resurrection will go hand in hand with commitment to 'literal' speech about it. But why should this follow? The mystery and novelty of the resurrected body (see point 2 above) may require the coinage of new metaphors to express it (and obviously did) without implying any lack of realism. Could Alston not concede this possibility? If so, why do certain elements (and which elements?) need to be guarded as 'literal'? Those familiar with Alston's essays on metaphor in *Divine Nature and Human Language*[2] will know that his main bane is the liberal 'pan-metaphoricist': the one who denies that *anything* other than metaphor is appropriate to God, and is insensitive to what he sees as the 'literal' *residuum* of metaphorical utterance. But I remain puzzled by his apparent resistance to the ontological *seriousness* of metaphorical speech. Is this finally just a sleight of hand, whereby any ontologically serious claim is one Alston *chooses* to call 'literal' (rather than anything else)? Since he denies (p. 25) that 'literal' for him evokes 'precise', 'univocal', 'specific', 'factual', 'empirical', or 'ordinary', I am left wondering exactly what is at stake when he so urgently requires that resurrection language be 'literal'.

4. *Resurrection and epistemic transformation.* Here we come to the main nub, at least for me. In his defence of the Matthean, Lucan, and Johannine resurrection accounts, Alston glosses over two features of the narratives that I have always regarded as highly revealing and theologically telling: namely (i) the problem of recognizing the risen Christ for who he was (see especially Luke 24: 13 ff., but also John 20: 15b, 21: 4), and (ii) the possibility of even being present at an appearance but still 'doubting' (Matt. 28: 17b). What this strongly suggests to me is a possibility Alston does not seriously consider (so busy is he seeing off the New Testament sceptics): that the apprehension of the risen Christ (then and now) requires some responsive recognition 'deeper' than normal cognition or visual perception. To say this is *not* to trivialize or side-line the reality of

---

[2] (Ithaca, NY: Cornell University Press, 1989), chs. 1 and 2.

Christ's risen body; but it is to complexify the epistemic picture in ways that Alston's *Perceiving God*, it seems, would rather not do—despite the suggestive mention of 'spiritual senses' in chapter 1 (pp. 51–4, a subject never developed further, however). Yet the tradition of 'spiritual senses' (in Origen, Gregory of Nyssa, and later medieval exponents) is all about a mode of cognition that transcends normal epistemic functioning and in which Christ is fully and finally embraced. It is, of course, understandable that a contemporary apologist such as Alston should want to keep Christian epistemic claims on a par with normal perceptions in order to counter the sceptical response. But is this finally profound enough *spiritually*, especially where the resurrected Christ is concerned? When Alston writes of spiritual practice elsewhere (for example, in his 1988 essay 'The Indwelling of the Holy Spirit', reprinted in *Divine Nature and Human Language*, ch. 11), he is not afraid to admit the place of the *unconscious* in the Spirit's cracking open of the human heart. Could he not also admit in the case of the recognition of the resurrection a crucial role for deepened and *transformed* epistemic functioning (see Luke 24: 32)? If so, how could this best be expressed?

5. *The resurrection and gender.* I cannot, lastly, forbear making a point about the gender themes encoded in the above (a matter I have discussed in more general reference to the discourses of analytic philosophy of religion in an entry on 'Feminism' for the forthcoming Blackwell's *Companion to the Philosophy of Religion*). In this context I merely want to underscore the point (mentioned briefly by Gerald O'Collins in his chapter, and discussed at length in Elisabeth Schüssler Fiorenza's *In Memory of Her*,[3]) that it was in all probability women who first witnessed the resurrection, first 'saw' the risen Christ. A more interesting but speculative question (following from point 4) is what *epistemic* significance this might have. What was it about Mary Magdalene's testimony that was both formative and yet in need of being downplayed? Even Thomas Aquinas argues (in gender-stereotypical mode) that woman's greater capacity for 'love' (witnessed in the women's fidelity to Jesus at the cross and their first presence on Easter morning) will earn them a quicker share than men in the beatific vision (see *ST* 3a, 55, 1 ad 3). And it is surely not a coincidence that the 'spiritual senses' tradition requires of *men*

[3] (New York: Crossroad, 1983).

the development of a 'feminine' role in relation to Christ. Naturally I do not want to answer my own question in ways that shore up these gender stereotypes. I am more interested in questioning the resistance, in philosophical circles, to probing *beneath* the level of epistemic functioning taken as normative for the 'generic male'—that is, the vision of selfhood supposedly abstracting from gender differentiation, but actually showing a marked predilection for characteristics honoured culturally as 'male'. That seems to me quite important for understanding the appropriate mode for recognizing the risen Christ. What levels of the self—what affective or intuitive depths, what interpersonal mysteries of human response, what dimensions of bodily existence (themes normally downplayed in 'masculinist' philosophical discussion)—are unavoidable in their epistemic implications if the true *richesse* of encounter with the risen Christ charted in the New Testament is to be grasped? How are 'normal' understandings of perception and rationality to be *revised* in the light of the resurrection narratives, and to what extent is that necessary revision entangled with questions of gender? In this, as in other areas of current analytic philosophy of religion, my suspicion is that no spiritually profound advances can be made here unless some of the lessons of feminist critique (both theological and philosophical) are assimilated.

I would much welcome Alston's response on this matter, as on the others.

8

Evidence for the Resurrection

RICHARD SWINBURNE

In assessing what happened on some particular occasion in the past, we have to take into account both detailed historical evidence and general background evidence. The detailed historical evidence may be of three kinds: our own personal (apparent) memories, the testimony of witnesses, and physical traces. The general background evidence will be evidence of what normally happens. This may be free-standing (some generalization about cases similar to that under investigation, confirmed solely by observing such cases) or a consequence of some deeper theory, confirmed by observations over a wide range of cases, some of them rather unlike the case under investigation.

Let me illustrate with a detective example. A detective investigating a safe robbery may himself have a relevant memory. By a 'memory' I mean what should be called, more strictly, an 'apparent personal memory', one which seems to the subject to be a genuine memory of having done something or having perceived something. The detective may have thought that he saw Jones robbing the safe. More likely, there may be other witnesses who report that they saw Jones robbing the safe. And there will often be physical traces—fingerprints on the safe or money stashed away in Jones's garage. The detective's own apparent memories or the testimony of witnesses may, more likely, be not of seeing the safe being robbed but of other events which in turn provide evidence of who robbed the safe.

That memories and testimony are to be trusted—that is, that they make it probable that what they report occurred—in the absence of counter-evidence, are a priori principles. You might think that memory is to be trusted only if independently confirmed. But what could confirm a memory except another memory, or some generalization about how the world works, itself confirmed by memories of it working on various occasions? You might say that no one memory is to be trusted until confirmed by another. But think how little knowledge we would have if we really thought thus. A memory would only be trustworthy if we simultaneously had another memory (for example, of what someone else said that he saw) confirming the first memory. We don't think that, and we must draw the consequences of our secular thinking: that memory as such, all memory, is to be trusted in the absence of positive counter-evidence that is untrustworthy—for example, that it concerns an occasion on which the subject was drunk, or concerns a matter on which he tends to misobserve, or that there is strong independent evidence that what the subject reports did not happen. That positive counter-evidence will come ultimately from other memories (or the testimony of others—see below) which clash with the given memory and are stronger or more numerous.

The principle of testimony, that we should believe what others tell us that they have done or perceived—in the absence of counter-evidence—is also a priori. Clearly most of our beliefs about the world are based on what others claim to have perceived—beliefs about geography and history and science and everything else beyond immediate experience are thus based. We do not normally check that informants are reliable witnesses before accepting their reports. And we *could* not do so because we form our beliefs about what they are saying, the meaning of the claims which they are making, on the assumption that other people normally tell the truth. We can see this by considering how an anthropologist comes to learn the language of a native tribe. He listens to what the natives say, and observes correlations between what they say and how things are; for example he finds that on the day before a festival natives often say '*p*' but that they do not say '*p*' at any other time. If he takes this as evidence that '*p*' means 'there will be a festival tomorrow', he must already be assuming that normally natives tell the truth. What applies to the anthropologist applies to a child learning his first language or additions to it. When people point to a colour and say 'This is green', the child believes that 'green' is the name of that colour—because he has already made (implicitly) the assumption that people normally tell the truth. The assumption itself cannot be tested—because if it is up for test whether people normally tell the truth, then we would have to see whether there are correlations between the propositions people utter and how things are—yet we should not know what proposition they were uttering (that is, what they meant by their sentence) unless we had already made the assumption up for test.

But again there can be positive evidence that certain witnesses, or witnesses positioned in certain circumstances, or a particular testimony by a particular witness, are unreliable. But the evidence will have force only on the assumption that most other witnesses are trustworthy. We can show that Smith is an utterly untrustworthy witness on certain matters only if we can trust the combined testimony of other witnesses about what happened. Conjoint testimony can defeat single testimony.

That physical traces are evidence of this or that is, however, an a posteriori matter. That fingerprints of the same pattern as those of Jones are (strong) evidence that Jones put his fingers where the prints are, follows from the theory that fingers leave prints uniquely characteristic of their owner, established in the last century on the basis of a very wide range of evidence. This evidence itself is available to us by the testimony (written or oral) of those who have studied it. That a particular piece of physical evidence, *a*, shows what it does, *b*, is something to be established inductively (that is, as something entailed or rendered probable by a theory which is itself rendered probable by other pieces of evidence). We need to show that *a* would probably not have occurred unless *b* occurred; and that will be so only if *a* would probably not have occurred unless *b*, or a cause of *b*, had caused *a*. And to show that, you need a theory of what causes what. Such a theory is to be accepted in so far as it is a simple theory rendering probable the occurrence of many observed data which there would otherwise be no reason to expect.

The observed data in the fingerprint example are a very large random sample of 'fingerprints' (identified as such by their shape), many of which have been seen being caused by fingers (and none of which can be attributed with any significant probability to any cause other than fingers), each fingerprint uniquely correlating one to one with the fingers of a different human being. The theory of unique fingerprints is a simple theory leading us to expect these observations which we would not otherwise expect, and has the consequence that Jones's fingerprint is evidence of Jones having put his fingers where the fingerprint is found. But this connection is established a posteriori on the basis of trusting what witnesses say about their observations of the large random sample.

Apparent memories, testimony, and physical traces will often be evidence of certain other things, which in turn are evidence of the matter of interest to us—say, that Jones robbed the safe. Here the above pattern of inductive inference will again be evident. Two witnesses may report that Jones was in the neighbourhood of the robbery at the time it was committed; another one may report that a little later Jones boasted about having won the Lottery, and had a lot of money to spend (and Lottery officials witness that he did not win the Lottery). The traces may include fingerprints on the safe and the discovery of much of the stolen money in a garage of which he possessed the key. And so on. A theory immediately suggests itself which leads us to expect all these data, when the combination of all the data together would be otherwise unexpected—namely, that Jones robbed the safe. And the theory is a simple one—that one person caused all these effects. Another theory which would also lead us to expect the data with equal probability would be that the fingerprints were planted by Smith, the goods stolen by Robinson, who dropped them, and Brown picked them up and hid them in the garage of which, coincidentally, Jones had the key; and so on, to deal with the other data. But the latter theory is not supported by the data, because it is complicated—and the former theory is simple.

All the detailed 'historical' data considered so far are causal evidence in the sense that the event reported by our hypothesis, if true, would (in part) have caused those data (or would have been caused by a cause of those data). Thus if Jones had robbed the safe, he would have caused the fingerprints to be on the safe. But now background evidence enters in. The background evidence is not, in the sense delineated, causal evidence, but evidence from a wide area supporting a theory or theories about what normally happens. It shows how likely it is on other grounds that an event of the kind alleged could have occurred. In our example it will include evidence of Jones's behaviour on other occasions, supporting a theory of his character, from which it would follow that he is or is not the sort of person who normally robs safes.

All these kinds of evidence are relevant to determining whether some historical event occurred, and need to be weighed against each other; and the most interesting clashes of evidence, for our purposes, occur when detailed historical evidence points to something which background evidence suggests is most unlikely to have occurred. Consider the sixteenth-century Danish astronomer Tycho Brahe making observations of comets and measuring their angular distance from various stars at different hours of the night. The background evidence in the form of all that had ever been observed in the heavens, and especially the movements of the sun and moon and planets relative to Earth and relative to the 'fixed stars', supported the Aristotelio–Ptolemaic astronomy which held that the heavenly regions beyond the moon were occupied by crystalline spheres in which there were no changes, and which carried sun, moon, and planets around the Earth. Now it followed from Tycho's observations that comets changed their apparent positions relative to the stars and planets during the year in such a way that if they existed in the heavenly regions, and the Aristotelio–Ptolemaic theory were true, they would be passing through the crystalline spheres—which would of course be impossible. But if comets are sublunary phenomena, they should show a diurnal parallax: that is, as the Earth (or the outer heavenly sphere of the stars) rotates daily, they should change their position during the course of the night relative to the background of the stars. Tycho Brahe in the sixteenth century had very accurate apparatus by which he could have detected any diurnal parallax. He observed the absence of such a parallax. The detailed historical observations supported the theory that any given comet was a body moving far beyond the moon's orbit.[1] In this situation of a clash between the historical evidence and the theory supported by background evidence, it must be the case either that the background theory is false or that the historical evidence is misleading. In any such clash, we must weigh the two types of evidence against each other, and it may not always be clear where the balance lies, although often it may. In the example which I have just discussed it was of course the background theory which was at fault, and eventually (whether or not that was evident at the time) it became evident that the balance of evidence was against the background theory.

In his discussion of miracles, Hume was concerned with just such a clash. He understood by a miracle 'a transgression of a law of nature by a particular volition of the Deity, or by the interposition of some invisible agent'.[2] Here we are concerned with a situation

---

[1] For this story, see e.g. S. Sambursky, *The Physical World of the Greeks* (London: Routledge and Kegan Paul, 1956), 218–20; and T. S. Kuhn, *The Copernican Revolution* (New York: Random House, 1957), 206–9.

[2] D. Hume, *An Enquiry Concerning Human Understanding*, 1777 edn., ed. L. A. Selby-Bigge, 2nd edn. (Oxford: Clarendon, 1902), 115 n. 1.

where the background evidence supports a theory, not just about
what normally happens (most of the time, on the whole) and so is
not all that powerful as evidence of what happened on the given
occasion, but rather with a situation where the background evidence powerfully supports a theory about what laws of nature make
(almost) inevitable. I write 'almost', for if we are to have a coherent notion of a 'transgression' or 'violation' of a law of nature, we
cannot understand a law of nature as a law determining what
inevitably happens. For in that case there could not be a 'violation'
of a law of nature, since a 'violation' implies an event contrary to
what follows from the operation of a law. An event contrary to
what is predicted by a purported law would only show the purported law to be no real law. If a purported law of gravity rules out
levitation, and a levitation occurs, then the purported law can be
no true law. To make the notion of a violation coherent, we must
amend our understanding of 'law of nature' along such lines as the
following. We should understand by a law of nature a principle
which determines what often happens, and by a fundamental law
a principle which determines what happens, when what happens is
determined by law at all. Derivative laws (such as Kepler's laws of
planetary motion) determine what happens in certain regions for
certain periods of time, subject to non-interference by other laws or
powers beyond law. Derivative laws are consequences of fundamental laws, which operate always and everywhere and without
exceptions (no other law prevents their operation)—when what
happens is determined by law. A violation of a law of nature is then
to be understood as an event contrary to the predictions of a fundamental law of nature (or very improbable given that law). Such
laws thus determine what happens (either of physical necessity or,
if they are indeterminate laws, with physical probability)
inevitably—in so far as laws operate at all. But they may be violated
by something which has the power to set aside the principles governing the natural behaviour of things. An understanding of a law
of nature of this qualified kind is not merely compatible with anything scientists wish to claim, but, more than that, is required, once
you allow the possibility of laws of nature (for example, those of
quantum theory) which determine what happens only with physical probability, and not necessity, and so you allow the possible
occurrence of the physically improbable.

Hume would, I think, have been satisfied with such an amended understanding of a law of nature, because he did not wish to rule out the notion of a miracle as logically impossible. What he did claim was in effect (to fill out his words a little) that to be justified in claiming some generalization to be a fundamental law of nature, we need to show that it operates without exception in a wide range of cases. That evidence will be evidence that it holds in the case in question. If the historical evidence suggests that some event occurred contrary to a fundamental law, we have at best a stand-off: we cannot say what happened, certainly not with enough certainty to provide 'a just foundation for any . . . system of religion'.[3] And the normal situation, Hume considers, is that the background evidence, in the form of evidence of the universal conformity to the purported law in many different areas investigated, will outweigh the historical evidence, and so show that what happened accorded with a law of nature, and so was no miracle.

Hume's discussion suffers from one minor deficiency, one medium-sized deficiency, and one major one. The minor one is that the only kind of historical evidence of which he takes account is testimony. He doesn't consider what someone who thinks that he himself has seen a miracle ought to believe. Nor does he consider the possibility of physical traces—for example, X-rays of the internal state of someone before and after a purported healing (whose status as X-rays taken at the time and of the patient is evidenced by many witnesses and much theory). But the addition of these important kinds of historical evidence would not affect the shape of Hume's argument. Far more important is the point that Hume seems to regard the situation as static. We have a certain number of witnesses, and their testimony has a certain limited force against the background evidence, and that's that. But that need not be the situation at all. Evidence can mount up both for the background theory and for the reliability of the detailed historical evidence. Evidence could mount up not merely that people do not pass from the kind of state recorded by the earlier X-ray to the kind of state recorded by the later one, but that it is contrary to some well-established biochemical theory they should. Evidence could also mount in favour of a healing having occurred. True, there could not be an indefinite increase in the number of physical traces and witnesses in favour of a healing; but what could mount up indefinitely is

[3] D. Hume, *An Enquiry Concerning Human Understanding*, 127.

evidence in favour of the reliability of X-rays of the kind in question (and of the reliability of the witnesses who testified to their status). Evidence could mount up that X-ray pictures are, interpreted in a certain way, never misleading, and hence that the two pictures show how things were. And evidence could mount up that certain witnesses or certain kinds of witnesses (for example, those testifying to events of great importance to them, where affirming the event could lead to their execution) are reliable. And when the evidence on both sides does mount up, the situation—given the logical possibility of miracles—would be not a stand-off, but evidence both that the purported law is a law and that there has been a unique exception to its operation.

But Hume's worst mistake was to suppose that the only relevant background theory to be established from wider experience was a scientific theory about what are the laws of nature. But any theory showing whether laws of nature are ultimate or whether they depend on something higher for their operation is crucially relevant. If there is no God, then the laws of nature are the ultimate determinants of what happens. But if there is a God, then whether and for how long and under what circumstances laws of nature operate depend on God. Any evidence that there is a God, and, in particular, evidence that there is a God of a kind who might be expected to intervene occasionally in the natural order will be evidence leading us to expect occasional violations of laws of nature. And any evidence that God might be expected to intervene in a certain way will be evidence supporting historical evidence that he has done so. To take a human analogy, suppose we have background evidence supporting a theory about some human person that he behaves normally in highly regular ways—Kant, say, going for a walk at totally predictable times through the streets of Königsberg (so that citizens could set their watches by his walk). Then suppose that there is historical evidence of many witnesses that on one day his walk was half an hour late, and other witnesses reported that he delayed because he visited a sick friend first. We might at this point have a stand-off. But suppose that we have other evidence strongly supporting a theory that Kant was a compassionate friend; then we might expect him to change his otherwise inflexible habits to respond to a friend's sickness. The total background evidence supports the historical evidence that on the occasion in question the regularity was broken.

So what of the core physical element of the resurrection under-stood in the traditional sense: of Jesus being dead for thirty-six hours, coming to life again in his crucified body (in which he then had superhuman powers—for example, to appear and disappear)? Of course, the resurrection is traditionally supposed to have a cosmic significance which goes infinitely far beyond this core physical element. The Jesus who died and is risen is Jesus Christ, Messiah and the Word of God, the second Person of the Trinity. His resurrection constitutes God the Father's acceptance of the sacrifice of Christ on the cross for the sins of the world, and the initiation of a process of redeeming humanity and nature in respects both physical and spiritual. But the resurrection has this cosmic significance, it is traditionally supposed, only because of its physical core. The Word of God is risen from the dead only because the human Jesus is risen from the dead (only *qua* human can the Word rise); a human can only be resurrected fully if he is resurrected in an embodied state (for although, I believe, we can exist without bodies, bodies make for the fullness of human existence—such is the traditional Christian and Jewish view), and although he could have risen in an embodied state with a totally new body, resurrection of a changed old body would manifest 'resurrection', as opposed to mere coming to life again, most eminently. The Father accepts the sacrifice of Christ by bringing to life what has been sacrificed; thereby he proclaims that suffering and death have been overcome. To initiate the redemption of humanity and of the natural order, he needs to bring to life a previously damaged body, not only a soul. And he gives his signature of approval to the teaching and sacrifice of Christ by doing an act which God alone can do—of interfering in the operation of the natural laws by which he controls the universe. For the coming to life again of a body dead for thirty-six hours is undoubtedly a violation of natural laws, and if brought about by an agent, requires God's action. The core physical element in the resurrection of Jesus has for these reasons been supposed to be a very important element in the Christian tradition. So what detailed historical evidence is there for the physical core?

There are no apparent memories of having seen it happen, and no currently available physical traces. But there is the testimony of witnesses—of an indirect character. There is the testimony of witnesses (the writers of the various books of the New Testament) to the testimony of other witnesses. It looks as though St Paul, St

Luke, and the rest purport to tell us what they have been told, both by witnesses who purported to see the tomb empty and by witnesses who purported to have met the risen Jesus. (There are those who deny that the main New Testament writers claim to report the testimony of direct witnesses of the resurrection events; but time requires me to leave that issue to others. It certainly does look initially as if that is their claim, and so I shall assume.) Let us call the New Testament writers the indirect witnesses, and their informants the direct witnesses. The principles of credulity and testimony require us to believe the indirect witnesses, and so in turn the direct witnesses. No doubt the testimony of one witness about what another witness claimed to have happened is not as strong evidence about what happened as is more direct testimony; but any diminution of trustworthiness by indirectness is compensated by quantity. In this case there are several indirect witnesses, and two at least of them claim to have heard their news from more than one direct witness.[4] In such circumstances positive counter-evidence is needed for not believing the news. The most obvious such counter-evidence of a historical kind in this case is discrepancy in the detailed testimony: and there is certainly some of that. (For a small example, consider the clash between Luke 24: 50, which implies that the ascension occurred on the same day as the resurrection, and Acts 1: 3, which states that it occurred forty days later.) Discrepancies in the details require explaining by the witnesses being deceitful, bad observers, careless reporters, or people whose testimony is not intended to be taken in a fully literal sense; and any such explanation casts some measure of doubt on other details of their testimony, and to some extent (dependent on the kind of explanation given) on the whole testimony. But evidence can only fail to render a hypothesis probable if it renders probable instead the disjunction of all alternative hypotheses. And if none of these has any great probability, the original hypothesis must retain its overall probability— which is only a more careful and precise way of putting Sherlock Holmes's famous remark: 'When you have eliminated the impossible, whatever remains, *however improbable*, must be the truth.'[5]

Alternative hypotheses will need to explain both why false testimony was given and also the absence of any positive testimony in

[4] See Luke 1: 2 and Gal. 1: 18–19.
[5] A. C. Doyle, *The Sign of Four*, *The Complete Sherlock Holmes*, i (Garden City, NY: Doubleday, 1930), 111.

their own favour—for example, testimony of having seen the dead body of Jesus after the first Easter Day.[6] But they may have evidence best explained by them, including, perhaps, the absence of certain evidence which one would expect if the traditional account is correct—for example, the failure of St Mark's Gospel to proceed beyond 16: 8. However, when all that is taken account of, I can only say that alternative hypotheses have always seemed to me to give far less satisfactory accounts of the historical evidence than does the traditional account—in the sense of leading us to expect the evidence we find with much smaller probabilities. Those who think that the total evidence is against the traditional account do so because they think the background evidence makes a resurrection very improbable. There is, in my view, so much testimony to the main outlines of the traditional account that if this event was of a kind which we might expect to happen, one licensed by our overall background theory, we would have no problem whatever in accepting the main point of that testimony. If it were testimony to Jesus having woken from sleep, rather than to Jesus having risen from the dead, there would be no problem (despite the discrepancies of detail) in accepting it.

The problem arises because the (physical core of) resurrection is supposed to be contrary to laws of nature—and, as I suggested earlier, rightly so. Although we are far from clear about what are the laws of biology and their consequences, in comparison with our clarity about some of the consequences of the laws of physics, it seems to me pretty clear that resurrection of the traditional kind is ruled out by the laws of biology very well established by a whole range of background evidence. So if the laws of nature are the ultimate determinants of what happens, there is at least a stand-off, and maybe not even that. True, we could multiply evidence about the reliability of the witnesses or kinds of witnesses with whom we are concerned. The witnesses include some whose life was in danger if they testified to the resurrection and (plausibly) some whose religious upbringing would not have led them to expect that a

---

[6] A. C. Doyle, 'Silver Blaze', in *The Memoirs of Sherlock Holmes* (London: George Newnes, 1894), 24:

'Is there any other point to which you would wish to draw my attention?'
'To the curious incident of the dog in the night-time.'
'The dog did nothing in the night-time.'
'That was the curious incident,' remarked Sherlock Holmes.

crucified rabbi would rise again. And if the evidence became
immensely strong that people of that kind could never have testified
to the resurrection unless they believed it to have occurred after
having checked the matter out thoroughly, then maybe the detailed
historical evidence would be so strong, despite the fact that such a
resurrection would have been a violation of natural laws, that Jesus
had risen that the balance of probability would favour the latter,
which would then constitute a miracle.

I am, of course, not an expert on the New Testament, but my
own limited acquaintance with it suggests that that is not our situation. There is a significant balance of detailed historical evidence
in favour of the resurrection, but it is not strong enough to equal
the very strong force of the background evidence—if the latter is
construed only as evidence of what are the laws of nature. But in
my view that is not the right way to construe the background evidence. My belief is that there is a lot of evidence for the existence of
God—a being essentially omnipotent, omniscient, and perfectly free.
This evidence is the evidence of the existence of a complex physical
universe, the (almost invariable) conformity of material bodies to
natural laws, the evolution of animals and humans (souls connected to bodies), the providential ordering of the world in various
ways, and the widespread phenomenon of religious experience (in
the form of people seeming to be aware of the presence of God). In
my view these phenomena are best explained by the causal agency
of a God (with the properties stated), and hence provide good inductive evidence for his existence; they make it more probable than not.
I have argued this case at length elsewhere,[7] and cannot do so here.
But suppose that I am right. It would then follow that the laws of
nature depend for their operation from moment to moment on God,
who, in virtue of his omnipotence, can suspend them as and when
he chooses. But what reason would he have for doing so?

In general, God has good reason to conserve the laws of nature.
For by so doing he creates a beautiful universe, a dance of moving
material bodies; and only by doing so can he give to us embodied
creatures power over nature and power to learn how to extend our
powers. For embodiedness involves having under our control the
chunk of matter which is our body, and being able to influence the
world only by moving it. But only if there are regular laws govern-

---

[7] Richard Swinburne, *The Existence of God* (Oxford: Clarendon, 1979).

ing how material bodies behave, which we can come to know, can we come to know which bodily movements to make to produce which results. Only regularities in the behaviour of air will enable me to communicate with you by sound, and only regularities in the behaviour of bricks will enable me to construct a building. And by studying such regularities we can learn to extend the range of our powers—by learning the laws of electromagnetism, we can learn to communicate with distant persons by radio, and so on.

In any household, secure rules give control to those under them. If children know that if they do this, they will be punished, and if they do that, they will be rewarded, that gives them control over their future—which a parent who acted on whim would prevent them from having. But a parent whose every interaction with his children was governed by rules and who never yielded to a plea to bend a rule would cease to be a loving person with whom the child interacted. And the same would be true of a God who never responded to prayer by acting in non-rule-governed ways or by breaking his own rules. Despite all the advantages of the predictable, God would wish to interact with his children—and that means doing things at their request which he would not otherwise do, and responding in non-automatic ways to what they have done—very occasionally. And he would want to show them things directly, not only through a book of nature which he had written in advance.

All this provides reason for God responding to the particular requests and needs of individuals in ways which manifest his presence only to them. But it also provides reason for God to respond to a common need of the human race. There are, I suggest, a number of reasons for God to intervene in a big way in human history and show that he has done so, some of them being reasons for intervening by himself becoming incarnate as a human. The first reason is to make available an atonement for human sin. When humans have badly abused the good life which he has given them, and so wronged him and each other, God will naturally seek to do something about it. He will want us to take our sin seriously, not just ignore it; and so he will want us to make reparation. But we have corrupted each other, and have no serious commitment to making reparation at all, let alone the means wherewith to make it; for we owe so much to God anyway in gratitude for all the good life he has given us. So just as a human parent may provide a child who cannot pay for the damage he has caused with the means to make reparation, so God may provide for humans a human life which they can offer back to him as the life they ought to have led—a human life, which being the life of God, was not the life of one created voluntarily by God who would owe a great debt to God anyway. So God has the reason of providing atonement to intervene personally in the course of human history by becoming incarnate as a human and living so generously as to be prepared to be killed for his teaching (a not unlikely consequence of totally honest and challenging teaching in many a society). But if we are to join in offering a sacrifice, we have to know which sacrifice to offer, for many human lives which might seem to be holy on the outside may not be. God needs not merely to accept the sacrifice, but to show us that he has done so. You accept an offer by taking it over, using it, and making it fruitful. What more obvious way of doing this than by bringing to life the human killed for living a holy life?

Other reasons for God to become incarnate are to identify with us by sharing the hardships of life needed for our perfection, to show us what a good thing humanity is, and that he regards us as friends and not as servants. Also, we need teaching. Reason may show us with some degree of probability that there is a God, and it may teach us some basic moral truths. But we need to know so much more in order to live and worship in the right way. The teaching will need to include teaching that a certain human life was the life of God incarnate; for if we are ignorant that God has become incarnate, we cannot utilize the benefits of divine incarnation. The teaching will need to be handed on to new generations and cultures, and so, whether in oral or written form, it will need to be entrusted to a community, a church, which can interpret it.[8] But how are we to know that a church's teaching about a certain human being is the teaching of God about God incarnate? God must authenticate it, put his signature on the original teaching and the community which resulted from it. Only God who keeps the laws of nature operative

---

[8] For a fuller justification of the claims that God has reasons of these various kinds to intervene in human history, especially by himself becoming incarnate, and a further consideration of what kind of evidence additional to a resurrection would show that he had done so, see my *Responsibility and Atonement* (Oxford: Clarendon, 1989), ch. 10; *Revelation* (Oxford: Clarendon, 1992), pt. ii; and *The Christian God* (Oxford: Clarendon, 1994), 216-23. These passages include some argument for supposing that we might expect such an incarnation only once in human history.

can set them aside, and if they are set aside in such a way as to vindicate the life and teaching of a human whose outer life was holy, and forward the teaching of a church which teaches that the incarnate one was God, that indeed is God's signature. So God has abundant reason to intervene in human history to cause a human being to rise from the dead—not just any human, but a human who had lived (outwardly) a certain sort of sacrificial life and proclaimed deep and plausibly true news from God and was killed for doing so.

Now if there is a God of the kind which, in my view, arguments from the vast range of natural phenomena mentioned strongly support, that God, being omnipotent, has, as I mentioned earlier, the power to bring about anything coherently describable, including a resurrection of the cited kind. God is an intentional agent; he performs actions because he has a reason for doing them—that is, he believes that they serve some good. We too do actions because we believe that they serve some good. But we humans are subject to desires, inclinations which lead us to do actions less than the best. If we were freed from those inclinations, nothing but reason would motivate us to act; we would therefore always act for what we believed the best, or equal best. God, as a perfectly free being, is subject to no desires of the stated kind; he will act for what he believes to be the best or equal best, and, being omniscient, will have true beliefs about what is the best or equal best. It may be, however, that there is no best or equal best; that God often has an infinite range of mutually incompatible actions open to him at any time, each better than some other, but no best. In that case God will do a good action (that is, one in favour of doing which there is a balance of reasons), but not the best. I have sketched a case for supposing that among the good actions open to him are to effect an incarnation leading to a likely death followed by a resurrection, and so for supposing that his goodness would lead him to bring about a resurrection. It is always possible that at every time some other incompatible action would always be as good or better. But at any rate my arguments indicate that a resurrection is the sort of thing which there is significant probability that a God might bring about.

I have not argued here my case for the existence of God; nor have I done more than sketch the case for supposing that if there is a God, he might well be expected to intervene in recorded and historically evidenceable human history in this sort of way. My main point is that we need that sort of background theory well supported by evidence if our evidence overall is to give a significant overall probability to the resurrection. Given that theory, we still require detailed historical evidence of a prophet who lived a holy life, proclaimed that he was the chosen of God and was offering his life for the sins of the world, and proclaimed that he was God himself—or at any rate that his church proclaimed this to be the implication of his teaching. But we don't require too much detailed historical evidence, in view of the background evidence that such an event might well be expected, in order to make it probable that the event occurred, and so rational to believe that it did.

If such a background theory as I have described were much less well supported, or a rival theory (for example, that there is no God and that the laws of nature are ultimate) were well supported, then we would need much more detailed historical evidence in favour of the resurrection to make our belief in it rational. New Testament scholars sometimes boast that they enquire into their subject-matter without introducing any theological presuppositions. If they mean that they investigate without taking into account any background theory, then they misdescribe their enterprise. This simply can't be done. An infinite number of theories are such that they lead you to expect the historical evidence with equal probability— be they theories of invisible visitors from outer space or of the powers of sacred mushrooms. No scholar could decide between these theories on mere historical evidence alone; he must take into account wider evidence (including a priori considerations of simplicity) for supposing such theories to be true or false. What is worrying is that New Testament scholars seem to think that they can do without background theories. But if a theological theory (that there is a God who has certain properties) is well established, that must be taken into account. And even if we could reach some conclusion without taking into account 95 per cent of the relevant evidence (which includes the existence of a universe, its conformity to scientific laws, etc.), we would be highly irrational if we tried to do so. Knowledge is a web, and when some event—if it occurred— would have cosmic significance, the threads of the web stretch to the ends of the cosmos.

I should make clear that in saying that we have evidence supporting a certain background theory, I do not mean that the Jews of the first century AD, or even highly secularized humans today, do in fact expect a sacrificing Messiah, or even could normally be expected to expect such a Messiah, if they had not been familiar with the Christian tradition. I mean that evidence for the existence of God (of a certain kind) is publicly available and supports that theory (by objective criteria of evidential support), and that this theory of the divine nature has the implications which I have drawn out about what we might expect to find in history. But we humans may be too stupid or sinful to see the strength of the evidential support or the implications of the theory until familiarity with the Christian tradition draws this whole line of reasoning to our attention. Yet the fact that it needs a causal stimulus to make us aware of the force of certain evidence does not cast any doubt on the strength of that evidence. Inspector Lestrade and the bumbling police of Victorian Scotland Yard often saw everything which Sherlock Holmes saw. But they could not see its inductive implications, what it made probable. It needed Sherlock Holmes to suggest a theory to account for the data; and once they heard his theory, then they came to see that the background evidence and historical evidence supported that theory. But the evidential relations were there, whether or not they saw them. We may need the Christian tradition of the divine nature and of what a being with that nature might be expected to do (for example, as worked out in St Athanasius' *De Incarnatione* and St Anselm's *Cur Deus Homo*)—that is, an available theory—before we can see that the evidence supports that theory well. But it does support it very well, and the detailed historical evidence for the resurrection also gives it a modest amount of support. The other participants in this conference will assess the latter amount of support in far more detail and with far more competence than I can. But as one with a mere amateur's interest in New Testament scholarship, I can only say that my own belief is that the historical evidence is quite strong enough, given the background evidence, to make it considerably more probable than not that Jesus Christ rose from the dead on the first Easter Day.

Appendix: Sunday

I wish to illustrate my account of how evidence for the resurrection should be assessed by bringing into the picture some detailed historical evidence which is very seldom mentioned in this connection.[9] This is the evidence that there was a universal early Christian custom of celebrating the Eucharist on a Sunday, which is in turn to be explained most simply by a very early belief (within much less than a decade of the crucifixion) of many of the original Christian community, including the eleven, that Christ had risen on a particular day. This, in its turn, could only be explained in a simple way by the fact that particular witnesses remembered (apparently) that they had seen either the empty tomb or the risen Jesus on the first Easter Day. I add this further detailed historical evidence to the evidence more normally adduced in this connection as data showing that these were indeed the apparent memories of many of the original community, including the eleven, about events which had happened a very short time beforehand, and thus to be believed in the absence of counter-evidence.

Acts 20: 7 is from one of the 'we' passages in Acts, and so probably reflects the author's participation in the events that occurred. It records for a 'first day of the week' the breaking of bread—κλᾶν ἄρτον was the expression used by St Paul (1 Cor.) and the Synoptists for what Jesus did at the Last Supper,[10] and was always used later as a description of the common Christian meal which included the Eucharist. 1 Corinthians 16: 1-2 suggests that the first day had an important place in the Christian calendar, and Revelation 1: 10 suggests that the 'Lord's day' (ἡ κυριακὴ ἡμέρα) has central theological significance.[11] The Sunday Eucharist was not a custom merely of Pauline churches. All references in early literature to when the Eucharist was celebrated refer to a weekly Sunday celebration—see the *Didache* (n. 14) and Justin's *First Apology* (nn. 65-7). Eusebius records of one of the two groups of Ebionites (a Jewish Christian sect who separated from mainstream Christianity in the reign of Trajan) that they 'celebrate the Lord's

---

[9] Much of this appendix consists in rearranging the evidence assembled in W. Rordorf's *Sunday* (London: SCM, 1968), ch. 4, on the origin of the Christian Sunday, into the form of evidence for the resurrection. I am most grateful to Christopher Rowland for his valuable criticism of an earlier draft of this appendix. Note that I am not concerned with the issue of when or why Sunday became the Christian Sabbath, only with the origin of the custom of celebrating the Eucharist on Sunday.

[10] The other uses of κλᾶν ἄρτον in the NT (e.g. Acts 2: 46) are also all plausibly taken as referring to a Eucharist, with the exception of Acts 27: 35.

[11] For argument that the 'Lord's day' is Sunday, and not Easter Day, see R. J. Bauckham, 'The Lord's Day', in D. A. Carson (ed.), *From Sabbath to Lord's Day* (Grand Rapids, Mich.: Zondervan, 1982), 230-2.

days very much like us in commemoration of his resurrection'.[12] A group so dedicated to Jewish discipline would not have preserved the custom of Sunday worship if they had regarded it as of non-Palestinian origin. Christians left Jerusalem to found Christian churches in many other parts of the Near East within the first Christian decade. They carried with them not merely a body of doctrine, but a practice of worship. If the practice of celebrating the Eucharist on Sunday had arisen subsequently to the foundation of these churches, one would expect to find some in which the Eucharist was celebrated on some other day (for example, on the day of the original Last Supper—probably a Thursday, and certainly not a Sunday, or annually rather than weekly). No such are known. There is no plausible origin of the sacredness of Sunday from outside Christianity.[13] There is only one simple explanation: the Eucharist was celebrated on a Sunday from the first years of Christianity because Christians believed that the central Christian event of the resurrection occurred on a Sunday. Yet such early practice would have included that of some of the eleven themselves, and so could only go with a belief of theirs that they had seen either the empty tomb or the risen Jesus on the first Easter Day. This practice gives powerful support to the New Testament witness to the latter.

But a further interesting question then arises: who in those very early days decided that the Eucharist was to be celebrated on a Sunday? One obvious explanation is that some very early gathering of apostles decided, in view of what they believed to have happened on a Sunday, that Sunday would be the most appropriate day on which to hold regular worship in the form in which Jesus instituted it at the Last Supper. But we find no hint in the New Testament of such a decision being taken,[14] analogous to the reported decisions of the apostles about the conditions under which Gentiles were to be admitted to the Church.

The New Testament contains quite a number of hints in favour of a different answer to the 'who decided?' question. A number of the resurrection appearances of Jesus to disciples together are associated with a meal at which Jesus presided or was present (on

---

[12] Eusebius, *Ecclesiastical History*, III. 27.
[13] See Rordorf, *Sunday*, 180–93.
[14] Mark 16: 9; the opening verse of the new ending of St Mark's Gospel sees this phrase as capturing a central part of the Christian message.

particular occasions—Mark 16: 14; Luke 24: 30, 35; 24: 43; John
21: 13—and in general—Acts 10: 41).[15] The descriptions of these
occasions have associated with them the Eucharistic phrases which
St Paul and St Luke recorded in their accounts of the institution in
1 Corinthians 11 and Luke 22—Luke 24: 30 and 35 speak of Jesus
'breaking bread' and being 'known' in the 'breaking of the bread'.
Luke 24: 43 speaks of Jesus 'taking' ($\lambda\alpha\beta\acute{\omega}\nu$—see 1 Cor. 11: 23) the
fish; John 21: 13 speaks of Jesus 'taking' the bread and 'giving'
($\delta\acute{\iota}\delta\omega\sigma\iota\nu$—see Luke 22: 19) it to his disciples, and 'in a like way'
($\acute{o}\mu o\acute{\iota}\omega\varsigma$—see Luke 22: 20, $\acute{\omega}\sigma\alpha\acute{\upsilon}\tau\omega\varsigma$) the fish. Although only the
additional chapter of the Fourth Gospel mentions a meal, the author
of the main body of the Fourth Gospel was unwilling to record the
Eucharistic details of the Last Supper, although the wealth of
Eucharistic references earlier in the Gospel shows his clear knowledge of them.[16] (St John's unwillingness[17] to record the details of
the original Last Supper may be attributed to various reasons,
including his awareness that his Christian readers would already
know the details of the rite by heart, his desire that non-Christians
should not be given details which would allow them to parody the
sacred rite (*disciplina arcani*), and consequently his preference for
telling a story which showed the 'true meaning' of the Eucharist.)
Hence it is not to be expected that he would mention a Sunday meal
of Eucharistic character explicitly. But note that the two appearances which St John records, to the disciples as a group, are both
Sunday appearances.

St Matthew's account of post-resurrection events, of course, does
not include even the hint of a meal, but there is some reason to
think that even he was aware of a post-resurrection Eucharist. The
three Synoptic Gospels and 1 Corinthians contain accounts of the
institution at the Last Supper in words so similar to each other that
it is reasonable to suppose that they were used at subsequent celebrations. The three Gospels all include among the words of Jesus
that he will not 'drink again of the fruit of the vine until that day
when [he] drinks it anew' in the kingdom of God. These words

[15] O. Cullmann (*Essays on the Lord's Supper* (London: Lutterworth, 1958), 11–12)
understands Acts 1: 4 as speaking of Jesus 'being assembled together' with his apos-
tles, $\sigma\upsilon\nu\alpha\lambda\iota\zeta\acute{o}\mu\epsilon\nu o\varsigma$, as 'taking salt' with them, and so referring to a meal.
[16] e.g. John 6: 51b, 'The bread which I will give is my flesh for the life of the
world', surely alludes to the Eucharistic words.
[17] John 13: 2.

would not have been preserved as part of Eucharistic celebration unless some common meaning or other was attached to them by the Christian communities which used them. Now the Lucan tradition mentioned earlier records that Jesus did eat and drink (Acts 10: 41) with the disciples after the resurrection (and I have given reasons for thinking of such meals as Eucharists). Hence Luke must have thought of those as occasions when Jesus drank again of the fruit of the vine.[18] So the post-resurrection meals must be what the phrase 'anew in the kingdom of God' was seen by St Luke as referring to. And plausibly, therefore, St Matthew also saw his similar phrase as referring to a post-resurrection meal (and, since the 'vow of abstinence' was made in a Eucharistic context, to a Eucharist). All this suggests an explanation of the universality of the tradition of Sunday celebration—not merely in the belief that Jesus rose on a Sunday, but in the belief of the apostles that they had joined with Jesus in post-resurrection Eucharists which he commanded them to continue on Sundays.[19] By previous arguments, these memory beliefs must be taken as true—especially in virtue of the fact that they are the beliefs of many about what happened on a public occasion—in the absence of strong counter-evidence.

A further important piece of evidence that the source of the tradition is Jesus himself is that St Paul lists instructions on how to celebrate the Eucharist as among the things which he 'received from the Lord' (1 Cor. 11: 23)—that is, as part of a body of central teaching believed (c.55) to have come via an oral tradition from the mouth of Jesus himself.[20] It would be very odd if such detailed

[18] The vast majority of commentators interpret Jesus as vowing to abstain from the fruit of the vine until some final, more distant establishment of his kingdom. But whatever Jesus may have meant by his words, it is hard to suppose that St Luke could have so understood them unless he also supposed that no wine was drunk by Jesus on any of the occasions when Jesus ate and drank after his resurrection. But it is not plausible to claim that St Luke did suppose that—wine was an ordinary enough drink, and was above all to be drunk on an occasion of a new meal with old friends; further, I have given some reason to suppose that he thought of some of these meals as Eucharists.

[19] It is true that if there had been one formal Eucharist at which all eleven disciples were present on the first Easter evening, most of the Gospels would inevitably have mentioned it. (See the objection in Bauckham, 'The Lord's Day', 235.) But that is reason only for supposing that the first post-resurrection Eucharists did not involve all the disciples, and were occasions somewhat unexpected for their participants—both points made in the Gospels (e.g. John explicitly mentions the absence of Thomas on the evening of Easter Sunday).

[20] The suggestion that St Paul understood 'received from the Lord' as describing the contents of a private vision is not plausible; there would have been no universal

instructions came with no hint as to when the Eucharist should be celebrated. What detailed instructions as to how to celebrate a rite were ever laid down or handed on without some indication of when the rite should be performed? Yet there is no record in the accounts of the Last Supper of such an instruction being given then. And if Jesus had given that instruction only at the Last Supper, that would only have made sense to the disciples if he had also told them that he would rise again on Sunday—and in that case they would certainly have checked out the tomb on that day and not have celebrated on a Sunday unless they had found it empty. But if the instruction did come from the mouth of Jesus himself, I suggest that a post-resurrection instruction is more plausible.

So there is some reason to suppose that the universal custom of Sunday Eucharist derives from the post-resurrection practice and command of Jesus himself, and thereby contributes further evidence of the resurrection. But whichever detailed account of the early origin of the Sunday Eucharist be accepted, it constitutes one further piece of evidence either that witnesses found the tomb empty on the first Easter Sunday, or that witnesses believed that they had seen and probably eaten and drunk with Jesus on or shortly after that day, and hence is further evidence for the resurrection itself.

detailed conformity of Christian communities to Eucharistic practice without that practice having roots earlier and stronger than a Pauline vision. That what were received were in effect instructions for subsequent celebration is made clear by v. 26.

9

The Resurrection of Jesus and Roman Catholic Fundamental Theology

FRANCIS SCHÜSSLER FIORENZA

This essay seeks to examine the affirmation of Jesus' resurrection as the ground of Christian faith and theology within Roman Catholic fundamental theology. The question concerns not only the apologetic demonstration with its various arguments, but also the function and the role of such an apologetic demonstration to provide a foundation for theology. In my opinion, any discussion of the resurrection of Jesus within contemporary Roman Catholic fundamental theology should take into account the critique of foundationalism. Such a critique obviously has consequences for fundamental theology to the extent that fundamental theology claims to be an independent discipline that demonstrates the foundations of Christian faith and of Christian theology.[1]

I CRITIQUE OF FOUNDATIONALISM

Within current epistemology the critique of foundationalism has been applied both against the Cartesian search for a firm and secure transcendental foundation upon which to base all knowledge and against a positivist and empiricist conception of scientific knowledge.[2] This critique has been argued against transcendental approaches to fundamental theology based upon self-consciousness and against the historical objectivism of some versions of neo-Scholastic fundamental theology. The question remains whether such a critique affects the treatment of the resurrection of Jesus

---

[1] See Francis Schüssler Fiorenza, *Foundational Theology: Jesus and the Church* (New York: Crossroad, 1984).

[2] Wilfrid Sellars, *Science, Perception and Reality* (Atascadero, Calif.: Ridgeview Publishing Co., 1963, 1991).

within fundamental theology, with its attempt to provide certain historical demonstrations of Jesus' resurrection as the foundation of Christian revelation.

What is at issue is not simply the metaphor of foundations, because the critique of foundationalism does not deny that there are foundations; rather, the issue is the isolation of a particular foundation from its general context of knowledge and interpretation. What is at stake is whether one can seek in fundamental theology an absolute certitude independent of faith that can provide an independent and certain foundation of theology. In explicating this critique of foundationalism, I argue that fundamental theology should not be understood as a discipline that completely prescinds from faith, that can be based purely on 'secular reasons', and that will persuade the 'religiously unmusical'. Instead, I have argued that a holistic conception of criteria, the interrelation between pre-understanding and interpretation, between practice and meaning, entails a fundamental theology that is intrinsically related to the systematic exposition of belief. Since I have argued this in general for fundamental theology elsewhere, I shall not repeat the arguments here.[3]

What does it mean to interpret Jesus' resurrection within the framework of a fundamental theology that takes seriously the critique of foundationalism, the intertwinement between the ground and object of faith, and interrelation between fundamental and systematic theology? The answer can be elucidated only in relation to several distinct questions and issues: The first question is that of the *meaning* of the resurrection of Jesus. What does one mean by the resurrection of Jesus when one affirms it? Is it exaltation, transformation, or resuscitation of Jesus? A second question concerns the *genetic* historical origin of the belief that God raised Jesus from the dead. How did the first disciples come to their belief in the resurrection of Jesus? A third question is the *historical apologetic* question: can one historically demonstrate the resurrection of Jesus? To what extent is a historical demonstration of the resurrection of Jesus possible and credible? A fourth question is the *foundational* theological issue: what is the 'foundational character' of Jesus' resurrection to Christian faith? How does his resurrection serve as a foundation of

---

[3] See my *Foundational Theology* and 'The Critique of Foundationalism and Fundamental Theology' and 'The Relation between Systematic Theology and Foundational Theology', forthcoming, *Irish Theological Quarterly* (1996).

Christian faith?' What role does the historical demonstration of the
resurrection have in this foundational question?

II Two Distinct Approaches

Roman Catholic fundamental theology has recently changed in its
approach to these issues, as two contrasting directions indicate. One
seeks to interpret the resurrection by historically reconstructing the
origin of resurrection belief, with an apologetic intent of producing
a historical demonstration of the resurrection as the foundation of
faith. However, it modifies traditional fundamental theology
through its sophisticated awareness of recent developments in the
historical analyses of the New Testament materials. The other
approach interprets the resurrection of Jesus in such a way that the
earthly life of Jesus becomes the foundation of faith and revelation,
rather than the resurrection. Instead of taking either of these directions, I shall argue for a fundamental theological approach based
upon the affirmations and disclosures of the New Testament testimonies as disclosing Christian identity in its beliefs and affirmations
and thereby serving as a non-foundational basis of faith that rests
on the faith of the early community. It is non-foundational because
only in the context of other beliefs and assumptions do they serve
to explicate the basis of Christian faith.

A. From Demonstration to Convergence

Interestingly, Roman Catholic fundamental theologians have
moved in a different direction from some recent trends within
Protestant theology. Traditionally, Roman Catholic fundamental
theologians have emphasized the function of a rational natural theology and a historical demonstration within fundamental theology
in order to secure the independence and objectivity of its argumentation. By historically demonstrating the resurrection of Jesus and
the foundation of the Church by Jesus, traditional fundamental theology sought to provide a foundation of Christian faith and theology. In so far as fundamental theology sought to provide a historical
demonstration independently of a faith perspective, it sought to provide a foundation for both Christian faith and systematic theology.
The change away from such a demonstration can be seen in the

Lexikon für Theologie und Kirche, a classic Roman Catholic theological encyclopedia.[4] The third edition asserts: 'The Resurrection of Jesus is not a fact that can be historically demonstrated.' Instead, it is a 'reality (mysterium) that is accessible only in faith'. The statement claims that the resurrection is not a fact that can be verified historically; it does not provide an independent empirical foundation of faith, but one that is accessible only through faith.[5] Many contemporary Roman Catholic theologians have moved from a 'strong' to a 'weak' claim about the ability to demonstrate Jesus' resurrection historically. Some have even rejected such a fundamental theological approach to the resurrection, and sought to ground Christian faith in the life and death of Jesus.

By contrast, some protestant theologians have moved in the opposite direction. Wolfhart Pannenberg, a German Lutheran theologian, has reacted to the neglect of history within neo-orthodox theology and to the relegation of the correspondence theory of truth to secondary status by Martin Heidegger and by his students Rudolf Bultmann and Hans-Georg Gadamer.[6] Pannenberg has sought to provide a historical demonstration to ground Christian belief in the resurrection, and has argued that this historical demonstration is independent of faith.[7] William Craig has expressed even more confidence than Pannenberg in a historical demonstration in so far as he has argued that the appearances are 'fundamentally reliable historically'[8]—a thesis that Pannenberg is hesitant to

---

[4] Hans Kessler, 'Auferstehung Christ', II, *LThK* i, 3rd edn. (Freiburg: Herder, 1993), 1183-90. For a fuller treatment see *idem, Sucht den Lebenden nicht bei den Toten: die Auferstehung Jesu Christi in biblischer, fundamentaltheologischer und systematischer Sicht*, 2nd edn. (Düsseldorf: Patmos, Verlag, 1987).

[5] Kessler, 'Auferstehung Christ', III.

[6] See Wolfhart Pannenberg, *Revelation as History* (New York: Macmillan, 1968); *Jesus—God and Man* (Philadelphia: Westminster, 1968); *Theology and the Philosophy of Science* (Philadelphia: Westminster, 1976); *Systematic Theology*, (Grand Rapids, Mich.: Eerdmans, 1994).

[7] For contrasting evaluations of Pannenberg's argument, see Herbert Burhenn, 'Pannenberg's Argument for the History of the Resurrection', *JAAR* 40 (1970), 368-79; Fred H. Klooster, 'Historical Method and the Resurrection in Pannenberg's Theology', *Calvin Theological Journal*, 11 (1976), 5-33; Gordon E. Michalson, 'Pannenberg on the Resurrection and Historical Method', *Scottish Journal of Theology*, 33 (1980), 345-59; Sarah Coakley, 'Is the Resurrection a "Historical" Event? Some Muddles and Mysteries', in P. Avis (ed.), *The Resurrection of Jesus Christ* (London: Darton, Longman & Todd, 1993), 85-115.

[8] William Lane Craig, *Assessing the New Testament Evidence for the Historicity of the Resurrection of Jesus* (Lewiston, NY: Mellen, 1989), 380, *idem*, 'On Doubts about the Resurrection', *Modern Theology*, 6 (1989), 53-75.

affirm.[9] Likewise, Richard Swinburne, in his various defences of Christian revelation, has taken up arguments with new tools that are remarkably similar to those of the anti-Enlightenment argument of neo-Scholastic fundamental theology with its appeal to miracles and probability.[10]

Among leading contemporary Roman Catholic fundamental theologians, no one has written more extensively and more often on the resurrection of Jesus than Gerald O'Collins. He has significantly advanced the discussion beyond the traditional Roman Catholic fundamental theology. He has moved away from the foundationalism of the traditional neo-Scholastic historical demonstration in so far as he acknowledges the complex hermeneutical issues of the texts and the intertwinement of internal and external reasons. Moreover, he has argued for probability and convergence of probability, rather than for the absolute certainty. He notes that many apologists assess the evidence for the appearances of the risen Jesus, evaluate the narratives about the discovery of the empty tomb, and consider the exceptional growth of Christianity in order to establish the truth of the resurrection of Jesus and the truth of Christianity. Yet, as O'Collins notes, a difficulty remains: 'One difficulty, however, will not go away: how can the probable or even highly probable conclusions of such historical investigation alone legitimate the unconditional and certain decision of faith?'[11]

Such a question reformulates the relationship between faith and historical knowledge that has haunted theology since Lessing posed the dilemma in the eighteenth century. O'Collins's proposed answer is that historical conclusions alone do not justify such a decision. Instead, he proposes a theory of convergence: that is, 'convergent signs that legitimate Easter faith'. These convergent signs include historical evidence, but are not limited to such evidence.[12] But what does 'convergent signs' mean? The convergence takes place in several ways. On the one hand, O'Collins proposes a cumulative

---

[9] Pannenberg, *Systematic Theology*, ii. 352–9.

[10] Richard Swinburne, *The Concept of Miracle* (New York: St Martin's Press, 1970), and *idem, Revelation: From Metaphor to Analogy* (Oxford: Clarendon, 1992).

[11] Gerald G. O'Collins, *The Resurrection of Jesus Christ: Some Contemporary Issues*, The Père Marquette Lecture in Theology, 1993 (Milwaukee: Marquette University Press, 1993), 32. See also his earlier books, *Interpreting the Resurrection: Examining the Major Problems in the Stories of Jesus' Resurrection* (Mahwah, NJ: Paulist, 1988); *Jesus Risen* (Mahwah, NJ: Paulist, 1987); *The Resurrection of Jesus* (Valley Forge, Pa.: Judson, 1973).

[12] O'Collins, *Resurrection of Jesus Christ*, 32.

convergence of 'external' historical evidence. The multiplicity of historical arguments coalesce to build the historical argumentation. On the other hand, he is aware of the role of 'internal' arguments. Hence, he points to the need for subjective reasons, and he employs the transcendental arguments. Quoting William Blake, 'the heart is a bottomless gorge', O'Collins looks for 'signs "from the inside" '. These consist in the human yearning for life in the face of our mortality, the yearning for a love that cannot be fulfilled in this mortal and transitory life, and the existential yearning for meaning in the face of the absurdity and isolation in human life.[13] The convergence of the external and internal signs points to the resurrection.

Critical observations. Historical demonstration is asserted as a complex set of converging arguments. The convergence combines historical arguments that lead to probability with existential and transcendental arguments for the resurrection. This argument is a definite advance over the emphasis on facticity and historical certainty in traditional Roman Catholic fundamental theology. In replacing historical certainty with probability from a convergence of arguments, it acknowledges that no one argument is strong enough to establish the historical facticity of the resurrection, and that, taken together, the arguments provide the demonstration with a much stronger case.

The question that I would like to raise briefly is: what is the role of certain background theories and assumptions in the weighing of historical evidence and arguments? In dealing with historical arguments, assumptions about the significance of the laws of nature and the use of analogies, and so on, play a significant role in the weighing of the evidence. One can advance a coherent historical argument (consisting of many historical arguments) for the resurrection; but what is one doing if one's argument presupposes assumptions about the relationship between the divine act and historical reality? Is one demonstrating the resurrection in a fundamental theological sense as providing a ground for faith if such a demonstration rests on assumptions about the relationship between God and historical reality? In addition, the question must be asked: how does one justify the claim that internal reasons are complementary and have probative values? Does my desire for continued life and meaning

---

[13] O'Collins, *Resurrection of Jesus Christ*, 34–5.

add to the historical demonstration of the resurrection, or does it make the argument susceptible to a Feuerbachian critique so that, rather than complementing it, desire could be seen as undermining the argument? I raise these questions not so much to disagree with O'Collins's arguments for convergence and complementarity, as to suggest that they have to be argued differently.

B. *Foundation of Faith in the Life of Jesus*

A second transformation of traditional fundamental theology is much more radical. Instead of advancing a convergent or 'weak form' of demonstration of the foundation of faith in the resurrection of Jesus, it seeks to relocate the foundation of Christian faith in the life of Jesus. Despite considerable differences among individual authors, this general direction can be seen in the work of the early Rudolf Pesch, Edward Schillebeeckx, Lorenz Oberlinner,[14] and, more recently and more explicitly, Hansjürgen Verweyen.[15]

The early Rudolf Pesch focuses on the genetic origin of the belief in the resurrection, and draws conclusions from his thesis on the genetic development of the belief to issues of foundational theological significance.[16] Pesch departs from the traditional fundamental theological conviction that the resurrection of Jesus is a supernatural miracle that demonstrates Jesus' divinity and thereby provides the foundation for the Christian faith.[17] Moreover, he seeks to undermine the very arguments that traditional fundamental theology appealed to in its argument. He argues that the traditions concerning the empty tomb are historically unreliable. Nowhere in the Gospel narratives about the empty tomb is the claim made that the

---

[14] See Lorenz Oberlinner (ed.), *Auferstehung Jesus—Auferstehung der Christen: Deutungen des Osterglaubens*, QD 105 (Freiburg: Herder, 1986).

[15] Hansjürgen Verweyen, 'Die Sache mit den Ostererscheinungen', in Ingo Broer and Jürgen Werblick (eds.), *'Der Herr Ist Wahrhaft Auferstanden' (Lk 24, 34): Biblische und systematische Beiträge zur Entstehung des Osterglaubens*, Stuttgarter Bibelstudien, 134 (Stuttgart: Katholisches Bibelwerk, 1988), 63–80. See also *idem*, 'Der Glaube an die Auferstehung. Fragen "Zur Verherrlichung" Christi', in Bernd Jochen Hilberath, Karl-Joseph Kuschel, and Hansjürgen Verweyen (eds.), *Heute Glauben: Zwischen Dogma, Symbol und Geschichte* (Düsseldorf: Patmos Verlag, 1993), 71–88, and *idem* (ed.), *Osterglaube Ohne Auferstehung? Diskussion mit Gerd Lüdemann*, QD 155 (Freiburg: Herder, 1995).

[16] Rudolf Pesch, *Zwischen Karfreitag und Ostern: Die Umkehr der Jünger Jesu* (Zurich: Benzinger, 1983).

[17] Rudolf Pesch, 'Zur Entstehung des Glaubens an die Auferstehung Jesu', *Theologische Quartalschrift*, 153 (1973), 201–28.

events surrounding the empty tomb are the basis for Christian faith in the risen Jesus.[18] That faith is to be sought elsewhere. The narratives about the empty tomb express the early Christian faith in the resurrection of Jesus, but they do not provide either a historical or a genetic account of that faith.

If the discovery of the empty tomb provides one pillar of the traditional fundamental theological argument, the appearances of the risen Jesus constituted the other pillar upon which the argument rested. Pesch seeks to knock down this pillar also. The Gospel accounts of appearances of Jesus are not historical descriptions of the origin of the Christian faith. Instead, they are *Legitimationsformeln*—that is, 'legitimation formulas': they serve as warrants of authority. They are narratives that validate the authority of Peter and other early Church leaders.[19]

How, then, did the Easter faith historically and genetically emerge? Pesch bases his historical argument in large part upon the research of Klaus Berger concerning the resurrection of eschatological prophets and the exaltation of the Son of Man.[20] This direction of historical research maintains that during the time of Jesus there was a widespread expectation of an eschatological prophet who would meet a violent death and whom God would exalt. Jesus not only had this conviction, but shared it with his disciples. The disciple's faith in Jesus during his lifetime continued after his death.

Some of the historical interpretations upon which Pesch has built his conception—for example, the theses of Klaus Berger—have been challenged by Johannes Nützel and Martin Hengel.[21] They do not accept the evidence that Berger provides to support his contention that the expectation was widespread during Jesus' lifetime. They do

---

[18] See also Ingo Broer, *Die Urgemeinde und das Grab Jesu* (Munich: Kösel, 1972). For a different viewpoint see E. L. Bode, *The First Easter Morning: The Gospel Accounts of the Women's Visit to the Tomb of Jesus* (Rome: Biblical Institute Press, 1970).

[19] See Ulrich Wilckens, *Resurrection. Biblical Testimony to the Resurrection: An Historical Examination and Explanation* (Atlanta: John Knox Press, 1978). See the critical comments by Gerhard Delling, 'The Significance of the Resurrection of Jesus for Faith in Jesus Christ', in C. F. D. Moule (ed.), *The Significance of the Message of the Resurrection for Faith in Jesus Christ* (London: SCM, 1968), 77-104.

[20] Klaus Berger, *Die Auferstehung des Propheten und die Erhöhung des Menschensohnes: Traditionsgeschichtliche Untersuchungen zur Deutung des Geschickes Jesus in frühchristlichen Texten*, SUNT 13 (Göttingen: Vandenhoeck & Ruprecht, 1976).

[21] See Johannes M. Nützel, 'Zum Schicksal des eschatologischen Propheten', *Biblische Zeitschrift*, 20 (1976), 59-94, and Martin Hengel, 'Ist der Osterglaube noch zu retten?' *Theologische Quartalschrift*, 153 (1973), 252-69.

not accept that this expectation influenced early Christian experience and interpretation of Jesus. In recent work, Pesch has retracted elements of his thesis. Nevertheless, his position has become quite influential, especially through the work of Edward Schillebeeckx.

Edward Schillebeeckx takes up elements of Pesch's thesis but modifies them in *Jesus: An Experiment in Christology*.[22] He concurs with Pesch that the genetic origin of the early Christian belief in the risen Jesus was neither the narratives surrounding the empty tomb nor the accounts of the appearances. However, in distinction to Pesch, he asserts that the 'Easter experience' is a new act of God, an act of divine grace, a conversion experience. It is not merely an interpretation of the pre-Easter life of Jesus, but a new experience by the disciples after Jesus' death.[23] This conversion experience is a post-Easter act of divine forgiveness and grace.[24]

Hansjürgen Verweyen, Professor of Fundamental Theology at the University of Freiburg, who wrote his dissertation under Joseph Ratzinger on the ontological presuppositions of the faith, begins by distinguishing two questions: how faith in Jesus' resurrection historically and originally came about and what the objective basis of the Christian faith in Jesus is. Though his position differs from those of Pesch and Schillebeeckx, especially regarding the interpretation and assessment of the Gospel accounts of the Easter appearances, the direction of his fundamental theology is to ground the Christian faith in Jesus' life rather than in his resurrection.[25] Verweyen's arguments are much more systematic than historical in character. He fears that an emphasis on the resurrection of Jesus as the foundation of the Christian faith would minimize God's self-revelation in and through Jesus' life and death. If the revelation of God in the

---

[22] (New York: Crossroad, 1979). For a clear affirmation of the reality of the resurrection, see also Edward Schillebeeckx, *Interim Report on the Books of Jesus and Christ* (New York: Crossroad, 1981), 74–93, 134–8.

[23] Schillebeeckx, *Jesus*, 379–97, and *Interim Report*, 77–81.

[24] This emphasis on God's post-Easter act leads some to classify Schillebeeckx separately from Pesch. See e.g. Thorwald Lorenzen, *Resurrection and Discipleship. Interpretive Models, Biblical Reflections, Theological Consequences* (Maryknoll, NY: Orbis, 1995), 52–4, 74–7.

[25] See Hansjürgen Verweyen, 'Fundamentaltheologie: Zum "Status Quaestionis" ' *Theologie und Philosophie*, 61 (1986), 321–35. For Verweyen's treatment of fundamental theology, see his *Gottes Letztes Wort. Grundriss der Fundamentaltheologie* (Düsseldorf: Patmos Verlag, 1991). Most recently, see Verweyen (ed.), *Osterglaube ohne Auferstehung?*, and earlier, Broer and Werbick (eds.), 'Der Herr ist wahrhaft Auferstanden'.

appearances of Jesus was the decisive revelation of God, then it would constitute a different revelation than that revealed in the life and death of Jesus. Such a theology would be a theology of glory that would too easily pass over the meaning of suffering as exhibited in the life and death of Jesus. In Verweyen's opinion, a fundamental theology that argued solely from the events after Jesus' death as the basis of the Christian faith would contradict the fundamental Christian belief in the incarnation as the basic revelation of God. The decisive revelation of God would then not be the incarnation, if the content of that revelation were revealed only after Jesus' death. In addition, Verweyen argues that by rooting the basis of Christian faith in the life of Jesus, one roots faith in events that are closely similar to ours, and Christians today are not relegated to the status of second-hand disciples.

Critical observations. This approach has merit to the degree that it precludes a reduction of Christian faith to the specific kerygma of the death and resurrection of Jesus and precludes the neglect of the revelatory character of Jesus' life and death. Moreover, it draws the lines of continuity between faith in Jesus during his ministry and faith in Jesus after his death and resurrection, thereby affirming the importance of the life of Jesus for the foundation of Christian faith.

It does represent a sharp departure from traditional fundamental theology when Ohlig aligns himself with Verweyen by affirming the thesis: '*Die Auferstehung bzw. das Zeugnis über Erscheinungen des Auferstandenen können eine Begründung von Christologie und Christentum nicht bieten.*'[26] When, however, the life of Jesus of Nazareth is proposed as the foundation of Christianity, then this position results from a historical reconstruction of theological texts of a believing community. Likewise, it seems to me that Verweyen does not explore sufficiently the extent to which affirmations of Jesus' resurrection should be seen not as a different revelation, but rather in relation to his life as a further reception of the meaning of that life and a continuation of God's act in history. If the life of Jesus is made the ground of faith, how, then, is Jesus' life accessible? The life of Jesus of Nazareth is accessible to us through theological inter-

---

[26] Karl-Heinz Ohlig, 'Thesen zum Verständnis und zur theologischen Funktion der Auferstehungsbotschaft', in Verweyen (ed.), *Osterglaube ohne Auferstehung?*, 90; emphasis original. See Ohlig's fundamental theology, *Fundamentalchristologie. Im Spannungsfeld von Christentum und Kultur* (Munich: Kösel, 1986).

pretations of Jesus. Is one not basing the ground of one's faith on a historical reconstruction of the life of Jesus from the New Testament testimonies in a way analogous to how the early Pesch sought a historical reconstruction of the genetic origin of the faith? Does one then interpret the explicit testimonies of the New Testament in such a way that these testimonies do not so much provide the foundation in what they affirm, but rather, the historical reconstruction of the life of Jesus becomes the ground of faith?

III THE NEW TESTAMENT TESTIMONIES

In the following sections, I would like to advance a fundamental theological approach to the resurrection of Jesus that does not seek primarily to ground the contemporary Christian's faith in the resurrection either in a historical reconstruction of the origin of post-Easter faith or in the historical reconstructions that the second approach takes. Instead, I propose that we seek first of all to take into account what the diverse New Testament testimonies affirm and disclose. Rather than examine these texts as possible proof-texts, or as sources for the reconstruction of the historical genesis of the emergence of the post-Easter community, I suggest that we first ask what these texts disclose. What is the rhetorical power and disclosure of the language and metaphors about God and Jesus? What do they affirm about the resurrection of Jesus? It is not only as a Christian with a commitment to Christian Scriptures that my first step is to ask what the New Testament texts themselves affirm about the resurrection of Jesus; it is also the case for any singular historical event of the past: its occurrence and meaning have first of all been disclosed through testimony. Testimony is not simply a source for the reconstruction of historical knowledge, but has a rhetoric of its affirmations.

In taking this approach, I have limited my reflections to the earliest formulas and to the narrative accounts of the appearances. The traditions about the empty grave and the final redactional element in the individual Gospels concerning the appearances narratives, such as the different theological intents in Luke's, Matthew's, and John's accounts, are not included. Such an analysis could help me develop my argument further in so far as it would link the formal critical analyses of the appearances with the theological intent of the individual evangelists. For example, Matthew's interpretation of Jesus' resurrection as the fulfilment of the Jonah sign.[27] Luke links the Easter traditions with Jerusalem, sharply distinguishes resurrection and ascension, emphasizes God's act of raising Jesus as the presupposition of the exalted Lord's reign, and seeks to avoid interpretation of the appearance of Jesus as a 'ghost' so as to secure the resurrection of the dead.[28] Likewise, the interpretation of Jesus' resurrection in John's Gospel and in the redacted chapter 21 intertwines several significant motifs of discipleship, faith, and community in relation to Jesus' resurrection.[29]

Dealing with such issues would, however, double the size of this essay. Moreover, I think I can make the fundamental theological point without including these issues. The omission should not be interpreted in any way as a historical judgement on the accounts of the empty grave. I am convinced that there is some very early material within these accounts as well as later developments. Both would have to be examined as examples of the rhetoric of the New Testament testimonies to the reality of Jesus' resurrection. 'The texts of the empty tomb tradition take suffering and death seriously but do not see them as having the "last word" or as a religious-theological value in themselves.'[30] Instead, they announce not an absence, but a presence ahead.

In approaching the goal of examining the testimony of the New

---

[27] Paul Hoffmann, 'Das Zeichen für Israel', in Hoffman (ed.), *Zur neutestamentlichen Überlieferung von der Auferstehung Jesu* (Darmstadt: Wissenschaftliche Buchgesellschaft, 1988), 416–52. Cf. Ferdinand Hahn, 'Der Sendungsauftrag des Auferstandenen, Matthäus 28, 16–30', in H. J. Becker and B. H. Willeke (eds.), *Fides pro Mundi Vita: Festschrift für H. W. Gensichen* (Gütersloh: Gerd Mohn, 1980), 28–43.

[28] Gerhard Lohfink, *Die Himmelfahrt Jesus. Untersuchungen zu den Himmelsfahrts- und Erhöhungstexten bei Lukas* (Munich: Kösel, 1971); Gerhard Friedrich, 'Die Auferweckung Jesu, eine Tat Gottes oder ein Interpretament der Jünger?', *KD* 17 (1971), 153–87; *idem*, 'Lk 9, 51 und die Entrückungschristologie des Lukas', in J. Blinzler, O. Kuss, and F. Mussner (eds.), *Orientierung an Jesus. Festschrift für Josef Schmid* (Freiburg: Herder, 1973), 305–24.

[29] For an analysis of John's Gospel and ch. 21, see Raymond E. Brown, *The Gospel According to St. John*, ii (Garden City, NY: Doubleday, 1970), and Rudolf Schnackenburg, *The Gospel According to St. John*, iii (New York: Crossroad, 1982). For a comparison between John's Gospel and the *Gospel of Thomas*, see Gregory J. Riley, *Resurrection Reconsidered. Thomas and John in Controversy* (Minneapolis: Augsburg/Fortress, 1995).

[30] Elisabeth Schüssler Fiorenza, *Jesus: Miriam's Child, Sophia's Prophet* (New York: Continuum, 1994), 125. See also *idem*, *In Memory of Her: A Feminist Theological Reconstruction of Christian Origins* (New York: Crossroad, 1983).

Testament, I am aware that such a goal presents me with a hermeneutical dilemma. For I am acutely mindful of the degree to which our pre-understandings, preconceptions, and pre-questions influence our interpretation of past testimony and texts. The question is: how can our reading and interpretation proceed in a way that is self-consciously and critically aware of our standpoints and at the same time seeks to broaden and open our horizons, so that our perspective and horizons can both confront and join the horizons of a different period and time? Such a merging of horizons may take place from the horizon of our own perspectives, but it should entail an expansion of our horizons. Since the apologetic and foundational task is central to fundamental theology, there is an interest in approaching the texts with the apologetic questions in the forefront. It becomes important to reflect on this interest, and to ask whether it is adequate to interpret the texts primarily as a source or resource for these apologetic tasks without at the same time reflecting that these texts have a different rhetorical context and intent. While apologetic and fundamental theological questions are indeed legitimate questions, it is important to ask whether bringing such questions to the texts constitutes not only a gain, but also a loss. It may fail to explore the vision and surplus meaning of the text itself. Consequently, it becomes important to treat the New Testament texts as more than sources for our historical and apologetic reconstructions. It becomes important to attend to language, literary form, and the rhetorical situation of the texts. We cannot avoid the hermeneutical circle,[31] but we enter it by becoming aware of the limitations of our perspectives, especially our apologetic and foundational perspectives.

A. Hymnic Language

God has raised Jesus from the dead. It is generally acknowledged that the one-member verses represent the earliest tradition.[32] Examples are Romans 10: 9; 1 Corinthians 6: 14; 15: 15; compare

---

[31] Martin Heidegger, *Being and Time*, trans. J. Macquarrie and E. Robinson (New York: Harper, 1962), 55-8.

[32] See Jürgen Becker, 'Das Gottesbild Jesu und die älteste Auslegung von Ostern', in Georg Strecker (ed.), *Jesus Christus in Historie und Theologie. Neutestamentliche Festschrift für Hans Conzelmann zum 60. Geburtstag* (Tübingen: Mohr, 1975), 105-26. See also Klaus Wengst, *Christologische Formeln und Leider des Urchristentums* (Bonn: Friedrich-Wilhelms Universität, 1967).

Acts 2: 32; 13: 34; Colossians 2: 12; 3: 1; Ephesians 2: 5. Recent research has been influenced by Hans Conzelmann's distinction between the homology to the risen Lord in worship and the credo formulas that refer to the saving work of Jesus and his death and resurrection.[33] God is the agent of the action, and in the action 'ek nekron' Jesus is taken out of the world of the dead. Its stark theocentric orientation, praising God, differentiated it clearly from the later Christological statements. The closest form-critical parallel are the predicates of God in the Hebrew Scriptures' worship and confession traditions. The second benediction of the Eighteenth Prayer reads: 'you are praised Jahweh, who makes the dead alive.' The Christian formulas praise God as the creator who raised Jesus. God, who is the creator of the world, who has acted through saving actions in history on behalf of Israel, has now acted on behalf of Jesus. He has raised Jesus; he made Jesus living. The majority of the earliest formulas are formulas of 'God raising Jesus' rather than 'resurrection' formulas. They envision the raising of Jesus as an eschatological act of God in parallel with God's creative and saving acts.

A series of verses contain phrases of more than one member. Whereas the one-member phrase refers singularly to God's act, the many members refer to a series of saving acts: death, being raised from the dead, and exaltation. These statements have Christological and baptismal motifs. In Ephesians 1: 20 (see also 1 Pet. 1: 21) the raising of Jesus is associated with his elevation to a status of power, or Lordship. The resurrection is also related to the baptism. God has raised him and placed him in the heavens (see Col. 3: 1). Romans 8: 34 has a four-member statement with Jesus as the subject, concerning Jesus' death and resurrection, exaltation to the right hand of God, and his action for us. The four-member statement in 1 Corinthians 15: 3–5 expands the text in so far as Jesus' death is expanded through reference to his burial and his resurrection through the appearance before Peter. An apologetic motive is introduced with the experience of the witnesses.

What do these earliest texts state regarding the four questions listed at the beginning of the first section? Concerning the question of *meaning*, liturgical statements are the earliest affirmations of God's relationship to Jesus. But it is clear that they entail a distinc-

---

[33] Hans Conzelmann, *Theologie als Schriftauslegung* (Munich: Kaiser, 1974).

tive understanding of reality and history. God has created the world, and acts in our history in a saving manner. The Jesus whom we confess is someone on whose behalf God has acted, whose life is, therefore, justified. A more specific affirmation about the meaning of this action is not immediately evident from these texts. What is clearly affirmed is that God has acted and that God has raised Jesus: the how or what is less clearly articulated.

What about the *genetic or historical* question concerning the emergence of the early Christian belief? These verses are form-critically very early texts. They show that the belief in God's action on behalf of Jesus was present very early in Christianity. However, they do not answer the historical and genetic question: how did the early Christian faith in Jesus' resurrection emerge? The narratives about the appearances and empty tomb are not only later, but also represent different traditions.[34] Regarding the genetic question: to argue that because the appearances are textually later, they were therefore deduced from these is unwarranted from the form-critical evidence. What these earliest texts affirm is expressed in the belief in God's definitive action on behalf of Jesus. The historical, apologetic, and foundational theological significance will be discussed later.

B. Appearance Narratives

Form-critical analyses of the appearances generally go back to Martin Dibelius's thesis that the accounts of the appearances of Jesus have the literary form of illustrations, examples, and paradigms that were used within missionary proclamations and sermons.[35] Dibelius's thesis was for quite some time widely accepted, though modified by the work of Lyder Brun, Martin Albertz, and Rudolf Bultmann. The form-critical point is that the stories were formed as illustrations for the kerygma. However, such a form-critical analysis and results should be interpreted within the limitations of a literary analysis. To argue simply from a form-critical analysis to the historicity or lack of historicity is unwarranted without further evidence and argumentation. Dibelius used the traditional folklore terminology of 'legends' and 'stories'. Although such

---

[34] Pheme Perkins, *Resurrection: New Testament Witness and Contemporary Reflection* (Garden City, NY: Doubleday, 1984).

[35] Martin Dibelius, *From Tradition to Gospel*, trans. B. L. Woolf, rev. 2nd edn. (Cambridge: James Clarke, 1971).

terminology is used without prejudice to historicity of the form, it is an unfortunate choice because the terms 'legends' and 'stories' have the connotation that they are not historical.[36]

In Anglo-Saxon literature, Charles H. Dodd has advanced the form-critical analysis of the appearance narratives by nuancing Dibelius's theses.[37] Accepting the form-critical folklore designations of 'novellas' or 'tales' (not a historical judgement), Dodd advances the analysis by distinguishing between two formal types: a 'concise' and a 'circumstantial' type. (He also profiles a third intermediary type.) The concise type is a stereotyped list, whereas the circumstantial type is much more embellished and has the 'art and craft' of the story-teller. The concise type is earlier, and represents a tradition that came to be embedded in the later embellished developments.

Taking this insight one step further, John Alsup argues that it was only later, at the editorial or redactional stage, that the stories were integrated into the early Christian kerygma as illustrations and paradigms.[38] Consequently, the stories did not originate as illustrations of the kerygma. Alsup is interested in analysing the preredactional versions of the appearances in order to determine their form, content, and origin. He carefully distinguishes the historical question (which was the historical nature of the event) from both the form-critical question of the nature of the literary form and the history of traditions question (the history of the tradition of the form). Among the narrative accounts of appearances, Alsup distinguishes between narratives of an appearance to a group in which a missionary task or mandate is given[39] and narratives which describe a new recognition of Jesus. Nevertheless, he seeks to combine both forms into an encompassing narrative form of appearance in which the element of missionary task is predominant.

---

[36] Lyder Brun, *Die Auferstehung Christi in der urchristlichen Überlieferung* (Oslo: H. Aschehoug, 1925); Martin Albertz, 'Zur Formgeschichte der Auferstehungsberichte', *Zeitschrift für neutestamentliche Wissenschaft*, 21 (1922), 259-69, repr. in P. Hoffmann (ed.), *Zur neutestamentlichen Überlieferung*, 259-70; Rudolf Bultmann, *History of the Synoptic Traditions*, rev. edn. (New York: Harper & Row, 1976).

[37] Charles H. Dodd, 'The Appearances of the Risen Christ: An Essay in Form-Criticism of the Gospels', in D. E. Nineham (ed.), *Studies in the Gospels: Essays in Memory of R. H. Lightfoot* (Oxford: Oxford University Press), 102-33.

[38] John E. Alsup, *The Post-Resurrection Appearance Stories of the Gospel Tradition* (Stuttgart: Calwer Verlag, 1975), 266-7.

[39] Ibid. 147-90.

The affirmation that Jesus was not dead but risen does not fully express the basis for these narratives. Alsup's conclusion is that this affirmation alone does not supply the reason for the use of the appearances. Nor is Dibelius's specification of the *Sitz im Leben* adequate to the theological complexity of the stories which did not emerge as kerygmatic illustrations, though there are some connections on the redactional level (Luke 24: 34 and Acts 10 and 13). The appearance narratives have an independent tradition alongside that of the hymnic material referred to above. They also represent traditions independent of kerygma and tomb traditions. Their specific intent is one of anchoring the new in continuity and identity with the earthly Jesus. They speak of a divine intervention in a situation of crisis.

The form of the appearance narratives shows a set pattern with set elements: the doubts and despair of the disciples, an identity which is not immediately recognized, then the significance of the revealed identity, and the affirmation of both the continued existence and the divine character of the hero. The narratives of the appearances describe the doubts and despair. In attempts to interpret these appearance narratives, the question of literary parallels has been prominent. Contemporary Hellenistic literature has been examined for the source of the literary form. The Hellenistic literature of the time does in fact have examples of 'appearances'. Parallels have been drawn between the resurrection appearances of Jesus and appearances of Hellenistic figures such as Apollonius of Tyana, Romulus, Aristeas of Proconnesus, Cleomedes of Astupaleia, Peregrinus Proteus, and others. These stories belong very much to the context of the genre of *theios aner,* and as answer to the question of where one who is no longer with us and can no longer be found has gone. The literary parallels are striking, especially for the Emmaus story. It is difficult to rule out any literary influence or dependence. Nevertheless, significant differences are also evident. While they are, as in the case of Jesus, accounts of someone who has been exalted or transferred to another sphere or level, they have not first died. They are less accounts of resurrection from the dead than accounts of the appearance of an absent person who has been exalted.

The Hebrew Scriptures provide the other literary parallel for the anthropomorphic appearances. A correspondence or coherence exists between the early Christian belief that God's presence is revealed in Jesus and the belief in the revelation of God's presence in the Old Testament that makes it probable that the theophanic appearances there provided a tradition and form for the New Testament accounts. The divine initiative, the unexpectedness of this initiative to the recipient, the promises to the individual and to the people, and the ensuing mission or task for both the individual and the people are characteristic of this theophanic narrative. The form-critical analysis points to the relation between the appearance narratives as affirming divine initiative and calling (Gen. 18; Exod. 3; Judg. 5: 13; Tobit 5: 12). The relation of the literary form of the appearances to the Old Testament theophanies helps to illuminate the meaning, significance, and affirmations of these testimonies of appearance narratives. Obviously consideration of the literary form of the Old Testament theophanies needs to be complemented by an analysis of the structural differences in the texts and of social and cultural influences on their formation in early Christianity.[40]

C. *Testimony and Historical Reconstruction*

Several distinct historical questions are often conflated in a fundamental theological approach to Jesus' resurrection. One historical question is: did the appearances lead to the origin of the Christian faith, or did the appearances of the risen Lord cause the post-Easter faith of the disciples? Another partly historical, partly metaphysical question is: did the risen Lord 'really' appear to the disciples? The conflation consists in the identification of the question of the genetic origin of the Christian faith with the question of the 'reality' of the appearances and with the fundamental theological question of the foundation of Christian faith. An affirmative answer to the second question does not necessarily mean that the appearances were the cause of the faith of the first disciples. It is questionable whether the death of Jesus led to a despair that would require this. Moreover, traditional theology (that is, theology prior to the emergence of historical-critical exegesis) always assumed that Jesus had promised his death and resurrection, and that the disciples believed him, so that the origin of the faith existed prior to the appearances. But the question remains: how does one interpret the appearance narratives?

These texts are difficult to interpret because they use established literary forms to affirm the truth of the faith and experience of the

[40] See Paul Hoffmann, 'Auferstehung', II/1, in *TRE*, iv. 501.

early Christian communities. They adopt a specific form, in order to express the identity of the disciples' faith in relation to God's continued act in history. My point is that we should first explore the meaning disclosed by these texts as part of a fundamental theological argument before we reduce them to sources for a historical reconstruction of the genesis of Christian faith. Moreover, we should not make a theoretical historical reconstruction of the meaning of these texts as if the meaning of the language and metaphors in these texts were determined by historical reconstruction.

Today, one line of interpretation follows the road paved by David Friedrich Strauss, and engages in a specific historical reconstruction to explain the meaning of the resurrection.[41] Gordon Kaufman takes these texts and interprets the appearances as 'hallucinations'.[42] Gerd Luedemann develops a historical reconstruction to offer a theory of psychological compensation for earlier guilt as an explanation.[43] Such approaches fail to take seriously the affirmation and meaning that these texts seek to disclose. They overlook the meaning of the appearance narratives and how they seek to anchor the ongoing faith of the early Christian Church. They move too quickly to historical reconstruction of the origin of a text without first exploring the meaning disclosed there.

If one seeks to argue from these texts that they provide a historical demonstration of the resurrection of Jesus, one is not at first sight primarily asking what is the meaning and truth that these

[41] David Friedrich Strauss, *The Life of Jesus Critically Examined*, trans. by George Eliot from 4th German edn. (Philadelphia: Fortress, 1972), 709-44. There is also a persistent sexism in Strauss's view: 'Lastly, how conceivable is it that in individuals, especially women, these impressions were heightened, in a purely subjective manner, into actual vision?' Strauss is usually considered as the first representative of the hypothesis of subjective visions in contrast to the rationalist assumption of deceit (Reimarus) or only 'apparent death' (H. E. G. Paulus and F. D. E. Schleiermacher). Nevertheless, Strauss's view reminds one of Celsus's criticism (see Origen, *Contra Celsum*, 2, 55, in Henry Chadwick, *Origen: Contra Celsum. Translated with an Introduction and Notes* (Cambridge: Cambridge University Press, 1965)). For the early epistemological debates see Robert J. Hauck, ' "They Saw What They Said They Saw": Sense Knowledge in "Early Christian Polemic" ', *Harvard Theological Review*, 81 (1988), 239-49.

[42] Gordon Kaufman, *Systematic Theology: A Historicist Perspective* (New York: Charles Scribner's Sons, 1968), 418-34. Hallucination is defined by Kaufman 'as a nonpublic privately *extremely significant experience*' (424 f. n. 29).

[43] Gerd Luedemann, *The Resurrection of Jesus: History, Experience, and Theology* (Minneapolis: Fortress, 1994). For recent responses to Luedemann, compare Wolfhart Pannenberg, 'Die Auferstehung Jesu—Historie und Theologie', *ZTK* 91 (1994), 318-28, with Verweyen (ed.), *Osterglaube ohne Auferstehung?*

texts are affirming. Instead, one is using these texts as a source for a historical reconstruction of the origin of the Christian faith. The conclusion of the form-critical analysis, as formulated by Alsup, is: 'these stories participate in a specific form as *theological statements* and the consequence of this radical tenacity in form seems to indicate that they were not primarily interested in or capable of delivering essentially historical information as eyewitness reports.'[44] The basic question, then, remains: how does one decide between certain alternatives? Does one reconstruct the texts to a genetic origin of the Christian faith and interpret the appearances as 'holy hallucinations', or 'conversion experiences', on the one hand, or as 'God's raising of Jesus' or 'experiences of the risen Lord', on the other? (Can we as Christians imagine 'A Sunday Feast of the Holy Hallucinations?')

How does a fundamental theological approach deal with adjudicating among such diverse reconstructions? Historical reconstructions depend upon a complex relationship among several elements: the hermeneutic reconstruction of the meaning of the texts, historical and literary reconstructions, relevant background assumptions, and the relation to the praxis.[45] These are intertwined to the degree that if one's background assumption is that there is a closed natural world and if one's hermeneutical reconstruction of the text is resuscitation, then the historical reconstruction is such that the conversion experience or holy hallucination appears as the most appropriate interpretation.

In short, what counts as the most responsible interpretation and explanation depends upon certain background assumptions. A hermeneutical circle exists that has to be faced. On the one hand, the historical reconstruction of the text is to serve as the fundamental theological argumentation grounding the Christian faith. On the other, presuppositions or background theories about the nature of reality and history that affect the historical interpretation are dependent upon faith. The question is whether a historical reconstruction can ground the Christian faith, or whether historical reconstruction presupposes certain beliefs. For this reason, we have to rethink the relationship between fundamental theology, experience, and historical reconstruction.

[44] Alsup, *Post-Resurrection Appearances Stories*, 273; emphasis original.
[45] Elsewhere I argue that such intertwinement entails a broad reflective equilibrium; see *Foundational Theology*, sect. IV.

IV   FUNDAMENTAL THEOLOGY AND THE RESURRECTION OF JESUS

It has been claimed that systematic theology and fundamental theology have distinctive modes of argument. Whereas systematic theology uses the disclosure model of truth, fundamental theology appeals much more to arguments that are employed in other disciplines, especially philosophical and transcendental arguments.[46] I would like to examine how fundamental theology could combine both these arguments and the disclosure model, and so maintain that the appeal to disclosure should not be limited to systematic theology. Instead, it should also be employed in fundamental theology. Disclosure is not simply a way of being in the world, or an existential self-understanding, but rather the disclosure involves a vision of reality, God, and Jesus. Transcendental deductions and existential interpretations take place only within a specific understanding of the world and totality.

Fundamental theological arguments are much more closely related to a rhetoric of disclosure than to a transcendental deduction. Moreover, historical arguments and the historical evidence are partially dependent upon background theories and assumptions about the nature of history and reality. Background theories can be open or closed to affirmations of God's creative act within history. Therefore, it is important to ask the fundamental theological question: how does one speak responsibly about God's action in history and on behalf of Jesus, in view of such divergent background theories? I would like to suggest that one begins not so much with a transcendental appeal to the experience of self-transcendence, but with an appeal to an openness to the other and to the transcendence of testimony as a testimony to transcendence.

A. From Transcendental Self-transcendence to the Transcendence of Testimony

Gotthold Lessing's 'On the Proof of the Spirit and of Power' (1777) contains a critique and downplaying of the value of testimony that has had enduring influence. Distinguishing between fulfilled

---

[46] For the division of argumentation, see David Tracy, *The Analogical Imagination* (New York: Crossroad, 1981), 54–82.

prophecies and miracles that one experiences and those that one knows about only from the reports of others, Lessing argues that he can readily believe what he has experienced, but not what relies on the reports of others. Experience gives us an immediacy, a reliability, and a certainty that reports do not and cannot give.[47] Faced with this critique of historical testimony, theologians, from Schleiermacher onward, emphasized the importance of experience, and have thereby, seeking to bypass Lessing's critique, implicitly accepted it. Or there has been the attempt to provide a historical demonstration that supports the veracity of testimony, and therefore its objectivity. There has been less of an attempt to rethink and revalorize the very nature of testimony, independently of using it as a source for historical reconstruction and historical certainty.

Roman Catholic fundamental theology has sought to combine a transcendental analysis of the experience of self-transcendence with a philosophical theological conception of revelation. Karl Rahner's fundamental theology points to the openness of human subjectivity, and correlates Jesus' resurrection with human transcendental orientation. His transcendental explication of human freedom, responsibility, and love correlates with his fundamental theological interpretation of the resurrection. He offers an interpretation in relation to the finality and definitiveness of human freedom.[48] Much within this transcendental analysis involves a combination of Joseph Maréchal's openness to transcendence with Martin Heidegger's existential of authentic potentiality for being and with Heidegger's understanding of the relationship between pre-apprehension and meaning within interpretation. [In what follows 'transcendence' denotes either what is 'transcendent of the consciousness of the subject' or 'what transcends the natural world and pertains to God'. The context will make clear whether the former or the latter meaning is intended—eds.] In this transcendental approach Rahner has made important contributions to the fundamental theological understanding of God and of Jesus' resurrection. Language about God and the Christian proclamation concerning the resurrection is meaningful in relation to a transcendental open-

---

[47] Henry Chadwick (ed.), *Lessing's Theological Writings*, A Library of Modern Religious Thought (Stanford, Calif.: Stanford University Press, 1956).

[48] See Karl Rahner, *Foundations of Christian Faith: An Introduction to the Idea of Christianity* (New York: Crossroad, 1982), 264–85. Rahner is, of course, hermeneutically sophisticated, and carefully emphasizes that the transcendental expectation and Christian belief in the resurrection of Jesus mutually influence each other.

ness that constitutes a pre-apprehension of its meaning. This approach attempts to follow Schleiermacher's emphasis on experience, while at the same time demonstrating an openness to revelatory acts of God in history.

I shall suggest an approach that revalorizes testimony and its fundamental theological significance. Transcendental and phenomenological approaches in theology that seek to combine Kant's notion of transcendental subjectivity with Heidegger's analysis of the historicity of *Dasein* need to reflect on Emmanuel Lévinas's critique of Heidegger's analysis of *Dasein*.[49] Lévinas attacks Heidegger's existential interpretation of conscience as *Dasein*'s potentiality and projection. He analyses Heidegger's understanding of transcendence as the manifestation of conscience in *Being and Time* as reductionistic in so far as it lacks the otherness of moral transcendence. The fundamental issue at stake is whether transcendence, conceived of in terms of the projection of the self, allows for an adequate encounter with the otherness of transcendence.[50] In his essay 'Truth as Manifestation and Truth as Testimony,' Lévinas attempts to articulate the value of testimony as an alternative to the philosophy of consciousness with its certitude.[51] His reflections are echoed by Paul Ricoeur when he opposes testimony to the certitude of representation that encompasses both self-certainty and manifestation and argues for testimony in relation to the absolute.[52] The fundamental theological question is: how does one experience the transcendence of the Divine within human history? How does a human person become open to the otherness of God? How does one encounter God as transcending our expectations and desires? Lévinas's phenomenology of the face and of the other exemplifies the attempt to develop the experience of transcendence in terms of intersubjectivity, rather than in the categories of transcendental self-projection of consciousness.

---

[49] See Emmanuel Lévinas, *Otherwise than Being or Beyond Essence* (Boston: Kluwer, 1981), 131-68; originally published in part as 'Vérité comme dévoilement et vérité comme témoignage', in Enrico Castelli (ed.), *Le Témoignage* (Paris: Aubier, 1972), 101-10.

[50] See Lévinas, 'Meaning and Sense', in his *Collected Philosophical Papers* (Boston: Kluwer, 1986), 75-107.

[51] *Otherwise than Being*, 142-52.

[52] Paul Ricoeur, *Figuring the Sacred: Religion, Narrative, and Imagination* (Minneapolis: Fortress, 1995), 123. See also the essay on testimony in *idem*, *Essays on Biblical Interpretation*, ed. Lewis S. Mudge (Philadelphia: Fortress, 1980), 199-54.

A locus of transcendence is the encounter with the other. One receives life and experiences love through the unmerited self-giving of another. One experiences human finiteness primarily through the death of the other, not through one's own death. It is the death of the other—parent, friend, loved one—that raises questions about meaning and finiteness. When one accepts another, one does so not through a transcendental self-projection, but rather through a trust in the words and actions of the other. Precisely our trust in their testimony of love and faith opens us to transcendence, because through our trust, through our faith, and through our acceptance of their word and testimony we overcome our attempts to manipulate our lives and to control our destiny. The Scriptures, in Christian as well as other religious traditions, underscore how in care for the poor and oppressed or concern for the widow, orphan, and stranger, one encounters the divine. Precisely by going beyond one's self to care for that which appears as anything but divine, one encounters the divine.

In short, what I am arguing is that the testimony and witness of the *other* is what makes possible the encounter and openness to transcendence. There is what I would like to call a 'hermeneutical experience' of a religious tradition and its testimonies that informs and shapes our horizons, which makes it possible for us to envision what is disclosed in our tradition. Our experience within a religious community or church is not merely an intersubjective encounter with other individual members of that community; it also entails an encounter with religious testimonies that forms not only the way we interact with one another, ethically, but also our historical expectations and eschatological hope.

A fundamental theological grounding of the resurrection of Jesus that extrapolates from transcendental 'excess' is not sufficient to get at the transcendence of Jesus' resurrection to which the New Testament testifies, because it runs the danger of reducing the resurrection to our expectation. In my book on fundamental theology I have argued that the affirmation of the resurrection presents us with a problem of meaning as well as of truth. Conditions of truth and conditions of meaning are interrelated.[53] In a review Gerald O'Collins argued that the resurrection is not totally new, because human persons do experience life and are aware of death. They can,

---

[53] Fiorenza, *Foundational Theology*, 292–4.

therefore, understand the meaning of Jesus' resurrection and of Jesus in relation to this experience.[54]

Here I disagree. Testimony plays a much more significant role with regard to the resurrection of Jesus than it does with other common historical events, and our subjective anticipation is less helpful as an interpretive key. Obviously, we have access to all historical events only through testimony, but the situation is not parallel or absolutely similar with the resurrection. Many events we can understand independently of testimony. For example, it is well known that Mark reports that Jesus took a nap on the boat before the storm, whereas Luke and Matthew do not. Historians have the problem of reconciling the differences among these accounts. They may never be able to do this with certainty, though they tend to give Mark's version the benefit of the doubt and see Luke and Matthew as eliminating what might appear to detract from the dignity of Jesus. The situation with the resurrection is quite different. Independently of how one judges the historicity of Jesus' nap, we all know from our daily lives what a nap is. But we do not know what Jesus' resurrection is, because this transcends our experience.

If we think of Jesus' resurrection in terms of our own categories and expectations, we will most likely misunderstand it. If we think of it in terms of a continuation of life as we know it, then we are likely to think of it as a 'resuscitation' of the body and a return to this life. Yet it is quite clear that the resurrection of Jesus cannot be reduced to the Johannine account of Lazarus's revival. Jesus does not return to his family, friends, and relatives as Lazarus did. If we think of exaltation, we tend to think of exaltation in spatial terms, but it is obvious from the New Testament testimony that Jesus' exaltation cannot be reduced to spatial metaphors, for it is viewed as an eschatological act. If we think of the resurrection of Jesus as a transformation of Jesus' bodily existence into a new 'spiritual body', then we have to ask, 'what does this mean?' The Pauline idea of body is a complex concept that can in no way be reduced simply to what we understand by the term 'body' today.[55] We should not use our customary images—for example, images drawn from Shakespeare

---

[54] See Gerald O'Collins, review of my *Foundational Theology*, *Heythrop Journal*, 26 (Apr. 1985), 201.

[55] See Francis P. Fiorenza, 'Der Mensch als Einheit von Leib und Seele', in Johannes Feiner and Magnus Löhrer (eds.), *Mysterium Salutis. Grundriss Heilsgeschichtlicher Dogmatik*, ii. (Einsiedeln: Benzinger, 1967), 584-636.

about Hamlet's father—as if Jesus was some ghost-like figure. The interpretive question is indeed difficult.[56] We have to be open to the New Testament testimonies to ask what they disclose. What is the power of their vision that breaks into our everyday expectation of continued existence, spatial transcendence, and ghostly existence, and proclaims to others that Jesus' resurrection is an eschatological act of the Creator God?

B. Resurrection: Ground and Object of Christian Faith

To deal with the resurrection of Jesus from a fundamental theological perspective requires that we ask the question about what the ground of contemporary Christian faith in the resurrection is. The question should not simply be identified with the genetic question as to how the first Christians came to their belief in the resurrection of Jesus. The early Christians had direct experiences of the earthly Jesus, and they had experiences after Jesus' death that led them to the affirmation that God had raised Jesus from the dead.

A traditional fundamental theology usually separated quite distinctly the ground and object of Christian faith. It relied primarily on a historical demonstration of the resurrection as a supernatural miracle that showed the divinity of Jesus, and that demonstration provided the ground and basis for the Christian belief in the resurrection of Jesus. It is the extrinsicism of such an argument that led Karl Rahner to develop a transcendental approach to the resurrection, led to the development of an approach that combines external and internal reasons, and led to the attempt to ground the resurrection of Jesus in the life of Jesus.

These approaches entail important correctives to the extrinsicism of a traditional apologetic based upon historical demonstration. Against such extrinsicism, it is important to argue not only for the interrelation between object and ground of faith, rather than their separation, with the latter being the foundation of the former, but also for the role of the faith and testimony of the early Christian community as the ground of faith today.

---

[56] For diversity in the conception of resurrection, see Gisbert Greshake and J. Kremer, *Resurrectio mortuorum. Zum theologischen Verständnis der leiblichen Auferstehung* (Darmstadt: Wissenschaftliche Buchgesellschaft, 1986), and Gregory J. Riley, *Resurrection Reconsidered: Thomas and John in Controversy* (Minneapolis: Fortress, 1995), 7-68.

The faith and testimony of the early Christian community are in many respects the ground of the contemporary Christian's faith. It is primarily—almost exclusively—through the faith of the early Christian community that the earthly Jesus has become accessible to history and to the contemporary Christian. This early Christian faith is based on more than the earthly Jesus, because it is an interpretation of Jesus which includes a reception of the reality of Jesus as an ongoing reality.[57] It affirms that the reality of Jesus includes the earthly Christian reception of Jesus. Moreover, it is through the faith of the early Christian community that we have access to Jesus, and this early Christian faith is that God has raised Jesus. To argue that fundamental theology has as its object the earthly Jesus rather than the resurrected Jesus would be possible if we had independent access to the earthly Jesus, but we do not.

The Christian faith not only makes explicit what is implicit in the life of Jesus, but also draws out implications of the life of Jesus in view of early Christians' understanding of God's saving act of raising Jesus from the dead and constituting the early Christian community. Narratives of Jesus' death and resurrection together spell out the identity of Jesus.[58] Events crucial to Christian identity, such as the foundation of the Church and of the early Christian mission, are rooted in this intertwinement of interpretation and reception.[59]

Metaphorical language is one of the most complex and debated issues in contemporary philosophy and hermeneutical theory.[60] Although these debates cannot be aired here, I would like to point to the inadequacy of existential interpretation of metaphors. When

[57] For the distinction between the historical and the earthly Jesus, see Van A. Harvey, *The Historian and the Believer* (New York: Macmillan, 1967).

[58] Hans W. Frei, *Theology and Narrative: Selected Essays*, ed. George Hunsinger and William C. Placher (New York: Oxford University Press, 1993), 45-116, and *idem*, *The Identity of Jesus Christ: The Hermeneutical Bases of Dogmatic Theology* (Philadelphia: Fortress, 1975).

[59] Fiorenza, *Foundational Theology*, 230 ff.

[60] See Paul Ricoeur, *The Rule of Metaphor: Multi-Disciplinary Studies in the Creation of Meaning in Language*, University of Toronto Romance Series, 37 (Toronto: University of Toronto Press, 1975). See also Sheldon Sacks (ed.), *On Metaphor* (Chicago: University of Chicago Press, 1979; repr. of autumn issue of *Critical Inquiry*, 5/1); and Andrew Ortony (ed.), *Metaphor and Thought* (Cambridge: Cambridge University Press, 1979). For the debate in the North American context see Richard Rorty, 'Unfamiliar Noises: Hesse and Davidson on Metaphor', in his *Philosophical Papers*, vol. 1: *Objectivity, Relativism and Truth* (Cambridge: Cambridge University Press, 1991), 161-72; Brøjn T. Ramberg, *Donald Davidson's Philosophy of Language* (Cambridge, Mass.: Blackwell, 1989).

Romeo states that Juliet is the sun, the meaning of his metaphorical statement cannot be interpreted simply as a literal statement. Nor can the statement be reduced to Romeo's existential self-understanding in the face of Juliet. He is making a statement about Juliet. One can, of course, point out that such a statement is metaphorical and not literal, and that one should not understand it as a total identification between Juliet and the sun. But it is wrong to conclude from that qualification to a purely existential interpretation of the metaphorical language.[61] A recent essay contains the following explanation: 'This would also enable us to accept the Christian affirmation of the resurrection of Jesus for what it is, namely, an extension of its symbolic use whereby the Christian community affirms that the same experience of liberation from bondage and new life in the Spirit ". . . continues to be experienced even now, after his crucifixion . . ." .'[62] In my opinion, one can argue against such a statement on the basis of the rhetoric of the New Testament testimonies that I have cited. They are not simply symbolic interpretations of liberation from bondage, but affirm God's act on behalf of Jesus and the post-Easter reality of Jesus. Existential interpretations make the move from linguistic text to existential meaning without sufficiently exploring the structure, form, and metaphors of the texts and the multiplicity of signification and connotation.

A metaphor, in contemporary philosophy, is defined either as a secondary use of language or as essential to language itself, so that the question emerges as to whether all language is metaphorical and how metaphorical language has meaning and is to be interpreted.[63] It is important in my opinion to understand how metaphors are meaningful in so far as they create meaning. Samuel R. Levin argues that one should not rationalize the meanings of metaphors by reducing and conforming their meaning to predetermined rules and conditions. Instead, one should take metaphors at

---

[61] For a critique of existential interpretations of religious metaphors see Frei, *Theology and Narrative*, 117-52, and Janet Martin Soskice, *Metaphor and Religious Language* (Oxford: Clarendon, 1985).

[62] Robert F. Scuka, 'Resurrection: In Search of Meaning', *Modern Theology*, 6 (1989), 90.

[63] For the literal use, see John R. Searle, *Expression and Meaning: Studies in the Theory of Speech Acts* (New York: Cambridge University Press, 1979), chs. 4 and 5. Compare Donald Davidson, 'What Metaphors Mean', *Critical Inquiry*, (1986), 273-94.

their face value to envision a reality in a new way.[64] To the degree that language is metaphorical, including philosophical language, even alternative accounts entail metaphorical language.[65] Moreover, most importantly for our testimonies, metaphorical language displays a surplus of meaning not only through the extension and range of reference and new reference, but also through the very last line or through referents to the very creative process of the metaphor that entails a creation of meaning and language.[66]

In affirming that contemporary Christian faith is grounded in the faith of early Christians, and that the vision of this faith is disclosed in the metaphors of its testimony, one must attend to the meaning and rhetoric of those testimonies. The meaning of language cannot be reduced either to an existing self-understanding or to referents independent of the meaning expressed in language. One can ask, and ask legitimately: why do you prefer to use the language 'God has raised Jesus' or the 'resurrection of Jesus' rather than the language of 'conversion experience' or 'holy hallucination'? The reason is that the metaphorical talks about the reality of Jesus, whereas the other language talks primarily about the reality of existential self-understanding of the community. If the meaning of language is reduced to existential understanding or referential object, then the very creativity, the surplus meaning of the metaphorical language, is not captured. Metaphorical language in itself and in its rich diversity in the New Testament is essential to point to, but not capture, an understanding of God's creativity that surpasses our understanding and proclaims the exaltation and resurrection of Jesus. The diverse metaphors expressing the post-Easter faith are indispensable. This is a problem in dealing with the mystery of God and God's acts. And it is no wonder that it is our poets, rather than our historians, who speak more about God.

I would like to use the example of the application of personal language to God. Since Fichte and the atheism controversy of the early nineteenth century, modern theologians have recognized the

---

[64] Samuel R. Levin, *Metaphoric Worlds: Conceptions of a Romantic Nature* (New Haven: Yale University Press, 1988).

[65] Jacques Derrida, 'White Mythology: Metaphor in the Text of Philosophy', *New Literary History*, 6 (1974), 5–74.

[66] See M. C. Beardsley, 'The Metaphorical Twist', *Philosophy and Phenomenological Research*, 22 (1962), 293–7, and especially Ricoeur, *Rule of Metaphor*.

inadequacy of personal language when applied to God.[67] The limitation of the relationality of our notion of person would conceive of God as person in relation to a finite model of personhood. However, the problem is that if we refuse to use personal language to describe God and exclusively use other language, such as 'ground', 'principle of creativity', and so on, an equal danger exists that we will not understand God as more than what we understand as personal or personhood, but as less than the personal. I suggest the same is true of the metaphorical language about the resurrection of Jesus. An attempt to use different vocabulary in order to avoid misinterpreting the resurrection runs the risk that it does not affirm more but, rather, less about the reality of the risen Jesus.

Is it necessary to use the same basic metaphors that the early Christian community used? There is a tendency among some contemporary Roman Catholic theologians to pick up a notion that was prevalent in modernism: namely, the interchangeability of concepts to express the same reality. This conviction is evident even in Pope John XXIII's opening of the Second Vatican Council when he called for new formulas to express the substance of ancient truths.[68] Such a position approximates the inadequate linguistic assumption that the meaning of a word consists in its referent, so that different words have an identical meaning if they refer to the same thing. But the meaning and use of vocabulary are much more intertwined than such a view assumes. Shifts in vocabulary necessarily entail shifts in meaning. In addition, we do not have any access to the referent, the resurrection of Jesus, independent of the New Testament metaphors. Consequently, the New Testament metaphors are irreplaceable metaphors not only in so far as they express our continuity with early Christian faith, but also in so far as they bring to the fore the meaning of that testimony.

C. Historical Reconstruction or Hermeneutics of Testimony

Is there then no room for historical reconstruction of the origins of early Christian belief? The function and role of such historical

---

[67] Johann Gottlieb Fichte (ed.), *Der Herausgeber des philosophischen Journals gerichtliche verantwortungsschriften gegen die Anklage des Atheismus* (Jena: C. E. Gabler, 1799). See the collection Franz Bockelman (ed.), *Die Schriften zu J. G. Fichtes Atheismus-Streit* (Munich: Rogner & Bernard, 1969).

[68] Pope John's 'Opening Speech to the Council', in Walter M. Abbott and Joseph Gallagher (eds.), *The Documents of Vatican II* (Chicago: Follett Publishing, 1966), 715.

reconstructions are quite different from those of a hermeneutical reconstruction of the diverse testimonies and narratives. The early credal formulas show how early and widespread was the belief in Jesus' exaltation. The appearance stories, though in theological and literary forms, are at the same time affirmations of the reality of Jesus. The hymnic material and appearance narratives are independent literary forms with a different rhetoric from that of fundamental theology, and this rhetoric shows the distinctiveness of their theological affirmations. The hermeneutical reconstruction of the testimonies underscores the meaning and rhetoric of the texts. The analysis also points to the existence of a belief in Jesus' resurrection at the very beginnings of early Christianity.

1. *Demonstration or Explication.* Analysis of the literary forms of the appearance narratives makes it very difficult to draw isolated conclusions from one or another aspect of the appearances, to arrive at a definitive historical conclusion as to the nature of the appearances. Literary analyses that distinguish an earlier concise form from a more detailed form speak against interpreting the appearances exclusively as later theological embellishments or interpretations for illustrative purposes within the kerygma. Instead these analyses point to the existence in primitive Christianity of Christian accounts of the appearances of Jesus and to the early Christian faith in the resurrection of Jesus. Does this demonstrate historically the resurrection of Jesus in a fundamental theological sense, so as to provide an independent foundation of Christian faith? In my opinion, it does not. It does provide some warrants for that conviction, but not an independent grounding of it. It points us back to the early Christian faith in the resurrection of Jesus. Again, I would contend that it shows that the foundation of our Christian faith in the resurrection is the faith of the early Christian community.

The hymnic material and the appearance narratives explicate the early Christian faith, rather than provide a singular or objectively secure foundation of its truth. The content of the hymns and narratives speaks against the fundamental theological view of Verweyen and others who appeal primarily to the life of Jesus as the foundation of faith. It is not a question of a theology of incarnation versus a theology of resurrection. Nor should it be framed simply as a question of a theology of glory versus a theology of the cross. The post-Easter narratives of the risen Jesus function to proclaim the reality of God's action on behalf of Jesus, so that God's act is seen in its continuity as well as its newness. The appearances are often linked to a calling and a mission. This post-Easter mission cannot be grounded simply in a pre-Easter earthly Jesus, but has to be understood as an ongoing reception of God's historical initiative with regard to Jesus. The emergence of the Church is not grounded simply in the life of Jesus, but entails a post-Easter Christian experience and reception.[69] This is not to separate or downplay the significance of the life of Jesus; one can interpret the resurrection not as an alternative or new revelation, but rather as a further reception and implication based on a faith in God's continuing act.

In short, by making the New Testament testimonies, rather than historical reconstructions, the foundation of Christian faith, I am taking an alternative position to both the fundamental theological trends that I described at the beginning. The fundamental theological approach that makes the case for convergence of probability as a historical argument which combines external and internal evidence needs to take into account how what it calls internal and external are historically mediated through a tradition and practice within a community of faith and interpretation, and how that tradition and practice form the horizon of the Christian. My interpretation of the appearance narratives also suggests a hermeneutics of reception that entails a development of faith in the early Christian community and in ensuing generations of Christianity, rather than the fundamental theological thesis that minimizes this post-Easter development of faith. My proposal thereby takes issue with the fundamental theological approach which, in seeking to ground Christian faith in the life of Jesus, downplays the significance of the resurrection narratives for the interpretation of the meaning and significance of that life.

In a recent study of the resurrection and historical rationality, Georg Essen disagrees with my position. He notes: '*Geht der Skopus der Ausführungen doch eindeutig in die Richtung, daß erst die im Zeugnis überlieferte Interpretation dem Ereignis die Bedeutung beilegt. Die Auffassung aber führt den christlichen Auferstehungsglauben zu der weitreichenden und m. E. problematischen These, daß die "biblischen Zeugnisse selbst der Glaubensgrund für den Glauben an die Auferstehung Jesu sind" und eben nicht mehr das im biblischen Zeugnis bezeugte*

---

[69] Fiorenza, *Foundational Theology*, sect. III.

Geschehen der (den neutestamentlichen Zeugen offenbaren) Auferweckung Jesu.[70] I am not sure whether such an objection is more substantial or verbal. It reminds me of the classical theological position about the propositions of faith. St Thomas affirms that the object of faith is not the doctrinal propositions themselves, but God.[71] Moreover, as he further notes, a foundation is first not only as isolated, but also as connected with what adheres to the foundation.

In the same manner, I would affirm that the ground of faith as the object toward which the intentionality of the act of faith is directed is the act of God on behalf of Jesus. But we know of God's act upon Jesus only through the New Testament testimonies—this essay highlights the hymnic material and the appearance narratives—and therefore these testimonies are the ground of our faith. It might be clearer if one were to distinguish between an epistemological ground of faith and an ontological ground of faith. Such a distinction would allow the claim that the epistemological ground of faith is the New Testament testimonies, whereas the ontological ground is God's act. Nevertheless, to the extent that the resurrection of Jesus is a historical event, to that extent the ontological ground is accessible to Christians today only through New Testament testimonies.

2. *Resurrection as Historical Event: Ambiguity of the Term 'Historical'.* Obviously some might ask of my position: what am I saying about the resurrection as a historical event? My arguments for the normativity of the early Christian metaphors and for the inadequacy of purely subjective or existential interpretations already contain an answer to this question. Is the resurrection of Jesus a historical event? A certain ambiguity exists in the term 'historical event' in so far as the term is employed in either an 'ontological' or an 'epistemological' sense, and each of these is in itself understood

---

[70] Georg Essen, *Historische Vernunft und Auferweckung Jesu: Theologie und Historik im Streit um den Begriff geschichtlicher Wirklichkeit.* Tübinger Studien zur Theologie und Philosophie, 9 (Mainz: Matthias-Grunewald-Verlag, 1995), 384–5. He kindly notes that his emphasis on the intertwinement of facticity and interpretation approximates mine.

[71] *ST* 2a. 2ae. 4. 6. In a. 7 ad 4, Thomas makes an important observation: 'To be a foundation a thing requires not only to come first, but also to be connected with the other parts of the building unless the other parts adhere to it.' He uses this to illustrate the connection between faith and charity. To disconnect an event from its testimony and make the event exclusively the foundation overlooks how an event is connected to the rest: viz. the history of the Christian community.

differently. The former uses 'historical' to assert that an event really happened, in distinction to an event that did not occur or is only imagined. A person's claim that they were abducted by a space alien is not historical, because it did not happen. The epistemological sense asserts that a historical event is historical to the degree that such an event can be asserted with some degree of certainty as historical according to certain canons of historical method. There is, of course, widespread disagreement about what constitutes a proper degree of certainty and what constitute the canons of historical method. Some might require higher degrees of certainty and stricter canons than others, especially in the case of an unusual event. Nevertheless, from this perspective, the available evidence determines what is historical. Suppose someone were to claim that Julius Caesar took a nap before he walked into the Roman Senate and was murdered. The nap may indeed have taken place, but it is not a historical event, because there is no evidence for it. This distinction between an event as has having happened and an event for which there is sufficient evidence is important, because the claim is made that the resurrection is not a historical event, not because one is contesting the reality of the event, but because one is contesting whether it is historical in the sense that it can be historically demonstrated or verified. In view of the distinction, which can be drawn between warranted assertability and truth, someone may be warranted to assert something on the basis of historical evidence, but those warrants may be false, so it can be historically warranted without necessarily being true.

In addition to ontological and epistemological assertions of the historicity, there is often a third notion that is difficult to characterize. One person denies that the resurrection is historical, while another asserts that it did indeed happen, but that one cannot objectively and scientifically verify the event.[72] On this view, the ontological is either 'empirical' or 'trans-empirical', and on this view the resurrection did take place, but it did not take place in empirical space and time. This latter distinction is somewhat difficult to understand. Whereas it is clear what is meant by an event that takes place in space and time, it is difficult to fathom such an event, if it is an event, that transcends space and time. It seems to

---

[72] For a survey of the neo-orthodox views (esp. Bultmann and Barth) on the relation of the resurrection to history, see Peter Carnley, *The Structure of Resurrection Belief* (Oxford: Clarendon, 1987), 96–147.

me that such an event, if it is even to be considered, must in some specific way be related to historical time and empirical space. Otherwise one can question whether it is an 'event' or even historical.[73]

My argument is that the early Christian testimonies do affirm the reality of God's raising Jesus from the dead. They affirm an act that has taken place, one that is at the same time an eschatological act. These testimonies of early Christian faith proclaim and entail that the resurrection of Jesus took place. How to describe in detail this event is a more complex matter, at least for someone who attends to the literary analysis of the narrative forms. Is it historical in the sense that it can be historically demonstrated? Yes and no. When one is writing history and one is attempting to deal with an event about which one does not have immediate evidence—for example, no neutral or even believing witness saw the act of resurrection—then one has to develop a narrative account that weaves together the various elements: death of Jesus, early Christian hymns, appearance narratives, empty grave stories, in order to come up with the most coherent and cohesive account. As a Christian, I consider the conviction that God raised Jesus to be the most coherent historical account. Nevertheless, I am aware that certain background assumptions about God's action in history might lead me to give one account, another Christian a different account, and an atheist a still different account. Consequently, I can offer my historical account as to how the events fit together in order to justify my conviction that God raised Jesus. Yet, at the same time, I am aware that others with different background assumptions will weigh the evidence and various warrants differently, and may not be convinced. Consequently, I do not think that fundamental theology can demonstrate even with probability that God raised Jesus. It can offer—and argue—its historical narrative as a probable and possible narrative to those who accept, as I do, that God can act in history.

3. *Praxis and Testimony*. In arguing for the valorization of testimony and its disclosive power as the foundation of the Christian faith, I would like to point to the importance of praxis as a retrospective warrant for the authenticity of testimony. Within traditional

---

[73] See Karl Barth, *Church Dogmatics*, iii/2 (Edinburgh: T. & T. Clark, 1960), 446.

fundamental theology, the lives of the witnesses were often considered an important factor in the veracity of the testimony. Today, we have come too much under the sway of analytical philosophy and its formal distinctions. In dealing with truth claims, we distinguish the genesis of an idea from the justification of its truth. Therefore, we also distinguish the practice and authenticity of a witness from the veracity of his or her testimony. These are indeed important distinctions that analytical philosophy has taught us.

However, such distinctions should not be allowed to rule out the role of praxis. Praxis as a retrospective warrant is indeed significant in the face of interpretations of the resurrection as holy hallucinations or as psychological compensation for the experience of guilt. The life and practice of the disciples become, then, important criteria for discounting such a psychological dependency theory of the resurrection.

The task of fundamental theology on this view is not only a theoretical task, but also a hermeneutical and practical task. It involves initiation into the religious imagination and practice of a community and its tradition of testimonies. The testimony to the resurrection of Jesus challenges the adequacy of our understanding of reality and history, and at the same time institutes a historical process and historical imagination of a community. The testimony of early Christians to God's power and justice in raising Jesus proclaims a creativity over despair and death. The disclosive power of this vision of God both as a vision and as a praxis is the object of our Christian faith, and it provides the foundations of faith, even if not an isolated foundation.

10

John Dominic Crossan on the Resurrection of Jesus

WILLIAM LANE CRAIG

I Introduction

As the view of the chairman of the Society of Biblical Literature's Historical Jesus Section, the opinions of John Dominic Crossan on the historicity of the resurrection of Jesus demand attention, and as the views of the co-chairman of the highly publicized Jesus Seminar they cannot in any case be ignored. According to Crossan, after the crucifixion Jesus' corpse was probably laid in a shallow grave, barely covered with dirt, and subsequently eaten by wild dogs; the story of Jesus' entombment and resurrection was the result of 'wishful thinking'. In this essay, I wish to evaluate critically Crossan's reconstruction of the events of Easter as well as his interaction with evidence allegedly supporting the fact of Jesus' resurrection.

Immediately we encounter a difficulty. Crossan presents no specific evidence, much less probative evidence, for his hypothesis concerning the fate of Jesus' corpse. Rather, the above scenario represents his hunch as to what happened to the body of Jesus based on customary burial procedures.[1] Since he does not accept the historicity of the discovery of the empty tomb (not to speak of the resurrection), Crossan surmises that Jesus' corpse was laid in the graveyard normally reserved for executed criminals, but he offers no specific evidence for this surmise. Instead, he seeks to undercut the

---

[1] John Dominic Crossan, *Who Killed Jesus? Exposing the Roots of Anti-Semitism in the Gospel/Story of the Death of Jesus* (San Francisco: HarperSan Francisco, 1994), ch. 6; idem, *The Historical Jesus: The Life of a Mediterranean Jewish Peasant* (San Francisco/Edinburgh: HarperSan Francisco/T. & T. Clark, 1991), 392–3; idem, *The Cross that Spoke: The Origins of the Passion Narrative* (San Francisco: Harper & Row, 1988), 21, 235–40; idem, *Four Other Gospels* (Minneapolis: Winston, 1985), 153–64.

credibility of the Gospel accounts of Jesus' burial and resurrection by means of a general analysis of the Gospel texts and traditions. Unfortunately, his tradition-historical analysis is so bizarre and so contrived that the overwhelming majority of New Testament critics find it wholly implausible.[2] For this reason it is difficult to engage Crossan in a conversation concerning the historicity of the resurrection of Jesus, since the presuppositions from which he works are so at odds with the consensus of New Testament criticism concerning the development of the Gospels in general. Discussion of specific points of evidence is rendered difficult because that evidence is being viewed by Crossan through a significantly different lens.

Crossan's theory of the formation of the passion and resurrection narratives in the Gospels is founded on his claim that the *Gospel of Peter* has embedded within it the most primitive Gospel of all, the so-called Cross Gospel, which Crossan identifies as the story of Jesus' crucifixion, entombment, and resurrection. The author of the Gospel of Mark had no other source for Jesus' passion and resurrection than the Cross Gospel, but he invented additional details of the passion and burial based on Old Testament passages—what Crossan calls 'historicized prophecy'. For the resurrection narratives virtually nothing was available from the Old Testament, but out of his theological conviction that Jesus' passion was to be followed immediately by his coming again in glory, without any intermediate manifestation of the resurrection, Mark retrojected the Cross Gospel's resurrection appearance back into his Gospel in the form of Jesus' transfiguration. But canonical Mark was not the original form of this Gospel. Crossan accepts Morton Smith's claim that canonical Mark is based on an earlier 'Secret Gospel of Mark', which Crossan believes ended with the centurion's confession in 15: 39 (itself a retrojection of the guard at the tomb's confession in the Cross Gospel). Canonical Mark, in addition to cleaning up the poten-

---

[2] In a blistering critique Howard Clark Kee hails Crossan's procedure as 'a triumph of circular reasoning' (Kee, 'A Century of Quests of the Culturally Compatible Jesus', *Theology Today*, 52 (1995), 22; cf. 24). Slightly more charitably, N. T. Wright says that Crossan's *Historical Jesus* 'is a book to treasure for its learning, its thoroughness, its brilliant handling of multiple and complex issues, its amazing inventiveness, and above all its sheer readability. . . . It is all the more frustrating, therefore, to have to conclude that the book is almost entirely wrong' (Wright, *Jesus and the Victory of God* (Minneapolis: Fortress, 1996), 44). Similarly, Ben Meyer praises the book for its readability, rapid pace, and useful information, but concludes: 'As historical-Jesus research, it is unsalvageable' (Meyer, critical notice of *The Historical Jesus*, *CBQ* 55 (1993), 576).

tially offensive texts in secret Mark, also created 15: 40-16: 8. The other canonical Gospels are based on both the Cross Gospel and canonical Mark (see Fig. 10.1).

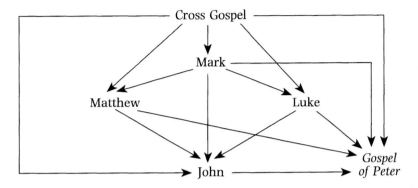

Fig. 1 Crossan's diagram of the tradition history behind the Gospels (*Cross that Spoke*, 18). The diagram needs to be supplemented by Crossan's subsequently embraced 'Secret Mark' hypothesis. Reproduced by permission of the author.

On the basis of this analysis, Crossan identifies several strata of tradition behind the passion and resurrection narratives and, in reconstructing the historical Jesus, adopts the methodological principle of refusing to allow as historically authentic any passage not attested by multiple, independent sources, even if that passage is found in the first stratum of tradition. This ensures agnosticism concerning Jesus' burial and resurrection, since, on Crossan's analysis, we lack multiple, independent accounts of the exact sequence of what happened at the end of Jesus' life. Given this idiosyncratic approach to the Gospels, it is small wonder Crossan comes to conclusions so radically diverse from those of the majority of critics, who deny the existence of the hypothesized Cross Gospel, reject any dependence of canonical Mark on a secret Mark, hold that the Gospel traditions concerning the burial and empty tomb of Jesus are rooted in history rather than in the Old Testament, regard the *Gospel of Peter*, even if it contains some independent tradition, as a composition basically compiled from the canonical Gospels, and maintain that multiple attestation is not a necessary condition of

judging a passage to be authentic.[3] It would be a hopeless under-
taking to try to provide in the limited space available a critical analysis of Crossan's presuppositions; but I think that it is important at
least to mention them because so doing will serve both to facilitate
our understanding of Crossan's peculiar perspective as well as to
underline the fact that much of Crossan's scepticism *vis-à-vis* the
resurrection of Jesus is predicated upon presuppositions which most
critics would regard as extremely dubious.[4]

II EVIDENCE FOR THE RESURRECTION OF JESUS

In my previous work, I have found it convenient to consider the evidence pertinent to the alleged resurrection of Jesus under three
main headings: (A) the empty tomb, (B) the post-mortem appearances of Jesus, and (C) the origin of the disciples' belief in Jesus' resurrection. In the following I shall consider the evidence under each
head only in so far as Crossan interacts with it, with a view to
assessing the success of his proposed reconstruction.

---

[3] On the purported Secret Gospel of Mark as a pastiche of elements drawn from
the canonical Gospels, see F. F. Bruce, *The 'Secret' Gospel of Mark* (London: Athlone,
1974); for a critique of Crossan's hypothesis that canonical Mark revises secret
Mark, see Robert H. Gundry, *Mark: A Commentary on his Apology for the Cross* (Grand
Rapids, Mich.: Eerdmans, 1993), 613–23; on the *Gospel of Peter* being a late com-
pilation containing no primitive Cross Gospel, see Raymond E. Brown, 'The Gospel
of Peter and Canonical Gospel Priority', *NTS* 33 (1987), 321–43, which is expanded
in appendix 1, 'The Gospel of Peter—A Noncanonical Passion Narrative', of Brown's
magisterial *The Death of the Messiah: A Commentary on the Passion Narratives in the
Four Gospels*, Anchor Bible Reference Library (2 vols.; New York: Doubleday, 1994);
on the illegitimacy of making multiple attestation a necessary condition of authenticity, see C. F. D. Moule, *The Phenomenon of the New Testament* (London: SCM, 1967),
71.

[4] The extremity of Crossan's scepticism is perhaps best illustrated by his remark
that he firmly believes that Jesus was crucified under Pontius Pilate, because his crucifixion is attested by Josephus (AD 93–4) and Tacitus (AD 110/120), two 'early and
independent non-Christian witnesses' (*Historical Jesus*, 372)! This is quite amazing.
We have on the one hand a NT chock full of early and independent references to
Jesus' crucifixion, including Paul's citation of the very early tradition in 1 Cor. 15:
3, and on the other hand a doctored reference a half-century later in Josephus and
a reference no doubt dependent on Christian tradition by Tacitus, and Crossan
accepts the crucifixion on the basis of the latter! This evinces a prejudice against the
NT documents which can only be described as historically irresponsible.

A. The Empty Tomb

Crossan recognizes that if the story of Jesus' burial is fundamentally reliable, then the inference that Jesus' tomb was found empty lies very close at hand. For if the burial story is basically accurate, the site of Jesus' tomb would have been known to Jew and Christian alike. But in that case, it would have been impossible for resurrection faith to survive in the face of a tomb containing the corpse of Jesus. The disciples could not have adhered to the resurrection; scarcely any one else would have believed them, even if they had; and their Jewish opponents could have exposed the whole affair by pointing to the occupied tomb, or perhaps even displaying the body of Jesus, as the medieval Jewish polemic portrays them doing (*Tolĕdot Yeshu*). Hence, as Crossan recognizes, it would seem to be unfeasible to affirm the historicity of the burial story and yet deny the historicity of the empty tomb.

But the burial story is widely recognized as a historically credible narrative. In 1 Corinthians 15: 3-5 the tradition received and delivered by Paul refers in its second line to the fact of Jesus' burial. The grammatically unnecessary fourfold '$ὅτι$', the chronological succession of the events, and particularly the remarkable concordance between this tradition and both the preaching of Acts 13 and the Gospel narratives with respect to the order of events (death, burial, resurrection, appearances) make it highly probable that the tradition's mention of the burial is not meant merely to underscore the death, but refers to the same event related in the Gospels—that is, the laying of Jesus in the tomb. If this is so, then it seems very difficult to regard Jesus' burial in the tomb as unhistorical, given the age of the tradition (AD 30-6), for there was not sufficient time for legend concerning the burial to significantly accrue. Remarkably, Crossan overlooks entirely this early tradition concerning Jesus' burial.

Moreover, it is generally acknowledged that the burial account is part of Mark's source material for the story of Jesus' passion. Even Crossan's hypothesized Cross Gospel includes Jesus' being sealed in a tomb, not buried in the criminals' graveyard (*Gospel of Peter* 8: 30-3). Apart from his methodological requirement of multiple attestation, Crossan provides no reason why this putatively pre-Marcan source is not to be trusted in this regard. In any case the burial is multiply attested, as we have seen, since the tradition delivered by

Paul also refers to it. Thus, on Crossan's own principles, we have good reason to accept the burial as historical. The age of Paul's tradition and the age of the pre-Marcan passion story support the fundamental historical credibility of the burial story.

Furthermore, the burial story itself is simple, and in its basic elements lacks theological reflection or apologetic development. Most scholars would concur with Bultmann's judgement to this effect.[5] Crossan, on the other hand, thinks that the burial story is a fictitious account manufactured out of Deuteronomy 21: 22-3 and Joshua 10: 26-7. Now since the supposed Cross Gospel contains no burial story at all—Crossan attributes *Gospel of Peter* 6: 23-4 (Joseph's entombment of Jesus) to a later stratum based on the canonical Gospels—it must be Mark's account that is supposed to be manufactured out of these Old Testament texts in conjunction with the Cross Gospel. Wholly apart from the question of whether early Christians felt free just to invent incidents without any historical basis, two problems with Crossan's hypothesis arise.

First, such an approach to the Gospels is in danger of repeating with Jewish texts the same error committed by the old *Religions-geschichtliche Schule* with pagan texts. That nineteenth-century movement sought to find parallels to Christian beliefs in pagan religions, and some scholars sought to explain Christian beliefs, including the resurrection of Jesus, as the product of pagan influences. The movement collapsed, however, largely because no genealogical link could be shown between the pagan beliefs and Christian beliefs. Crossan's Jewish parallels are similarly devoid of significance unless a causal connection to incidents narrated in the Gospels can be shown. In the case at issue, it is very doubtful that this can be done, since one only notices the parallels if one reads the relevant texts in the light of and with full knowledge of the Gospel narratives. The parallels are too distant to think that a first-century Christian with knowledge only that Jesus was crucified would find such texts relevant to Jesus' fate.[6]

Second, the dissimilarities between the burial story and Joshua

[5] Rudolf Bultmann, *The History of the Synoptic Tradition*, trans. John Marsh, 2nd edn. (Oxford: Blackwell, 1963), 274.

[6] In his most recent book Crossan seems to concede this point, remarking, 'The burial stories are not history remembered, but neither are they prophecy historicized. What prophecies were present to be historicized?' (Crossan, *Who Killed Jesus?*, 188). Rather, the burial story is Mark's free invention designed to shift the responsibility for Jesus' burial from his enemies to his friends.

10: 26–7 suggest that Mark's account is not based on the latter. Joshua speaks of a cave, whereas Mark makes a point of the man-made, rock-hewn sepulchre in which Jesus is laid (cf. Isa. 11: 16); Joshua has a guard at the cave, whereas Mark has no guard; Mark has Joseph of Arimathea, the scene with Pilate, and the linen shroud, no parallels to which occur in Joshua. Details like the stone over the entrance and burial before nightfall are features which belong to the attested historical Jewish milieu, and so provide no genealogical clue. Crossan thinks that the Cross Gospel simply took it for granted that the Jews buried Jesus, but that the Joshua passage provided the buried body, the great rolled stone, and the posted guards for the Cross Gospel's guard at the tomb story. But surely the buried body is already provided by the fact of the crucifixion coupled with Jewish customs with respect to burial of the dead; the stone is an archaeologically confirmed feature of tombs of notable persons in first-century Palestine; and the guard is more plausibly derived from Matthew than Joshua, particularly in light of the *Gospel of Peter*'s heightening of the guard story by identifying it clearly as a Roman guard (complete with the name of the commander), having it posted on Friday rather than on Saturday, so that the tomb is never left unguarded, and emphasizing that the soldiers did not fall asleep, but were constantly on watch.[7] We appear

---

[7] Crossan provides one argument in support of the priority of the *Gospel of Peter*'s guard story: it is less likely that the *Gospel of Peter* would preserve Matthew's three-day motif but drop its connection with Jesus' prophecy of his resurrection than that Matthew would connect the three-day motif already present in *Peter* with prophecy. Crossan argues that the reason why the Jewish elders in *Peter* ask that the tomb be guarded for three days is that by then Jesus would be 'really and irrevocably a corpse so that the disciples cannot resuscitate Jesus and remove him', leading the people to infer that Jesus was risen from the dead (Crossan, *Who Killed Jesus?*, 177–81). This is an enormously implausible explanation of the three-day motif in *Peter*. (i) It ignores the fact that the three-day motif was already normative in primitive Christian belief (1 Cor. 15: 4) and is there associated with OT prophecy. (ii) There is no reason to think that the elders were concerned (in line with the Jewish belief that the soul of the deceased lingered about the grave until the fourth day) with Jesus' resuscitation; on the contrary, their concern is that 'his disciples come and steal him away' (*Gospel of Peter* 8: 30), a threat which, as Crossan notes, is not limited to three days' time. Therefore, the three-day motif in *Peter*, even if primitive, cannot be understood in isolation from the normative Christian belief that Jesus was raised on the third day. But in that case there is no reason to think that the same explanation should not suffice for *Peter*'s retention of that motif in the likelihood that *Peter* is late and derivative. He gives his own free account of the guard in any case, and, for all we know, may have included Jesus' prophecies of his resurrection on the third day earlier in his Gospel, so that the motif plays implicitly the same role as in Matthew. Crossan's argument for Petrine priority is therefore without weight.

to have in Mark a primitive tradition recounting Joseph's begging the body of Jesus and his laying it, wrapped in linen, in a tomb, a tradition which has not been significantly overlaid with either theology or apologetics.

With respect to Joseph of Arimathea in particular, even sceptical scholars agree that it is unlikely that Joseph, as a member of the Sanhedrin, was a Christian invention. Again Crossan disagrees, asserting that Mark invented Joseph of Arimathea to take Jesus' burial from his enemies to his friends, and so winds up with 'an impossible creation: one with access to power but still on the side of Jesus'.[8] Unfortunately, Crossan gives no evidence for his assertion that such was Mark's intent, nor an explanation as to why a person such as Joseph is impossible. Since neither the Cross Gospel nor Mark say clearly that Jesus was buried by his enemies or that Joseph was a friend of Jesus, it is dubious that Mark's intent was to shift the burial from Jesus' enemies to his friends. Even more simply, if Mark was so inventive, why should he create a figure like Joseph rather than just have the disciples bury Jesus? If he wanted more historical verisimilitude, he could have had Jesus buried by his family. Or why not just stick with burial by his enemies? As for Joseph himself, Raymond Brown judges that Joseph's being responsible for burying Jesus is 'very probable', since a Christian fictional creation of a Jewish Sanhedrist who does what is right for Jesus is 'almost inexplicable', given the hostility toward the Jewish leaders responsible for Jesus' death in early Christian writings.[9] In particular, it is unlikely that Mark invented Joseph in view of his statements in 14: 55, 64 and 15: 1 that the whole Sanhedrin voted for Jesus' condemnation. Brown notes that the thesis of Joseph's invention is rendered even more implausible in light of his identification with Arimathea, a town of no importance and having no scriptural symbolism. To this may be added the fact that the later descriptions of Joseph receive unintentional confirmation from incidental details in the Marcan narrative: for example, his being rich, from the type and location of the tomb. His being at least a sympathizer of Jesus is not only independently attested by Matthew and John, but seems likely in view of Mark's description of his special treatment of Jesus' body as opposed to those of the thieves. I see no reason to agree

---

[8] Crossan, *Who Killed Jesus?*, 172.   [9] Brown, *Death of the Messiah*, ii. 1240.

with Crossan that it is 'impossible' that a Sanhedrist could have been a sympathizer of Jesus.

On the other hand, if the burial of Jesus in the tomb by Joseph of Arimathea is legendary, then it is very strange that conflicting traditions nowhere appear, even in Jewish polemic. That no remnant of the true story or even a conflicting false one should remain is hard to explain unless the account is substantially the true account. Crossan attempts to find other burial traditions in the *Epistula Apostolorum* (a Coptic document from the second century) and Lactantius *Divine Institutes* 4. 19 (from the early fourth century). That Crossan thinks that these late, derivative, and sometimes fanciful sources are more trustworthy purveyors of historical tradition than the New Testament documents is a comment on his methodology. In any case, these sources do not in fact offer alternatives to the account. The *Epistula Apostolorum* 9 (20) speaks of Jesus' body being taken down from the cross along with those of the thieves, but then singles him out as being buried in a place called 'skull', where Mary, Martha, and Mary Magdalene went to anoint him. The summary nature of the passage no more excludes burial by Joseph of Arimathea than does the Apostles' Creed. The same is true of Lactantius' summary, in which he says in reference to the Jews, 'they took his body down from the cross, and enclosing it safely in a tomb, they surrounded it with a military guard' (4. 19). The desire to polemicize against the Jews leads Lactantius to include Joseph under the general rubric 'the Jews'. The same motive governs Acts 13: 27–9, to which Crossan also appeals. Finally, John 19: 31 has only to do with a request, not with actual burial. That Crossan has to appeal to passages such as the above only serves to underline how strained is the attempt to find competing burial traditions.

It is thus not without reason that the majority of New Testament critics today agree, in the words of Wolfgang Trilling, that 'It appears unfounded to doubt the fact of Jesus' honorable burial—even historically considered.'[10] But in that case, the conclusion that the tomb was found empty lies close at hand.

Consider now the empty tomb narrative itself, as we find it in Mark. It has frequently been observed how theologically unadorned

---

[10] Wolfgang Trilling, *Fragen zur Geschichtlichkeit Jesu* (Düsseldorf: Patmos Verlag, 1966), 157; see also Raymond E. Brown, 'The Burial of Jesus (Mark 15: 42–47)', *CBQ* 50 (1988), 233–45.

and non-apologetic in nature this account is. The resurrection is not described, and later theological motifs that a late legend might be expected to incorporate are wholly lacking. Comparison of Mark's account with those in the apocryphal gospels like the *Gospel of Peter* underlines the simplicity of the Marcan story. The *Gospel of Peter* inserts between Jesus' being sealed in the tomb and the visit of Mary Magdalene early Sunday morning an account of the resurrection itself. In this account, the tomb is surrounded not only by Roman guards but also by the Jewish Pharisees and elders, as well as by a multitude from the surrounding countryside. Suddenly, in the night, there rings out a loud voice in heaven, and two men descend from heaven to the tomb. The stone over the door rolls back by itself, and they go into the tomb. Then three men come out of the tomb, two of them holding up the third man. The heads of the two men reach up into the clouds, but the head of the third man reaches up beyond the clouds. Then a cross comes out of the tomb, and a voice from heaven asks, 'Have you preached to them that sleep?' And the cross answers, 'Yes'. In contrast to the Marcan account, this narrative is brightly coloured by theological and apologetic motifs that display its unhistorical character.

Crossan agrees that the above account found in the Cross Gospel (= *Gospel of Peter* 9: 35–10: 42) is theologically determined, but he thinks that Mark's account is, too. For Mark's closely linking Jesus' passion and parousia leads him to suppress the Cross Gospel's colourful account of the resurrection (and, presumably, the guard) so that his simple narrative results. For Mark, 'The resurrection was simply the departure of Jesus pending a now imminent return in glory.'[11] The retrojected appearance from the Cross Gospel became the transfiguration, which functions as a foretaste of Jesus' parousia, not his resurrection.

Crossan's hypothesis hinges crucially on the widely rejected idea that Mark's Gospel envisions no resurrection appearances, but only Jesus' parousia (Mark 13: 26; 14: 62). Now clearly, Jesus' predictions of his glorious return do not preclude resurrection appearances after he rises from the dead, as he predicted he would (Mark 8: 31; 9: 9, 31; 10: 34). And in 14: 28; 16: 7 Mark gives us clearly to understand that such resurrection appearances will take place. Jesus' going before the disciples to Galilee and the restricted

---

[11] Crossan, *Historical Jesus*, 296.

circle of the witnesses make it clear that Mark is not envisioning Jesus' second coming in Galilee (not to mention the problem that Mark knows that such did not occur).[12] Crossan cannot retreat to the position that these verses were not part of the original, secret Mark, for the issue is the simplicity of Mark 16: 1–8, which was supposedly added by canonical Mark. If canonical Mark contemplates resurrection appearances, then no reason remains for him not to give a resurrection narrative akin to the *Gospel of Peter*'s. As for the transfiguration, most critics regard this narrative as so firmly embedded in its context that it is not plausibly thought of as a retrojected resurrection narrative. Crossan confesses that the parallels between Mark's transfiguration narrative and the *Gospel of Peter*'s resurrection story (for example, the height of the heads reaching to heaven becomes the high mountain) are 'not very persuasive' in themselves, but blames this on Mark's having 'incompletely recast' the narrative.[13] But this explanation serves only to lend an air of unfalsifiability to his hypothesis. In any case, Mark 16: 1–8 lacks any theological reflection on Jesus' glorious return, as well as other theological motifs, like his descent into hell, victory over his enemies, and so forth, which bespeaks its primitiveness.

Furthermore, the discovery of the empty tomb by women is highly probable. Given the relatively lower status of women in Jewish society and their lack of qualification to serve as legal witnesses, the most plausible explanation, in light of the Gospels' conviction that the disciples were in Jerusalem over the Easter weekend, of why women and not the male disciples were made discoverers of the empty tomb is that the women were in fact the ones who made this discovery.

At this point Crossan's speculations really go off the rails. The Secret Gospel of Mark, he says, lent itself to an erotic interpretation which the author of canonical Mark wished to avoid. But rather

---

[12] Perhaps Crossan would attempt to elude the force of these considerations by holding that Mark does envisage resurrection appearances, but implies that they never occurred due to the women's failure to convey the angel's message to the disciples. This strange interpretation is unavailing, however, since Mark's audience is led to infer that these predictions, like all the rest of Jesus' prophecies in the Gospel, will be fulfilled, despite the women's stunned silence. Moreover, Crossan's hypothesis hinges on his assumption that Mark is writing to a community that has experienced persecution and defeat, and so needs to see the disciples' failures, an assumption which needs to be re-examined in light of Gundry's commentary.

[13] Crossan, *Four Other Gospels*, 173; cf. idem, *Who Killed Jesus?*, 202.

than simply remove the offending text, Mark dismembered it and scattered its parts throughout his Gospel. For example, the angelic figure of the young man in the tomb (Mark 16: 5) derives from the young man in secret Mark who comes to Jesus for instruction in the mystery of the Kingdom of God. More relevant to the present point, the three women who discover the empty tomb (Mark 16: 1) are the dismembered residue of secret Mark 2r: 14–16, which followed canonical Mark 10: 46a and reads: 'And the sister of the young man whom Jesus loved and his mother and Salome were there, and Jesus did not receive them.' Thus, the women's role in the empty tomb narrative does not undergird its historical credibility.

In an extensive discussion of Crossan's hypothesis, Robert Gundry has shown that the supposedly dismembered elements do not intrude unnaturally in canonical Mark, as Crossan claims, leaving the theory without any positive evidentiary support.[14] Moreover, one might ask, why in the world would Mark scatter these various figures and motifs throughout his Gospel, rather than just delete them if he found them potentially offensive? Crossan's ingenious answer is that Mark did this so that if someone should come upon a copy of secret Mark with the offending passages, then orthodox Christians could claim in response that the passages were just a pastiche assembled from disparate elements in the original Mark! Now this answer is just scholarly silliness. Not only does it ascribe to Mark prescience of redaction criticism, but, more importantly, it tends to render Crossan's hypothesis unfalsifiable, since evidence ostensibly disconfirmatory of the theory is reinterpreted in terms of the theory itself to be actually confirmatory—compare Freudian psychology, which takes someone's claim not to have experienced Oedipal desires as evidence that that person is, in line with the theory, suppressing such experiences. To critics who assert that the Secret Gospel of Mark passages are not primitive, but look like amalgamations drawn from other Gospel stories, it is said, 'Aha! that's just what Mark wanted you to think!' In any case, the answer will not work, because some elements of the pastiche are drawn from John's Gospel (the beloved disciple, the raising of Lazarus), which secret Mark is supposed to antedate. With respect to the women at the tomb, Crossan's hypothesis still fails to explain why Mark would insert them here, rather than elsewhere in the

---

[14] Gundry, *Mark*, 613–21.

Gospel, when he could have made male disciples (perhaps even the young man!) discover the empty tomb.

In his most recent book, Crossan does provide an explanation of why the women are assigned the role they play in the empty tomb story: Mark invents their role here to show that the female followers of Jesus, like the men, fail him. They do so in two ways: first, they fail him by coming to the tomb to anoint him, thus evincing their failure to believe his prediction of his resurrection, in contrast to the unnamed woman in 14: 3-9, who, says Crossan, 'believes Jesus and knows that, if she does not anoint him for burial now, she will never be able to do it later' because he will have risen; and second, the women fail him by fleeing from the tomb, so that the angel's message is never delivered or received. Thus, on Crossan's view, the role of the women is not to bear witness to the empty tomb, but to serve as female illustrations of failure, and so their presence in the narrative is not surprising.

It seems to me that this is a serious misinterpretation of the empty tomb story. I see no evidence for Crossan's assertion that 'Male and female followers of Jesus are important for Mark, and the inner three from each group are especially important for him.'[15] Mark does not show a great deal of interest in women, and none whatsoever in female followers of Jesus up until their introduction in 15: 40-1, and it is fatuous to speak of obscure figures like Salome and the two Marys as an inner trio comparable to that of Peter, James, and John. There is no reason to think that Mark is exercised to provide peculiarly feminine examples of failure. Moreover, the role of the women in the stories of the cross, burial, and empty tomb is not to serve as illustrations of failure. Mark does not give us to understand that the anonymous woman of 14: 3 consciously believed in Jesus' resurrection and so wanted to anoint him now before it was too late; that sort of prescience is reserved for Jesus, and it is he who interprets the woman's action in light of his impending death. As for the women at the tomb, Gundry rightly points out that

The women cannot be faulted for having failed to believe the predictions of Jesus that he would rise. They had never heard those predictions, and neither here nor in 14: 3-9 has Mark hinted at their knowing the remark of Jesus that the pouring of perfume on his head had amounted to an anticipatory preparation of his body for burial. Besides, differences in diction and

---

[15] Crossan, *Who Killed Jesus?*, 184.

substance make doubtful that Mark wished his audience to draw any sort of comparison between 14: 3–9 and 16: 1–8. . . . At no point does Mark signal that he is comparing the women's intention unfavourably with the woman's act.[16]

As for their failure to report to the disciples, the emphasis here lies not on their failure but on the overwhelming awesomeness of the resurrection, which induces trembling, astonishment, and stupefaction in them. Thus the role of the women as the principal witnesses to the crucifixion, burial, and empty tomb of Jesus cannot be plausibly reinterpreted along the lines of Crossan's hypothesis.

According to the Gospels, the male disciples of Jesus did go to the tomb later to confirm the women's report. Crossan says—without argument—that Peter's visit to the tomb is Luke's creation (from which he seems to infer non-historicity). But the visit of Peter and another unnamed disciple to the empty tomb is attested by both Luke and John (Luke 24: 12, 24; John 20: 3); and, as I have tried to show elsewhere, the hypothesis of Lucan creation and Johannine copying in this case is less plausible than the hypothesis of independent sources.[17] The story is thus multiply attested, and so cannot be written off even on the basis of Crossan's own strict standard of historicity. Moreover, the historicity of the disciples' visit is also made likely by the plausibility of the denial of Peter tradition (Mark 14: 66–72), for if he were in Jerusalem, then, having heard the women's report, he would quite likely check it out. Crossan, on the other hand, embraces without argument the hypothesis of the flight of the disciples, who knew nothing more than the fact of the crucifixion, back to Galilee, a hypothesis which most scholars today would regard, in von Campenhausen's words, as 'a fiction of the critics'.[18] The inherent implausibility of, and absence of any evidence for, the disciples' flight to Galilee render it highly likely that they were in Jerusalem, which reinforces the plausibility of their inspecting the empty tomb.

[16] Gundry, *Mark*, 998.
[17] William L. Craig, 'The Disciples' Inspection of the Empty Tomb (Lk. 24, 12: 24; Jn. 20, 2–10)', in A. Denaux (ed.), *John and the Synoptics*, BETL 101 (Leuven: Leuven University Press, 1992), 614–19.
[18] Hans F. von Campenhausen, *Der Ablauf der Osterereignisse and das leere Grab*, 3rd edn. (Heidelberg: Carl Winter, 1966), 449. Intriguingly, the Jesus Seminar also endorses this hypothesis (R. W. Funk, R. W. Hoover, and the Jesus Seminar, *The Five Gospels: The Search for the Authentic Words of Jesus* (New York: Macmillan, 1993), 468).

Further evidence could be adduced in support of the fact of empty tomb, but Crossan does not interact with it. What is clear from his limited interaction with the evidence is that Crossan is forced again and again to adopt extremist positions which the wide majority of scholars would reject, thus bearing out the truth of D. H. Van Daalen's comment that it is extremely difficult to object to the fact of the empty tomb on historical grounds; most objectors do so on the basis of theological or philosophical considerations.[19]

B. The Post-mortem Appearances

Turning from the empty tomb to the second category of evidence pertinent to Jesus' alleged resurrection—namely, his post-mortem appearances—we want to see how Crossan handles the evidence that Jesus appeared alive after his death to his disciples.

As we all know, Paul's citation of the traditional formula in 1 Corinthians 15: 3-5 closes with references to various post-mortem appearances of Jesus to both individuals and groups. The age alone of the traditions in 1 Corinthians 15, which probably reach back to within the first five years after the crucifixion, seems to preclude regarding the appearances of the list as legendary. Crossan himself states that it would take five to ten years just to discover the Old Testament motifs necessary to invent the passion story alone.[20] Yet the tradition delivered by Paul antedates even the lower limit assigned by Crossan, and already knows not only the Old Testament warrant for the passion, but also the resurrection with its scriptural warrant. Incredibly, Crossan scarcely touches on 1 Corinthians 15: 1-11, and he adopts the old interpretation of von Harnack that the list of witnesses reflects rival factions looking to Cephas and James as their respective leaders.[21] Of the resurrection appearances, Crossan says, 'None . . . was an illusion, hallucination, vision, or apparition. Each was a symbolic assertion of Jesus' continued presence *to the general community, to leadership groups*, or to specific and even competing

---

[19] D. H. Van Daalen, *The Real Resurrection* (London: Collins, 1970), 41.

[20] Crossan, *Jesus*, 145; cf. *idem*, 'The Historical Jesus in Earliest Christianity', in Robert Ludwig and Jeffrey Carlson (eds.), *Jesus and Faith: A Conversation with John Dominic Crossan* (Maryknoll, NY: Orbis, 1994), 16—and this is said to be the case even when 'You know, first of all, exactly what you are looking for'.

[21] Crossan, *Historical Jesus*, 397-8; *idem*, *Who Killed Jesus?*, 203. It is noteworthy that the Jesus Seminar adopts Crossan's interpretation to explain away the denial of Peter tradition (Funk and Hoover, *Five Gospels*, 119).

individual leaders.'[22] The interpretation of the list as reflecting com-
petitive leadership has been rejected by virtually all contemporary
commentators, not only because there is no evidence of first-
generation factions centred on Peter and James, but also because
the chronological ordering of the list as well as the great age of the
tradition Paul hands on precludes such an interpretation. Virtually
every contemporary New Testament scholar thus agrees that the
original disciples had apparitional experiences of Jesus alive after his
death. As for Crossan's claim that belief in the resurrection was a
purely symbolic assertion, I shall have more to say when we examine the origin of the disciples' belief in the resurrection.

The fact that the disciples experienced appearances of Jesus is also
independently attested in the Gospels. Though it may be impossible
to prove that any single appearance narrative is historically accurate, there are nevertheless good grounds for holding to the credibility of the Gospels' claim that that the disciples did experience
post-mortem appearances of Jesus, given their breadth of tradition
in the Gospel records. Trilling compares in this respect the appearance stories to the Gospel miracle accounts:

From the list in 1 Cor. 15 the particular reports of the gospels are now to
be interpreted. Here may be of help what we said about miracles. It is
impossible to 'prove' historically a particular miracle. But the totality of the
miracle reports permit no reasonable doubt that Jesus in fact performed
'miracles.' That holds analogously for the appearance reports. It is not possible to secure historically the particular event. But the totality of the
appearance reports permits no reasonable doubt that Jesus in fact bore witness to himself in such a way.[23]

From these reports we may infer with good probability that both
groups and individuals under varying conditions witnessed post-
mortem appearances of Jesus.

All Crossan has to contribute on this head is to carry over to the
Gospels his unfounded inference from 1 Corinthians 15: 5–8 that
the resurrection appearances 'have nothing whatsoever to do with
ecstatic experiences or entranced revelations', but with 'questions
of authority' and leadership.[24] According to Crossan, 'Followers of

---

[22] Crossan, *Historical Jesus*, 407; emphasis original.
[23] Trilling, *Fragen zur Geschichtlichkeit Jesu*, 153. Trilling notes that the fact that
miracles in general belong to the historical Jesus is widely recognized and no longer
disputed.
[24] Crossan, *Who Killed Jesus?*, 208; cf. 210.

Jesus also sought to be brokers of the kingdom, contrary to Jesus' own teaching. . . . [T]he last chapters of the Gospels . . . are carefully constructed stories which try, for the most part, to establish who's in charge by naming those to whom he appeared.'[25] Wholly apart from the illegitimacy of this inference in 1 Corinthians 15, it is unclear how all the Gospel appearance stories, such as those to the women, can be forced into this mould,[26] or how the disciples' abandoning Jesus' vision of the brokerless kingdom is consistent with Crossan's claim that the reason why Jesus' death did not spell the end of the disciples' faith was because that faith was not lodged in Jesus but in the brokerless kingdom.

As one reflects on this second category of evidence concerning the post-mortem appearances of Jesus, what is most striking about Crossan's treatment is his relative silence on this important issue.[27] When he does speak to it, it is only to adopt once again outmoded, long-refuted positions. Especially astonishing is his assertion that the disciples did not have *any* post-mortem, apparitional experiences of Jesus at all, a position which is not defended by any other contemporary scholar in my acquaintance.

C. Origin of the Disciples' Belief in Jesus' Resurrection

Finally, let us turn to the third category of evidence concerning the alleged resurrection of Jesus: the very origin of the disciples' belief

[25] John Dominic Crossan, 'The Historical Jesus: An Interview with John Dominic Crossan', *Christian Century*, 108/37 (18 Dec. 1991), 1203.

[26] I consider it extremely dubious whether even the most frequently cited instance of questions of authority being played out—viz. the supposed competition between Peter and the Beloved Disciple in John 20-1 is not a scholarly fiction (see William L. Craig, *Assessing the New Testament Evidence for the Historicity of the Resurrection of Jesus*, Studies in the Bible and Early Christianity, 16 (Lewiston, NY: Mellen, 1989), 237-41).

[27] Crossan does try to play off Paul's assertion that 'flesh and blood cannot enter the kingdom of God' (1 Cor. 15: 50) against a physical resurrection (Crossan, *Historical Jesus*, 404-5). But such an opposition is spurious. 'Flesh and blood' is a typical Semitic word-pair connoting frail, mortal human nature (cf. Gal. 1: 16; Eph. 6: 12), so v. 51b expresses in parallel form the same idea: 'neither does the perishable inherit the imperishable'. Paul is not talking about anatomy. The resurrection body will be an immortal, powerful, glorious, Spirit-directed body suitable for inhabiting a renewed creation. A *soma* which is unextended and intangible would probably have been a contradiction in terms for the apostle. All commentators agree that Paul did not teach the immortality of the soul alone; but his affirmation of the resurrection of the body becomes vacuous and indistinguishable from such a doctrine unless it is understood to mean the tangible, physical resurrection.

that Jesus had been raised from the dead. Whatever they may think of the historical resurrection, even sceptical scholars admit that at least the *belief* that Jesus rose from the dead lay at the very heart of the earliest Christian faith. Without prior belief in the resurrection, belief in Jesus as Messiah would have been impossible in view of his death. Without the resurrection, Jesus' death could only have meant humiliation and accursedness by God, but in view of the resurrection it could be seen to be the event by which forgiveness of sins was obtained. The origin of the Christian Way thus hinges on the disciples' belief that God had raised Jesus from the dead.

Crossan's position on this issue is ambiguous. On the one hand, he seems to agree with the undeniable fact that the earliest disciples proclaimed the resurrection of Jesus and that that doctrine was crucial to the origin of the Christian faith. On the other hand, he reinterprets the belief in Jesus' resurrection to be the symbolic assertion of Jesus' continued presence. He writes, 'That *is* the resurrection, the continuing presence in a continuing community of the past Jesus in a radically new and transcendental [sic] mode of present and future existence';[28] the problem the disciples faced was 'how to *express* that phenomenon'. Crossan thinks that in order to express their sense of Jesus' ongoing, invisible presence with them, Christians appropriated the language of resurrection from the dead. He explains:

Those who had originally experienced divine power through his vision and example still continued to do so after his death. Jesus' followers, who initially fled from the danger of the crucifixion, talked eventually of not just continued affection, but of resurrection. They tried to express what they meant by telling, e.g., of the journey to Emmaus. They were disappointed and in dejected sorrow. Jesus joined them unrecognized and explained that Hebrew scripture 'should have prepared them for his fate.' Later they recognize him by the meal, as of old. Then they go back to Jerusalem in high spirits. The symbolism is obvious, as is the metaphoric condensation of the first years of Christian thought and practice into one parabolic afternoon.[29]

Thus, on Crossan's view, in a literal sense the first disciples did not really believe in the resurrection of Jesus.

Crossan's view thus raises two questions: (i) When the earliest Christians said that Jesus was raised from the dead, did they mean

---

[28] Crossan, *Historical Jesus*, 404.   [29] Ibid., p. xii.

it literally or not? (ii) Can the origin of their belief be explained as a result of their reflection on Hebrew Scripture?

With respect to (i), I think there can be no doubt that the earliest Christians asserted a literal resurrection of Jesus. Paul's earnest declarations in 1 Corinthians 15: 12–23, 29–32 about the essentiality of Jesus' being raised from the dead, and especially his linking it with our own resurrection from the dead (which cannot be interpreted in terms of continuing presence), show how literally and seriously this event was taken. So do Paul's disquisitions about the nature of the resurrection body in answer to the questions 'How are the dead raised? With what kind of body do they come?' (1 Cor. 15: 35). The sermons in the book of Acts also present Jesus' resurrection as a literal event, which could only present gratuitous obstacles to their hearers if no such event were being asserted (Acts 17: 31–2). The empty tomb tradition would be superfluous and pointless were not a literal event in view, since mere continuing spiritual presence does not require an empty tomb. Moreover, the earliest Christians were perfectly capable of expressing the idea of Jesus' spiritual presence with them without recourse to the misleading language of resurrection from the dead (cf. 1 Cor. 5: 3; Col. 2: 5). Indeed, in the notion of the Holy Spirit of Christ the Christians had the perfect vehicle for expressing in a theologically rich way the idea of Jesus' continuing, numinous presence with and in them (Rom. 8: 9–11). But they were not content to assert merely the presence of Christ through the Spirit with them; they also believed in Jesus' resurrection from the dead, the harbinger of their own resurrection (Rom. 8: 11, 23).

As for (ii), it is now widely agreed that the disciples' belief in Jesus' resurrection cannot be plausibly explained as the result of their reflection on the Old Testament. For as Crossan himself admits,[30] the Old Testament furnishes very little that could be construed in terms of Christ's resurrection, much less prompt such a belief in the absence of any experiences of appearances or an empty tomb. When Crossan says that the Hebrew Scripture should have prepared the disciples for Jesus' fate, what that refers to is his death; but there is almost nothing there to prepare them for his resurrection. For this reason most critics concur that Old Testament

---

[30] Crossan, *Four Other Gospels*, 174.

proof-texts of the resurrection could be found only after the fact of
the disciples' coming to believe that Jesus was risen, not before.

In his more recent book *Jesus*, Crossan takes an even more radical line: the primitive Christians did not even express their sense of
Jesus' continuing presence in terms of his resurrection, but held
simply to belief in Jesus' passion and second coming. 'Where, then
did all the emphasis on resurrection come from? In a word, from
Paul. . . . For Paul . . . bodily resurrection is the only way that continuing presence can be expressed.'[31] Crossan considerably compli-
cates this remarkable hypothesis by positing at least four different
Christian groups responding to the historical Jesus by the 50s:
Thomas Christianity (an ascetic group behind the *Gospel of Thomas*,
for whom Jesus' death and resurrection held no interest), Pauline
Christianity (which focused on Jesus' historical execution and held
to his bodily resurrection as the first-fruits of the general resurrection), Q Christianity (a pre-Easter community behind the Q document, which had no interest in the death and resurrection of Jesus,
but saw him as living according to Wisdom and empowering others
to do so), and Exegetical Christianity (a scholarly group which
searched the Scriptures to invent the passion story and concentrated on passion–parousia, not passion–resurrection).[32] Even if we
concede the existence of such groups, however, it is not at all clear
how the belief in resurrection is supposed to have originated. Belief
in Jesus' continuing presence sounds most characteristic of the Q
community, as Crossan describes it:

---

[31] Crossan, *Jesus*, 163, 165.

[32] Crossan, *Historical Jesus*, 12. Wright observes that this 'mind-blowing reconstruction' lies at the heart of Crossan's work, for without it his use of the sources
makes no sense; nor does his highly idiosyncratic interpretation of the passion and
resurrection narratives. 'Yet', says Wright, 'it is, arguably, the most threadbare part
of his whole rich tapestry' (*Jesus and the Victory of God*, 63). Specifically, to imagine
that Paul's Corinthian opponents were a recognized group identified with the *Gospel
of Thomas* strains credibility beyond the breaking-point. To separate Paul from
Exegetical Christianity is extraordinary, given Paul's own earnest search of the
Scriptures. In order to postulate the existence of Q Christianity, Crossan has to distinguish an early Q from a later Q in order to separate out the apocalyptic elements
in Q so as to render it purely sapiential; but he has no non-question-begging criteria for such a division. There is in any case no reason to suppose that Q (the extent
of which is literally unknowable) represents the beliefs of a group within Christianity.
So-called Exegetical Christianity is a simple fiction, since the examples Crossan gives
of it are notable precisely for how unlike the writings of the evangelists and Paul they
are.

To believe that the Wisdom of God appeared performanically [sic] in Jesus' life meant, for them, to live likewise. That faith was there before he died and continued not so much despite, but because of it. He had warned them to expect refusal and even persecution, to live the life of Wisdom spurned. I wonder if anyone ever told them that they had lost their faith on Good Friday and had it restored by visions on Easter Sunday?[33]

But obviously belief in Jesus' resurrection did not originate in such a group, since the ongoing validity of Wisdom did not require such a metaphor; nor is it in evidence in Crossan's Q. Obviously it did not originate among Thomas Christians, since they were ostensibly Paul's opponents in Corinth, and resurrection plays no role in the *Gospel of Thomas.* Crossan admits that Exegetical Christianity did not invent the resurrection, since there were no Old Testament proof-texts available for that event, and this group conceived the passion to be followed by the parousia rather than the resurrection. So it could only have come from Pauline Christianity. But how is this hypothesis consistent with the view that the resurrection is just the symbolic assertion of the continuing presence of Jesus? Crossan admits that Paul wrote to Corinth to defend 'the possibility and actuality of bodily resurrection' and that Paul held Jesus' resurrection to be the first-fruits of the general eschatological resurrection of the dead. Crossan wants to maintain both that 'resurrection is the only possible way to articulate the presence of Jesus for Paul, but it is also inextricably linked to the imminent general resurrection at the end of the world'.[34] If we are to bring consistency into Crossan's view, he must hold that Paul believed in the literal, bodily resurrection of Jesus because he believed that Jesus was present and that Jesus could only be present if he had been raised. Now if Pauline Christianity is supposed to have originated with Paul, this means that none of the original followers of Jesus believed in or even used the language of resurrection symbolically prior to Paul. But in light of the early tradition received and delivered by Paul in I Corinthians 15: 3–5 alone, not to mention Paul's declaration that this is the *kerygma* proclaimed by all the apostles (I Cor. 15: 11), such a view is simply impossible, for the normative belief in Jesus' resurrection antedated Paul. Moreover, the claim that Paul was at a loss to express the notion of Jesus' continuing presence other than through the language of resurrection is incredible, since it was Paul

---

[33] Crossan, *Historical Jesus*, 15.   [34] Ibid. 7, 8.

himself who wrote so eloquently of Christ's presence in the believer through his indwelling Holy Spirit. Paul could have held Jesus to be present in spirit or, as divine, present even as God is present. If we try to rescue Crossan's hypothesis by holding that Paul did not originate 'Pauline' Christianity, but merely represented it, having inherited the belief in Jesus' resurrection from what we might more accurately call resurrection Christianity before him, then the origin of this group's belief is left unexplained by anything Crossan says. Apart from the event of the resurrection itself, it remains mysterious how the Christian belief in Jesus' resurrection from the dead, and the movement founded on that belief, should have come into being at all.

III CONCLUSION

In conclusion, I think that it is evident that Crossan has not been able to render plausible his reconstruction of the events of Easter, including Jesus' burial, empty tomb, post-mortem appearances, and the origin of the disciples' belief in Jesus' resurrection. His entire approach is predicated upon idiosyncratic presuppositions concerning sources and methodology which would not be accepted by any other major New Testament critic. Like an inverted pyramid, Crossan's whole reconstruction balances on the putative existence of the Cross Gospel, in the absence of which the whole structure collapses.

More specifically, we saw with respect to the burial story that, even if we concede the existence of the primitive Cross Gospel, the burial account meets Crossan's demand of multiple attestation, and is therefore to be accepted as prima facie historical. Crossan was unable to make a plausible case for regarding Mark's account as historicized prophecy; nor could he render doubtful the historicity of Joseph of Arimathea's role in the burial.

With respect to the empty tomb, Crossan's attempt to construe Mark's account as a distillation of the account of the resurrection in the *Gospel of Peter* forces him to adopt a number of untenable hypotheses, such as Mark's envisioning no resurrection appearances prior to the parousia and the transfiguration story's being a recast version of the resurrection appearance related in *Peter*. Crossan is also forced to embrace without evidence the fanciful hypothesis of the flight of the disciples to Galilee. The *reductio ad absurdum* of his position, however, is his treatment of the role of the women in the empty tomb account, the explanation of which forces Crossan to what can only be described as desperate lengths.

With respect to the post-mortem appearances, Crossan's treatment is surprisingly brief and superficial. Again we see the desperation, as Crossan denies without argument that the disciples experienced any post-mortem appearances of Jesus, despite the multiple attestation enjoyed by the appearances, and embraces without evidence the long-refuted interpretation of the appearances as solely authority-conferring constructs of the early Church.

Finally, with respect to the origin of the disciples' belief in Jesus' resurrection, Crossan's developing views seem to be self-contradictory, at first ascribing to the disciples a purely symbolic use of resurrection language, but later attributing to Pauline Christianity the original application of the notion of resurrection to Jesus' fate. The first hypothesis is merely enormously implausible; the second is absurd. None of Crossan's hypothetical Christian communities, even if they existed, can be plausibly thought to have originated the idea of Jesus' resurrection.

Crossan has announced that his next project will be a book dealing with the events following Jesus' death. It is greatly to be hoped that his more studied reconstruction will be more substantial, more plausible, and more consistent than what he has heretofore produced.

Response by Paul Rhodes Eddy

In his critique of John Dominic Crossan's views on the resurrection of Jesus, William Lane Craig begins by offering a summary, with brief critical remarks, of Crossan's source- and tradition-critical 'presuppositions'. The bulk of the paper then goes on to assess Crossan's views in the light of three major strands of evidence for a historical resurrection: (1) the empty tomb, (2) the post-mortem appearances of Jesus, and (3) the origin of the disciples' belief in Jesus' resurrection.[1] In the end, Craig's analysis leads him to conclude that 'Crossan has not been able to render plausible his reconstruction of the events of Easter' (p. 270).

On the whole, I find Craig's line of argument and critique of Crossan to be convincing. The following critical comments, then, should be construed as suggestions for refining and polishing an already strong case. I shall begin by noting two points at which revision of the argument might be considered. Next, I shall briefly discuss several points at which further support and/or development of particular strands of the argument might serve to strengthen the cumulative force of the whole. Finally, I shall return to the crucial, and vexing, issue which Craig raises in the opening section of his paper: that of presuppositions.

I TWO SUGGESTIONS FOR REVISION

My first concern involves an issue of the form rather than the content of the argument. Here I refer to Craig's wide-ranging use of statements regarding 'scholarly consensus' and the like. There is, of

---

[1] As Craig notes, he has made use of these same three lines of evidence in structuring his most comprehensive defence of the historical resurrection of Jesus; see his *Assessing the New Testament Evidence for the Historicity of the Resurrection of Jesus* (Lewiston, NY: Mellen, 1989).

course, nothing necessarily problematic with such statements; it is always possible that they simply represent an accurate statistical report of the state of the discussion. Unfortunately, the claim of 'scholarly consensus' within New Testament studies today has at times become little more than an unsubstantiated rhetorical ploy, rather than simply the reporting of a documented state of affairs. One recent and glaring example of this is the claim of the Jesus Seminar that one of the seven 'pillars' of contemporary 'modern critical scholarship' is the conclusion that Jesus' message—contrary to John the Baptist and much of the early Church—was fundamentally 'non-eschatological' in nature.[2] Thus, given this tendency toward overstatement among some within New Testament studies today, scholars should take extra precautions when making claims of 'consensus'.

Within Craig's paper, there are two types of cases where claims of 'consensus' serve to raise questions: (1) instances of inadequate documentation of a purported 'consensus',[3] and (2) instances where, given the status of the question in the field today, a claim of consensus is at least questionable.[4] In regard to instances of the

[2] See R. Funk, R. W. Hoover, and the Jesus Seminar, *The Five Gospels: The Search for the Authentic Words of Jesus* (New York: Macmillan, 1993), 3, 4. The strength of this 'pillar' is called into question in light of the many scholars today who argue for the very opposite conclusion. In fact, J. H. Charlesworth has recently stated that the view that Jesus preached an apocalyptic message is 'one of the strongest consensuses in New Testament research'; 'Jesus Research Expands with Chaotic Creativity', in J. H. Charlesworth and W. F. Weaver (eds.) *Images of Jesus Today*, (Valley Forge, Pa.: Trinity, 1994), 10. Some of Alan Padgett's thoughts on the 'consensus Jesus' in his contribution to this volume (pp. 296–8) are relevant here.

[3] e.g. p. 254: 'Most scholars would concur with Bultmann's judgement' that the Marcan burial story 'lacks theological reflection or apologetic'—here only Bultmann is cited; p. 259: 'most critics regard this [transfiguration] narrative as so firmly embedded in its context that . . .'—no representative scholarship is cited here at all. Documentation is particularly crucial here since at least one other scholar has claimed the opposite conclusion as the majority position; see E. Klostermann, *Das Markusevangelium* (Tübingen: Mohr, 1950), 86; p. 262: 'most scholars today' reject the 'flight-to-Galilee' thesis as 'in von Campenhausen's words . . . "a fiction of the critics" '—only von Campenhausen's 1966 work is cited; pp. 267–8: 'most critics concur that Old Testament proof-texts of the resurrection could be found only after . . .'—again, no representative scholarship is cited.

[4] e.g. the claim that 'sceptical scholars agree' that Joseph of Arimathea was not a Christian invention (p. 256). For 'sceptical' (and one generally not so) scholars who question the historicity of Joseph of Arimathea see e.g. B. Lindars, 'Jesus Risen: Bodily Resurrection but No Empty Tomb', *Theology*, 89 (1986), 93–4; R. Mahoney, *Two Disciples at the Tomb* (Bern: Lang, 1974), 112; G. Scholz, 'Joseph von Arimathäa und Barabbas', *Linguistica Biblica*, 57 (1985), 81–94. Likewise, the claim that Crossan's 'presuppositions concerning sources and methodology' are 'idiosyncratic'

former, the addition of supporting documentation should be no problem. In fact, at certain points Craig could simply refer to the relevant discussion, with documentation, as found in his book, *Assessing the New Testament Evidence for the Historicity of the Resurrection of Jesus*. On the other hand, instances of the latter should be reworded so as to more accurately reflect the present state of the field.

My second suggestion for revision involves Craig's attempt to catch Crossan in a self-contradiction concerning his thesis on the origin of resurrection belief in the early Church. According to Craig, the self-contradiction occurs in 'first ascribing to the disciples a

and 'would not be accepted by any other major New Testament critic' (p. 270). With the exception of one aspect of his 'source' theory—viz. his Cross Gospel thesis (on which see n. 22), Crossan's source-critical conclusions and much of his overall methodology are (for better or worse) shared by a significant wing (represented by the driving force within the Jesus Seminar) of the NT scholarly community in North America today. For example, Crossan is far from alone in his support of the following source/method presuppositions:

(1) The dependence of canonical Mark upon secret Mark; see e.g. H. Koester, 'History and Development of Mark's Gospel (From Mark to Secret Mark and "Canonical" Mark)', in B. Corley (ed.), *Colloquy on New Testament Studies: A Time for Reappraisal and Fresh Approaches* (Macon, Ga.: Mercer University Press, 1983), 35-57; M. W. Meyer, 'The Youth in the Secret Gospel of Mark', *Semeia*, 49 (1990), 129-53; H.-M. Schenke, 'The Mystery of the Gospel of Mark', *Second Century*, 4/2 (1984), 65-82.

(2) The earliness and/or essential independence of the *Gospel of Peter* from the canonicals; see e.g. P. Vielhauer, *Geschichte der frühchristlichen Literatur*, GLB (Berlin: De Gruyter, 1975), 646; B. A. Johnson, 'The Empty Tomb Tradition in the Gospel of Peter' (diss., Harvard University, 1965, under Koester's direction); J. Denker, *Die theologiegeschichtliche Stellung des Petrusevangeliums*, EHS 36 (Bern: Lang, 1975); N. Walter, 'Eine vormatthäische Schilderung der Auferstehung Jesu', *NTS* 19 (1972-3), 415-29; and esp. H. Koester, *Ancient Christian Gospels: Their History and Development* (Philadelphia: Trinity, 1990), 216-40. Incidentally, two other critiques (beyond Brown's work cited by Craig in n. 3) of an early and/or independent *Gospel of Peter* are worthy of mention: F. Neirynck, 'The Apocryphal Gospels and the Gospel of Mark', in J.-M. Sevrin (ed.), *The New Testament in Early Christianity*, BETL 86 (Leuven: Leuven University Press, 1989), 140-57; A. Kirk, 'Examining Priorities: Another Look at the *Gospel of Peter*'s Relationship to the New Testament Gospels', *NTS* 40 (1994), 572-95.

(3) The claim that the burial and/or empty tomb traditions are rooted in history rather than in early Church fabrication; whether he is right or not, R. Morton (review of G. Luedemann, *Die Auferstehung Jesu* (Göttingen: Vandenhoeck & Ruprecht, 1994), *CBQ* 57 (1995), 599) has recently referred to the view that the empty tomb traditions are 'late' and 'ultimately irrelevant for Christian faith' as 'the consensus of the majority of NT scholars'. For arguments in this vein see Lindars, 'Jesus Risen', 90-6; and, more recently, Luedemann's *The Resurrection of Jesus: History, Experience, Theology*, trans. J. Bowden (Minneapolis: Fortress, 1994), 45-7, 109-21.

purely symbolic use of resurrection language, but later attributing to Pauline Christianity the original application of the notion of resurrection to Jesus's fate' (271; see pp. 266-70 for the extended argument). However, in my reading of Crossan, I do not find him claiming that Pauline Christianity—or even Paul himself—'originated' the notion of Jesus' resurrection. Rather, he merely claims that Pauline Christianity 'emphasized' and *literalized* it.[5] In terms of actual origination, Crossan's thesis would suggest that the expression arose as an admittedly less-than-appropriate metaphor by which the disciples could symbolically voice their sense of Jesus' lingering presence among them.[6] Thus, against Craig (p. 268), Crossan could conclude that a group very much like the supposed Q or Thomas people did inaugurate the use of resurrection *language*, though not the literal belief, when they coined this overly potent metaphor.[7] Paul, then, having inherited this tradition, would have simply literalized and idealized it. I see no 'self-contradiction' in this general proposal.

However, what I do see here—along with Craig—is massive implausibility. Thus, I want to emphasize that to revise the claim of self-contradiction here is not to free Crossan from the real problem. He is still left with the heart of the dilemma posed by Craig, namely: (a) can Crossan's thesis adequately explain the quite strong evidence suggesting that Jesus' earliest disciples held to a belief in a *literal* resurrection (evidence which Craig nicely summarizes on pp. 265-6); and (b) why, on Crossan's thesis, would the purported pre-Pauline, Q- or Thomas-like disciples (for that is what they would have most looked like on Crossan's reconstruction) have chosen the ill-fitting metaphor of 'resurrection' for their expression of a generic 'continuing presence' of Jesus, especially with so many more appropriate ones within the tradition just waiting to be used in a literal fashion (e.g. Wisdom, the Holy Spirit, and so on)? I don't see that Crossan's

---

[5] See J. D. Crossan, *Jesus: A Revolutionary Biography* (San Francisco: HarperSanFrancisco, 1994), 163, 165.

[6] Crossan, *The Historical Jesus: The Life of a Mediterranean Jewish Peasant* (San Francisco: HarperSanFrancisco, 1991), pp. xiii, 404.

[7] In a lengthier critique of Crossan, one would want to devote more space to an examination and critique of the driving force behind Crossan's proposal here: viz. the thesis that the earliest Christian groups—i.e. the supposed Q (as derived from J. Kloppenborg's Q redactional stratigraphy) and Thomas (as derived from the now-standard North American post-Bultmannian arguments for the early and independent nature of the *Gospel of Thomas*) people—had no real knowledge of and/or concern for a passion–resurrection soteriology.

reconstruction can furnish a credible answer to either of these questions.

II SUGGESTIONS FOR DEVELOPMENT

Next, I turn to three matters related to Craig's arguments regarding the burial and empty tomb (ET) traditions.

First, then, to what may just be a matter of clarification. In the course of his discussion of the evidence for the historicity of the burial tradition, Craig writes, 'Moreover, it is generally acknowledged that the burial account is part of Mark's source material for the story of Jesus' passion' (p. 253). To make a claim about the nature of 'Mark's *source material* for the *story* of Jesus' passion' could sound like a claim regarding a pre-Marcan passion narrative. Given the current debates regarding the existence and/or possible content of such a narrative, some clarification and/or support of this potentially controversial claim is called for.[8] It may be that Craig is merely claiming here that Mark received the burial tradition in *some unspecified form*, be it oral or written, and thus simply that Mark did not 'create' it himself. If so, this can be clarified, thereby avoiding any need to address the nest of complex disputes surrounding the pre-Marcan passion narrative question.

Second, I would add a brief supportive note to Craig's detailed and effective critique (pp. 256–7) of Crossan's rejection of a historical Joseph of Arimathea. Crossan, of course, claims that Joseph is simply a Marcan creation designed to function as 'the perfect in-between figure, at once within the Jewish leadership elite . . . and still connected to Jesus', and thus as a character who could explain how Jesus ended up being buried by his friends and not his enemies.[9] A central problem with this thesis is that, contrary to Crossan's scenario in which Mark creates Joseph with 'a solid and

---

[8] There are at least two issues that arise here: (1) the question of the *existence* of a pre-Marcan passion narrative; and (2) even among those who do hold to its existence, the question of its *content*: i.e. whether it contained a burial account. Recently, both J. B. Green and A. Yarbro Collins have argued against such a claim on genre and other grounds; see J. B. Green, *The Death of Jesus*, WUNT 2/33 (Tübingen: Mohr (Siebeck), 1988), 311–13; A. Yarbro Collins, *The Beginning of the Gospel: Probings of Mark in Context* (Minneapolis: Fortress, 1992), 117; idem, 'The Genre of the Passion Narrative', *Studia Theologica*, 47/1 (1993), 18–19.

[9] Crossan, *Historical Jesus*, 393.

powerful foot in both camps', Joseph's 'power' in either camp appears to have been something less than robust—certainly less than Crossan's fictionalized mediatorial role theory would anticipate.[10] As Fathers O'Collins and Kendall have pointed out, it is clear that, on the one hand, Joseph 'obviously lacked the power needed in the Jewish court to prevent the condemnation of Jesus'; while on the other, his 'lack of "power" in the Christian camp may be gauged by the fact that, outside the burial story in the gospels, the NT nowhere mentions him'.[11] This way of starting the problem could assist Craig in situating Crossan more firmly—and uncomfortably—in that cramped, imaginary space between two sharp horns. For the more 'powerfully' Joseph is presented (in order to function as the effective middleman), the less historically plausible he becomes—a serious consideration for a creative author (i.e. Mark) who wants his fictional character to be believable. On the other hand, the less powerful he appears (and thus the more historically plausible), the less reason Crossan would have for questioning his historical existence in the first place. Whichever way Crossan moves on this dilemma, the general plausibility of his thesis begins to unravel.

Third, and more importantly, I think the essay could be strengthened by adding a section offering a focused response to Crossan's most recent and explicit argument against the historicity of the private burial of Jesus, as presented in his *Who Killed Jesus?*.[12] In his critique, Craig notes that Crossan offers 'no specific evidence, much less probative evidence' for his own thesis regarding the fate of Jesus' body. Rather, Crossan's scenario merely 'represents his hunch as to what happened to the body of Jesus based on customary burial procedures' (p. 249). While Crossan's arguments here do not emphasize 'specific' evidence in the sense of appeals to particular historical data from the Gospels tradition, he does propose several broad arguments in defence of his claim that Jesus' body would most likely have been left on the cross, or, at best, have been buried in a shallow, unmarked grave. According to Crossan, in either case wild dogs or birds of prey most likely disposed of Jesus' corpse.

Crossan begins his argument by noting Martin Hengel's careful

---

[10] Ibid.

[11] G. O'Collins and D. Kendall, 'Did Joseph of Arimathea Exist?', *Biblica*, 75/2 (1994), 241 n. 18.

[12] J. D. Crossan, *Who Killed Jesus? Exposing the Roots of Anti-Semitism in the Gospel Story of the Death of Jesus* (HarperSanFrancsico, 1995), 163–8.

description of ancient crucifixion practice, including his observation that 'quite often its victims were never buried'.[13] According to Crossan, this general observation holds true even for crucifixion victims within Jewish Palestine, a claim, he suggests, that is corroborated by the fact that only one victim of crucifixion has ever been found buried in a family tomb in the Jewish homeland.[14] Thus, Crossan concludes that non-burial for the crucified Jesus must be our probable conclusion, unless credible evidence to the contrary is forthcoming.

The remainder of Crossan's argument comes in the form of five 'steps' of consideration, wherein he raises and considers lines of evidence that could serve as rebutting defeaters of his conclusion. In each case, Crossan counters such evidence with what he considers to be undercutting defeaters of sufficient magnitude. In the end, he suggests that each rebuttal can be effectively undercut, and thus that his original contention regarding Jesus' body remains the most plausible conclusion.[15] Though they are largely based on general

---

[13] Ibid. 162. Here Crossan is citing Hengel's *Crucifixion* (1976), trans. J. Bowden (Philadelphia: Fortress, 1977), 87.

[14] The 1968 discovery of the skeleton of a Palestinian crucifixion victim, the young man, Yehochanan; see J. Zias and E. Sekeles, 'The Crucified Man from Giv'at ha-Mivtar: A Reappraisal', *IEJ* 35 (1985), 22–7.

[15] Crossan's five 'steps' analyse and attempt to undercut several lines of potential rebutting evidence: (1) *Rebutting evidence*: those who defend Jesus' private burial point to the proscription in Deut. 21: 22–3 against leaving a dead corpse upon a tree overnight; burial on the same day is called for. This command is also exemplified in two narratives in Joshua (8: 23–9; 10: 26–7). *Crossan's undercutting evidence*: this OT proscription applies explicitly only to those executed and then *subsequently* 'hung on a tree': 'Removal by evening of one crucified *after* death is very different from removal by evening of one crucified *before* death. Could Deuteronomy 21: 22–23 prevail against *live* crucifixion?' (Crossan, *Who Killed Jesus?*, 164). His second step serves to support this undercutting question. (2) The older practice of crucifixion of the dead *did* give way to the Roman practice of live crucifixion under the Jewish Hasmonean dynasty (last centuries BC). Thus the theoretical question posed above becomes practical: did the Romans and their Jewish vassals worry about the Deuteronomic proscription in such cases? (3) *Rebutting evidence*: the Temple Scroll (11QTemple) records a command to bury the body of one who has been crucified on the same day, and applies it to *both* dead and live crucifixion cases. Here, Crossan is faced with documentary evidence that would answer his earlier question in a way that counts against his thesis. *Undercutting evidence*: Crossan writes: 'I consider the laws of the Temple Scroll to be ideals for what Essenes would do if and when they controlled Jerusalem. As such they tell us more what was *not* being done than what was being done at the time of their composition. I cannot presume, therefore, that Deuteronomy 21: 22–3 was followed in Roman crucifixion in the first-century Jewish homeland' (ibid. 166). *Response*: Crossan's thesis must be seriously challenged at this point. One line of questioning that could quickly test the plausibility of

and quite speculative considerations, Crossan's arguments call for a more sustained response. To my mind, such an addition to Craig's essay would strengthen it considerably.

The thrust of such a critique could be a demonstration of the claim that Crossan's proposed undercutting defeaters simply do not work. For instance, take Crossan's response to the fact that Josephus *does* mention the command to bury *on the same day* one who has been hung on a tree after being stoned to death, and this in a first-century Jewish context.[16] Crossan's response is to drive a wedge between what he considers to be this recital of 'ideal Jewish law' and the actual practice of the day.[17] Specifically, he argues that the few instances of Josephus' own accounts of actual first-century crucifixion in the Jewish homeland never explicitly mention removal of the body by sunset. This is, of course, at best an argument from silence. But in actuality it is much less! Not only does Josephus mention the Deuteronomy 21 proscription in a general, possibly 'idealized' form in the *Antiquities* passage, but in his account of the Zealots' abuse of corpses during their seizure of the

Crossan's speculation here would be to analyse the various commands and proscriptions in the Temple Scroll to see if it is the case that they revolve solely around Essene concerns regarding things that were *not* being practised by the Jews in Jerusalem at the time. (4) Next, Crossan attempts to quarry support for this conclusion from Josephus (argument presented in body of text). (5) *Rebutting evidence*: Crossan introduces a text from Philo (*Against Flaccus*, 83) wherein he mentions that, on holidays, good governors have been known to grant burial permission to the survivors of the victims of crucifixion. This is, of course, the very case which the Gospel tradition offers with regard to Jesus (the Joseph of Arimathea incident). The 1968 discovery of the crucified young man, buried in the family tomb, supports this type of event. *Undercutting evidence*: Crossan softens any hopes here, with regard to Jesus, by noting that only *one* such victim has ever been unearthed to date; thus, he concludes, the practice must have been extremely rare.

Crossan's conclusion to all this is that, given the priority of Cross Gospel and the fact that it states that those who crucified Jesus buried him (since Crossan locates the Joseph of Arimathea reference in the *Gospel of Peter* to a secondary, post-canonical redactional layer), Jesus' followers themselves had no first-hand knowledge of the burial. Rather, the Cross Gospel simply writes in the enemy burial as a 'hope' (based on the Deut. 21 proscription) that Jesus did get a dignified Jewish burial. A later (post-canonical) redaction writes in a new twist: Joseph of Arimathea and a burial by friends in a private, marked tomb. Thus, 'history' was eclipsed by 'hope' as the story was transformed from the *probable* (Jesus' body was left on the cross . . . and was devoured by wild animals) to the *possible* (Jesus' body was buried by his enemies in a shallow, unmarked grave . . . and was devoured by wild animals) to the *fictional* (Jesus' body was buried by friends in a private tomb).

[16] Crossan cites two passages: *Antiquities* 4. 202 and *Jewish War* 4. 317; see *Who Killed Jesus?*, 166.

[17] Ibid.

Temple in the First Roman War, he notes that 'the Jews are so careful about funeral rites that even malefactors who have been sen-
tenced to crucifixion are taken down and buried before sunset'
(*Jewish War* 4. 317). In order to avoid the clear implications of this
report of actual first-century practice in the Jewish homeland,
Crossan must make the unjustified, *ad hoc* move of labelling this
report as purely an instance of Josephan anti-Zealot polemic, thus
robbing it of its historical credibility. Only then does his single argument—the one from silence—gain any possible plausibility. Finally,
a critique of Crossan's arguments here could, I think, clearly win
the day after Crossan's controlling presupposition—that the passion
tradition is almost entirely 'prophecy historicized' rather than 'history remembered'—has been dismantled. And with this I turn to
the final section of my response.

III On 'Presuppositions'

The first issue I want to address here is Crossan's driving presupposition mentioned above: namely, that the passion tradition is essentially 'prophecy historicized', not 'history remembered'. I will
broach it by posing a few questions. First, what would Crossan, or
anyone in his general camp, have to say in response to Craig's critique? Would they ever be convinced by his line of argument? And
if not, why not? I submit that they would not, and the reason has
very little to do with the relative strength or weakness of the specific historical evidence that Craig presents. We are now back to
Craig's observation that Crossan offers little in the way of specific
historical evidence for his claims regarding Jesus' body, but rather
presents only what amounts to conjectural extrapolations from
quite general considerations. But this is, I think, Crossan's very
point. In his eyes (and not his eyes only) there just are no specific
historical data for the passion. There is only the bare historical fact
of a crucifixion,[18] and then the rampant fabrication of fictional
details—leading eventually to an imaginative narrative—via 'creative' pseudo-exegetical exercises. In Crossan's words, there is
'prophecy historicized', but certainly 'not history remembered'.[19] It
is this presupposition of the fundamentally fictional (or, more

---

[18] Crossan, *Historical Jesus*, 387.   [19] Crossan, *Who Killed Jesus?*, 10.

euphemistically, 'creative'), and thus historically unreliable, nature of the passion tradition that undergirds Crossan's entire enterprise. Thus it is this presupposition that requires a focused analysis in any critique of Crossan's work.

Craig does address this general approach as it appears in the form of one specific claim: namely that the burial tradition is a fictional creation based upon Deuteronomy 21: 22-3 and Joshua 10: 26-7 (pp. 254-5). Here, his critique is right on the mark, and goes to show just how vulnerable Crossan's speculative proposals can be to careful scrutiny, when taken on an individual basis. Craig's overall critique might be enhanced, however, by including at least a brief summary statement of the evidence against Crossan's guiding background assumptions about the *general non-historicity* of the Gospels tradition. Here, two points worthy of focus would be: first, the remarkable observation that, just when Crossan and his fellow critics within the North American post-Bultmannian wing of New Testament scholarship[20] have coalesced around a resurgent scepticism with regard to the canonical Gospels tradition, a growing trend among a much more diverse group of biblical scholars suggests that this same tradition offers a generally reliable historical base from which to launch a 'Third Quest'.[21]

---

[20] By this term 'North American post-Bultmannian scholarship' I mean to signify that stream of scholarship, most visible in the Jesus Seminar, that derives from the transplantation of Bultmannian seeds from German to North American fields of NT study, primarily in the form(s) developed by Bultmann's two former students Helmut Koester and James Robinson. See J. M. Robinson, 'The Q Trajectory: Between John and Matthew via Jesus', B. A. Pearson (ed.), *The Future of Early Christianity: Essays in Honor of Helmut Koester* (Minneapolis: Fortress, 1991), 173. W. Farmer has referred to this movement under the rubric of 'the Harvard–Claremont connection'; see *The Gospel of Jesus: The Pastoral Relevance of the Synoptic Problem* (Louisville, Ky.: Westminster/Knox, 1994), 163.

[21] On the recent rise and growth of the conviction that the canonical Gospels tradition is generally reliable see e.g. J. H. Charlesworth, 'From Barren Mazes to Gentle Rappings: The Emergence of Jesus Research', *Princeton Seminary Bulletin*, 7 (1986), 221-4; idem, 'Jesus Research Expands with Chaotic Creativity', 5-7; C. A. Evans, 'Life-of-Jesus Research and the Eclipse of Mythology', *Theological Studies*, 54 (1993), 14-15, 34-6; B. F. Meyer, *The Aims of Jesus* (London: SCM, 1979), 16-17; E. P. Sanders, *Jesus and Judaism* (Philadelphia: Fortress, 1985), 2; W. R. Telford, 'Major Trends and Interpretive Issues in the Study of Jesus', in B. Chilton and C. A. Evans (eds.), *Studying the Historical Jesus: Evaluations of the State of Current Research*, NTTS 19 (Leiden: Brill, 1994), 33-74; B. Witherington, *The Christology of Jesus* (Minneapolis: Fortress, 1990); idem, *Jesus the Sage: The Pilgrimage of Wisdom* (Minneapolis: Fortress, 1994); N. T. Wright, *Jesus and the Victory of God* (Minneapolis: Fortress, 1996), esp. ch. 3; idem, *The New Testament and People of God* (Minneapolis: Fortress, 1992).

In this regard, it is interesting to note the influence of Birger Gerhardsson's work

Second, Crossan's entire project rests upon the claim that first-century Jewish-Christian exegetes would have felt virtually no constraints in using the Old Testament as a springboard for the wholesale fabrication of fictional tales of Jesus, and then presenting them to the early community as remembrances—often 'eye-witness' in nature—of very *recent* 'history'. Incidentally, I believe it is this thesis of 'prophecy historicized', rather than his Cross Gospel thesis, as Craig suggests, that functions as the central and glaringly precarious base upon which his entire reconstructive enterprise teeters like an 'inverted pyramid' (p. 270).[22] Here, the critical remark by Joel Green (in his *JBL* review of *The Cross that Spoke*) points to a conclusion that, once substantiated in detail, could thoroughly undermine Crossan's reconstructive project:

Crossan failed to consider substantial work of the last decade on the hermeneutics of late Judaism, specifically on the question whether the creation of current history from OT texts was an accepted and widely-practiced phenomenon. In fact, while more work needs to be done, study of *pesharim* texts from Qumran, postbiblical historiography, and selected apocalyptic writings is already suggesting that the direction of influence was *from event to biblical text*.[23]

on many within the 'Third Quest': see e.g. J. H. Charlesworth, *Jesus within Judaism* (New York: Doubleday, 1988), 204; B. F. Meyer, 'Some Consequences of Birger Gerhardsson's Account of the Origins of the Gospel Tradition', in H. Wansbrough (ed.), *Jesus and the Oral Gospel Tradition*, JSNTSS 64 (Sheffield: JSOT Press, 1991), 424–40; Sanders, *Jesus and Judaism*, 14–16; Wright, *New Testament and People of God*, 422. For two sharp critical assessments of the foundational presuppositions that support a sceptical approach to the canonical Gospels tradition see Meyer, *Aims of Jesus*, 16–17; Witherington, *Christology of Jesus*, 3–22.

[22] Craig's assessment of Crossan's Cross Gospel thesis as 'idiosyncratic' is accurate; virtually no one has followed Crossan in the specifics of his highly speculative reconstruction of the origin and history of the passion tradition. However, Craig's attendant claim, that 'Like an inverted pyramid, Crossan's whole reconstruction balances on the putative existence of the "Cross Gospel," in the absence of which the whole structure collapses' (p. 270), is questionable. See Crossan's comments on this point in *Who Killed Jesus?*, 10.

[23] *JBL* 109/2 (1990), 257–8. For similar concerns regarding Crossan's approach to the passion tradition see the reviews of *The Cross that Spoke* by C. C. Black, *JR* 69 (1989), 398; R. H. Fuller, *Inter.*, 45 (1991), 72. As Green notes, more work needs to be done here. However, for observations which suggest that the sequencing in Jewish exegesis of the day *generally* moved from 'history' to 'text', and not vice versa, see the following: F. F. Bruce, 'Biblical Exposition at Qumran', in R. T. France and D. Wenham (eds.), *Studies in Midrash and Historiography*, GP 3 (Sheffield: JSOT Press, 1983), 77–98; J. D. G. Dunn, *Unity and Diversity in the New Testament*, 2nd edn. (Philadelphia: Trinity, 1990 (1977)), 99–101; J. A. Fitzmyer, 'The Use of Explicit Old Testament Quotations in Qumran Literature and in the New Testament', in his

In short, Crossan gives precious little evidence of demonstrated parallels to support his thesis of the rampant *creation* of supposedly *very recent* 'historical' events from Old Testament texts by early Jewish Christians, as opposed to the quite common practice of the subsequent *interpretation* of actual historical events in the light of Old Testament texts.[24] This, I would suggest, is where a critique of Crossan's thesis on the passion–resurrection tradition must focus its attention most strongly.

My final concern related to Crossan's presuppositions involves the fact that his explicit religio-philosophical presuppositions preclude a priori his taking seriously the Gospel resurrection accounts as evidence of an historical event.[25] This is to raise a question that is too often treated as a non-issue in contemporary biblical scholarship.

Essays on the Semitic Background to the New Testament (London: Chapman, 1971), esp. 30-1, 53; R. T. France, 'Jewish Historiography, Midrash, and the Gospels', in France and Wenham (eds.), *Studies in Midrash and Historiography*, 99-127; idem, 'Postscript—Where Have We Got To, and Where Do We Go from Here?', in France and Wenham (eds.), *Studies in Midrash and Historiography*, esp. 290-2; M. P. Horgan, *Pesharim: Qumran Interpretations of Biblical Books*, CBQMS 8 (Washington: Catholic Biblical Association of America, 1979), 229, 248-9; J. Marcus, 'The Old Testament and the Death of Jesus: The Role of Scripture in the Gospel Passion Narratives', in J. T. Carroll, J. B. Green, *et al.*, *The Death of Jesus in Early Christianity* (Peabody, Mass.: Hendrickson, 1995), esp. 212-13; D. J. Moo, *The Old Testament in the Gospel Passion Narratives* (Sheffield: Almond, 1983), esp. 378-81.

On ancient writers as aware of, and concerned about, the distinction between 'fact' and 'fiction' in their historical writings see A. W. Mosley, 'Historical Reporting in the Ancient World', *NTS* 12 (1965), 10-26; Wright, *New Testament and People of God*, 67-9, 83-7, 377-8. On the claim that the Gospel writers (and early Christians in general) were very concerned with *history* see R. P. C. Hanson, 'The Assessment of Motive in the Study of the Synoptic Gospels', *Modern Churchman*, 10 (1967), 265-6; P. Minear, 'Gospel History: Celebration or Reconstruction?', in D. G. Miller and D. Y. Hadidian (eds.) *Jesus and Man's Hope* (2 vols.; Pittsburgh: Pittsburgh Theological Seminary, 1971), ii. 21; C. F. D. Moule, 'The Intention of the Evangelists', in A. J. B. Higgins (ed.), *New Testament Essays: Studies in Memory of T. W. Manson* (Manchester: Manchester University Press, 1959), 165-77; G. N. Stanton, *Jesus of Nazareth in New Testament Preaching*, SNTSMS 27 (Cambridge: Cambridge University Press, 1974), 186-90; N. T. Wright, 'Jesus, Israel, and the Cross', in K. H. Richards (ed.), *SBLASP 1985*, (Atlanta: Scholars, 1985), 90; Idem, *New Testament and People of God*, 137, 377-8.

[24] In personal conversation, Crossan has indicated that, with regard to the passion tradition, the two most important illustrations of this phenomenon are (1) the redactional activity of Matthew, Luke, and John on the Marcan tradition, and (2) the *Epistle of Barnabas*, esp. ch. 7 (see *Historical Jesus*, 376-83).

[25] Craig himself has taken issue with Crossan on this in the format of a public debate with him on the resurrection, (23 Sept. 1995 in Chicago). Here, Craig suggested that Crossan's presuppositions were fundamentally tied to a 'naturalistic' world-view, a label that Crossan adamantly rejected.

Thankfully, a number of scholars have begun to highlight the important ramifications of such generally unstated and even unconscious presuppositions for what are often taken to be the disinterested and 'objective' results of New Testament exegesis.[26] Crossan, for instance, explicitly states: 'I do not think that anyone, anywhere, at any time brings dead people back to life'; such an event never 'did or could happen'.[27] Surely this a priori metaphysical assumption will have a direct bearing upon his presumably a posteriori conclusions regarding the historical evidence for the Gospel tradition's claims of resurrection. This is, of course, simply one more instance of the ongoing discussion about the nature and inherent limitations of the historical-critical method. But it is a topic that deserves ongoing attention and analysis, given the tendency in the field toward allowing such considerations frequently to vanish beyond the horizon of the critical exegete at work.

Tied to this matter of religio-philosophical presuppositions is a final question regarding Crossan's hermeneutical method. In a number of writings, Crossan explicitly sketches the contours of his religious world-view, one which is best described as a radical negative theology. Beginning with the notion of the divine as 'Wholly Other',[28] nearly every aspect of his early parables study led him fur-

---

[26] See e.g. H. J. de Jonge, 'The Loss of Faith in the Historicity of the Gospels: H. S. Reimarus (*ca.* 1750) on John and the Synoptics', in A. Denaux (ed.), *John and the Synoptics*, BETL 51 (Leuven: Leuven University Press, 1992), 409–21; E. E. Ellis, 'Gospels Criticism: A Perspective on the State of the Art', in P. Stuhlmacher (ed.), *The Gospel and the Gospels* (1983), trans. J. Bowden (Grand Rapids, Mich.: Eerdmans, 1991), 26–33; E. Schüssler Fiorenza, 'The Ethics of Biblical Interpretation: Decentering Biblical Scholarship', *JBL* 107/1 (1988), 11; I. H. Marshall, 'Historical Criticism', in I. H. Marshall (ed.), *New Testament Interpretation: Essays on Principles and Methods* (Exeter/Grand Rapids, Mich.: Paternoster Press/Eerdmans, 1977), 126–38; T. C. Oden, 'The Critique of Criticism', in his *After Modernity . . . What?: Agenda for Theology* (Grand Rapids, Mich.: Zondervan, 1990), 103–47; G. N. Stanton, 'Presuppositions in New Testament Criticism', in Marshall (ed.), *New Testament Interpretation*, 60–71; P. Stuhlmacher, *Historical Criticism and Theological Interpretation of Scripture: Towards a Hermeneutics of Consent* (1975), trans. R. A. Harrisville (Philadelphia: Fortress, 1977).

[27] Crossan, *Jesus*, 95, 94. Comparison of this confident claim with the more restrained comment of E. P. Sanders, another 'liberal' scholar, is instructive: 'That Jesus' followers (and later Paul) had resurrection experiences is, in my judgment a fact. What the reality was that gave rise to the experiences I do not know' (*The Historical Figure of Jesus* (New York: Allen Lane/Penguin, 1993), 280).

[28] J. B. Crossan, *In Parables: The Challenge of the Historical Jesus* (New York: Harper & Row, 1973), 13.

ther into 'negation and darkness'.[29] Crossan's negative theology—
his '*via negativa* in a modern translation'—is self-consciously rooted
in a deconstructive 'philosophy of absence'.[30] None the less,
Crossan strives to avoid the wholesale atheology of deconstructionism, placing his hope instead in a radical negativity which still offers
some shadow of transcendental experience, however fleeting.
Noting Derrida's destructive conclusions for *all* theology, Crossan
concludes that 'those theologians who believe, as I do, in the necessity of a breakout from ontotheology and who have been research-
ing the foundations of our tradition, as I have been, to locate the
best place for its deconstruction, may be more willing to accept
Derrida's comments on positive than on negative theology'.[31] Aside
from the question of whether or not one can embrace Derrida's
deconstructionist theory and still retain anything remotely 'theological', negative or otherwise (a claim, incidentally, that Paul
Ricoeur has explicitly challenged[32]), another troubling problem
arises. Can such an approach to reality support the kind of historical reconstruction project that Crossan has been investing himself
in over the last decade? More specifically, can the pre-1985/Jesus
Seminar Crossan (whose work evinces a clear movement from
structuralism to post-structuralism[33]) be reconciled with the post-
1985/Jesus Seminar Crossan (whose work reveals an apparent
commitment to a non-deconstructive, even asymptotically 'objective', approach to history and its texts)? What are we to make of

---

[29] F. B. Brown and E. S. Malbon, 'Parabling as a *Via Negativa*: A Critical Review
of the Work of John Dominic Crossan', *JR* 64 (1984), 532.

[30] J. D. Crossan, *Cliffs of Fall: Paradox and Polyvalence in the Parables of Jesus* (New
York: Seabury, 1980), 11.

[31] J. D. Crossan, 'Difference and Divinity', *Semeia*, 23 (1982), 38.

[32] For Ricoeur's critical response to Crossan's attempted appropriation of Derrida
for a negative theology, see 'A Response' (to Crossan's 'Paradox Gives Rise to
Metaphor: Paul Ricoeur's Hermeneutics and the Parables of Jesus', 20-37), *Biblical
Research*, 24-5 (1979-80), 71-6. For a counter-response from Crossan, still maintaining assistance from Derrida for his negative theology, see J. D. Crossan, 'Stages
in Imagination', in E. Winquist (ed.), *The Archaeology of the Imagination*, JAARS 48/2
(Ann Arbor: Edwards, 1981), 49-62.

[33] This process can be traced through the chronological unfolding of the follow-
ing works: *In Parables* (1973); *The Dark Interval: Towards a Theology of Story* (Niles,
Ill.: Argus, 1975); *Raid on the Articulate: Comic Eschatology in Jesus and Borges* (New
York: Harper & Row, 1976); *Finding is the First Act: Trove Folktales and Jesus' Treasure
Parable* (Philadelphia/Missoula Mont.: Fortress/Scholars, 1979); *Cliffs of Fall* (1980);
'Difference and Divinity' (1982). For a more detailed discussion of Crossan's pil-
grimage see G. A. Boyd, *Cynic Sage or Son of God?* (Wheaton, Ill.: BridgePoint, 1995),
ch. 3.

the fact that, analysed as a whole, Crossan's corpus betrays a radical hermeneutical rupture: namely, an earlier, post-modern,
deconstructive 'C-1' layer on the one hand and a later, classical,
historical-critical 'C-2' layer on the other? I will end with simply
posing these questions: but I think that they are questions worthy
of further consideration.

11

Advice for Religious Historians: On the Myth of a Purely Historical Jesus

ALAN G. PADGETT

Once again Western thought has turned to the 'historical Jesus', both in the popular media and in many academic volumes speeding from the presses. A 'Third Quest' for the historical Jesus has begun, and the so-called Jesus Seminar has produced a new version of the Gospels, the 'Scholars Version' of *The Five Gospels*, dedicated to Galileo (among others).[1] Such general interest in historical scholarship provides us with an opportunity to reflect on the legitimacy of this enterprise, and indeed, to reflect on the character of our academic approach to religious studies. In this essay I will pursue two goals at once. First, I wish to debunk a powerful and influential myth, arising from the Enlightenment divorce of religion and science, which assumes that a purely neutral, value-free 'scientific' approach to the historical Jesus is desirable and possible.[2] Second, I hope to provide an alternative, post-modern approach which integrates faith and science, as indeed the real Galileo did.[3]

[1] R. Funk, R. W. Hoover and the Jesus Seminar, *The Five Gospels: The Search for the Authentic Words of Jesus* (New York: Macmillan, 1993). By the 'Jesus Seminar' I will always mean the corporate authors of this book and its introduction. I am not talking about the scholars as individuals, many of whom I know and respect. For a good introduction to the work of the Jesus Seminar and the 'Third Quest' for this historical Jesus, see Marcus Borg, *Jesus in Contemporary Scholarship* (Valley Forge, Pa.: Trinity, 1993).

[2] In this essay I use 'science' in a very broad sense, as it is used in Latin (*scientia*), Greek (*epistēmē*), and German (*Wissenschaft*), to refer to any academic, rigorous enquiry that is based upon evidence, reason, and argument. I do not reduce 'science' to mean the natural sciences, as many Americans do.

[3] Mine is a mild sort of post-modernism. By 'post-modern' I only mean a view that is critical of the Enlightenment. Relativism is not implied in this term as I use it. After completing this essay, I discovered that my basic thesis is advocated by Robert Morgan in his contribution to the G. B. Caird memorial volume, 'The Historical Jesus and the Theology of the New Testament', in L. D. Hurst and N. T. Wright (eds.), *The Glory of Christ in the New Testament* (Oxford: Clarendon, 1987), 187–206. However,

Like earlier theologians reflecting on the problem of faith and history, such as Alan Richardson, Richard R. Niebuhr, and Wolfhart Pannenberg, I have found that reflection upon the early Christian claim that Jesus rose from the dead is a powerful place from which to consider the relationship between faith and historical research.[4] I will propose no new interpretation of the data, but rather reflect on the very practice of historiography in the face of the historical claim that Jesus rose from the dead. I hope to show, furthermore, that reflection on the difference between historical and theological explanation clarifies the sense in which the resurrection is a 'historical' event.

At one time in our Western universities we were certain of how history should proceed, as a rigorous, value-free, scientific discipline. But that era is now over. How shall we now proceed? Does 'anything go' in historical research now that modernity is over? How shall we understand the discipline of religious history in a post-positivist, post-modern situation? For modernity, with its faith in reason and its myth of neutral, scientific scholarship, is well and truly dead. *Requiescat in pace*.

We stand at the end of the twentieth century asking much the same question as religious thinkers at the end of the nineteenth century in Europe: what is the right method by which to approach the history of religion? The answer given in particular by that brilliant German scholar Ernst Troeltsch is this: the proper method for the study of religion is a purely scientific historiography that is value-

---

Morgan's elegant argument pertains only to NT theology. I believe it applies (*mutatis mutandis*) to any historical approach to Jesus from any faith perspective. Morgan in turn points us to Adolf Schlatter, who anticipated many of the points I make here. See Robert Morgan (ed.), *The Nature of New Testament Theology*, SBT, 2nd ser., 25 (London: SCM, 1973), which contains Schlatter's 1909 essay, 'The Theology of the New Testament and Dogmatics'.

[4] I am referring to Alan Richardson, *Christian Apologetics* (London: SCM, 1947); Richard R. Niebuhr, *Resurrection and Historical Reason* (New York: Scribner's, 1957); and W. Pannenberg, 'Redemptive Event and History', first published in German (*KD*, 1959), trans. S. Guthrie, in *Basic Questions in Theology*, i (Philadelphia: Fortress, 1970), 15–80, also partly found in C. Westermann (ed.), *Essays on Old Testament Hermeneutics* (Atlanta: John Knox Press, 1963), 314–35. Each of these works was published independently of the others in the 1940s or 1950s, each in its own way responding to Barth and Bultmann on this topic. See also Pannenberg's later work, *Jesus—God and Man*, trans. L. L. Wilkins and D. A. Priebe (Philadelphia: Westminster, 1968).

free and religiously neutral.[5] I have traced this answer and this method back to its sources in Western intellectual history. This 'purely historical' approach to religion was first applied specifically to Jesus. The argument of scholars like H. S. Reimarus, David Strauss, and William Wrede was that the only proper, scholarly approach to Jesus was a purely historical, purely scientific one that rejected all religious belief as distorting and unscientific.[6] Because the Enlightenment was a Western movement, and because Christianity was the dominant religion of the West, the Enlightenment was forced to answer the question of what a proper, scholarly, 'enlightened' approach to Jesus was. Their answer, which is followed by the Jesus Seminar, I am going to label 'the myth of a purely historical Jesus'.

I am going to use the specific issue of the resurrection of Jesus as a basis for examining the myth of a purely historical approach to religious studies. The resurrection is a fascinating claim made by early Christians, for it is at once both a claim about history and a claim about religious truth. How then shall we academics, we 'scientific' investigators of religion, approach such a claim?

One easy and common answer is quite simple: dismiss the claim at once as impossible, and perhaps begin a historical and sociological investigation of why early Christians would create such a mythological tale. After all, we all know (don't we?) that dead people stay dead, and that resurrections are in fact scientifically impossible. This is the approach of Rudolf Bultmann and his followers, along with the vast majority of academics in religious studies today. This easy and common response to the claim that Jesus actually rose from the dead points to something important: the role

---

[5] See his essay, 'Historiography', in J. Hastings (ed.), *Encyclopedia of Religion and Ethics* (Edinburgh: T. & T. Clark, 1913), vi. 716–23. Troeltsch's philosophy of history is in fact very nuanced. He rejected the certainty of historical judgement, arguing that world-views and historical science are sometimes in tension. Nevertheless, for Troeltsch as I read him, scientific historiography is an absolute value, arising within a particular context, that all academics should adopt *qua* academics. See further his *Religion in History*, trans. J. L. Adams and W. E. Bense (Minneapolis: Fortress, 1991). So even when he is striving 'to recognize an influence of faith on science', Troeltsch cannot help but write, 'the empirical sciences in themselves are wholly independent of faith and follow their own laws' (p. 130).

[6] See H. S. Reimarus, *Fragments* (c.1775), ed. C. H. Talbert (London: SCM, 1971); David F. Strauss, *The Life of Jesus Critically Examined*, trans. George Eliot (1846; London: SCM, 1973). For Wrede, see Morgan, *Nature of New Testament Theology*.

of presuppositions and bias in historiography.[7] This influence of world-views upon academic and scientific investigation has many names, and is widely believed today. Any quest for knowledge, and considerations of argument and evidence, will be biased by the investigator's world-view. For want of a better name, I will call this 'the prejudice of perspective'. Bultmann himself would agree with us, of course. In a famous paper he asked: 'Is Exegesis without Presuppositions Possible?'[8] The right answer, of course, is 'No', and this was indeed Bultmann's answer, much to his credit. My problem with Bultmann is that he imports presuppositions that are antithetical to Christian faith, especially those that lie behind the myth of a purely historical Jesus.[9]

I THE MYTH EXPOSED

Behind the myth is a basic assumption we need to examine: that religious faith corrupts scientific research. This powerful and attractive ideology in Western culture is still responsible for much of the rhetoric in biblical and religious studies about 'scholarly' approaches to our topic. For example, the Jesus Seminar shows its arrogance and prejudice in this false claim: 'The Christ of creed and dogma, who had been firmly in place in the Middle Ages, can no longer command the assent of those who have seen the heavens through Galileo's telescope.'[10] In my analysis of this myth, I have discovered three underlying assumptions:

(1) That religious faith distorts scientific, critical scholarship.
(2) Because this is true, the only proper, academic, scientific methodology in religious studies is one that rejects religious faith itself.

---

[7] Numerous scholars have noticed this before, including Schlatter and Richardson (cited above). More recently, among others, G. N. Stanton, 'Presuppositions in New Testament Criticism', in I. H. Marshall (ed.), *New Testament Interpretation* (Exeter/Grand Rapids, Mich.: Paternoster Press/Eerdmans, 1977), 60–71. See also the next note on Bultmann. On world-views and belief in miracles see R. G. Swinburne, *The Concept of Miracles* (London: Macmillan, 1970), who argues that background beliefs influence our judgements of historical probability.

[8] The English translation of this paper is found in R. Bultmann, *Existence and Faith*, ed. S. Ogden (Cleveland: Meridian Books, 1960), 289–98.

[9] For a careful critique of Bultmann see R. C. Roberts, *Rudolf Bultmann's Theology* (Grand Rapids, Mich.: Eerdmans, 1976).

[10] Funk *et al.* (eds.), *Five Gospels*, 2.

(3) That a purely historical, scientific, faith-free and value-neutral methodology is available to us in what we might broadly call the social-scientific disciplines.

I will argue that each of these ideas is false, and, even more, that this ideology as a whole is deluding and distorts the quest for truth about religion. Finally, the myth of a purely historical and faith-free approach to religion is part of an ideology which is destructive of human flourishing, because it seeks to separate faith and values on the one hand and science and reason on the other.

Troeltsch, Wrede, and their many followers were working against another, earlier approach to religious history, called the dogmatic method or 'apologetics' in the negative sense of these terms. In this method, one assumes the truth of a religion, and then finds this truth in the historical sources (surprise!). This kind of vicious circular reasoning can in fact prove anything to be true. So I completely agree with modernity and its rejection of the earlier, dogmatic approach to religious history. Furthermore, I do believe that we must continue to study religions in an academic, scholarly way that accepts criticism and argument as necessary correctives to our biases and prejudices. I do not want to be heard as suggesting that we throw out rigorous, scientific research. The canons of historical criticism are a lasting contribution to our civilization. My concern is not with our methods, but rather with our attitudes toward them and toward religious faith. I want to examine the myth of a purely historical Jesus, and consider its shortcomings. I will suggest that we must replace this attractive and powerful ideology (the 'myth') with one that is more humble, holistic, and accepting of religious belief.

Such a claim obviously needs substantiation, so we will look at the basic assumptions of the myth. First of all, supposedly, Christian faith distorts the quest for a purely historical Jesus. The Jesus Seminar participants, and many others intend to 'liberate' Jesus research from the 'oppression' of dogmatism. For example, Ed Sanders in his book *Jesus and Judaism* writes that 'I have been engaged for some years in the effort to free history and exegesis from the control of theology' and 'I aim only [!] to be a historian and an exegete'.[11] Both aims are, alas, impossible, for we simply substitute one 'theology' (or 'mythology' as Burton Mack calls it) for another!

---

[11] E. P. Sanders, *Jesus and Judaism* (Philadelphia: Fortress, 1985), 333 f.

The myth of a purely historical Jesus helps the exegete fool herself about this substitution (that is particularly obvious in the work of the Jesus Seminar[12]).

Because of the prejudice of perspective there is no such thing as a purely historical, value-free, neutral scientific approach to the historical Jesus. Indeed, I would argue that there is no purely historical, value-free, neutral scientific approach to any great religious figure or controversial person from the past. The truth of this point is made clear by a controversial (but hardly religious) figure known to all of us: Richard Nixon. If you watch the Oliver Stone film *Nixon* and follow it with a visit to the Nixon Library, you find yourself asking, 'Will the real Richard Nixon please stand up?' And it is very obvious that the political biases of both the Nixon Library and Oliver Stone have influenced their quite distinct interpretations of the real Nixon of history. If the prejudice of perspective is true for our interpretation of Nixon—a very famous leader in our own country and our own time, about whom many, many facts are known—imagine how much more it must influence our treatment of Jesus or, for that matter, Buddha or Confucius.

The myth of a purely historical Jesus, of course, has had tremendous cultural appeal, especially among academics, for some time now. For almost 200 years academics have sought this El Dorado, this powerful but ultimately elusive and deluding mythology, and like De Soto have often lost their way. I am not suggesting that no important advances have been made in the quest for the historical Jesus; they have. Rather, my point is that this mythology of a purely neutral, faith-free approach has deluded scholars concerning the importance, character, and meaning of their results.

I will examine two versions of this myth, and criticize each one. The first version I call 'the neutrality two-step' in which the prejudice of perspective is recognized, but then we try and step around it back into scientific neutrality. For the 'neutrality two-step' version of the myth, the problem of perspective is a problem only for faith— not for the scientific, rational scholar who of course has no faith! A second version of the myth is one I call 'the consensus Jesus', in

---

[12] For a good critique of the work of the Seminar, see Luke T. Johnson, *The Real Jesus* (San Francisco: Harper, 1995). I agree with much of what Johnson has to say, but in the end his own view still divides faith and science. Our spiritual knowledge of the real, risen Jesus must be subject to critical, scientific reflection and historical examination (I do not say historical 'verification'—I agree with Johnson that such verification is impossible for historical science).

which a consensus theory of truth is supposed to lead us to the real Jesus of history.

I will start with the most important version of the myth, the neutrality two-step. Many scholars today are sophisticated enough to realize that hermeneutic theory, epistemology, and the philosophy of science all converge at one point: namely, what I have called the prejudice of perspective. A purely neutral science is both undesirable and not possible in the first place.[13] Having recognized the prejudice of perspective, however, scholars still seem to hope that our biases and prejudices can be overcome through careful religious neutrality and scientific method. Let us pay attention to the facts and hope that all this interpretation stuff goes away, they seem to be saying. As long as we focus on the right methodology, are rigorously sceptical of the sources, and are as neutral and scientific as possible, excluding religious presuppositions, then the prejudice of perspective will not affect our results. This, of course, is simply self-delusion of the part of scholars.

An example of the neutrality two-step would be the work of either Ed Sanders or Burton Mack.[14] For both men, 'theology' is a bad word, and theological commitments tend to distort and warp neutral, scientific research. That their own world-views distort and warp their own work is, of course, equally obvious, at least to us. For all of us approach our work with some sort of faith stance. Mack and Sanders have their own agendas, which distort their interpretations of Jesus, as does the Jesus Seminar.

Another example of the neutrality two-step would be Gary Habermas, a conservative apologist. He writes: 'The best approach to take towards history is one of caution, as we should try and recognize this subjective bias and then make the proper allowance

---

[13] The separation of faith from science is the major problem I have with Peter Carnley's otherwise excellent book *The Structure of Resurrection Belief* (Oxford: Oxford University Press, 1987). Carnley wants to add to pure scientific facts about Jesus a mythopoetic appropriation of the Spirit of Christ by faith (see pp. 352–8). The fusion of faith and science I have in mind presumes Christian faith *in the midst of* careful scientific work.

[14] Sanders, *Jesus and Judaism*; Burton Mack, *A Myth of Innocence: Mark and Christian Origins* (Philadelphia: Fortress, 1988), and *idem*, *The Lost Gospel: The Book of Q and Christian Origins* (San Francisco: HarperSan Francisco, 1993). For Mack it is not so much theology as 'mythology' that is the problem (these words denote, for him, pretty much the same thing). A balanced reply to Mack is found in Pheme Perkins, 'Jesus before Christianity: Cynic or Sage?', *Christian Century*, 110 (28 July–4 Aug. 1993), 749–51; and Paul Eddy, 'Jesus as Diogenes', *JBL* 115 (1996), 449–69.

for it.'[15] This sentence is an almost perfect example of what I mean by the neutrality two-step, in fact. Of course, Habermas and other apologists have their agenda, too, and want history to be neutral so that they can use it to prove that Christianity is true. Allow me one final example: Willi Marxsen, a follower of Bultmann and a well-known New Testament scholar, defines 'the historical Jesus' as 'Jesus before anyone has ventured an interpretation of him'.[16] This might be the true Jesus, but it is hardly the historical Jesus. Of course no such Jesus can be known, for the knowing process is itself an interpretation.

The neutrality two-step is close to being right. I agree that religious and historical claims must be subject to critical, scientific examination. The fundamental flaw in the neutrality two-step is this: all data is already infected by theory. World-views don't just give us the questions we ask; they also affect our understanding of the evidence and our historical judgement. There just is no such thing as data apart from some interpretation. The question of what counts as 'evidence' or 'data' is already biased by our prior interests, theories, and world-views. So the neutrality two-step just trips us up as we reflect upon the relationship between faith and science.

The neutrality two-step is also self-deluding. It leads to a bias against theological commitments in historical science, without recognizing the distorting elements in the researcher's own world-view. The rhetoric of the Jesus Seminar is a good example of what I mean by the self-deluding character of myth.

The best-known and most sophisticated version of the neutrality two-step is found in a book dedicated to Professor Bultmann, Van Harvey's *The Historian and the Believer*.[17] Harvey develops a 'morality of knowledge' in which the religious faith of the believing historian so distorts and warps her judgement that the validity of her reasoning process is called into question. Harvey's book downplays two important factors: first, the secular unbeliever is just as distorted and warped by his prejudice and world-view as the believer is; second, who is to say that Christian faith does not give us better

---

[15] Gary Habermas, *Ancient Evidence for the Life of Jesus* (Nashville: Nelson, 1984), 18.

[16] W. Marxsen, *Jesus and Easter*, trans. V. P. Furnish (Nashville: Abingdon, 1990), 16. Of course Marxsen is not a slavish follower of Bultmann, and disagrees with him on several points (these are helpfully outlined in G. O'Collins, *Jesus Risen* (Mahwah, NJ: Paulist, 1987), 65 f.).

[17] Van A. Harvey, *The Historian and the Believer* (New York: Macmillan, 1966).

insight into the data than unbelief does? Why should unbelief, rather than faith, lead to the best explanation of the evidence? Would it be so strange if the followers of Jesus have an inside track in the understanding of Jesus? Why is faith so damaging to reason, anyway?

Granted that faith is a kind of prejudice, perhaps it is a helpful prejudice. Helpful prejudices can give us insight into data, and clear the way for understanding. For example, the planet Neptune was discovered because of prejudice on the part of astronomers in favour of classical mechanics. And the Marxist prejudice of liberation theologians has helped us to see what the Bible really does say about poverty and liberation. As Gadamer has argued, we all stand in some tradition, and have some prejudice, when we approach the task of interpretation.[18] Not all tradition and prejudice is bad: some can be helpful. All reasoning is based upon some prejudice; all insight and research takes place from a particular position, and in the light of a particular world-view and tradition of enquiry. There is 'no view from nowhere' to borrow a phrase from Thomas Nagel.[19]

The question of whether a certain prejudice is helpful or harmful in the evaluation of evidence cannot be decided a priori as Harvey wants it to be.[20] It is only in the give and take of dialogue and in the evaluation of reasons, arguments, and evidence that our pre-understanding will be found to be helpful or harmful. I am not suggesting that we abandon rational enquiry or scientific historiography. Nor do I suggest that biblical scholarship return to the Christian dogmatism of a previous age. Rather, I suggest that the myth of a neutral, scientific history, which Harvey assumes throughout his book, distorts the relationship between faith (or lack of it!) and historical research. The casual dismissal of the claim that Jesus may indeed have risen from the dead is not a helpful prejudice, for it is founded upon a fallacious conception of natural

[18] Hans-Georg Gadamer, *Truth and Method*, 2nd English edn. (New York: Continuum, 1991; original German edn. 1960).

[19] Thomas Nagel, *The View from Nowhere* (Oxford: Oxford University Press, 1985).

[20] See e.g. Harvey, *The Historian and the Believer*, 213. All of Harvey's discussion of 'hard and soft perspectivism' is interesting just because he misunderstands the point being made that there are no objective standards of historical reasoning. Note his prejudice in favour of 'what any historian would accept as a legitimate claim' (p. 218), or again, 'events that are otherwise known in the way any event can be known' (p. 242).

science and the 'laws' of nature (which are purely descriptive, not
prescriptive). It is no accident that Van Harvey's book is dedicated
to Professor Bultmann, and perpetuates the misunderstanding of
faith and science one finds in Bultmann and his school.

The implications of the myth of a purely historical Jesus are in
fact a road-block to historical knowledge of the real Jesus. For it is
part of the myth that religious faith distorts our knowledge of reality. Since the New Testament is written, in part, from a faith perspective, it must be questioned at every turn. For example, in his
book *A Future for the Historical Jesus*, Leander Keck writes (correctly
in my view) that 'every believer and every theologian has central
things at stake in the historical study of Jesus'.[21] I applaud Keck's
rejection of the attempt to divorce faith and science, characteristic
of the Bullmann school. But when Keck insists that 'a skeptical attitude toward the sources' is necessary, he has obviously bought into
the myth of a purely historical Jesus.[22] Why is a sceptical attitude
necessary? Only because, as a hidden premiss, we must doubt any
historical claim that could come from a faith perspective. But all historical writing comes from a faith perspective. We must, indeed,
accept a critical attitude toward all historical sources and artefacts.
But a critical attitude which looks for reasons and evidence is not
the same thing as a *sceptical* attitude, based upon a prejudice against
religious faith in the sources. Such a scepticism, the 'guilty until
proved innocent' modern attitude toward the New Testament, actually blocks good historical research. Once again we can cite the
Jesus Seminar:[23] 'methodological skepticism' was a working principle of the Seminar; 'when in sufficient doubt, leave it out'. In fact
the Seminar seems to work on the principle, 'when there is any
doubt, leave it out'. There is much we can learn historically from
the New Testament, but not if we insist on doubting every line of it
until we can prove it to be true. In logic, we would call this the fal-
lacy of 'poisoning the well'. In the history of philosophy, it represents Descartes' approach to epistemology, and that is a blind alley.
So, ironically, the myth of a purely historical Jesus ends up distorting what the very quest for the true Jesus was created to assist.
Such is the human condition!

Another version of the myth of a purely historical Jesus is
the 'consensus Jesus'. Once again, some scholars recognize the

[21] L. Keck, *A Future for the Historical Jesus* (Nashville: Abingdon, 1971), 38.
[22] Ibid. 21.   [23] Funk *et al.* (eds.), *Five Gospels*, 37.

prejudice of perspective, but then try to dance around it. In this version, they hope that a consensus of New Testament scholars will provide us with the 'true' Jesus of history. A brilliant example of this method, which I admire very much, is *A Marginal Jew*, by John Meier.[24] While Meier's historical judgement is excellent, and his scholarship and knowledge are profound, his presentation of method is quite flawed. To see why this is so, let us first make some distinctions in our terminology. By 'the true Jesus', 'the real Jesus', or 'the Jesus of history' I will mean Jesus of Nazareth as he really was in the past. However, by 'the historical Jesus' I will follow common usage and understand these terms to designate Jesus as we can know him through historical research. Finally, by 'consensus Jesus' I will understand the Jesus who is known to us through a consensus of current New Testament scholarship.

There is very little hope that the consensus Jesus will yield to us the real Jesus. This is so for both theoretical and practical reasons. As any first-year philosophy student knows, the consensus theory of truth is bogus. Just because a group of humans think something is true does not make it true. At the practical end, we always have to ask the critical or Marxist question: who defines the consensus? The so-called consensus of the Jesus Seminar is obviously based upon personalities and a priori ideology, as anyone who is aware of the history and personalities behind the group knows. Or again, in his very interesting book *The Quest for a Post-Historical Jesus*, William Hamilton tells us that there is a consensus among current scholars that no historical knowledge of the real Jesus is possible.[25] As a factual statement about the academy of biblical scholarship, this 'consensus' is obviously false. I am afraid that the consensus Jesus will yield us nothing, and cannot lead to any sound, scientific results about history, or indeed about any scientific topic.

Now consensus is important, of course, in many areas of life. We are wise to rely upon a consensus of experts, when there is such, for topics in which we are not well versed ourselves. But in our own areas of expertise, scientific investigators must ignore the 'consensus' in favour of the evidence and arguments themselves. At best, a consensus might provide a beginning for our own careful examination of the issues. Unlike the Jesus Seminar, which is 'pop'

[24] John P. Meier, *A Marginal Jew* (2 vols.; Garden City, NY: Doubleday, 1991-4).
[25] W. Hamilton, *A Quest for the Post-Historical Jesus* (London/New York: SCM/Continuum, 1994), 19.

scholarship, Meier is better than the methodology he espouses. Like so many other scholars, he is aware of the prejudice of perspective, but does not realize the implications of this prejudice for his own work. He writes, 'we abstract from Christian faith because we are involved in the hypothetical reconstruction of a past figure *by purely scientific means*'.[26] In another place he indicates that, 'to be sure, *A Marginal Jew* works with presuppositions, but they are the general presuppositions of historiography'.[27]

The point that must be made against the 'consensus Jesus' version of the myth of a purely historical Jesus is that our presuppositions are pluralistic, and that they inevitably influence our gathering of the data, our grasp of what counts as 'evidence', and our interpretation of that evidence. None of the natural or historical sciences has as criteria or indices of truth a consensus among investigators, and for very good reasons. We may try to be as reasonable and rational as possible, but we cannot escape from our own prejudices. And since our perspectives are so pluralistic, the consensus Jesus becomes a minimalist Jesus. If we were really to base a book on Jesus just upon what all, or 90 per cent, of 75 per cent (how shall we define 'consensus'?) of what all New Testament scholars agree upon, the resulting book would be a lot shorter than *A Marginal Jew*! And honestly, of what scientific value would such a purely sociological study be? At best it might give us a starting-point for our own investigations, based upon our own faith and our own methods, but we would still have to reinvestigate each point for ourselves. And this consensus Jesus would be a jaundiced, emaciated Jesus, for there are so few facts we can all agree on. The consensus Jesus is not even the historical Jesus, much less the real Jesus of history.

I hope I have said enough to indicate that the myth of the purely historical Jesus is a false ideology imposed upon religious studies by the Enlightenment. It is self-deluding, and it also distorts the attempt to come to know the real Jesus. The myth 'poisons the well' with respect to the only significant sources we have to study the historical Jesus. Now it is certainly true that a dogmatic method, which presumes the results of critical enquiry before the give and take of evidence, argument, and reasoning takes place, is destructive of true critical scholarship. But religious faith does not have to lead to

[26] Meier, *Marginal Jew*, i. 30 f.; my italics.   [27] Ibid. ii.

dogmatism of this kind, and it often does not. I have met many dogmatic atheists, who arrogantly assume that scientific materialism is the only rational world-view, and that Christian theology is just another kind of ancient myth. Belief that all truth is God's truth, that God is the maker of heaven, earth, and my neighbour, can and does lead to open enquiry, toleration, understanding, and careful scholarship. Adolf Schlatter would be a good example of this in New Testament studies. Moreover, have we forgotten that the founders of natural science were men of faith? For Copernicus, Kepler, Galileo, and Newton belief in a rational Creator was a fundamental assumption for the scientific quest. So the first assumption of the myth, that religious faith corrupts scientific research, is both false as an idea, and self-deluding as an ideology. It allows researchers to believe about themselves—falsely, of course—that their own faith stance and their own world-view do not corrupt their research.

The assumption, left over from Enlightenment prejudice, that religious faith corrupts science is self-deluding, and it distorts the quest for religious truth; but finally, it is part of the divorce between science and faith. The idea that the only proper approach to religion is one that ignores or brackets religious faith is part of an overall attempt to 'free' science from the 'biases' of religion and morality, an idea we can trace to the French encyclopedists. And this divorce has been destructive in our own century, to our own people. It leads to bad religion, and to bad science and technology. Who wants a religion divorced from reason, or scientific experiments and application that ignore moral truth? We know now that science and technology are not autonomous realms, free from such biases as respect for life and love for people of other cultures and classes. I would like to point out that the myth of a purely historical Jesus is part of the overall attempt to separate faith and moral values from science. This attempt has been destructive to the human race, to religious faith, to good scientific methods, and to the environment. Science and technology, divorced from religious wisdom and moral values, constitute not only a myth, but the nightmare of the twentieth century.

II TOWARD A DIALOGUE BETWEEN FAITH AND SCIENCE

I have indicated several reasons for dropping the self-deluding myth of a purely historical approach to religious studies. But if we drop this ideology, what shall replace it? This, I think, is the major reason why so many scholars continue to have faith in the myth. They feel that if they drop the idea of a purely neutral, value-free approach, then history will be left in a quagmire of subjectivity. To quote from Meier again, 'Whether we call it a bias, a *Tendenz*, a worldview, or a faith stance, everyone who writes on the historical Jesus writes from some ideological vantage point; no critic is exempt. The solution to this dilemma is neither to pretend to an absolute objectivity that is not to be had nor to wallow in total relativism.'[28] Notice two things in this quotation: first, that a faith stance creates a dilemma for the historian, and second, the fear of relativism if we drop the myth of a purely historical Jesus. In fact, Meier accepts here some version of the neutrality two-step: let us admit our bias, follow a rigorous methodology, and try to be as objective and religion-neutral as possible. But this assumes, all along, that faith is a problem for scientific objectivity. There is, as Ben Meyer puts it, a fear of subjectivity here. We are afraid as scholars that a post-modern perspective will lead to 'anything goes'. Any view of Jesus will be just as good as any other. We will, in fact, be out of a job, no longer needed to guide young minds into the truth about religious history. Ben Meyer points us to the proper way out of this fear in his review of criteria or indices of authenticity: not to shun subjectivity, but to embrace it as a moment on the way toward objectivity.[29]

I have myself been involved in the study of the philosophy of science, so please forgive me if I put this whole issue in terms of the relationship between faith and science. In this brief essay I can, of course, only suggest a way forward. First of all, let us recognize the prejudice of perspective. This means that I, as a scientist (social or natural), recognize that my world-view is bound to influence what I call data, and how I weigh the evidence in reaching toward the

---

[28] Meier, *Marginal Jew*, i. 5 f.
[29] Ben Meyer, 'Objectivity and Subjectivity in Historical Criticism of the Gospels', in D. L. Dungan (ed.), *The Interrelations of the Gospels*, BETL 95 (Macon, Ga./Leuven: Mercer University Press/Leuven University Press, 1990).

best explanation. Second, we recognize pluralism in world-views. There are many different ways of understanding reality. Pluralism and the prejudice of perspective should lead us to humility, but not to despair or to relativism. Cognitive relativism does not follow from plurality or from the prejudice of perspective.[30] There is a real world out there to know, and a real past, too. We do know things about reality, after all. It does, however, lead to humility. Our results are not certain. They are not purely neutral. They may be 'scientific', but that does not grant them certainty as Troeltsch himself knew.

Let us embrace our faith, and recognize it for what it is. And of course, by 'faith' I do not mean only religious faith, but would include all world-views, such as Marxism or scientific materialism. They, too, operate on faith or trust. We accept that faith may distort our judgement, but at the same time, it may give us deeper understanding. There just is no way to tell, except in the give and take of pluralistic and public dialogue, whether our faith is distorting or helpful to understanding the object of study. So, in the end, we subject our conclusions to public scrutiny and careful scientific examination, then revise them in the light of what we learn in that process.

So I am not abandoning the quest for truth and reality. Relativism is just as destructive of true historical and scientific research as the myth of a purely historical Jesus. I affirm objective truth; it is the claim to objective knowledge I object to. Nor am I suggesting a return to the old dogmatic method of presuming the truth of our faith and refusing to change in the light of evidence. But let us face the facts. The evidence about Jesus is slight, and capable of many equally reasonable interpretations. The social sciences do not have the same objective status as the natural sciences, for they cannot do experiments (except in a few cases) to test which theory or interpretation is true. Measurements and mathematical theories are few and far between in history. So the social sciences draw more fully on subjective judgement. But this does not mean that they are unscientific. And in the case of Jesus, the evidence is so slight and so capable of many interpretations that our faith

---

[30] This is argued well by Gadamer in hermeneutics (*Truth and Method*), by Alasdair MacIntyre (*First Principles, Final Ends and Contemporary Philosophical Issues* (Milwaukee: Marquette University Press, 1990)) for ethical principles, and by Larry Laudan for the philosophy of science (*Science and Relativism* (Chicago: University of Chicago Press, 1990)).

stance is bound to have a tremendous influence on our reconstruction of the historical Jesus. But this does not mean that the quest is in vain, or that faith is not at risk. It is. For Christianity has made certain historical claims, and must demonstrate to a public, pluralistic audience that it has reasons, arguments, and evidence for them. We can prove that Christianity is reasonable, even if we cannot prove it is true in the open market-place of ideas.[31]

I am arguing, then, that we must integrate faith and science, reason and religion, in an overall coherent and rational world-view. Each aspect of our world-view, both faith and science, has its place. Each is open to modification in the light of the other. Faith and science must be in dialogue and mutual modification, as we seek an overall world-view that is rationally satisfactory and existentially meaningful.

There is one point at which the old myth of a purely historical Jesus was correct. This has to do with the distinction between history and the other sciences. While history does investigate the past, its explanations are created in terms of psycho-social understanding. History is limited to the human, to human events and artefacts, and to explanations in terms of psycho-social forces and institutions. There is, in fact, a precise parallel here with natural science. Take as an example the initial expansion of the universe at the Big Bang. This is clearly a past event, but it is not a historical event (in the sense of history as an academic discipline). Indeed, I think the term 'historical event' is a misleading one, since it can mean either a past event or an event subject to historical explanation. More precision can be had if we stick to natural-scientific explanations versus historical explanations. The Big Bang is subject to natural-scientific explanations, but not to historical explanations. The American Revolution, on the other hand, is an event that cannot be adequately explained by natural science. We need historical explanations, based on psycho-social causal factors, to understand it fully.

---

[31] This position represents what Stephen T. Davis calls 'soft apologetics'. See his debate on the resurrection with Gary Habermas and James Keller, in the pages of *Faith and Philosophy*: Davis, 'Is it Possible to Know that Jesus was Raised from the Dead?', 1 (1984), 147–59; Habermas, 'Knowing that Jesus' Resurrection Occurred: A Response to Davis', 2 (1985), 295–302; Davis, 'Naturalism and Resurrection: A Reply to Habermas', 2 (1985), 303–8; Keller, 'Contemporary Christian Doubts about the Resurrection', 5 (1988), 40–60; Davis, 'Doubting the Resurrection: A Reply to James A. Keller', 7 (1990), 99–111. See also Davis, *Risen Indeed* (Grand Rapids, Mich.: Eerdmans, 1993).

Now the myth of a purely historical Jesus insisted on a distinction between theology and history. And this distinction is a valid one. But it is best understood on the model of levels of explanation in the sciences.[32] When teaching about Jesus in an academic and pluralistic context, therefore, we should say this: our class is limited to events in the life of Jesus that are subject to historical explanation or verification. We focus on normal historical explanations for the life of Jesus, and exclude from consideration any theological explanations. In fact, this is what we do in any case, but let us be open and up front about it. It is important to distinguish history from theology, in terms of the goals and methods of each discipline. But we can separate history and theology without the arrogance of the myth of a purely historical Jesus. In terms of scholarly publications, on the other hand, let us return to John Meier. His conclusions are better than the methodology he espouses. His results are not based upon a mythological consensus among scholars. What he should say about his methodology is this: it is limited to events in the life of Jesus that are subject to historical explanation, focuses on normal historical explanations for the life of Jesus, and excludes from consideration any theological explanations. In fact, this is what he does in any case.

With this difference between history and theology in mind, let us take the resurrection of Jesus as an example. If this event happened at all, it is a past event. Some have suggested that it did not take place in space and time; yet, if it took place at all, it surely did so in space and time. If Jesus rose from the dead, this event has a date, and it took place at a certain location in space, just outside Jerusalem. However, if it did happen, it is not subject to natural-scientific explanation. Likewise, it is not subject to historical explanation. Historical science is incapable of making a theological judgement about whether or not God could or did raise Jesus (at the same time, historical scientific judgement is important to the theological issue, of course). Rather, if the resurrection did take place, only a theological explanation, based upon the causal powers of God, will be fully

---

[32] For more on levels of explanation in the sciences, see D. M. McKay, ' "Complementarity" in Scientific and Theological Thinking', *Zygon*, 9 (1974), 225–74; J. Polkinghorne, *One World* (London: SPCK, 1987); Ian Barbour, *Religion in an Age of Science* (San Francisco: Harper, 1990); A. G. Padgett, 'Levels of Explanation in Theology and Science', *Glaube und Denken: Jahrbuch der Karl-Heim-Gesellschaft*, 7 (1994), 184–201, and idem, 'The Mutuality of Theology and Science', *Christian Scholars' Review* (forthcoming).

satisfactory to human reason. Social science cannot explain how someone rose from the dead. So we can and should accept the difference between natural-scientific, social-scientific (including historical), and theological explanations. When John Meier writes about the resurrection, he will no doubt limit himself to natural and historical explanations of the event. And that is very helpful and important. But we can separate history and theology without the myth of a purely historical Jesus and all its arrogant and self-deluding properties. Rather, we must insist that faith and science respect and learn from each other, while recognizing that they are not the same thing (you can learn exactly this same lesson by reflecting critically upon the debate between evolution and 'creation science').

A good example of how the myth of a purely historical Jesus can delude and confuse biblical scholars is the recent book on the resurrection by Gerd Luedemann. There are a host of problems with this book, but one of them is surely that Luedemann insists, against both reason and faith, that historical explanation is the only legitimate kind of explanation for past events. He rejects any idea that God might actually do anything in history that could be known by people. Buying into the prejudice of modernity, he labels any attempt to discuss theological explanation as 'apologetic manoeuvres to evade history. Here the historical question is demoted to a question which is marginal compared with theology.'[33] In fact, Luedemann's methodology reduces theology to mere social-scientific explanation. Reasons for past events based on the action of God (what I am calling 'theological explanation') are ruled out a priori. And that is just a piece of Enlightenment bias. The basic problem here is a positivist or empiricist notion of what counts as 'scientific explanation' (social or natural). Does this positivist bias lead, in his book, to a better understanding of the early Church's Easter faith? Hardly. Because he refuses to allow the resurrection to (possibly) be beyond historical explanation, he generates a so-called historical explanation that is patently absurd, based upon pseudo-historical 'depth psychology' as a source for understanding the myth of the resurrection, which Peter (in his grief) imagined to himself. Luedemann's treatment of New Treatment texts is a hatchet job, based on a sceptical (rather than critical) approach to the texts. He always finds some way to fit the texts to his anti-supernatural bias

---

[33] G. Luedemann, *The Resurrection of Jesus*, trans. J. Bowden (Minneapolis/London: Fortress/SCM, 1994), 180.

and psycho-historical prejudices. His so-called explanation is in fact far less likely than any miracle! Here we find yet another book shipwrecked on the shoals of the myth of a purely historical Jesus. Just to take one example, in discussing Paul's first encounter with the Risen One, Luedemann writes: 'the conversion of Paul *must* [his emphasis!] in principle be accessible to historical criticism, even if at present not all the details are yet known. Only through the mediation of an understandable [i.e. purely historical!] approach to the event of Paul's conversion is it possible to discuss its meaning and its significance.'[34] In his polemic against Martin Hengel (who correctly insists, as a Christian scholar, that the resurrection is not reducible without remainder to historical explanations) Luedemann demands that we attempt psycho-historical readings of the apostle. 'A really historical work cannot rest content', he insists, with a past event which cannot be fully explained by social science.[35] But why not? Is social science, rather than God, now omniscient? With prejudices and confusions like these, Luedemann's book provides an excellent example of the way the myth of a purely historical Jesus leads to both bad history and bad theology.

This leads me to one last issue, which again can only be touched upon briefly. I have been arguing that we should recognize and publicly admit our trust or faith during scientific investigations. Christian historians, then, should openly acknowledge their belief in the resurrection even while seeking careful historical and public evidence for this claim. But this avoids 'dogmatic' circular reasoning only if our faith is open to revision in the light of evidence. One objection to the view I am arguing for might come from a misunderstanding of 'faith'.

A major error in Western thought has been committed in the analysis of 'faith'. Because of the deep effect that faith has upon life, some thinkers such as Søren Kierkegaard have insisted that faith must have existential certainty.[36] Therefore, faith cannot be based upon the probability arguments of history, philosophy, and science. This error in analysis is at the root of the division between faith and science.

We must not separate faith and science again in our culture, for

---

[34] Ibid. 59. He refers here to 'Holsten's starting point' and clearly adopts it himself.

[35] Ibid. 80.

[36] e.g. S. Kierkegaard, *Concluding Unscientific Postscript*, trans. D. F. Swenson and W. Lowrie (Princeton: Princeton University Press, 1941), 28–33.

this leads to terrible destruction. But what, then, is the right understanding of the relationship between faith and reason? As a Christian I have faith in Christ, a faith which I would, under God's care, be willing to die for. Hopefully I will not be put to the test! But this strong existential certainty does not translate into epistemic certainty. That is the category mistake that Kierkegaard, Bultmann, Willi Marxsen, and so many others have made. Rather, my interpretation of the meaning of my faith in God must be open to rational reflection and revision in the light of reason, evidence, and argument. Of course, this rational reflection does not happen at the same moment, or in the same mood, as the experience of faith itself. My rational reflection and interpretation of faith constitute a different, critical moment, quite distinct from the personal and existential moment of faith. Few people hold their deepest faith because of arguments. And religious faith is certainly quite different in its logic and 'grammar' from a scientific hypothesis. Nevertheless, our faith itself, and especially our interpretation of the meaning of that faith, is open to revision in more critical and reflective moments. In the face of objections to faith, or in the face of terrible experiences of suffering or oppression, I may come to doubt. At that point my continued faith may well depend upon arguments, reasons, and evidence, as well as the private and personal grounds on which faith originally rose and continues to well up in my soul. I may also encounter difficult questions, or rational problems, with the implications of my faith. In such instances, I have a duty to myself and the truth to investigate the reasonableness of my beliefs. Fideism is in the long run unsatisfactory.

Let us take up the example of the resurrection of Jesus. Imagine that after careful historical research I concluded not only that there is limited evidence for a resurrection of a publicly available sort (which is compatible with belief in the resurrection), but that all the best evidence was against the resurrection. What then? Would that change my faith? It would certainly change my interpretation of Christianity. Gone would be any hope of my own real resurrection after death, for example. My understanding of biblical authority would no doubt weaken, if this central historical claim turned out to be false. But I would hope that my faith in God, and in Jesus, would still remain. I might become a liberal United Methodist theologian, but I would not cease to be a Christian.

Our interpretation of both faith and science must be open to revision in the light of reason, evidence, and argument. Of course, there is no one right understanding of reasoning or logic, or of what counts as evidence and a good argument. Here we have to do the best we can, with the tools and methods that are most appropriate to our quest for truth. But there can be no guarantees to truth, not in the area of faith and not in the area of science.

Let us therefore embrace our faith, and recognize it for what it is, but be willing to admit that others' faiths have insight we need. Let us use our best methodologies and scientific, critical thinking; but this does not mean that we have to be sceptical of the religion we are studying, or of its texts and sources. Let us, instead, seek to understand, sympathize with, and appreciate the religious faiths we study. In terms of education, this means that the job of religion and Bible teachers is not to destroy the faiths of our students. We have a moral duty not to use our position as teachers to undermine and shock the religious faiths of our students, however naïve or closed-minded they may be. Instead, let us help each student to integrate their own faith (not ours, theirs) with the methods, scholarship, and results with which vigorous academic training have provided us. I suggest that it is bad pedagogy to seek to 'blow away the funda-mentalists', however tempting it may be! Rather, college and uni-versity students need help in the integration of faith and science, whatever faith they may have.

The myth of a purely historical Jesus has distorted scholarship long enough. It has served as a mask to shield us from criticism, to delude ourselves and others, to confuse us as to the character of the historical method and the certainty of our historical results. In our post-modern situation, progress will be made only when we each embrace and understand our own faith stance, stake our claim in the public and pluralistic market-place of ideas, and give what reasons, evidence, and arguments we can for our conclusions. My plea, then, is this: let us take off the mask of pure objectivity, and speak to each other face to face.[37]

[37] The author is grateful for his kind reception by the American Academy of Religion, Western Region, and the Society of Biblical Literature, Pacific Coast Region, where he read an earlier version of this chapter as a Presidential Address for 1996. Equally kind was my reception at the Department of Theology in Durham, England, which heard another version of the chapter, a most happy occasion for me and my wife. A very early version of this essay was also read to the Joseph Butler Society at Oxford, in 1987. Finally, my thanks to the following colleagues for helpful criticism: Steve Davis, Gerry O'Collins, Sharon Pearson, Sarah Coakley, and Ralph Martin. I am grateful to Davis and O'Collins, in particular, for the invitation to the Resurrection Summit.

12

The Preaching of the Resurrection of Christ in Augustine, Luther, Barth, and Thielicke

MARGUERITE SHUSTER

INTRODUCTION

It can scarcely be doubted that proclamation of the resurrection of Jesus Christ was central to the earliest preaching of the Christian community, as indicated by the remembered sermons of Peter and Paul (Acts 2: 29–36; 3: 12–26; 5: 29–32; 10: 34–43; 13: 16–41; 17: 18, 22–31) and by Paul's unequivocal remark that if Christ be not raised, preaching and faith are in vain and Christians (who would then believe a delusion) are of all people most to be pitied (1 Cor. 15: 12–19). Nor can it be doubted that the idea of a resurrection was very nearly as implausible to people of the first century as it is to those of the twentieth, whether among followers of Jesus (for example, Thomas, John 20: 24–9) or among pagans (e.g. the Athenians, Acts 17: 32): they knew as well as we do that human life reliably, inevitably, and irrevocably ends in death. Thus, Christian preachers have always faced the problem that what is most existentially critical to their message is least credible to their hearers. Their best and potentially most life-changing news is their least believable news. Those who are thoughtful about the structure of Christian belief as a whole and about how to communicate essentials to others have always had, one way or another, to deal with this problem. The purpose of this chapter, then, is to examine how a sampling of significant theologians of the Church who also preached regularly handled the resurrection of Jesus.[1]

---

[1] This chapter is based upon the following primary sources, which represent an extensive though not completely exhaustive exploration of the materials available in English: Augustine—*The Works of St. Augustine: Sermons*, ed. J. E. Rotelle, OSA, trans. E. Hill, OP (10 vols.; Brooklyn, NY: New City Press, 1990–5); *Augustine of Hippo: Selected Writings*, trans. M. T. Clark, *Classics of Western Spirituality* (Mahwah,

NJ: Paulist, 1984); *Homilies on the Gospel of John, Homilies on the First Epistle of John, Soliloquies*, ed. P. Schaff, NPNF, 1 ser., vii (1888; repr. Peabody, Mass.: Hendrickson, 1994); *Expositions of the Book of Psalms*, ed. A. C. Coxe, NPNF, 1 ser., viii (1888; repr. Peabody, Mass.: Hendrickson, 1994); Martin Luther—*Sermons of Martin Luther*, 8 vols.; ed. J. N. Lenker, trans. J. N. Lenker *et al.* (8 vols.; 1905; Grand Rapids, Mich.: Baker, 1989); *Sermons on the Gospel of St. John, Chapters 1–4*, ed. Jaroslav Pelikan, trans. M. H. Bertram, in *Luther's Works*, xxii (St Louis: Concordia, 1957); *Sermons on the Gospel of St. John, Chapters 6–8*, ed. Jaroslav Pelikan, trans. M. H. Bertram, in *Luther's Works*, xxii (St Louis: Concordia, 1957); *Sermons on the Gospel of St. John, Chapters 14–16*, ed. Jaroslav Pelikan, trans. M. H. Bertram, in *Luther's Works*, xxiv (St Louis: Concordia, 1961); *The Catholic Epistles*, ed. Jaroslav Pelikan, trans. M. H. Bertram and W. A. Hansen, in *Luther's Works*, xxx (St Louis: Concordia, 1967); *Sermons I*, ed. and trans. J. W. Doberstein, in *Luther's Works*, li (Philadelphia: Muhlenberg Press, 1957); *Sermons II*, ed. Hans J. Hillerbrand, in *Luther's Works*, lii (Philadelphia: Fortress, 1974); Karl Barth—Karl Barth and Eduard Thurneysen, *Come Holy Spirit*, trans. G. W. Richards, E. G. Homrighausen, and K. J. Ernst (New York: Round Table, 1934); Karl Barth and Eduard Thurneysen, *God's Search for Man*, trans. G. W. Richards, E. G. Homrighausen, K. J. Ernst (Edinburgh: T. & T. Clark, 1935); K. Barth, *Deliverance to the Captives*, trans. Marguerite Wieser (London: SCM, 1961); *idem*, *The Word of God and the Word of Man*, trans. D. Horton (Gloucester, Mass.: Peter Smith, 1978); Helmut Thielicke—*Christ and the Meaning of Life: A Book of Sermons and Meditations*, ed. and trans. J. W. Doberstein (New York: Harper & Row, 1962); *Faith: The Great Adventure*, trans. D. L. Scheidt (Philadelphia: Fortress, 1985); *How Modern Should Theology Be?*, trans. H. G. Anderson (Philadelphia: Fortress, 1969); *How the World Began*, trans. J. W. Doberstein (Philadelphia: Fortress, 1961); *How To Believe Again*, trans. H. G. Anderson (Philadelphia: Fortress, 1972); *I Believe: The Christian's Creed*, trans. J. W. Doberstein and H. G. Anderson (Philadelphia: Fortress, 1968); *Life Can Begin Again*, trans. J. W. Doberstein (Philadelphia: Fortress, 1963); *Our Heavenly Father*, trans. J. W. Doberstein (New York: Harper & Bros., 1960); *The Silence of God*, trans. G. W. Bromiley (Grand Rapids, Mich.: Eerdmans, 1962); *The Waiting Father*, trans. J. W. Doberstein (New York: Harper & Row, 1959). The sources represent predominantly sermons that were actually preached, but also some material that probably was not delivered orally, despite its generally sermonic tone (e.g. part of Augustine's *Homilies on the Gospel of John*) and/or material that, while delivered orally to church people, was not in sermon form (e.g. the addresses in Barth's *The Word of God and the Word of Man*). Furthermore, in each case, hands and minds other than those of the theologians cited were involved: most of Augustine's and Luther's and a few of Thielicke's sermons were reconstructed from the transcriptions of scribes or the notes of listeners; and some of 'Barth's' sermons were preached by Thurneysen (though Barth himself read and approved the translation of the relevant 2 vols., and in neither is notation made of which man preached which sermon). Finally, particularly as regards Augustine and Luther, questions have been raised about the reliability of the various texts, and about the quality of Lenker's translation of Luther (one may note J. W. Doberstein's critique in his introduction to *Luther's Works*, vol. li, p. xv). However, this essay explores not minutiae and fine nuance, but rather the broad and general thrust of these theologians' preaching of the resurrection, an approach which somewhat mitigates the effect of these problems.

The reason for selecting Augustine and Luther for this exercise is, no doubt, sufficiently obvious: they were both major theologians who also preached a great deal. Deciding upon contemporary figures was more difficult, and was governed by the criteria that the persons must have done serious theological work, that they must also have been preachers, and that their sermons must be available in English. Lest the

Twelve centuries separate Augustine from Luther, and another four separate Luther from Barth and Thielicke. Obviously, differences in cultural setting are vast, as are differences in scientific understanding of the created order and differences in critical understanding of the nature of the biblical texts. Opponents differed, too. To oversimplify, Augustine fought against heretics who, he believed, wrongly construed the person of Christ and the nature of the Church. Luther struggled against the Church itself in its understanding of the relationship of faith and works. Barth and Thielicke faced a superficially self-confident liberalism, secularism, and scientism tempted to give final authority to their own powers and understanding. Their diverse historical settings and varied opponents naturally influenced the shape of these theologians' discussion of the resurrection; yet (to anticipate what follows) the fundamental content of their preaching on this subject differs less than one might guess.

No doubt there are some self-evident reasons for the similarities we shall shortly observe, not least being the high regard all of these men had for Scripture and the fact that, in that sense, they had some common data from which to work.[2] Also, there is a clear line of influence extending from Augustine to Luther to the Lutheran Thielicke. (The Reformed Barth was naturally somewhat closer to aspects of Augustine and further from the Lutherans.) But, just as important, the fundamental situation which the biblical texts—and the resurrection itself—address has in no relevant way changed: humanly speaking, sin and death continue to reign as they have from the earliest memory of humankind. Indeed, our long historical experience may be sobering in this respect. Surely, by now, we are past thinking that some new technique, some bit of 'progress', will enable us to 'rise above' our sins; surely we have noticed, to our sorrow, that all our efforts to conquer death have, if anything, made dying more grotesque, so that now the freedom to *take* one's own life at the end becomes a form of truncated hope. Today, as yesterday, only the resurrection and the triumph over sin and evil it

reader wonder, I did consider making a comparison between Easter (and funeral) sermons and these preachers' day-to-day work; but I found that themes and tone remained quite constant, so that the distinction did not appear to be important.

[2] Granting that one's cultural position and theological and critical presuppositions influence one's apprehension of texts, I am none the less refusing a radical reader-response view of their meaning and am assuming that they have content and referents that significantly determine what can (or should!) be read out of them.

entails gives a satisfactory response to these stark, limiting conditions of our lives. Of course, our experience of needs does not itself determine the truth of the answers that may be offered to them. None the less, there may also be unarguable truths that are too small to be adequate to the needs. The resurrection, if and only if it truly occurred and truly implies something for our own future, is a large enough answer—large enough for mind and heart alike. I will examine, then, how in their preaching Augustine, Luther, Barth, and Thielicke understood the centrality of the resurrection and the affirmation that it 'truly occurred', how they approached the problem of doubt, and the implications of each one's affirmation of the resurrection for the living of this life. I will close with some brief reflections on what today's preachers may learn from their approaches.

THE CENTRALITY AND REALITY OF THE RESURRECTION

All of the theologians we are considering preached unequivocally the centrality of the resurrection to Christian faith. Augustine not only affirmed that 'the resurrection of the Lord Jesus Christ is the distinctive mark of the Christian faith'[3]—indeed, that 'Christian faith consists in believing in His Resurrection[4]—but further asserted that the whole of Christ's work, including the incarnation, was in the service of the resurrection, and that his death would have profited us nothing had the resurrection not occurred[5] (a view that, incidentally, constitutes a rejection of the adequacy of the moral influence theory of the atonement that could hardly be more definite!).

Luther said, altogether similarly:

When one wants to preach the Gospel, one must treat only of the resurrection of Christ. For this is the chief article of our faith. . . . The greatest power of faith is bound up in this article of faith. For if there were no

---

[3] *Sermons*, vi. 295, 1. See also e.g. vi. 163-4, 6, and vii. 37, 3 (quoting 2 Tim. 2: 8); vii. 70, 1; *Homilies*, 407, 5 (referencing Rom. 10: 8, 9).

[4] *Augustine of Hippo*, 218.

[5] *Sermons*, vi. 295, 1; 305, 2; vii. 104, 3; *Expositions*, 306, 23. 'Even the pagan believeth that He died; and maketh this charge against thee, that thou believest in one dead. What then thy praise? It is that thou believest that Christ arose from the dead, and that thou dost hope that thou shalt rise from the dead through Christ' (*Expositions*, 501, 24).

resurrection, we would have no consolation or hope, and everything else
Christ did or suffered would be futile (1 Cor. 15: 17).[6]

Or again, 'We can better dispense with all the other articles than
this one.'[7] 'What shall they preach? Nothing else, he [Christ] says,
than just that I am risen from the dead and have overcome and
taken away sin and all misery. . . . The Gospel is nothing else than
preaching the resurrection of Christ.'[8]

Contemporary writers speak to the same effect. Barth says:

Strike out this word ['resurrection'] with all that it means, and we are striking from Jesus what He really was. From this viewpoint we can understand
why this word occupies the central point of importance in the New
Testament, why it is the word that contains in itself what the whole of
Christianity really is.[9]

Or again: 'A Jesus who failed to rise from the dead avails us nothing. . . . Were we to hear only of a God who, fortunately for him,
measures up to our rule and who is able to do what we can also do
ourselves without Him, what need have we of such a God?'[10]
Thielicke quite matter-of-factly refers to the resurrection as 'the
basic teaching of Christianity',[11] and avers that 'if Christ did not rise
from the dead, then his life and his work are refuted'.[12]

However, affirming the centrality and necessity of Jesus' resurrection for Christian faith does not in itself say what one means by
the term 'resurrection', as the labours of myriad theologians and
the very fact of our meeting in New York amply confirm. Although
they nuanced it slightly differently, had somewhat different auxil-

---

⁶ *Catholic Epistles*, 12–13. See also *Sermons of Martin Luther* ii. 249, 2; and
Sermons on John 14–16, 40-1, where Luther avers that if we see Christ only as
teacher and example, 'Then His whole suffering, His death, and His resurrection
would be lost and useless for us'; for while his example directs us correctly, it fails
to bear us along, to give us the help we require.

⁷ *Sermons of Martin Luther*, iii. 200, 14. While Luther appears generally to put
this emphasis simply on the resurrection, he occasionally includes the whole second
article of the Creed (e.g. *Sermons I*, 165, in one of his sermons on the catechism);
and at least once refers to John 1: 29 as being 'the chief article of our Christian doctrine', encompassing the whole work of Christ (*Sermons on John 1–4*, 170-1).

⁸ *Sermons of Martin Luther*, iii. 201, 17.

⁹ Barth and Thurneysen, *Come Holy Spirit*, 164–5.

¹⁰ Barth and Thurneysen, *God's Search*, 29–30.   ¹¹ *I Believe*, 176.

¹² *Christ and the Meaning of Life*, 49. Elsewhere (*I Believe*, 165) he says that had
Christ been simply a teacher, his dying would not have mattered critically; but for
one who claimed he could fill the gap between humankind and God and could challenge death, it would be a catastrophe.

iary theological agendas, and handled matters of doubt significantly differently (at least as regards tone and emphasis, as we shall see later), Augustine, Luther, Barth, and Thielicke all preached a bodily resurrection of Jesus. While they were certainly willing to grant Christ's resurrection body some additional and mysterious properties (like the ability to penetrate walls and exemption from dying any more), they emphatically rejected spiritualizing interpretations, holding to the position that the tomb was empty and Christ's true flesh rose. Augustine says, 'The Lord fears such thoughts [as that he, as risen, was just a spirit], afraid they may kill the faith of the disciples. So be afraid yourselves of having such thoughts. No patient is unconcerned about what the doctor fears.'[13]

What is more, scriptural imagery and assertions (first-fruits, head and body, statements like 'because I live, you also will live'; John 14: 19) prompted the preachers we are considering to draw conclusions about the essential unity of Christ's resurrection and our

---

[13] *Sermons*, x. 341, 3. References, especially for Augustine, could be multiplied at great length. Augustine states his basic principle thus: 'when you hear the hidden meaning explained of a story in scripture that tells of things that happened, you must first believe that what has been read to you actually happened as read, or else the foundation of an actual event will be removed, and you will be trying to build castles in the air' (*Sermons*, i. 179, 7; this sermon is not on the resurrection, but Augustine maintains both parts of the principle with respect to it: that it must be taken literally (e.g. *Sermons*, iii. 443, 4; *Homilies* 60, 7) and that it may be further interpreted, as of Christ rising in the Gentiles as they come to believe in his resurrection (*Expositions*, 145, 18)). That the resurrection was of Christ's true flesh—indeed, the very same body that had died—and not simply spiritual, see further, e.g., *Sermons*, iv. 204, 4; vi. 155, 8; 300, 1; vii. 57, 2, 3; 190, 4; 216, 1; 226, 2; *Expositions*, 179, 5; 614, 5. Luther claims that the disciples' failure to recognize Jesus on the road to Emmaus is to be attributed to their estrangement of heart and thoughts, not to any change in Jesus (*Sermons of Martin Luther*, ii. 284, 3). With his usual earthiness, he declares that Christ had to rise on the third day because after that, his body would have begun to decompose (ibid. 239, 3), and that he was quickened again and glorified 'that he might not be a spirit' as the disciples on the road thought (ibid. 311, 3). Barth refers to resurrection as 'fact' (*Come Holy Spirit*, 157) and says, for instance, 'He is raised. He is truly risen, not only does His spirit continue to live somewhere beyond death; "He Himself" the whole Jesus has come forth from the dead as the new man of God. If that fails, then the whole of Christianity fails' (ibid. 165-6). See also *God's Search*, 26-7, for the empty tomb. Thielicke is particularly cautious in his approach, but he repeatedly speaks of the empty grave—'That [Christ's] is *one* grave from which more than merely flowers grew' (*I Believe*, 247; emphasis original)—and energetically repudiates suggestions that the resurrection is myth or legend (see esp. ibid. 160-87). Even his remark that Jesus' presenting himself to sight and touch is 'a sort of icebreaker' (ibid. 185) acknowledges the physicality that he argues is not in itself enough to produce belief.

own, separated though they are in time.[14] (Indeed, Augustine's view of their unity was so strong that he justified this separation in time by alleging that Christ rose before his members in order that they might have something to hope for.[15] He further suggested that if we did not like the body, we should stop caring for it now, concluding, 'bodies will rise again, because Christ rose again'.[16]) Since these men were theologians even while they were preachers—theologians who adduced many arguments both for the concrete reality of Christ's resurrection and the unity of our own with his—one cannot accuse them of a merely homiletical or psychological motive for preaching a bodily resurrection, though they were all obviously and explicitly concerned with speaking to the human condition and human fears.[17] But in so far as Christ's resurrection and our own are 'one fact', and in so far as the relevance of that 'fact' is not cast in terms of some non-factual myth, symbol, or metaphor, that Christ's resurrection was bodily becomes intensely relevant at the

[14] Augustine relied most heavily on head and body imagery, along the lines of, 'where the head goes, there too go the other parts of the body' (*Sermons*, iv. 372, 1; see similarly e.g. *Sermons*, ix. 264, 3; *Homilies*, 62, 11; *Expositions*, 274, 1; 425, 4. He also argued, though, that in one sense our resurrection will be even more wonderful than Christ's, since our flesh will be restored from a state of ashes (*Sermons*, v. 230, 12). Luther, in a sermon on Col. 3: 1–7, wrote, 'The apostle . . . regards as one fact the resurrection of the Lord Jesus Christ, who brought his body again from the grave and entered into life eternal, and the resurrection of ourselves' (*Sermons of Martin Luther*, vii. 220, 6; see also, on John 14: 20, *Sermons on John 14–16*, 136, 139). Generally, however, he emphasized more Christ's actively bestowing upon us all that he has done on our behalf (which we must receive by faith and baptism); see e.g. *Sermons of Martin Luther*, viii. 144, 8, 13; ii. 255, 15, 16; iii. 355, 16. Barth said, 'The last word concerning the world of men is not Dust though art and unto dust thou shalt return: but, Because I live, ye shall live also' (*Word*, 279). Preaching on John 14: 19, Barth proclaimed, 'It is now all-important for us to cling to this truth that *he*, Jesus Christ, in his life, is our present'; and on Rom. 6: 23, 'his Easter story is our history as well' (*Deliverance to the Captives*, 32, 145; and in quite the same vein, see the much earlier *God's Search*, 9–10). Thielicke said, 'One might reduce the Gospel to the very simple formula that at the very deepest level Jesus Christ unites the destiny of us men with His own' (*Silence of God*, 86). He was fond of quoting the hymn lines, 'Could the Head/Rise and leave his members dead?', and attributed the great Easter jubilation to the fact that the grave can no longer hold us, either (*Christ and the Meaning of Life*, 37; see also *How the World Began* 179).

[15] e.g. *Sermons*, ii. 254, 15; vii. 70, 1; 233, 6; *Expositions*, 454, 7. (Luther, by contrast, says that the Lord delays the resurrection of people in order that he might raise all at once, defeating death with one blow (*Sermons of Martin Luther*, v. 155–6, 38)).

[16] *Sermons*, vii. 87, 13. He added that they would rise free of all needs and evils, which are brought about by sin.

[17] Note the tenderness of Augustine: 'We were anxious . . . about the soul, and he by rising again gave us assurance even about the flesh' (*Sermons*, vii. 208, 1).

human level. Most human beings, including non-Christians, do remain emotionally unsatisfied by the various 'demythologized' or spiritualized versions of the promise of survival: you may recall that Woody Allen, having considered various options of this latter kind, including fame and progeny, concluded that he himself would prefer to obtain immortality by not dying. Given that not dying is not an option, the promise of rising with that personal identity given by our bodies intact speaks powerfully to the human condition.

Strong similarities in fundamental beliefs and proclamation do not obviate significant differences in the way these theologians' arguments were developed, however. Augustine worked out of, and in defence of, basic Christological assumptions, and he spent enormous energy laying out the consequences of an orthodox Christology in the face of the challenges of a seemingly endless array of heretics. Because he affirmed the full divinity of the Son, he emphasized strongly (in a way quite foreign to much modern biblical scholarship and theological presupposition) the agency of the Son in his resurrection, repeatedly quoting John 2: 19 ('Destroy this temple, and in three days I will raise it up') and John 10: 18 ('No one takes it [my life] from me, but I lay it down of my own accord. I have power to lay it down, and I have power to take it up again'— an agency that did not exclude that of the Father but was not subordinate to it, either[18]. The Son could exercise this agency because, as divine, he could not in the nature of the case die. Only by assuming human flesh could he, as a human being, die; and while the flesh was also truly Christ, in view of its having been assumed by the divine Word it could not remain dead.[19] (In speaking of the work of Christ, Augustine repeated continually that Christ took on in the incarnation what he was not; he did not give up what he had;[20] so, 'you have Christ coming into the world, and yet he was already there; he rose again and ascended into heaven, and yet he

---

[18] 'When the Father raiseth, the Son also raiseth; so when the Son raiseth, the Father also raiseth: because the Son has said, "I and the Father are one" ' (*Homilies*, 73, 11; see also *Expositions*, 226, 7; *Sermons*, viii. 321, 2–4; and esp. iii. 55–6, in a sermon on the unity of the Trinity).

[19] *Homilies*, 264–5, 10–13; see also *Sermons*, ii. 48, 10. From the two natures of Christ, Augustine also drew the altogether curious conclusion that 'God raiseth up souls by Christ, the Son of God; bodies He raiseth by the same Christ, the Son of man' (*Homilies*, 129, 15).

[20] e.g. *Sermons*, iii. 353, 5; 467, 2.

had never left it. You think of him as a man? Don't think like that'.[21]) Thus:

The only one who could raise himself up was the one who didn't die, when his flesh died. Even in this case he raised up what had died. He raised himself up, because he was alive in himself, though he had died in his flesh which was to be raised. You see, it wasn't only the Father who raised up the Son, . . . but the Lord too raised up himself.[22]

Or again: 'He chose also the manner of His death. . . . On the very cross, when He pleased, He made his body be taken down and departed; in the very sepulchre, as long as it pleased Him, he lay; and, when He pleased, He arose as from a bed.'[23] In no way was his complete sovereignty to be compromised.

Luther reiterates most of these convictions in a manner so similar to that of Augustine that Luther's dependence upon him can scarcely be doubted (especially since we know that Luther spent much time studying Augustine). He affirms Christ's as well as the Father's agency in the resurrection;[24] emphasizes that 'an indivisible being, at the same time a Son of the virgin of the house of David and of God . . . cannot remain in death';[25] none the less attributes life to Christ as the eternal Word, not to Christ as the human being;[26] and says that Christ 'descended, ascended and all the while remained in heaven in divine essence and power'.[27] He further affirms that if Christ be not risen, then sin has overcome him; and

---

[21] *Sermons*, viii. 178, 3. The same principle applies to Christ's words to the thief on the cross, that he would that day be with Christ in paradise—while Christ's dead body was yet on earth (*Sermons*, iii. 218, 7; *Homilies*, 264, 10). The *extra calvinisticum* obviously antedated Calvin!

[22] *Sermons*, iii. 216, 2.   [23] *Homilies*, 242, 9; similarly, ibid. 62, 11.

[24] *Sermons of Martin Luther*, vii. 203, 1; *Sermons of John 1–4*, 116, 143, 247; also *Catholic Epistles*, 39, making causal reference to the Father raising Christ. Regarding the Son's equality with the Father, he says that the statement 'the Father is greater than I' 'is not said of the personal, divine essence of his own nature nor of his Father's . . . but concerning the difference between the kingdom which he shall have with his Father and his service or servile state in which he was before his resurrection' (*Sermons of Martin Luther*, iii. 336, 92).

[25] *Sermons of Martin Luther*, vii. 216, 23; see also ibid. ii. 298, 37.

[26] *Sermons II*, 61. He also says that the incarnation reveals the true manhood, while the resurrection reveals the true Godhead (*Sermons on John 14–16*, 376).

[27] *Sermons of Martin Luther*, iii. 449, 63 (see also ibid. 418, 21; *Sermons on John 1–4*, 321). Luther's statements in these three sermons are clear and unequivocal. The 'Logos non extra carnem' is a postulate of seventeenth-century Lutheran orthodoxy, developed in opposition to the pressing of the *extra calvinisticum* by the Reformed party. (See R. Muller, *Dictionary of Latin and Greek Theological Terms* (Grand Rapids, Mich.: Baker, 1985), 180.)

we too are left helpless before sin.[28] All this is basic to Luther's theological universe—essential, but not enough. The distinctive note ringing through his sermons is that none of these truths matters unless they are appropriated, unless the sinner not only knows them but receives the work on Christ as done on his or her behalf. He proclaims:

It is not enough that we believe the historic fact of the resurrection of Christ; for this all the wicked believe, yea, even the devil himself believes that Christ suffered and is risen. But we must believe also the meaning— the spiritual significance of Christ's resurrection, realizing its fruit and benefits, that which we have received through it, namely, forgiveness and redemption from all sins.[29]

When I come to understand the fact that all the works of Christ are done for me, nay, they are bestowed upon and given to me, the effect of his resurrection being that I also will arise and live with him; that will cause me to rejoice.[30]

Luther argued, in sum, that what everyone desires most deeply is to be free from death and hell, sin, and a bad conscience; that the conquering Christ has procured for us these supreme desiderata through his death and resurrection, having turned away the wrath of God; and that these great blessings come to us only through, and not without, faith.[31]

In sharp contrast to Augustine and Luther, neither Barth nor Thielicke cares to emphasize in his preaching the agency of the Son in the resurrection or the idea that he remains in heaven even while on earth. Barth goes so far as to say, 'What else did Jesus do toward resurrection than that he died?'[32] He none the less insists that while Christ was in death, death was not in him; and hence he could not remain in death,[33] which sounds a lot like the earlier theologians. His main concern, though, was to emphasize that the resurrection lifts the world and all our preconceptions of the possible off their hinges, in a divine encroachment that modern people resist

---

[28] *Sermons of Martin Luther*, iii. 199, 12.
[29] Ibid. 200, 13. See also ibid. ii. 216, 1; 220, 9; 249, 3; 354, 2. Luther's point is freshly confirmed by a recent 'Harper's Index' listing which says that 52 per cent of non-Christian Americans affirm that they believe in the resurrection of Christ (noted by Martin Marty in *Context*, July 1995, p. 4).
[30] *Sermons of Martin Luther*, ii. 241, 6.
[31] Ibid. i. 38, 51; v. 195, 26; vii. 197, 9.
[32] *Come Holy Spirit*, 251; see also ibid. 168, and *Deliverance to the Captives*, 149.
[33] *Come Holy Spirit*, 143.

mightily because it manifests to them their actual helplessness.[34] People can contribute nothing to this most important of all events, this in-breaking of God that promises renewal and transformation, this victory that is simply not a historical possibility.[35] (Note well, however, that when Barth says that the resurrection is not a historical event, he clearly does not mean that it did not occur in our time and space, but rather that it is not something that is some sort of 'hidden potentiality' in the created order, or something the import of which can be limited by that order. It is an act of the transcendent, sovereign God breaking into our world.[36]) Because of the resurrection, our earthly reality has been decisively altered—a truth that Barth sometimes says we have only 'to perceive, to accept, and to take to heart'[37]; sometimes almost seeming to imply that we have only not actively to reject or defend ourselves against[38]; and sometimes says means that Christ 'has already taken [our] life whether [we] know it or not'.[39] This seeming ambivalence of statement, which does *not* represent a clear line of temporal development in Barth's thought, would appear to be an aspect of his wider wrestling with his universalist insistence upon the divine sovereignty and yet his inability completely to put aside the significance of human apprehension and choice. Even so, the tone is entirely

---

[34] *Come Holy Spirit*, 167, 150–1.   [35] Ibid. 168 (and 146–70, *passim*).

[36] See e.g. *Word*, 90, where Barth speaks of 'an event which, though it is the only real happening in is not a real happening *of* history'. However, in this quite early piece (delivered in 1920), Barth does speak more abstractly (and allusively?) than he does later on, merging the resurrection with the second coming—which he can do because events that belong in their essence to eternity rather than to time are not subject to temporal sequentiality (which does not imply that persons yet in time do not come to them in sequence). Making a close tie between the two is of course unexceptional: Thielicke, e.g. says, 'the New Testament sees the secret of history in terms of its end, the "death of the world," as it were, from the perspective of him who rises victorious beyond that death' (*How Modern*, 62). (In the materials I am working with, I sense somewhat less reluctance on the part of the middle Barth to speak of the resurrection as occurring in history than does O'Collins (*Jesus Risen* (New York: Paulist, 1987), 36–7), though the difference may be one of nuance. Even in 1919, though, Barth can say, 'God applies the lever to lift the world. And the world is being lifted by the lever which he has applied. God in history is *a priori* victory in history' (*Word*, 297).)

[37] *Deliverance to the Captives*, 149.   [38] *Come Holy Spirit*, 135–6.

[39] *God's Search*, 221. See also, as something of a curiosity, the oddly concrete remark (as contrasted with Barth's frequent high level of abstraction) that 'these two thieves literally died with Christ, and theirs was the assurance that they were also literally to live with him' (*Deliverance to the Captives*, 82): one suspects that Barth's pastoral heart, desiring to give assurance to actual prisoners, got the better of his head here.

different from Luther's, where the fact is of no use whatever without personal appropriation of it.

Thielicke is impatient with modern world-views that define miracles or any transcendent interventions or acts of God, including the resurrection, as inherently impossible and hence refuse to entertain any evidence that would seem to suggest them: he says wryly that Jesus has consistently risen from the *conceptual* graves in which we have locked him.[40] Like Luther, he speaks of the importance of knowing that Christ died *for me*; but he is much clearer that this conviction is one that comes from within faith.[41] Like Barth, he recognizes that there is a great divide between those who welcome God's decisive intervention as a wonderful gift of new freedom and those who desire no encroachments on their management of their own lives.[42]

THE PROBLEM OF DOUBT

Anyone who supposes that twentieth-century people have unprecedented difficulty with the idea of resurrection might take note of Augustine's remark that 'nothing has been attacked with the same pernicious, contentious contradiction, in the Christian faith, as the resurrection of the flesh'.[43] Against the opposition and doubt of his day, Augustine marshalled in his preaching two principal kinds of argument: those from the nature of God and his creation and those relying on evidence supporting Christ's resurrection, including alleged prophecies of it and results stemming from it. With respect to the nature of God, Augustine reasoned that if one acknowledges that God is almighty, then the resurrection is, by definition, possible.[44] Furthermore, he says, birth is a greater miracle than resurrection: 'Look at God, think about the Almighty, and stop hesitating. I mean, if he could make you out of nothing when you

---

[40] *How Modern*, 5, 19.   [41] e.g. *Christ and the Meaning of Life*, 58.
[42] *Faith*, 57.
[43] *Expositions*, 437, 32; Augustine proceeds to contrast the idea of the immortality of the soul, which he says many defend. Elsewhere he berates doubters thus: 'Miserable man! Perverse and preposterous human heart! If his own grandfather rose again, he would believe him; the Lord of the world has risen again, and he is unwilling to believe' (*Sermons*, vii. 233, 6; see also ibid. v. 112, 6; x. 230, 8).
[44] *Sermons*, vii. 66, 2; 79, 1.

didn't exist, why could he not rouse from the dead his man whom he had already made?'[45]

However, for this kind of deductive argument to work, one must grant the premiss; so Augustine the preacher spent a great deal more time furnishing what he considered to be concrete evidence of the truth of the resurrection. More than anything else, he emphasized the forty days of post-resurrection appearances to the discouraged and doubting disciples, especially to the two on the road to Emmaus (Luke 24), to Mary and to Thomas (John 20), and to Peter and his companions (John 21), with particular attention to the physical solidity of Christ's body, the reality of his scars, and his ability to eat and drink.[46] He even went so far as to say, 'It would have been insufficient to present himself to the eyes for the seeing if he hadn't also offered himself to the hands for the touching.'[47] While Christ could certainly have risen without his scars, he kept them in order to heal the wounds of doubt in his disciples' hearts.[48] Similarly, he ate not because he needed to, but because he could, thus demonstrating the reality of his risen flesh and thereby giving his disciples hope for themselves.[49] But, of course, that hope had more important aspects than an overcoming of doubts about the reality of the resurrected body: 'It was a man being touched, God being understood; flesh being touched, wisdom being understood; weakness being touched, power being understood. The whole of it true and real.'[50]

[45] *Sermons*, vi. 163, 6 (note that here, 'he' refers to Christ the Word). See also ibid. vii. 87, 2; *Homilies*, 57, 1.

[46] That this solid body could pass through walls, he attributed quite frankly to miracle, which in the nature of the case cannot be understood (*Sermons*, vii. 108-9, 2). We may contrast this emphasis in the sermons on the appearances with O'Collins' observation that Augustine does not appeal to these in *The City of God* (Gerald O'Collins, 'Augustine on the Resurrection', in Fannie LeMoine and Christopher Kleinhenz (eds.), *St. Augustine the Bishop* (New York: Garland, 1994), 69).

[47] *Sermons*, vi. 304, 1. See also e.g. ibid. vii. 78, 1; *Expositions*, 162, 6. Christ stayed forty days in order to bring home the reality of the resurrection (*Sermons*, vii. 236, 1; 249, 1).

[48] e.g. *Sermons*, iii. 419-20, 2; iv. 203, 3.

[49] Esp. ibid. iv. 204, 3: 'How much the good builder adds to strengthen the structure of faith! He wasn't hungry, and he asked for something to eat. And he ate to show he could, not because he had to. So let the disciples acknowledge the reality of the risen body, which the whole world has acknowledged as the result of preaching.' See also e.g. ibid. vii. 79, 2; 90, 3; *Homilies*, 316, 2.

[50] *Sermons*, vii. 232, 6. Augustine wavers significantly on why it was that the risen Christ appeared only to his own: the Jews were not worthy (ibid. vi. 285, 1); Christ did not wish to appear to taunt his enemies (ibid. viii. 92, 6); Christ wished

Should the appearances fail to persuade, Augustine brings in prophecies of Christ and his work: he says that even a magician who could make himself appear could not, before he was born, create prophecies of himself in Scripture.[51] He claims further that all the prophecies which foretold the work of Christ also foretold the Church; and those who cannot see Christ in the flesh can see the Church: 'He [Christ] showed himself to the disciples, and promised them the Church; he has shown us the Church, and ordered us to believe about himself.'[52] These references to Scripture actually form a more significant part of his argument than it might at first appear; for despite his strong insistence upon the physical, visible, touchable reality of the risen Christ's body, he acknowledges that in the end seeing is not enough; we require the Spirit speaking through the Word if we are to believe in Christ as God: 'even if we were to see, should we not see that which the Jews saw and crucified?'[53]

When He [Christ] had given Himself to be handled by them that did not suffice Him, but He would also confirm by means of the scriptures the heart of them that believe: for He looked forward to us who should be afterwards; seeing that in Him we have nothing we can handle, but have that which we may read. For if those believed only what they held and handled, what shall we do?[54]

While the elements of Luther's treatment of doubt differ but little from Augustine's, his emphases differ considerably. In fact, he emphasizes doubt and physical proof less in all respects; and he does not argue from the divine omnipotence (although it is surely

---

to make clear to later believers that the promise of resurrection was to those who believed, not to those who simply saw (*Expositions*, 275, 5); or 'this is a great mystery'! (ibid. 85, 2).

[51] *Sermons*, vi. 306, 4. See also *Homilies*, 469, 1–2: 'For the firmness of faith is in this, that all things which came to pass in Christ were foretold.' Most often Augustine simply refers to Luke 24 without providing specifics; when he does offer suggestions of what OT texts prophesy about the resurrection, like Ps. 22: 6 (*Expositions* 56, 7), the modern reader may scarcely be convinced. The most casual approach to his *Expositions on the Psalms*, for instance, immediately reveals his conviction that the Psalms refer to Christ throughout, in a way that is completely foreign to a modern, critical reading of these texts.

[52] *Sermons*, iv. 170–1, 1; vi. 301, 2.   [53] *Expositions*, 180, 5.

[54] *Homilies*, 469, 1; see also *Sermons*, vi. 301, 2. Paul 'knew even the flesh of Christ, not according to the flesh but according to the spirit, seeing that he acknowledged the power of his resurrection with the certainty of a believing mind, not the curiosity of feeling fingers'; and 'we could in no way enjoy this blessing of not seeing and yet believing, unless we had received it from the Holy Spirit' (*Sermons*, iv. 427, 3, 4).

implicit). When he speaks of the disciples' striking and stubborn refusal of reports of the resurrection, it is often in service of an acknowledgement of Christians' frailties and in admiration of Christ's kindness none the less.[55] Similarly, he frequently interprets the post-resurrection appearances, the eating and drinking, the showing of the wounded hands and feet, in terms of Christ's intent to provide reassurance and comfort (obviously he is thinking in terms of proofs, but the tone is quite different from Augustine's).[56] He says that Christ came to the gathered disciples first in Thomas's absence so that we might have stronger evidence and documentary testimony of the resurrection.[57] Luther adduces Thomas's confession, the courage of the women in going to the tomb, and miracles wrought through the Holy Spirit after the resurrection as additional signs of Christ's power.[58]

However, Luther's primary concern is to demonstrate the necessity of the Word if people are to believe. Regarding the interaction with the two on the road to Emmaus, he insists that the resurrection is apprehended 'above all first through the Word and faith, rather than through bodily vision or sensation'; and he continues, 'So strange and unknowable had he [Christ] become to them that they would not have known him had he stayed with them ever so long, until he announced to them his resurrection and preached about it.'[59] 'His purpose is to show and teach us that the power of his resurrection and dominion will be exercised here on earth and manifest itself in this life, only through the Word, and through faith which holds fast to Christ.'[60] Indeed, an angel announced the resurrection to the women because Christ 'wanted to reveal his resurrection through the Word, even before they should see him and experience the power of his resurrection'.[61] Predictably, then, Luther, too, puts very heavy emphasis on Old Testament prophecies of Christ, though in a candid moment, speaking of Christ's exposition on the road to Emmaus, he acknowledges:

Now it is true we all would gladly know just the passages the Lord quoted referring to himself, by which he thereby enlightened, strengthened and

[55] *Sermons of Martin Luther*, ii. 284–7, 4–14; iii. 210–11, 2.
[56] Ibid. ii. 320, 1; 382, 8; 407, 8.   [57] Ibid. 403–4, 1.
[58] Ibid. 410, 14; 20, 4; *Sermons on John 1–4*, 118.
[59] *Sermons of Martin Luther*, ii. 284, 3 (not, as stated above, n. 13, because of any change in Jesus).
[60] Ibid. 284, 4.   [61] Ibid. 249, 1.

convinced these disciples, since Moses contains so little, or nothing, as it would seem, of a plain statement on that of which Christ here speaks, that it behooved him to suffer, and to rise on the third day. . . . [But] the Bible is a book that must not only be read and preached, but it also requires the true interpreter, that is, the revelation of the Holy Spirit.[62]

Thus, when Luther emphasizes the Word, he is not referring to some possibility of purely rational apprehension of truth, but, like Augustine, assumes the necessity of the work of the Spirit in and through the Word if human hearts are to be reached.

When we come to Barth, the weight of the argument shifts altogether away from alleged 'proofs' of any kind. He says, 'That One who was dead should rise from the dead is something impossible, incomprehensible and unprovable.'[63] Or again, 'We will never get beyond the experience that our faith is a constant struggle with our own overwhelming doubt.'[64] He says that the Lord's 'revelation as well as His resurrection will always appear to us as a logical and physical absurdity'.[65] 'Our reason pants for breath when it attempts to follow what the Scriptures say.'[66] Although Barth chastens those who, like Judas, have insufficient hope to cast themselves into the hands of God alone—and thus engages the human will by berating human unwillingness to cease relying upon one's own powers and recognize one's absolute lostness—his fundamental presupposition is the sovereignty of God.[67] Time may or may not be ripe for eternity; all we can do is wait for God to send his fire.[68] But whether or not we recognize and receive it, 'the resurrection of Christ from the dead is not a question but the answer which has been given us'.[69] Although one may resist quite so bald a way of putting it (and Barth's relentless emphasis on the divine initiative has certainly

---

[62] Ibid. 292–3, 24, 26. None the less, earlier in the same sermon he declares that Jesus upbraided the two disciples for their unbelief 'because they ought to have known the Scriptures' (ibid. 283, 1). For references to the theme that OT prophecies were used by Jesus both before and after his resurrection and also by Peter and Paul, see e.g. *Sermons on John 14–16*, 334; *Sermons on John 1–4*, 339; *Sermons of Martin Luther*, vii. 197, 8; 203, 2; 213, 20.

[63] *Come Holy Spirit*, 162.

[64] *God's Search*, 152–3. See also *Come Holy Spirit*, 147–9. Barth suggests from Paul's discourse in 1 Cor. 15 that some in the first Christian congregation must have found the idea of resurrection too strong, but Paul says, 'then everything is vain' (ibid. 165).

[65] *God's Search*, 152–3.   [66] *Come Holy Spirit*, 187.

[67] Ibid. 134, 150–1, 169. See also *Word*, 88.

[68] *Come Holy Spirit*, 228, 120.   [69] *Word*, 296.

been widely resisted!), one must recognize, I think, that his position is really implicit in Augustine's and Luther's, since both acknowledge that apart from the work of the Holy Spirit, people do not come to belief.

Thielicke, much exercised by modern barriers to belief, comes to essentially the same conclusion; though he uses a less apodictic tone, moderated by the affirmation that the truth of the Gospel must be presented in new ways to relate to the new questions of each generation, without simply capitulating to one world-view after another.[70] He takes with particular seriousness post-Lessing historical scepticism, acknowledging that nothing could, by modern standards, 'prove' Christ's resurrection, and yet insisting that if the Easter message is to help us come to terms with death, it must be at least as certain as death is, a level of certainty by no means easy to come by.[71] Thielicke makes a considerable point of the style of the biblical narratives: their striking lack of fanciful elements; their veiled, discreet, even cryptic language; the mysterious, indirect light in which they are bathed; the sense that the normal faculties and even the imaginations of those who had experienced the events were badly overtaxed.[72] He reiterates that none of the disciples thought Jesus could rise from the dead; nor were the people of Jerusalem recklessly credulous: they 'would have repudiated this maddest of all messages just as firmly as we would, if—*if* they hadn't been bowled over by the upsetting facts'.[73] But in the end, he affirms that 'A miracle has never yet brought anyone to faith, since it is always open to other interpretations'.[74] He speaks instead

[70] *How Modern*, 10. None the less, sometimes he does speak sharply: 'Where theologians sit poring over the Scriptures that dark power sows between the lines the seeds of man's own thinking, causing the wisdom of the Greeks to triumph over the foolishness of the Cross and spreading the gravecloths of human, all too human thoughts upon the open Easter grave and turning the mighty acts of God into the humbug of idle self-assertion' (*Waiting Father*, 72). He also makes the point that for many centuries it was not the resurrection so much as the incarnation that was a stumbling-block and suspected of being only legend (*Christ and the Meaning of Life*, 50).

[71] *Christ and the Meaning of Life*, 51. 'That Christ came to us through the night of the grave into eternal life—what experience could ever prove such a thing? Would we seriously doubt the certainty of the Pythagorean proposition if someone told us about a dream he had had in which he had experienced an entirely different kind of geometry?' (ibid.). See also *Silence of God*, 82; *I Believe*, 152–3; *How Modern*, 23.

[72] *I Believe*, 162–6, 249; *Silence of God*, 80.

[73] *I Believe*, 167; see also *Silence of God*, 81.

[74] *Silence of God*, 83. Jesus himself rejected 'proofs' from beyond in the parable of the rich man and Lazarus (*Christ and the Meaning of Life*, 52).

of the self-testimony of the risen Christ himself and of how, facing
the empty tomb and hearing the words of the angel, scales fell from
the disciples' eyes, so that they perceived how all of Jesus' words
and deeds pointed to the truth that death could not hold him.[75]
Thus it is not surprising that only those who had known Jesus
became witnesses to the resurrection: only they could make the
necessary connections. But even so, they were not permitted to see
the resurrection directly but had to believe the *word* of the risen
Lord.[76] True conviction over against doubt comes only from within
faiths, not from provision of outside evidence.

Have we yet difficulty believing? Thielicke adds one more caveat:

> If we cannot believe and the seed will not grow, the reason lies only in the
> rarest cases in the fact that we have intellectual doubts, that, for example,
> the relation of miracle and causality remains a problem to us, or that a per-
> son cannot understand from a medical point of view how a dead man can
> rise again. Rather, when we cannot believe, there is something in the back-
> ground of our life that is not in order.[77]

Though, again, the tone is different, this reference to sin as a bar-
rier to belief resembles significantly Barth's claim that we refuse God
because we refuse to admit our utter helplessness, and Luther's
insistence that to rest any confidence in our own works is to refuse
God's work on our behalf.

It results, then, that while the weight given to external evidence
varies significantly among these preachers (Augustine giving it the
most), and while none disavows the legitimacy, reality, and importance of the evidence, none believes that seeking to compel the intel-
lect will by itself solve the problem of doubt. Belief, faith, is
necessary—belief enabled somehow by the Spirit and entailing a
willingness to let go of human predilections of thought and behaviour.

---

[75] *I Believe*, 168–9; *Christ and the Meaning of Life*, 53–4; *Silence of God*, 83; *How Modern*, 55.

[76] *I Believe*, 170; *Silence of God*, 84. See also *Faith*, 54–5, for the necessity of the work of the Holy Spirit.

[77] *Waiting Father*, 58; note also the very interesting fact that in *How To Believe Again*, Thielicke makes no use of the resurrection for apologetic purposes, but rather stresses the link between obedience and faith.

THE RESURRECTION AND THE CHRISTIAN LIFE

If we believe the resurrection took place, it obviously has consequences for how we ought to live our lives: only by the oddest sort
of intellectual or psychological disjunction can one say that, yes, the
resurrection occurred; but, no, it makes no difference to one's perception of the nature of things and of what really counts. Preachers,
of course, are scarcely slow to make the connections. Augustine,
concerned for a Church that had known martyrdom, gave particular attention to how the resurrection bears on Christians' facing of
trials. If the Lord himself, the chief of martyrs, gave up his body to
be afflicted for a time but then raised it up, his followers may likewise stand fearless before those who can kill the body but cannot
kill the soul, for they know both what they must endure and what
they may hope for.[78]

In his sufferings Christ showed us one life that is laborious, full of troubles,
temptations, fears and griefs, the life with which this age runs its course;
while by his resurrection he demonstrated that life where nobody will
grieve, nobody be afraid, nobody be reconciled because nobody will
quarrel.[79]

If the work dismays us, we should consider the reward.[80] Christ has
gone before us, so we know what to expect; and the greatness of
our hope should give us a proper measure of disregard for this present life. In fact, Augustine goes so far as to claim that 'we are not
Christians, except on account of a future life'.[81] 'In this life', he
says, 'you cannot be happy. Nobody can.'[82] Instead of directing our
efforts to such a futile end, we may be empowered by the whole

---

[78] *Augustine of Hippo*, 228; *Sermons*, vi. 143, 5. Besides referring to martyrs of his
own time, Augustine was fond of using the example of Peter, who had denied Jesus
out of fear, but later, having seen the risen Christ, became fearless (e.g. *Sermons*, iv.
449, 3; vii. 149, 3; viii. 204, 3; *Homilies*, 445, 4).

[79] *Sermons*, ix. 246, 1; see also ibid. vi. 133, 1; *Expositions*, 175, 4.

[80] *Sermons*, iii. 165, 16: 'You are afraid of losing your money, because acquiring
your money has cost you a great deal of hard labor. If you haven't come into the
money, which you are going to lose some time or other, at least when you die, without labor, can you really expect to come into eternal life without labor?'.

[81] *Expositions*, 452, 1.

[82] *Sermons*, vii. 22, 5. Similarly, if we want peace, we should seek it not here but
by lifting up our hearts to where it has gone before, in the risen Christ, who is our
peace (*Expositions*, 77, 18; *Sermons*, ii. 85, 57).

work of Christ, as we believe in it, 'to gaze upon those invisible realities which our material eyes are unaware of'.[83]

A 'proper disregard' for this present life does not, however, entail withdrawal from its responsibilities or a shirking of the truth that the Lord cared about us and this world enough to become incarnate. While it is true that in key ways Christ does not present himself for imitation—for instance, we have no power to take up our lives once we have died, to slay death, or to shed blood for the remission of sins (though Augustine certainly lauded the martyrs)—we are to imitate Christ in reverent obedience.[84] We should note his humility and not seek to 'rise before him' or prefer ourselves to him by seeking to be exalted here rather than after our own deaths.[85] We should emulate his patience; for he remained on the cross not because he could not come down, but lest he seem to yield to insults and be unable to bear reproach.[86] We should recall how the apostle Peter, once he had been liberated from his dread of death, was taught by the Lord how to love.[87] In short, we are to live good lives, for we have no grounds for confidence that the resurrection of Christ is at work within us if we are making no progress in our daily living.[88]

[83] *Sermons*, iii. 424, 8. In a curious and very often repeated bit of allegorizing (with many variations), Augustine treats Jesus' words to Mary at the tomb—that she should not touch him (John 20: 17; most modern interpreters translate ἅπτω as 'hold on to' or 'cling to')—as meaning that Mary or the Church ought not to 'touch' or understand Christ materialistically but rather spiritually, as he is in his equality with the Father; she ought not to, 'by touching earth, lose heaven' (ibid. vii. 98, 3; see also e.g. ibid. i. 223, 7; iv. 427, 4; *Homilies*, 438, 3). Augustine makes exceedingly clear his conviction that it is neither because she was a woman nor because of some lack of concreteness of the resurrection body that Jesus spoke as he did.

[84] *Homilies*, 351, 1. 'So don't be ungrateful to your Redeemer, by not believing what he promised; but do what he commands, in order to receive what he promised' (*Sermons*, vii. 87, 3). The martyrs also follow Christ's example in their dying: 'Too little therefore it were for the Lord to exhort the martyrs with a word, unless he had enforced it by examples' (*Expositions*, 264, 3).

[85] *Expositions*, 607, 3, 4; see also *Sermons*, vi. 106, 1. Alternatively, he speaks of our humbling ourselves in penitence (*Expositions*, 636, 3).

[86] *Expositions*, 131, 12; Augustine also repeatedly claims that rising from the grave is harder than coming down from the cross; see also e.g. *Sermons*, iii. 412, 9. 'He suffered with a patience all his own, to teach us the patience we should have; and in his resurrection he showed us the reward of patience' (*Sermons*, v. 266, 3).

[87] *Sermons*, viii. 204, 3.

[88] Ibid. 28, 8; see also ibid. viii. 65, 9: 'because you can't choose here not to die, choose, while you are alive, not to die forever. . . . By dying [Christ] showed you what you are going to suffer, willy-nilly; by rising again he showed you what, if you live a good life, you are going to receive'; and ibid. vii. 19, 2: 'Now the resurrection of our Lord Jesus Christ is the new life of those who believe in Jesus. . . . He rose

However, though it is essential to Augustine that the lives of people be remade by Christ, he does not in his preaching of the resurrection extend this principle to promoting the remaking of society. He speaks frequently of the necessity of the unity of the one Body of Christ on earth (particularly in opposition to the Donatists) and of care for that Body, including reference to justice, charity, and the giving of alms; but his major concern is clearly for the preaching of the Gospel.[89] Now that Christ is risen and his power is no longer hidden, we have no excuse: he has called for labourers to make him known to all the earth.[90] Since Christ's resurrection makes his promises sure—which promises include the resurrection to an eternal life of perpetual bliss of their whole selves, with bodies no longer subject to pain or penalty, for all who believe in him—nothing could be more important than the preaching of Christ, that this supreme blessing might be made known.[91] 'The resurrection of my Lord being known, and mine own being promised me, my love, having been brought out of the straits of fear, walks abroad in continuance, into the expanse of liberty.'[92]

Luther, too, spoke of the resurrection nerving Christians in the face of present trials, and of how earthly appearances suggesting defeat deceive us: 'Christians . . . must have the vision which enables them to disregard the terrible spectacle and outward appearance of death, the devil, and the might, the swords, the spears, and the guns of the whole world, and to see Him who sits on high.'[93] However, by contrast with Augustine, one notices

again in order to demonstrate in his own life the newness of our life.' Augustine speaks of Christ's fasting as referring to his hungering for the good works that he enabled in his disciples by coming to them (*Expositions*, 83, 15). Not, of course, that God is somehow dependent upon human achievement: he works all to the good, as he did by the resurrection; rather, those who devise evil are judged by their intention (ibid. 130, 8; 257, 14). 'Let punishments terrify those, whom rewards win not. Of no value to thee is what God promiseth, tremble at what He threateneth' (ibid. 180, 7).

[89] *Sermons*, vii. 44, 1; iii. 404, 17; *Homilies*, 524-5, 8, 9.

[90] *Sermons*, iii. 412, 9; see also ibid. vii. 32, 1; *Homilies*, 396, 1; *Expositions*, 431-2, 8, 9. In the day of judgement, 'The form of a servant will be shown to servants: the form of God will be reserved for sons. Wherefore let the servants be made sons' (*Homilies*, 143, 14).

[91] *Sermons*, ii. 317, 22. iv. 185, 2; vi. 163-4, 6; vii. 66, 2; *Expositions*, 349, 22 (the resurrection included among many evidences of the reliability of God's promises); 545, 1.

[92] *Expositions*, 69, 9; see also *Homilies*, 85, 11.

[93] *Sermons on John* 14-16, 417; see also *Sermons of Martin Luther*, iii. 75, 5.

immediately the intense subjectivity of his approach, the emphasis on the internal more than the external aspects of the struggles of this life.[94] He suggests, indeed, that trials remain because were we not to feel the effects of sin and death, we would not experience our need for God and would miss the experience of his grace.

Just as a pig's bladder must be rubbed with salt and thoroughly worked to distend it, so this old hide of ours must be well salted and plagued until we call for help and cry aloud, and so stretch and expand ourselves, both through internal and through external suffering, that we may finally succeed and attain this heart and cheer, joy and consolation, from Christ's resurrection.[95]

But once we have attained this Christian hope and power, everything should change: 'your whole attitude toward those things of which the world is terrified should be different, and . . . you should have eyes, ears, senses, and thoughts which are different from those you had before from Adam, when you were frightened and sorrowful, as those who had no hope'.[96] In particular, we must resist all worldliness, for the resurrection of Christ does not avail for those who are worldly.[97]

---

[94] E. C. Kiessling speaks of Luther's 'doctrinal objectivity'. His point is not actually in conflict with mine, however, because he is contrasting preachers who, like Luther, gave predominance to 'topics of universal religious interest' with those who mirrored the times or addressed the crisis of the hour. He is not denying the personal engagement and concern for appropriation of the truth that I am noting (*The Early Sermons of Luther and their Relation to the Pre-Reformation Sermon* (Grand Rapids, Mich.: Zondervan, 1935), 109).

[95] *Sermons of Martin Luther*, ii. 253, 10. 'If now the Gospel teaches naught but that Christ has overcome sin and death by his resurrection, then we must indeed confess that it can be of service to none save those who feel sin and death' (ibid. 303, 3); see also *Catholic Epistles*, 126. One may contrast this dominant emphasis with Luther's affirmation that as Christ's brother or sister, 'like him, I obtain all, eternal righteousness, eternal wisdom, eternal strength, and become lord and reign over all. The stomach will not hunger, sins will not oppress, I will no more fear death, nor be terror-stricken by Satan, and I will never be in want, but will be like Christ the Lord himself' (ibid. 218, 5). If we still feel these things, it is because 'feeling and faith are two different things' (ibid. 244, 13).

[96] *Sermons I*, 245; see also *Sermons on John 14–16*, 137–8. 'Then a person thinks this way: Now, Lord Jesus, I will serve you, die and live for you, and patiently suffer all that is disagreeable from you and from men; do with me as you will' (*Sermons I*, 110).

[97] *Sermons of Martin Luther*, vii. 222–3, 11–14. In a way similar to some of Augustine's exposition, Luther interprets Jesus' prohibition of Mary touching him (John 20: 17) as a correction of her looking upon him wrongly, taking only bodily, fleshly pleasure in his being alive again (ibid. ii. 250-1, 5).

In everything we must rely wholly on Christ—which affirmation brings us to the centre of Luther's concern: that we above all put no confidence in our own works; for if we do, all is lost. We contributed nothing to that work of Christ by which he overcame sin, death, and the devil; therefore, to rely on our own efforts or to suggest any supposedly necessary additions to what Christ has done is poisonous.[98] We must not 'stay in Moses' school', for any effort at all to become holy through our own works is tantamount to denying the resurrection.[99] Indeed, the devil's 'whole skill consists in using this image of our goodness to snatch from our eyes the image of the Man who died and rose again'.[100] If we begin to look at ourselves, we will see our sins; and if we start to look at our sins, they will destroy us.[101] By contrast, looking to Christ we can say, 'No matter how much sin I have committed, even more than ten worlds can commit, I still know that Christ's death and resurrection is far greater. Swiftly fling out that defiance and boast, not of yourself or your righteousness, but of the fact that Jesus Christ died and rose again for you.'[102] Only by knowing that our sins have been laid upon Christ, where they cannot rest but are swallowed up by his

[98] *Sermons of Martin Luther*, iv. 274, 23; see also e.g. ibid. ii. 261, 29; iii. 57, 33; *Sermons on John 14–16*, 348; *Sermons I*, 63. 'By virtue of Christ's resurrection we obtain remission of sin, every namable element not from Christ being completely excluded, and the honor given to him alone. What does the work, the ability, of all mankind amount to when it comes to accomplishing or meriting a thing of such magnitude as remission of sins and redemption from death and eternal wrath? How will it compare with the death and shed blood of the Son of God, with the power of his resurrection? How will it divide honors with him?' (*Sermons of Martin Luther*, vii. 198, 10).

[99] *Sermons on John 14–16*, 295–6; *Sermons on John 1–4*, 139; *Sermons of Martin Luther*, iii. 199, 8. 'I shall suffer myself to be crucified and shall rise. Those who believe that I have died for them, I shall draw after me, although they cannot enter heaven by their own strength. Thus he places us on his shoulders and bears us up to the place to which he ascends. Hence, our salvation is not by our strength, but by that of another' (ibid. 450, 65).

[100] *Sermons I*, 240. In a particularly moving assertion, Luther claims that any thoughts that do not result finally in comfort come not from Christ but from the devil (*Sermons of Martin Luther*, ii. 331, 28).

[101] *Sermons of Martin Luther*, ii. 242, 9.

[102] *Sermons I*, 242. If, by chance, conscience should at some moment report something positive, we still should not count on it, for it is likely to be beset with doubts later. Rather, 'even though I may have lived a good life before men, let everything I have done or failed to do remain there under the judgment seat as God sees fit, but, as for me, I know of no other comfort, help, or counsel for my salvation except that Christ is my mercy seat. . . . Thus faith remains pure and unalloyed because then it makes no pretensions and seeks no glory or comfort save in the Lord Christ alone' (ibid. 282).

resurrection, can we achieve the peaceful conscience we so desperately need; for the righteousness he promises us is a concealed righteousness, hidden from us on this earth.[103]

Apparently, however, Luther is not satisfied that this righteousness remain *wholly* hidden, for he insists that if the miracle of the resurrection does not make a change in us, quickening our hearts and producing 'new thoughts, new knowledge, new forces, life, joy, comfort and strength', then 'the story has been learned in vain'.[104] We must both feel its power ('How is a dead man profited, however much life may be preached to him, if that preaching does not make him live?') and 'practice the apostles' teaching of its essential fruits'.[105] However, we must be careful to keep clear on the point that, for Luther, changes of heart and life that spring from the power of Christ's resurrection within us must by no means be confused with efforts to become righteous before God by our own strength.

With respect to the implications of the resurrection for our role in this world, Luther, like Augustine, puts much heavier emphasis on the preaching of the Gospel than upon other kinds of activism in society—in fact, he speaks even more explicitly to that effect, attributing to Christ the words: 'through my resurrection I have entered into that glory where I shall reign forever over all creatures at the right hand of my Father. Therefore I send you also forth in like manner to be my messengers, not to engage in temporal affairs,

---

[103] *Sermons of Martin Luther*, ii. 189-90, 13; 266, 39; iii. 151, 48; *Sermons on John 14-16*, 346-7. Luther makes frequent reference to Rom. 4: 24 and also to John 16: 10.

[104] *Sermons of Martin Luther*, ii. 285-6, 57. See also ibid. iii. 109, 33; viii. 144, 7.

[105] Ibid. vii. 217, 1; 218, 2. He goes so far as to say that the one who has experienced God's grace and forgiveness 'can now readily resist sin' (ibid. viii. 156, 1) and ought to 'strive to become more and more godly' (ibid. ii. 316, 6)—which seems to be at some distance both from Luther's insistence upon the hiddenness of Christ's righteousness in us and his vigorous denunciation of human effort. One suspects that, like most preachers, he handles the problem of formally conflicting but practically complementary imperatives by coming down now on one side, now on another (though he is consistent even at the formal level in so far as one keeps in mind his strong emphasis on the divine omnipotence and rejection of free will, such that anything the person in Christ achieves, he or she achieves only by the grace of God at work within, and in faith that the battle has already been won beforehand by Christ (see e.g. ibid. iii. 85, 31; also *Sermons on John 6-8*, 410; *Sermons on John 14-16*, 422).

but to . . . preach the Word.'[106] Luther interprets Christ's coming
to the disciples through closed doors as demonstrating not only his
ability to be present with us at all times, unhindered by worldly constraints, but, and very strikingly, 'he also shows that wherever he
comes with his government and rule, through the office of the
Word, he does not come with a great noise, with storm and com-
motion, but very orderly; not changing nor breaking anything in
the outward affairs of human life and government.'[107] Luther's
'two kingdoms' theory comes through clearly, for he insists that
while Christ ascended not to sit idly but to take charge and rule as
a king, and while we should think of him as being present and
reigning among us, yet his kingdom is spiritual and does not have
to do with temporal things.[108]

But to say that Christ's kingdom is spiritual is hardly to imply
that it lacks present-day consequence.

If I have Christ, the great treasure and Lord over death, sin, devil, and hell,
I shall not despair, and I know that I, too, shall be Lord over these things,
and I, too, have eternal life. . . . What could bring a person greater joy than
to be told that he need not die? That's why this assurance of Christ is
unfathomable.[109]

In the hour of our death and in any other moment of distress, we
may have comfort: any victory of death or the world is at worst
temporary.[110] The resurrection makes sure God's promise that we
shall at last be saved.[111] 'In contrast with death and the devil's

[106] *Sermons of Martin Luther*, ii. 388, 23. See also ibid. i. 57, 96; ii. 251, 6;
Catholic Epistles, 10. He thought the Pope erred in seeking to make converts by force,
since the Lord commanded only preaching (*Sermons of Martin Luther*, iii. 201, 18).
Like Augustine, Luther also believed that we rightly manifest the power of the resurrection when we serve the Church for its consolation and growth (ibid. ii. 289,
14, 15).
[107] *Sermons of Martin Luther*, ii. 384, 12, 13.
[108] Ibid. iii. 19, 6; 117, 15: ii. 385, 16-22. However, he also spoke of the great
works Christians would do because of Christ's Lordship, and gave Jesus to say: 'I
shall first leap from death into life, from the cross and the grave into everlasting
glory, divine majesty, and might. Then . . . all creatures will have to be subject to
me. Then I shall be able to say to you apostles and Christians: "You, Peter or Paul,
you must go forth and overthrow the Roman Empire if it refuses to obey My Word"'
(*Sermons on John 14-16*, 85-6). Like many great people, Luther was not entirely
consistent, as has often been remarked!
[109] *Sermons I*, 114.
[110] See e.g. *Sermons of Martin Luther*, i. 195, 58; ii. 27, 22; v. 156, 39; *Sermons
on John 1-4*, 359; *Sermons I*, 235, 240.
[111] *Catholic Epistles*, 116.

might we are small and slight; but if we cling to Him who says: "*I, I have overcome the world,*" we shall see whether all the world, death, and the devil have jaws large enough to swallow us.'[112]

Barth's well-known dialectical Yes and No to this world resound when he speaks of the work of Christ: 'Who can and dare seriously say *Yes* to a life for whose depravity the Lord could atone only on the cross? And who can and dare say *No* to a life for whose justification He rose from the dead?'[113] In such a world, we will inevitably come up against devastating limits: illness, sin, occurrences beyond our control, death. But if Jesus lives, then all of these do not have the finality we supposed. Indeed, all our calculations are then plainly off.[114] We do not really know this, though, until we have come to the absolute end of our own resources and of our hopes for assistance from progress, evolution, or enlightenment.[115] Thus, the Church fails at the essential point if it fails to bring us to the end of ourselves: if it does not bring us to the cross, the resurrection will be lacking as well.[116] But once we are raised together with Christ, we will know that God's tender mercy has visited us and has also given significance to the world we live in, bestowing upon it, as well as us, a new quality.[117] We will, then, take the world seriously without relying upon what it, apart from God, provides for us.

---

[112] *Sermons on John 14-16*, 416. In one sermon for the Sunday after Easter, Luther treats the advantages of the resurrection at some length: 'But what does the resurrection advantage us? It has already brought us this gain: our hearts are enlightened and filled with joy, and we have passed from the darkness of sin, error and fear into the clear light; the Christian is able to judge all sects, all doctrines of devils that may arise on earth. . . . Secondly, through Christ's resurrection we have a good, joyful conscience, one able to withstand every form of sin and temptation and to maintain a sure hope of eternal life. The great glorious gifts and blessings of the resurrection are these: the Gospel, Holy Baptism, the power of the Holy Spirit, and comfort in all adversity. . . . But these do not represent the consummation of resurrection blessings. We must yet await the real, the perfect, gifts. . . . If we continue in faith, not allowing ourselves to be turned away through wrath and impatience, God will bring us the real, eternal blessings, called "perfect gifts," the possession of which excludes error, stumbling, anger, and any sin, whatever' (*Sermons of Martin Luther*, vii. 293-4, 10-2).

[113] *God's Search*, 215. [114] *Come Holy Spirit*, 166-8.

[115] Ibid. 120, 149, 154. Regarding 'philosophical' approaches to death, he says, 'Do you really believe that is why Jesus came to earth, why He agonized and suffered, why He was crucified and rose again on the third day, to become merely a symbol for the truth—which reality is no truth that eventually everything will be all right?' (ibid. 153).

[116] Ibid. 198. [117] Ibid. 189; *Word*, 90-1.

Further, we will seek that God's touch might be manifest somehow in our lives—not that we can reproduce Christ's ways and
works, but just that some change might be worked in us.[118] This
change is not 'a new form of godliness' but the fruit of the resurrection, and in the resurrection we will discover a new motivation.[119] Barth's Easter words to prisoners are particularly moving:

> It is vitally important for us to let grow the tiny root of confidence, of
> earnestness, of joy, which seeks ground in our hearts and minds, in our
> thoughts and intentions and opinions. . . . It is truly impossible that Jesus
> Christ proclaims: 'I live,' without the answer arising from somewhere
> within us: 'yes, you live, and because you live, I shall live also, I may and
> I can and I want to live!' . . . It is all-important now that not one among
> us consider himself excluded, either too great or too insignificant or too
> godless.[120]

Barth, however, does not limit his understanding of the impact of
the resurrection to our personal life. He takes it as the standpoint
from which we must think about the whole society, with the functioning of which Barth is more engaged than are the other three
theologians. On the one hand, 'the place we have taken in Christ
over against life is so unique and preeminent, that we cannot limit
our conception of the Kingdom to reform movements and social rev-
olutions in the usual sense'; but still, 'we must enter fully into the
subversion and conversion of this present and of every conceivable
world, into the judgment and the grace which the presence of God
entails, unless, remaining behind, we wish to fall away from
Christ's truth, which is the power of the resurrection'.[121]

---

[118] *Come Holy Spirit*, 198.

[119] *Word*, 285–7; note, of course, the similarity to Luther's rejection of 'works'
but insistence that there be fruit in our lives. Says Barth: 'The new life revealed in
Jesus is not a new form of godliness. That is the reason why Paul and John are interested not in the personal life of the so-called historical Jesus but only in his resurrection. And that is the reason why the synoptic accounts of Jesus can really be
understood only with Bengel's insight: *spirant resurrectionem*' (ibid. 285–6).
Similarly, the reality of the cross that precedes resurrection will be seen in our lives
not through self-negation but through genuine repentance (*Come Holy Spirit*, 70–1).
Regarding self-negation: 'The cross is erected, but the resurrection is not preached;
and therefore it cannot really be the cross of Christ. It is some other cross. The cross
of Christ does not need to be erected by us!' (*Word*, 205).

[120] *Deliverance to the Captives*, 33.

[121] *Word*, 298, 318. 'The *resurrection* of Jesus Christ from the dead is the power
which moves both the world and us *because* it is the appearance in our corporeality
of a *totaliter aliter* constituted corporeality. More we cannot say' (ibid. 323; emphasis original).

The consequences of the Easter Gospel are so great that Barth finds it astounding that we ignore and strive against it.

Why is not the Gospel preached from every pulpit? Why is it not heard in all our human constraints, upon all deathbeds and at the side of all graves? Why do we not really know that all have been made alive through the mercy of God? And even when we do know it, why is it not the one and the only truth against which there is not anything of importance to invalidate it, because it pierces everything, suspends everything and renews everything? These questions are synonymous with the question: why do we still think that we can live our life without God, even for one hour?[122]

Thielicke adds little that is truly distinctive to the discussion of the resurrection and the Christian life, though he is as definite as the others that it changes everything, that its truth is quite literally a matter of life and death.[123] If we are in painful and perplexing circumstances, we can be assured by the resurrection that all the paths of life find their end at the throne of God.[124] Just to read the Gospel accounts of the resurrection in the presence of death is to feel their power.[125] Because the living Christ is with us, we know both his comfort and his summons in the present moment.[126] If we are irritated by 'weaklings and pests', we may find our love for them stirred by the fact that Christ rose on their behalf.[127] In sum, 'either Jesus Christ has breached the front of death—or the boundary of death defines the meaning of our life, delivering us over to the philosophy of Let us eat and drink, for tomorrow we die'.[128] 'If I were not also convinced that this One Man also carries his own, and therefore me too, right through the same death, then I wouldn't even dare to ask the question for what is being played out in my life.'[129]

REFLECTIONS

What may strike us most immediately about the preaching of the resurrection in Augustine, Luther, Barth, and Thielicke is that it never flinches when contemplating the power of God, in contrast to

---

[122] *Come Holy Spirit*, 156. [123] *I Believe*, 149; *Silence of God*, 78–9.
[124] *Faith*, 134. [125] *I Believe*, 162; *Christ and the Meaning of Life*, 49.
[126] *Silence of God*, 87; *How Modern*, 20.
[127] *Faith*, 32. One may note a strong similarity to Luther here.
[128] *How Modern*, 26. [129] *Christ and the Meaning of Life*, 49.

much contemporary discussion relating to the problem of evil. Historical evils have been so overwhelming that contemporary theologians of many stripes have bolstered their confession of the all-loving nature of God by suggesting that constraints of one kind or another prevent God from eliminating these evils, which he surely would at least mitigate if only he could. The short-term psychological gain from this procedure, however, obviously brings heavy long-term loss: if God can do nothing about historical evils except, perhaps, be present with sufferers, then it is hard even to conceive the hypothesis that he can ever give them meaning by bringing them to serve his sovereign purposes for good; and it is equally hard to believe that he has truly conquered that final evil, death. Hence, we are left to our own likewise impotent devices. If, however, we believe firmly in the finality of God's power as evidenced in the resurrection, we may have to hold in abeyance, not our moral horror at historical evil, but our tendency to use that horror to undo our confidence in the only one who can deliver us from it.

The strong, and doubtless related, contemporary tendency to do 'Christology from below' or to espouse some form of kenosis (and also to give little weight to the Gospel of John, as far as statements relating to anything pertaining to 'the historical Jesus' are concerned) similarly works against the attribution of full divine agency to Jesus that is so prominent in Augustine and Luther.[130] Feminist scholars and preachers who see substitutionary views of the atonement as both evidencing and fostering a kind of 'child abuse' might at least recall the possibility of free self-sacrifice rather than victimization on the part of one who has power both to lay his life down and to take it up again.

With respect to the nature of the resurrection, one might ask if it manifests not admirable courage and intellectual sophistication but, rather, a curious naïvety for some contemporary scholars to assert that the resurrection could not be any sort of bodily reality, on the grounds that such a thing is simply not a historical possibility. Of course it is not, and most serious theologians and preachers have never supposed it was. The issue is not what our created reality can generate, but who God is and what God can do. And, of course,

---

[130] Thielicke does not wish to espouse a 'Christology from above', but he also does not wish to have what Jesus can be understood to have done and to be limited by historically derived presuppositions (see *Evangelical Faith*, ii, trans. and ed. G. W. Bromiley (Grand Rapids, Mich.: Eerdmans, 1977), 268–73).

doubt about that is not going to go away; nor should it be punished or ignored.

On another side of the issue, it will be interesting to see how the disembodied interactions of cyberspace affect the felt *desirability* of a bodily resurrection. Various reports suggest not only that many relish the opportunity to try out identities to which their physical bodies offer opposition (for instance, persons may present themselves as being of a different gender or ethnic background, or as possessed of certain highly desirable attributes), but also that these new identities may intrude powerfully—often in confusing, confounding ways—on their daily lives as embodied persons. We may be seeing the beginning of a modern rejection of the body that rivals that of ancient Gnosticism. 'Netizens' may not share the apostle Paul's fear of final disembodiment (2 Cor. 5: 4) and might logically come to prefer a spiritualized interpretation of the resurrection of Christ.

I suspect, in any case, that the resurrection often may not be a good apologetic starting-point, since it invites endless intellectual debates on both the plausibility and, perhaps, the desirability fronts. As with most apologetic issues, the resurrection may best come to the fore when a needy or at least curious enquirer asks a reason for the hope that is in one (1 Pet. 3: 15). None the less, contemporary preachers would do well to emulate the intellectual seriousness with which all the figures we have considered tackled the particular forms that doubt (and heresy) took in their own time, rather than mumble evasively and resort to something entertaining. I am convinced that today's congregations, like earlier ones, *will* listen to serious theological discussion if they are persuaded that the issues at stake matter.

To take the questions of one's own day seriously, however, is by no means the same thing as meekly submitting to its criteria of judgement. The Gospel has always been in the business of breaking through world-views, not of baptizing them; and stopping with any version of the humanly or naturally 'possible' has ever been a means of losing all. To confess that the work of the Spirit is necessary in order that we might believe will no doubt continue to offend many as being undemonstrable and obscurantist; but to deny that possibility is one more way of refusing to allow God alone to be God—the ancient sin of pride.

Preachers who know that they must somehow, week by week, address how their congregations live their lives need to consider that unbelief at the centre—with reference to the resurrection—gives us nothing to preach that differs significantly from what is offered by therapists, entertainers, country club managers, and political visionaries. And let it be clear that to try to seize some existential 'meaning' from the resurrection without the fact of the resurrection will not do, for such a procedure does not carry conviction against the actual finality of death—a death that slays all merely earthly meanings as surely as it does those who cling to them. It is not that the preacher who believes in the resurrection will speak of nothing else, but rather that belief in the resurrection and in the kind of God the resurrection entails will put its mark on everything the preacher says and thinks, even as it should put its mark on the way the faithful view every aspect of their lives.[131] And perhaps that is the problem. On the one hand, we in our day have been told that it is not healthy (or, some may bravely assert, realistic) for us to feel that keen misery and helplessness that Luther thought it was necessary that we face if we are rightly to know our need of Christ and the true wonder of his grace. On the other hand, the part of us that obediently, but not quite successfully, hides from that misery and helplessness may be afraid to hope for too much. Our actual despair may be so deep that we dare not even entertain the idea that the Gospel means, as Barth said, that at last 'there will be resurrection, resurrection and life on the battlefield and final resting place of our existence; fullness of our emptiness; truth of our parables; the goal of pilgrimage; and God's work where our works are at an end'.[132] The Gospel is still better news than we can readily believe. And that is why we still need preachers.

---

[131] It may be noted that one can read not just individual sermons but, on occasion, a whole volume of sermons by, say, Thielicke or Luther, without the resurrection as such coming up for much, if any, discussion; but the sermons as a whole breathe the spirit of resurrection faith (see e.g. Thielicke's *How To Believe Again* and *Life Can Begin Again* and Luther's *Commentary on the Sermon on the Mount*, ed. and trans. Jaroslav Pelikan, in *Luther's Works*, xxi (St Louis: Concordia, 1956), 3-294).

[132] *Come Holy Spirit*, 187.

13

Transformation Ethics: The Moral Implications of the Resurrection

BRIAN V. JOHNSTONE, CSsR

'If Christ has not been raised, then our preaching is in vain and your faith is vain' (1 Cor. 15: 14). There can be no doubt that the resurrection of the crucified Jesus is the fundamental belief of Christians. Yet that belief does not seem to have left any mark on Christian ethics or moral theology, at least as this is portrayed in the standard texts. There is little here of the drama of those mysterious moments we read of in the New Testament, when consciousness moved from non-recognition to recognition of the risen Lord, and the disciples were transformed from unbelievers to believers and impelled to a mission in the service of others. These experiences were the beginning of Christianity, and must have an impact on the way in which Christians understand the moral life. The purpose of this chapter is to explore what that impact might be.

First, there is a need to explain some of the basic terms that will be used here. 'Christian morality' refers to the ways in which Christians actually live out their calling. The 'moral tradition' of the community would include the memories, stories, lives of the saints, songs, controversies, and doctrines which have been passed down from generation to generation and which have shaped the way people lived, and in turn have been shaped by their lives. 'Christian ethics' means the systematic reflection on that lived morality. 'Moral theology' is the endeavour to derive a way of life from the sources of Christian belief, Scripture and tradition. Although a distinction can be drawn between the two, this is not necessary for the purposes of this enquiry. The aim will be to suggest ways in which belief in the resurrection might shape how Christians understand and order their lives.

What is the meaning and task of ethics? Ethics is often under-

stood as a process of systematic reflection that seeks to describe, justify, and where appropriate, challenge and correct the customs that
regulate human life in community. It seeks, therefore, to distinguish
between what is merely customary and rules of action which can
be grounded on secure principles. Ethics is also concerned with
delineating the qualities of character or virtues which would mark
the kind of person one ought to become. In contemporary writing,
the ethics of virtue have become, for many, the primary object of
interest. Ethics has a further more fundamental, if less obvious, role
in shaping our vision of life; it trains us to see rightly, and thus to
appreciate the elements which make up a genuinely good life. In
this context, ethics may provide an account of what it means to
adopt a moral point of view, as distinct from mere interested calculation or a concern for aesthetic form. An ethic is displayed not
only, or primarily, in systematized prescriptions or tables of virtues,
but in narratives. Some of these offer 'experiments', ways of living
the good life which have been tested in the community and are
testified to as providing authentic fulfilment. While the narrative
has primacy, the development of an ethic calls for the elaboration
of the ontological implications of these narratives, specifically in
terms of the nature of the human person as a moral agent and the
nature of virtue and vice. This chapter will propose that the resurrection narratives and the doctrine that derives from them have a
threefold role with regard to Christian ethics. First, they modify the
moral point of view; second, they offer a new and distinctive vision
of life, which makes possible a Christian critique of culture; third,
the vision provides a principle for interpreting virtue in an authentic Christian way.

THE RESURRECTION IN CHRISTIAN ETHICS AND MORAL THEOLOGY

A review of some scholarly texts of Christian ethics and moral theology indicates that authors have given the theme of the resurrection
only a marginal importance, if that. In Christian theology there are
two major currents of reflection, one beginning with the divine, the
other with human experience. The first might be represented by
Gustafson's account of the ethics of Barth and Bonhoeffer in his *Christ*

d the Moral Life.[1] For these classic authors, reality is defined in terms
the language of faith: Jesus Christ *is* reality. However, even this
.ristological concentration does not lead to any specific focus on the
ent of the resurrection. It is not the salvific events which are para-
)unt, but those categories which are more readily recognizable as
1ics. For example, the first chapter of Barth's *Ethics*[2] is entitled 'The
ality of the Divine Command'. Among authors who begin their
lections with human experience we could mention James M.
istafson himself. In his personal version of Christian ethics, as devel-
ed in his *Ethics from a Theocentric Perspective*,[3] it is religious experi-
ce, specifically the experience of piety, taken in the sense of a
nerally available type of human experience, that provides the foun-
tion. In Gustafson's thought the person of Jesus has significance
ly as the one who incarnates theocentric piety and fidelity.[4] Here,
: might say, the realm of faith is defined in terms of a general
man reality. As might be expected, in the second approach the
ent of the resurrection does not figure at all.

In Roman Catholicism the manuals which dominated moral the-
)gy from after the Council of Trent (1545-63) were concerned
th instructing confessors in the adjudication of individual sins in
: sacrament of confession: they are concerned with command-
ents and individual sins, not with events such as the resurrection.
more contemporary Roman Catholic studies there is a division
alogous to that already mentioned in other than Roman Catholic
:ology. Broadly speaking one looks to a 'faith ethic', the other to
'autonomous ethic' founded on human reason. According to the
:t view, Christian morality derives from faith: it may indeed
:lude insights from more general ethical wisdom, but where it
es, these are transformed so as to become the proper material of
lief. The moral theology of Servais Pinkaers reflects this position.
his most recently published work[5] the resurrection is mentioned
ce or twice, but is by no means a major theme, and is not

James M. Gustafson, *Christ and the Moral Life* (Chicago: University of Chicago
ss, 1968).
Karl Barth, *Ethics*, trans. T. Bromiley (London: SCM, 1981).
James M. Gustafson, *Ethics from a Theocentric Perspective*, vol. 1: *Theology and*
ics (Chicago: University of Chicago Press, 1981).
Ibid. 276.
Servais Pinkaers, *The Sources of Christian Ethics* (Washington: Catholic
.versity of America Press, 1995).

even noted in the index. Bernard Häring's second text[6] rejects the autonomy view as represented, for example, by Franz Boeckle,[7] and considers the task of moral theology to be the exposition of the call to faith. Häring is strongly influenced by the theology of the cross, as expounded by Moltmann and Käsemann, and emphasizes this so much that it overshadows the brief mention of the resurrection. The resurrection itself is invoked by Häring to confirm the value of freedom: it is not seen to have any proper significance for moral theology in its own right.

For those who uphold the idea of an autonomous ethic, the material content is provided by reason, while faith provides motivation or intention.[8] Charles E. Curran develops a theological 'stance', and seeks to indicate the significance of the fundamental givers of faith for moral theology. For example, in social ethics he writes that the fullness of resurrection destiny emphasizes the imperfections of the present and the need for change and growth.[9] The resurrection thus serves to support a conviction that could well be grasped by human reason in a general, neutral sense, independently of faith. However, the link between resurrection and change is not explained; nor is it clear why precisely a resurrection belief would generate these insights. In the writings of Klaus Demmer, one expects to find a judicious care for methodological questions. However, in the one discussion of the resurrection that I have been able to find,[10] it has only an extrinsic role. It enables the believer to look beyond the reality of death, and so makes the moral life possible. More recently John Milbank[11] has written a work of extraordinarily wide scope and acute analysis, covering a vast range of theology (and social theory) but, strangely, with only a passing reference to the resurrection. There is only one major work in the field of moral theology dedicated to the resurrection: Oliver O'Donovan's

---

[6] Bernard Häring, *Free and Faithful in Christ, Fundamental Moral Theology* (New York: Seabury, 1978), 119-20.

[7] Franz Boeckle, *Fundamental Moral Theology* (New York: Pueblo, 1980).

[8] V. MacNamara, *Faith and Ethics* (Dublin: Gill and MacMillan, 1985).

[9] Charles E. Curran, *Directions in Fundamental Moral Theology* (Notre Dame, Ind.: University of Notre Dame Press, 1985), 52.

[10] Klaus Demmer, *Die Wahrheit Leben: Theorie des Handelns* (Freiburg: Herder, 1991), 32.

[11] John Milbank, *Theology and Social Theory: Beyond Secular Reason* (Oxford: Blackwell, 1990).

Resurrection and Moral Order.[12] Here the resurrection functions as a reinstatement of order in the world, which sustains the objective status of ethics. The resurrection belief itself does not shape or illumine the form of the moral life. F. X. Durrwell published *The Resurrection: A Biblical Study*[13] with the specific aim of restoring the resurrection to a central place in Catholic theology. Durrwell discusses at length the implications of this belief for the Christian life, but does so in such a way as to nourish religious sensibility or spirituality, rather than by addressing ethics as such. In dealing with relationships between the resurrection and ethics, we are therefore in an area without clearly marked paths, and what I offer here are merely tentative explorations.

Why might it be that authors have given so little attention to the theme of the resurrection, or even considered it worthy of inclusion in an exposition of the Christian way of life? In the Catholic tradition, moral theology was described as a work of reason illumined by faith. This meant that moral theology presupposed a theory of reason, even if this was rarely explained, and with that a set of notions which were considered specifically 'moral'. 'Faith' was usually taken to mean the data of 'revelation'—that is, Scripture and the tradition in the form of propositions. With its recognizable notions of the 'moral' such as commandments, virtues, and sanctions, moral theology could readily find corresponding material in revelation. However, since the resurrection was obviously something quite different, it appeared to elude consideration. Thus, as we have seen, on the few occasions when the resurrection was included, it was invoked to sustain general ethical themes such as freedom or change, and even here the connections were tenuous. It would have been anticipated that those styles of Christian ethics or moral theology that began 'from above'—that is, with the faith and with a theologically determined notion of reality ('Christ is reality')—would have been more likely to include the resurrection. But the authors do not appear to have adverted to the possibility that it is the resurrection belief above all which transforms a Christian interpretation of reality, and, because of this, must have a significant place in ethical reflection. Besides this, there is a further problem: if one begins with a theologically founded notion of 'reality', it is often very

[12] Oliver O'Donovan, *Resurrection and Moral Order: An Outline For Evangelical Ethics* (Grand Rapids, Mich.: Eerdmans, 1986).
[13] F. X. Durrwell, *The Resurrection: A Biblical Study* (New York: Sheed and Ward, 1960).

difficult to relate this to the concrete, contingent circumstances of life where ethical questions arise. And ethics 'from above' often seems formal and remote. No doubt it would seem all the more difficult to relate the reality of the resurrection to the situations of real life. Nevertheless, in what follows I shall attempt to do this.

THE RESURRECTION AND THE MORAL POINT OF VIEW: WHY BE MORAL?

In what has been said above, I have suggested that an ethics may provide either a particular way of construing the emergence of the 'moral point of view' or a response to the question, 'Why be moral?' However, before developing the argument, a clarification is needed. Should we regard the experience of the resurrection on the part of the women and the male disciples as an experience of a special— indeed, unique—kind, or should it be considered as essentially like a religious experience that any believer might have undergone in the past or that contemporaries might enjoy today?[14] The presupposition behind the latter claim (of essential sameness) is that religious experience is neutral with respect to traditions, so that such experiences can be detached from the traditions in which they occur, while still preserving their essential meaning. However, such a general notion of religious experience is neither attainable nor useful. To reduce the Easter experience to a general notion would be to leave out precisely what is most interesting about it, and precisely what engendered the kind of faith that could change the world. Such a reductive interpretation must be rejected as an example of untenable 'foundationalism'. The experience of the resurrection is the original experience, containing the specific dynamism within history that brought the tradition to life. To take tradition seriously requires that we take the originality and uniqueness of the initial experience seriously. The original experience is embedded in narratives which are handed on, providing the interpretations without which new experience cannot be recognized and encoded in the tradition.

The experience, as conveyed in the narratives of the New Testament, provides a way of interpreting the subsequent experience of Christians, and in so doing, modifies what we would call

---

[14] See Gerald O'Collins, *Jesus Risen* (Mahwah, NJ: Paulist, 1987), 115-17.

today the 'moral point of view'.[15] For much of modern philosophical ethics, the moral point of view must be expressible in terms of a rationality that is removed from any particular, historical tradition. Further, the rational principles on which morality is founded must be based on reciprocity.[16] Thus, ultimately, I choose to accept morality because there is something in it for me.[17] However, there is a radically different way of approaching the question. According to Emmanuel Lévinas, morality emerges primarily in encountering the face of the Other, prior to any ontology, and is characterized by absolute, non-reciprocal responsibility. I would suggest that we might say that morality emerges primarily in the encounter with the concrete presence, 'the face', of the other, especially the victim, and brings forth a response independent of any response on the part of the other.

Lévinas's account is developed in terms of Jewish prophetic eschatology.[18] I would suggest that Christians might learn from this, as we have done so often in the past, and discover therein how a Christian version of eschatology might contribute to an understanding of morality. The resurrection, for Christians, is the eschatological fulfilment, and contains within it the pledge of ultimate fulfilment. In the encounter with the risen Jesus, as presented in the narratives, there is a recognition of the face, identifiable as the victim, but now transformed. Such a meeting engenders a response which is total and absolute and expressed in terms of profound personal love. In the case of the human loved one, under the conditions of ordinary human life, love endures in an ongoing tension between potentiality and fulfilment, which ultimately yields to the reality of death. 'Death means that nothing will happen any more. No miracles, no surprises—no disappointments either.'[19] The play of love is finished, and nothing is left but memory shading into profound, irrevocable loneliness. However, in the resurrection narratives, something does happen after death: the interrelationship with Jesus, as person and not just as memory, continues. Further, the

---

[15] Cf. Kurt Baier, *The Moral Point of View* (Ithaca, NY: Cornell University Press, 1958), 210.

[16] John Rawls, *Political Liberalism* (New York: Columbia University Press, 1993), 17.

[17] Zygmunt Bauman, *Postmodern Ethics* (Oxford: Blackwell, 1993), 55.

[18] Emmanuel Lévinas, *Totality and Infinity* (Pittsburgh: Duquesne University Press, 1995), 22.

[19] Bauman, *Postmodern Ethics*, 100.

disciples' continuing love commitment to the person of Jesus is to be translated into service of those who are his (John 21: 15-17). This notion I draw from the New Testament apparition stories, which have a characteristic structure of recognition (of the risen Jesus by the disciples), followed by a sending on mission, sustained by personal love for the Risen One.[20] Thus, love for the risen Jesus generates responsibility, and this becomes absolute commitment to others, the victims and potential victims whom one encounters in the world. Christian morality, therefore, can never yield to forgetfulness and resignation to the fate of victims: it generates a love beyond the range of death, which moves the Christian to try to change the conditions which destroyed this victim, so that others may not be similarly destroyed. The victim rises again, not in vengeful memory, but in action to create a world where others may live. This, I would suggest, is the way in which the moral point of view emerges for Christian ethics. This does not prove that or why we should be moral; it displays what being moral ultimately means for a Christian: namely, to transcend oneself in the service of others, a transcendence which participates in the divine activity itself.

In Lévinas's account, the absolute, unlimited responsibility to the Other is projected by the infinite beyond ourselves. In the view which I have suggested, the absolute responsibility flows from an encounter with an Other who is divine: namely, the risen Lord Jesus. In meeting the Lord, a disciple encounters the divine power that raised him from the dead, and this power is communicated to her or him together with the mission to serve others. We participate in the divine activity which raised Jesus, and so participate in the absolute responsibility of the Father for the Son. This consideration also suggests a response, within a resurrection ethic, to the problem of ethical absolutes. Here I have taken the position that ethical reflection must begin and develop within a tradition. But this presents a serious problem: if ethical reflection functions within a historical tradition, and a living tradition is characterized by change, where is there a possibility for any absolute? A tradition which is 'radically open-ended'[21] would seem to have no absolutes, and without such lacks the ability to challenge all the distortions of responsibility which may appear in history and justify themselves as

---

[20] Xavier Léon-Dufour, *Resurrection and the Message of Easter* (London: Chapman, 1974), 235.

[21] Milbank, *Theology and Social Theory*, 416.

legitimate developments of the tradition at this historical moment. In the perspective which is being proposed here, absoluteness is grounded in the participation of human responsibility in divine responsibility, and established within history in the historical object of the divine responsibility: namely, Jesus, the one who is really risen. Responsibility to this real person founds our responsibility to all other persons, who are meant to share his destiny. It is, therefore, not so much a question of absolute norms, or absolute values, but primarily of absolute responsibility to persons.

As I shall explain more fully later, the power which raises Jesus is essentially non-dominative, non-violent. Thus, the love by which Christians seek to serve others cannot become the will to dominate and subtly coerce them, the kind of love impugned by Nietzsche,[22] without betraying its source. The will to serve is necessarily a will to raise up others, to fulfil their real needs and not the needs of those who serve.

THE RESURRECTION AND THE VISION OF LIFE

Lévinas contrasts what he calls 'the eschatology of messianic peace' and the 'ontology of war'.[23] We might follow this and suggest that for Christian theology it is the eschatology of the resurrection which points to an ontology of peace, as opposed to that of war or violence. By 'ontology' here I mean the constitutive structure of human, social reality, and with Lévinas, I propose that this is ultimately no irrevocable conflict, but reconciliation and concord. By violence is meant, in the first place, arbitrary domination over another, as in the Augustinian *libido dominandi*,[24] and, secondly, the 'violence' which separates all entities one from another in a world interpreted in terms of an ontology of difference.

Historically, the death of Jesus was brought about through the agency of the high priests carrying out their duties of preserving order under the Roman procurator. Jesus was considered dangerous because he might cause a disturbance, which Roman troops would suppress with great loss of life. Caiaphas then acted out of what he saw as his political and moral responsibility, to preserve peace.[25]

---

[22] Ibid. 288.   [23] Lévinas, *Totality and Infinity*, 22.
[24] See Milbank, *Theology and Social Theory*, 390.
[25] E. P. Sanders, *The Historical Figure of Jesus* (Harmondsworth: Penguin, 1992), 272.

From his perspective it was obvious that 'it is expedient for you that one man should die for the people, and that the whole nation should not perish' (John 11: 50). Pilate probably saw Jesus as a religious fanatic who could well cause serious disruption to law and order, and had him flogged and crucified. The whole episode, from a human point of view, was a banal, if brutal, act of judicial murder to preserve the structures of security and privilege which the powerful of this world call 'peace'. According to the perverted logic of the perpetrators, it was their role to preserve life, even if they had to kill to do so. Christian interpretation of the events gave them a very different significance. Jesus' death is a martyrdom through which 'he could vicariously set right a moral order disturbed by sin'.[26] His dying, therefore, completely subverts the pseudo-morality of Caiaphas and Pilate, and with that a large part of the political 'morality' of our world. The 'peace' of this world is declared a sham and perversion, and the vision of a new and authentic peace is opened up. This vision is displayed in the accounts of the resurrection and its meaning. The presence of the kingdom which he had announced and embodied in his preaching and healing had apparently been defeated and annulled by his condemnation and death. It is now triumphantly vindicated in his resurrection. The new order is established, and with it true, definitive peace. This new peace supplants, in principle, the false peace founded on violence, and opens up new possibilities for our world. Thus, I would suggest that we could say that the resurrection presents peace as a moral possibility in human history. It is something we can work towards, because it is already given in principle. It is not my intention here to identify the peace which is realized in the resurrection with 'worldly' peace: the latter must be constructed by human responsibility directing will and intelligence, which will never achieve a perfect result within human history. Nevertheless, because we are assured that the ultimate reality is peace, and that God is committed to realizing this, we can be sustained in our efforts to bring at least a minimum of peace into the apparently intractable circumstances of our world.

However, there is more to be said about the new order of peace, and to understand this, we follow Christian reflection in its movement from the resurrection to the doctrine of the Trinity. The Trinity can be understood, in the tradition, through the resurrec-

---

[26] O'Collins, *Jesus Risen*, 151.

tion.[27] The action realized in the event of the resurrection is the manifestation, in history, of the economic Trinity. The intimate link, in the tradition, between the resurrection and the Trinity, will be an important element in the argument to be developed here. With reflection on the Trinity, we move to the level of ontology and the ultimate nature of reality. Through its reflection on divine activity in history, manifest above all in the death and resurrection of Jesus and the conferring of the Spirit which followed, Christian tradition arrived at an understanding that the nature of the divinity, the absolutely ultimate reality, is one, and yet subsumes difference, specifically the distinction of the divine persons. In this vision of reality, difference is not constituted by violent self-assertion and opposition, but by relationship. The ultimate reality is that unity in relationship which is the Trinity itself,[28] in which there is relationship to another, but no domination, and differentiation without violence. Just as the resurrection narratives 'translate' into a way of being moral, so too, as developed into a Trinitarian theology, they provide a 'critical theory' which challenges the inherent violence of our culture and the philosophies which legitimate it. This they do by challenging the notion that violence is an ultimate, and therefore inevitable, element of our human world.

According to Milbank, there is a rift in our culture between the ontology of peace and the ontology of violence. The ontology of peace is borne by the tradition in the doctrine of the Trinity, where unity brings forth difference, and difference is held within unity.[29] This is in contrast with the ontology of violence, which is carried by a tradition arising from ancient paganism and articulated again and again throughout history. The most recent representatives of this Milbank sees in Nietzsche and his more recent epigones among the supporters of post-modernism.[30] There is an abiding element of violence deep within human cultures, and it may be worthwhile attempting to offer some explanation of this. There is an aspiration to transcend ourselves towards the Other in all of us; earlier, I tried to explain how this might be construed positively in terms of a resurrection vision and ethic. However, this aspiration frequently goes disastrously awry, perhaps when religion fails to lead us towards a

[27] Gerald O'Collins, *Christology: A Biblical, Historical, and Systematic Study of Jesus* (Oxford: Oxford University Press, 1995), 103.
[28] Milbank, *Theology and Social Theory*, 423.   [29] Ibid. 424.
[30] Ibid. 278.

genuine transcendence, and sweeps us towards a fascination with violence.[31] Such a cult of violence has shown itself many times in this century in bizarre and horrifying forms, very often justified by appeals to 'religion'. Against all such attempts to declare violence sacred stands the continuing challenge of the Trinitarian vision of genuine peace, which emerged from the resurrection of Jesus.

However, even the more familiar traditions that shape our society may not be immune from contamination by violence. The liberalism and neo-liberalism which increasingly dominate our politics may also be read as embodiments of ontological violence. This can best be explained by describing the historical context.[32] With the arrival of the Enlightenment, according to its philosophical expositors, humans were finally able to face the truth that the doctrine of the goodness of God, the world, and humankind were myths and nothing more. By accepting reason alone, man could discover the laws which really govern our world and human affairs. The basic law is that men seek to protect themselves against violence and death. If the whole society of human beings could recognize this, they would be willing to enter into a social contract, a rational society, a liberal democracy. In particular, they would establish rights so as to protect their safety, their property, and their lives. The ultimate aim is protecting the individual's property and security. Thus, our own dominant political culture, built essentially on repelling the (violent) intrusions of others by more violence is still committed to this dark view of reality as inherently conflicted, and founded on more violence, even if this is exercised in apparently pacific forms such as imposed contracts, bargaining which is less than truly free, and forced down-sizing. An ethic formed in the light of the resurrection would necessarily be critical of such a culture, and would impel its adherents to seek ways in which to transform it.

The second step in the argument was to show how the resurrection might engender a negative, critical theory, as a basis for challenging the inherent violence of our culture. The next step will be an attempt to show how, from the resurrection, a positive ethic can be constructed that might guide our efforts in the structuring of society. This will be an ethic of virtue, but virtue transformed in the light of the resurrection.

[31] Charles Taylor, 'Spirituality of Life—and Its Shadow', *Compass*, 14 (1996), 11.
[32] Gregory Baum, *Critical Theology* (Kansas City, Kan.: Sheed and Ward, 1994), 99.

RESURRECTION, JUSTICE, AND NON-VIOLENCE

The narratives and doctrine of the resurrection do not, of course, provide us with a particular account of virtues; but they may alert us to intimations of violence and oppression in some theories of virtue, and so provide a criterion by which to interpret and transform them. We can begin with a consideration of justice. Because it has its focus on one who was a victim of death-dealing oppression, a resurrection theology recognizes injustice particularly in this form. It establishes a ground of suspicion against all systems of order, in that it unveils the possibility that what is claimed to be order, may, in fact, be concealed violence, and what claims to serve peace may subvert it. In this way, it shares to some extent the determination of the early Nietzsche to expose unjust structures; it holds before our imagination always the collaboration of religion and state that killed the innocent Jesus. But it could never accept that the arbitrariness of institutionalized power reflects the definitive state of the human condition, as the later Nietzsche appears to have done. This would be to deny that the ultimate structure of reality is peace rather than violence. Further, Christian morality is sustained by belief in the divine power which overcomes the unjust sentence of death by resurrection. Accordingly, it aims at overcoming injustice by transforming the institutions which embody it and challenging the ideologies which legitimate it. I would suggest that authentic justice from the perspective of the resurrection must always be transformative justice. As such, it would be distinct from merely 'restorative' justice, which sees the proper work of justice as returning things to the way they were, presuming that the existing order must be just. Thus, the revelation of the in-breaking or ontological peace in the death and resurrection of Jesus radically transforms particular notions of justice.

How, then, might a resurrection ethic function in critically transforming particular notions of justice? We might consider some particular examples from the classic text of St Thomas Aquinas. Are there, perhaps, instances where elements that seem to be remnants of the past, embodying oppression and exclusion, have remained to distort complete justice? We might consider the following: St Thomas's arguments justifying the death penalty, arguments which appear to subordinate the individual to the community as part to whole (*ST* 2a. 2ae. 64. 2); his neglect of a specific discussion of non-combatant immunity (cf. *ST* 2a. 2ae. 40 ff.); and his view of the subordination of women in society (cf. *Supplement*, q. 39, a. 1). These positions may be attributable, at least in part, to a residue of Aristotelian notions of society. On the other hand, St Thomas's situating of the question of war specifically in the context of the context of the virtue of charity, and not that of law and justice, where later authors would have it, identifies the evil of war precisely as a violation of peace (*ST* 2a. 2ae. 39. introd.). His giving primacy to charity implies a transformation, in principle, of the antique notion of the virtue of justice.[33] Peace, as the peace of concord, consists of social order which reflects the interior ordering of the wills of the members of the community (*ST* 2a. 2ae. 29. 1 *ad* 1). In this social ontology, there is no place for that kind of order whereby prior disorder or violence is reduced to order by further violence. The resurrection ethic which I am seeking to develop would positively affirm this social ontology of peace. Thus, the resurrection and its implications might enable us to discern those features which must be rejected and those which could be accepted, as we seek to transform the traditions of the past and construct a more adequate notion of the virtue of justice.

There have been two traditions within the Christian tradition as a whole in relation to the questions of war and violence. Although the Catholic and main-line Protestant traditions came to adopt the 'just war' doctrine, there always remained currents deriving from the peace tradition of the earliest Christian communities. These were even institutionalized in the Catholic tradition by the division of vocations between 'lay' and 'religious', with the latter being committed to non-violence. The 'peace Churches' claim to have preserved the ancient tradition in a more authentic form. Christians have argued about whether or not they may go to war from at least the second century, and in so doing have cited the Scriptures to support their respective positions. Some passages were cited to support the case in favour (e.g. Luke 3: 14); others were cited against (Matt. 26: 52; Rom. 12: 19). However, whatever the force of such arguments, the real differences were not in the texts favoured, but in diverse visions of the world. If one conceives the role of politics as the maintaining of order in an actual or potential state of violence

---

[33] Milbank, *Theology and Social Theory*, 360.

by further violence, then one may well see war as a logical and legitimate extension of politics and a work of justice. On this view, a state which disturbs the balance of power endangers order in the world, and may be coerced by war, so that order may be restored. On the other hand, if one holds the priority of ontological peace, as has been explained previously, the violence of war must be seen as a tragic aberration, contrary to the fundamental nature of reality. This position would not inevitably lead one to absolute pacifism; this depends not only on one's vision of the world, but also on the ethical theory one adopts. Thus, a person may be committed to non-violence, but may not hold that this is an ethical absolute for all. Rather, a different vision leads to a different way of structuring the argument: in the first, the presumption is in favour of order and justice as sustaining order: in the second, the presumption is in favour of non-violence.[34] This was the position taken by the US Bishops in their document *The Challenge of Peace: God's Promise and Our Response*.[35] Some critics claimed that this was an implicit acceptance of the pacifist position, and thus an abandonment of the long tradition accepting the just-war theory. However, in view of the arguments which have been developed here, we might see it not as an abandonment of authentic tradition, but as an expression of a more fundamental current of the tradition: namely, the rejection of ontological violence in favour of ontological peace.

RESURRECTION AND EMANCIPATION

The goal of the Enlightenment was emancipation, and we cannot deny the gains it has brought, such as the recognition of human rights, freedom of religion, and democracy. Thus, while there has been much criticism of the Enlightenment both by post-modern philosophers and in recent Roman Catholic documents,[36] many still support its positive aspects.[37] Does the perspective which is being proposed here have any bearing on this question?

[34] cf. Brian V. Johnstone, 'Abandoning the Just-War Theory: The Development of B. Häring's Thought on Peace, 1954-1990', *Studia Moralia*, 33 (1995), 289-309.
[35] (Washington, 1983).
[36] Brian V. Johnstone, 'The European Synod: The Meaning and Strategy of Evangelization', *Gregoriamum*, 73 (1992), 469-87.
[37] Alain Finkielkraut, *The Defeat of the Mind* (New York: Columbia University Press, 1996).

Despite their rejection of the Enlightenment, post-modern philosophers—in particular, all the recent neo-Nietzscheans, if not Nietzsche himself, and Heidegger—want to affirm the emancipatory thrust of the Enlightenment. The question is whether the philosophical positions of these authors are consistent with such intentions. Milbank argues—rightly, I believe—that their commitment to emancipation is something they profess or will to believe, a *mythos*, but which ultimately cannot be shown to cohere with their own principles.[38]

What might be the position of Christians on this question? In the first place, I would suggest that it is precisely in the resurrection that, for Christians, liberty is manifested in its true significance. The self-gift of Jesus into death is a totally free act, as is the Father's raising of Jesus. Nevertheless, this freedom is not an unstructured freedom of arbitrary self-assertion. It is the expression of unity in community, of the ontology of peace, which finds its reality in the Trinity. It is actuated in the resurrection, and then becomes real in human history in the free response of faith of the disciples. For Christians, human freedom is participation in divine freedom, and thus shares analogously in the structure of that freedom. The realization of freedom is always in the direction of community, not the affirmation of one self against another. But neither is this community such that it would subsume the individual as a part of a greater whole. Thus, despite its failures in this respect in the past, the Christian tradition can sustain a commitment to freedom precisely by being faithful to its own fundamental beliefs.

These beliefs are carried through history by the tradition of the community. This tradition does not merely drift across time like a myth, however; it is rooted in history: namely, in the event of the resurrection of Jesus and the resurrection experiences of the disciples. These experiences engendered in them a commitment to mission, service, and the forming of community. Because the original experience of the free activity of God in raising Jesus is the experience of a reality, and because the experience of participating in this freedom led them to concrete acts of service in history, the Christian commitment to freedom is not mere myth, whatever may be the case with post-modern philosophy.

Belief in the resurrection does not, of course, supply reason with

---

[38] Milbank, *Theology and Social Theory*, 279.

a programme for the historical liberation of humankind; but the narrative of the divine freedom and the ensuing narratives of free human commitment to service stir imagination to discover how freedom may be further promoted, and moves reason to elaborate concrete projects on its behalf. Thus, because it calls on reason for practical guidance, the resurrection vision implies a trust in reason itself. In other words, the tradition sustains reason, and protects those who accept it from the profound loss of faith in reason which characterizes some versions of post-modernism. Reason in this case is sustained by a faith tradition, not by some 'foundation' outside tradition. Post-modern criticism has made it difficult to defend any such foundationalism; but, as I have tried to argue here, in the Christian tradition reason looks to no such extrinsic support. Indeed, we could say that faith in the resurrection sustains faith in reason.

With the discrediting of socialism, especially in its Marxist version, liberation theology seems to have lost something of its former vigour. Could the transformation theology which is being proposed here provide some support, or perhaps an alternative? The governing myth of liberation theology was the exodus, which gave faith a political orientation, relevant to the urgent need for political revolution in so many situations of oppression. However, precisely because it was so obviously relevant, it presented certain difficulties. There was a danger that it could legitimate certain concrete forms of political revolution as re-enactments of the exodus, and so confer on them a divine validity.

The 'myth' of resurrection, however, takes up and transforms the myth of the exodus. The resurrection experience, as I have tried to show, includes an experience of freedom and a commitment to bring freedom to others; it has an emancipative thrust. However, the resurrection cannot be linked immediately to any political programme, such as a liberating exodus in the shape of a revolution. Yet the resurrection is a real act of justice, and entails a radical judgement on all politics which is nothing but disguised violence in the interest of the powerful. This judgement frees us from the pseudo-claims of such a political order, and sets reason at liberty to discover strategies of change and new forms of communal order.

By way of introduction, we could take up a specific question raised by theologians in the past and today: namely, whether the women mentioned in some New Testament accounts were genuine witnesses of the resurrection.[39] O'Collins attributes at least some of the arguments against the validity of the experience and witness of women and in favour of the exclusive validity of male witness to prejudice against women. Following on from what I have suggested already, I would suggest that what is involved is not only prejudice, but a certain conception of social order, with its implied social ontology. As Milbank points out, the Greek conception of social order excluded women and children as participants.[40] This exclusive notion of society reflects that antique social ontology which is based on the suppression of (male) force or violence by greater (male) force or violence. This particular dispute about the validity of women's witness to the resurrection is, then, a reflection of a much more fundamental point. If one accepts the antique or contemporary ontology of violence, then one either accepts the prevailing of (male) force or seeks to defend the validity of women's social position in terms of modern rights theory, which is, as I have indicated, based on individualistic theories of rights, deriving from a version of the ontology of violence. If one adopts the Christian social ontology of resurrection and Trinity, then one will want to look elsewhere. The notion of complementarity is rejected by many women, and I would suggest that the reason is that it is often interpreted in terms of the prevailing of force over force. The social ontology of the resurrection may offer a quite distinct way of dealing with the question. In any case, the original experience of the Christian tradition includes the experience of women (in particular, that of Mary Magdalene), and the witness which flows from and is part of that experience includes the witness of women as much as that of men.

To pursue my suggestion that, at least sometimes, Christian theologians have accepted too much of the social ontology of the prevalence of force, I would point to the implied notion of social order in St Thomas's discussion of the ordination of women.[41] His argument is that since it is not possible in the female gender to signify eminence of degree, for a woman is in the state of subjection, it follows that she cannot receive the sacrament of orders.[42] Society is here conceived in terms of states of life in community, distinguished

[39] Gerald O'Collins, 'Mary Magdalene as Major Witness to Jesus' Resurrection', in *Interpreting the Resurrection* (Mahwah, NJ: Paulist, 1988), 22–38.

[40] Milbank, *Theology and Social Theory*, 368.

[41] Cf. William Shannon, 'Tradition and the Ordination of Women', *America*, 174/5 (17 Feb. 1996), 8–9.

[42] *Supplement*, q. 39, a. 1.

according to subjection. Perhaps St Thomas believed such subjection was of the order of nature. However, on examination, his argument here reveals elements of the ontology of violence. I have suggested that the feminist case is often presented in terms of a (modern) theory of rights, and so can be contaminated by the ontology of violence. It might be worth examining the possibilities of the ontology of peace as revealed in the resurrection. The fact that the experience of women was part of the historical elements of that original moment suggests that it may be worth following this up and discovering that the Christian tradition reflects the subjection of women not of itself, but when it has been infected by the ontology of violence and its implied notion of social order. Recognition of this would, of course, call for repentance for past failures and a determined effort to remove whatever elements of that ontology still remain.

LOVE AND ECOLOGY

Nietzsche, on the evidence, might be right. It might well be that there is sufficient reason to accept the ultimate interpretation of the world as ontological violence. If this were so, the will to power would rightly dominate all human relationships. If it is true that reality is characterized by ontological violence, that all desire carries within it the threat of its own destruction, and that identity is merely a rhetorical flourish, as post-modernists affirm, that relationships are the self-assertion of one against the self-assertion of the other, then the prospects of love are dim indeed.

The Christian hope is that love is not ultimately doomed. Rather, because Christians believe with resurrection faith that the person will not perish ultimately, but be realized in spirit and body—that is, in a fully personal way—they believe in the future of interpersonal love. Further, the person, through the body, is a telling of the story of the universe, the capacities of which have developed through evolution to the point of the emergence of a person who loves. That love is not only of the spirit, but of the body. The beloved is present to the lover as another self. In genuine love identity is not lost, but affirmed; yet in the mutual presence, identity is also shared. The sharing also includes the body, for it is only through the body that the spirit is present. When such presence is lost by the removal of one of the parties, by spatial separation, or even by death, personal love does not cease. Yet the story of that love is still bound to the story of the world. Only when the story of the world is complete will the story of that love be complete. And with the completion of the story of the world comes the resurrection of the body. Only then will that love be fulfilled, personally and bodily, by a body completely fulfilled. Death does not destroy that love. It has a future. Nor does the destruction of the body by the forces of nature after death destroy it. It will come to fruition. The fundamental assurance operating here is that the ultimate constitution of reality is not violence and destruction, but life and love. Dionysius the Areopagite (or, better, the author now identified as Pseudo-Dionysius of the sixth century) linked Neoplatonic Greek philosophy and the Christian mystical tradition. He taught that because of their unity all things are bound together in the intimacy of 'friendship'. It is because all things are united in this friendship that we can speak of the 'universe'. This word 'universe' indicates that the diversity of things exists not in separation but in comprehensive unity, whereby all things are bonded together in inseparable and everlasting unity.[43] The assurance of this is the resurrection of the Lord, body and spirit, and the promise of each person's ultimate resurrection, body and spirit. The form that the risen body will have, we do not know; that it will not be destroyed ultimately, we do know. In a resurrection theology, the desire of *eros* is not ultimately doomed by an inherent threat of destruction, but transformed.

Here I select just two questions that have been raised in contemporary debates, and relate them to the theology of the resurrection. One is the charge made against Christian theology by Thomas Berry and others that it has been guilty of anthropocentrism, and that it has been led to this by a theological concentration on redemption at the expense of creation.[44] Berry calls for a reversal of this one-sided emphasis.

However, I would reply that a theology of redemption which presented redemption in extrinsic legal terms referring only to humanity would indeed omit creation and nature and need to be corrected or replaced. But an adequate theology of redemption which includes

[43] *Oeuvres complètes du Pseudo-Denys l'Aréopagite*, trans. Maurice de Gandillac (Paris: Aubier, 1943), 107–8.
[44] Anne Lonergan and Caroline Richards (eds.), *Thomas Berry and the New Cosmology* (Mystic, Conn.: Twenty-third Publications, 1991), 15.

the resurrection, as it must if it is to be at all adequate, would include matter and nature. As O'Collins writes, the resurrection signifies the completion and personalization of matter, an ontological reality.[45] The need, therefore, is not to abandon the theology of redemption, but to develop an adequate theology of redemption as including resurrection.

The second problem is the basis of the positive value of nature. 'Deep ecologists' are concerned to establish the 'intrinsic value' of nature, as distinct from its merely instrumental value.[46] However, they seem to be at a loss when it comes to providing some ground for this intrinsic value. In a Christian theology of resurrection as transformation, nature is transformed, specifically in the person of the risen Lord, and will be definitely transformed in the kingdom. This transformation is the ground of nature's intrinsic value for a Christian believer.

An adequate theology of resurrection also provides a corrective to a theology which goes, in my view, to the opposite extreme. This seeks to overcome anthropocentrism and provide nature and the world with intrinsic value by 'divinizing' the world of nature itself. This would appear to be the approach taken by Sallie McFague.[47] While she insists on the transcendence of God, this seems to become lost or obscured as the argument progresses. It is interesting to note that although McFague deals with creation, incarnation, and eschatology at some length, she fails to mention the resurrection. A theology of the resurrection would see nature divinized in the body of Jesus as it enters in the most intense way into the divinity with the resurrection. Created reality and the world, however, do not themselves become the 'body of God' except in a derived and analogous sense. The uniqueness of Jesus and the transcendence of God are preserved. Created things are sacramental symbols, or icons, of the risen body of the Lord; but they are not themselves divinized.

The aim of this chapter was to offer arguments in favour of the thesis that the resurrection should have a central place in Christian ethics and moral theology, and to suggest how this might make a

---

[45] O'Collins, *Jesus Risen*, 178.
[46] Eric Katz and Lauren Oechsli, 'Moving beyond Anthropocentrism: Environmental Ethics, Development, and the Amazon', *Environmental Ethics*, 15 (1993), 49.
[47] Sallie McFague, *The Body of God* (London: SCM, 1993).

difference to those disciplines. The problem that has been addressed here is only an instance of a wider concern: namely, the unfortunate separation that has grown up between ethics and moral theology and the global vision of faith, embracing theology, spirituality, and scriptural studies. I am well aware that at least some of the arguments offered here may be found less than convincing. But at least what has been proposed may stimulate further reflection on that mystery on which our faith stands.

Index of Names

Abbott, W. 242 n.
Achtemeier, P. 14
Adams, J. L. 289 n.
Akiba, Rabbi 114, 117
Albertz, M. 227, 228 n.
Allen, W. 315
Allison, D. C. 18 n.
Alston, W. 12, 148-90
Alsup, J. E. 228-9, 232 n.
Anderson, B. W. 67 n.
Anderson, H. G. 309 n.
Anselm of Canterbury, St 207
Apollonius of Tyana 229
Aquinas, St Thomas 145, 168-9, 189,
    245, 351-2, 356-7
Aristeas of Proconnesus 229
Aristotle 101, 195, 352
Athanasius, St 168, 207
Audi, R. 47 n.
Augustine of Hippo, St 20 n., 43,
    308-38, 347
Aune, D. E. 16
Avis, P. 17 n., 55 n., 133 n., 134, 216 n.

Badham, L. 17
Badham, P. 17, 133-4
Baier, K. 345 n.
Bammel, E. 50 n.
Barbour, I. 303 n.
Barrett, C. K. 81 n.
Barth, K. 246 n., 247 n., 288 n.,
    308-38, 340-1
Barton, S. 7 n., 11 n., 28 n.
Bassler, J. M. 16
Bauckham, R. J. 208 n., 211 n.
Baum, G. 350 n.
Bauman, Z. 345 n.
Beardsley, M. C. 241 n.
Beasley-Murray, G. R. 73 n.
Becker, H. J. 224 n.
Becker, J. 225 n.

Beeck, F. J. van 28 n.
Beker, J. C. 81 n.
Bense, W. E. 289 n.
Berger, K. 220
Berry, T. 358
Berten, I. 14
Bertram, M. H. 309 n.
Betz, H.-D. 18 n.
Bietenhard, H. 70 n.
Black, C. C. 282 n.
Black, M. 69 n., 81 n.
Blake, W. 218
Blank, J. 14
Blinzler, J. 14, 224 n.
Bockelman, F. 242 n.
Bockmuehl, M. 49 n., 53 n.
Bode, E. L. 220 n.
Boeckle, F. 342
Boer, M. C. de 88 n., 103 n.
Bonhoeffer, D. 340
Borg, M. 287 n.
Bowden, J. 16 n., 28 n., 274 n., 278 n.,
    284 n., 304 n.
Boyd, G. A. 285 n.
Brahe, T. 194-5
Brennan, T. 145 n.
Briggs, C. A. 61 n.
Broer, I. 219 n., 220 n., 221 n.
Bromiley, G. W. 309 n., 336 n.
Brown, F. B. 61 n., 285 n.
Brown, R. E. 28 n.
    on burial of Jesus 15 n., 256, 257 n.
    on calling Jesus 'God' 75 n.
    on empty tomb 14
    on Gospel of Peter 252 n., 274 n.
    on the Q document 18
    on resurrection in John 224 n.
    on the risen body 165 n.
    on seeing the risen Jesus 135, 138 n.,
        142 n., 147, 154 n.
Bruce, F. F. 78 n., 81, 252 n., 282 n.

Brueggemann, W. 63 n.
Brun, L. 227, 228 n.
Buddha 292
Bultmann, R.:
  influence on North American
    scholarship 281
  on accounts of Jesus' appearances
    227, 228 n.
  on burial of Jesus 254, 273 n.
  on correspondence theory of truth
    216
  on criterion of dissimilarity 176
  on divine intervention 182
  on empty tomb 36 n.
  on faith 306
  on faith and history 288 n.,
    289-90, 294, 296
  on pre-Marcan traditions 181-2
  on resurrection and history 246 n.
  on Son of Man 72
Burhenn, H. 216 n.
Burrows, M. S. 51 n.
Bynum, C. W. 13 n., 20, 24

Caesar, Julius 246
Caiaphas 347-8
Caird, G. B. 287 n.
Campenhausen, H. von 14, 262, 273 n.
Capes, D. L. 76 n.
Caragounis, C. 71 n., 72 n., 73 n.
Carlson, J. 263 n.
Carnley, P. F. 28 n., 29-40
  on appearances of the risen Jesus
    160 n., 161 n., 165 n., 176 n.
  on experiencing God's Spirit 18
  on faith and science 293 n.
  on resurrection and history 246 n.
Carroll, J. T. 283 n.
Carson, D. A. 208 n.
Cartlidge, D. R. 143 n.
Casey, M. 70 n.
Castelli, E. 235 n.
Castelli, J. 90 n.
Cavallin, H. 20
Celsus 231 n.
Chadwick, H. 231 n., 234 n.
Charlesworth, J. H. 273 n., 281 n.
Chilton, B. 11 n., 281 n.
Clark, M. T. 308 n.
Clements, R. E. 65 n.
Cleomedes of Astupaleia 229
Coakley, S. 17 n., 19, 184-90, 216 n.,
  307 n.

Coats, G. W. 65 n.
Collins, J. J. 68 n., 103
Confucius 292
Conzelmann, H. 176 n., 226
Copernicus, N. 299
Corley, B. 274 n.
Coxe, A. C. 309 n.
Coypel, N. 19
Craig, W. L. 9, 140, 147 n., 216,
  249-83
Cranfield, C. E. B. 74 n., 81
Crossan, J. D. 14, 17, 249-86
Cullmann, O. 72 n., 210 n.
Curran, C. E. 342

Daalen, D. H. van 263
Dalferth, I. 26
Davidson, D. 239 n., 240 n.
Davies, W. D. 69 n.
Davis, S. T. 1, 3, 28 n., 157 n., 187,
  307 n.
  on analogy 13
  on apologetics 302 n.
  on the resurrection claim 8
  on seeing the risen Jesus 2, 9,
    126-47 *passim*, 160 n., 165 n.
Dean-Otting, M. 69 n.
Deichgräber, R. 82 n.
Delling, G. 220 n.
Delorme, J. 14
Demmer, K. 342
Denaux, A. 262 n., 284 n.
Denker, J. 274 n.
Derrida, J. 241 n., 285
Descartes, R. 296
Dibelius, M. 181, 227-8, 229
Doberstein, J. W. 309 n.
Dodd, C. H. 228
Donaldson, J. 143 n., 144 n.
Doyle, A. C. 200 n., 201 n.
Driver, S. R. 61 n.
Drury, J. 16
Dungan, D. L. 143 n., 300 n.
Dunn, J. D. G. 81 n.
  on Adam theology 79 n.
  on appearances of risen Jesus 35
  on Christianity's break with Judaism
    59 n., 60 n.
  on empty tomb 36, 37
  on moving from history to text 282 n.
  on reasons for Jesus' execution
    74 n.
Durrwell, F. X. 28 n., 343

Eddy, P. R. 272–86, 293 n.
Eichrodt, W. 63 n., 67 n.
Eliade, M. 66 n.
Eliezer, Rabbi 117, 118
Eliot, G. 231 n., 289 n.
Ellis, E. E. 78 n., 284 n.
Ernst, J. 16
Ernst, K. J. 309 n.
Essen, G. 244–5
Eusebius of Caesarea 208–9
Evans, C. A. 11 n., 281 n.

Farmer, W. 281 n.
Feiner, J. 237 n.
Feuerbach, L. 46, 219
Fichte, J. 241–2
Finkielkraut, A. 353 n.
Fiorenza, E. S. 189, 224 n., 284 n.
Fiorenza, F. S. 1–2, 18, 23 n., 28 n.,
    213–48
Fitzmyer, J. A. 14, 136 n., 282 n.
Flint, T. P. 15 n.
France, R. T. 282 n., 283 n.
Frederickson, P. 51 n.
Frei, H. W. 239 n., 240 n.
Frerichs, E. S. 60 n.
Freud, S. 96, 260
Friedrich, G. 224 n.
Fuller, R. H. 9, 14 131 n., 153–82,
    184, 185, 282 n.
Funk, R. W. 287
    on dying and rising gods 17 n.
    on faith and science 290, 296
    on the flight to Galilee 262 n.
    on Jesus' message 273
    on Peter's denials 263 n.
Furnish, V. P. 294 n.

Gadamer, H.-G. 216, 295 n., 301 n.
Gaffin, R. B. 80 n.
Galileo 287, 290, 299
Gallagher, J. 242 n.
Gallup, G. 90 n.
Gamaliel, Rabbi 122
Gandillac, M. de 358 n.
Gensichen, H. W. 224 n.
Gerhardsson, B. 281 n., 282 n.
Gerstenberger, E. 64 n.
Glasson, T. F. 73 n.
Gnilka, J. 14, 16
Goulder, M. 11 n.
Grant, R. M. 83 n.
Grass, H. 35, 135 n.

Green, J. B. 133 n., 276 n., 282, 283 n.
Gregory of Nyssa, St 189
Greshake, G. 238 n.
Grosheide, H. H. 66 n.
Grundmann, W. 14
Gundry, R. H.:
    on empty tomb 14
    on Mark's sources 16, 252 n., 260
    on the risen body 133 n., 140 n., 141 n.
    on women at Jesus' tomb 261–2
Gustafson, J. M. 340–1
Guthrie, G. H. 77 n.
Guthrie, S. 288 n.

Habel, N. 68 n.
Habermas, G. 293–4, 302 n.
Hadidian, D. Y. 283 n.
Hahn, F. 224 n.
Hamann, A. 20 n.
Hamerton-Kelly, R. 69 n.
Hamilton, W. 297
Hansen, W. A. 309 n.
Hanson, P. 66 n.
Hanson, R. P. C. 283 n.
Harakas, S. S. 27 n.
Häring, B. 342, 353 n.
Häring, H. 24 n.
Harnack, A. von 263
Harrelson, W. 67 n.
Harrington, D. J. 16
Harris, M. J. 75 n., 137 n.
Harrisville, R. A. 284 n.
Harvey, V. A. 239 n., 294–6
Hastings, J. 289 n.
Hauck, R. J. 231 n.
Hawthorne, G. W. 79 n.
Hay, D. M. 80 n.
Hebblethwaite, B. 21 n.
Heidegger, M. 216, 225 n., 234–5, 354
Heim, K. 303 n.
Henderson, E. 21 n.
Hengel, M. 59 n., 78 n., 84 n., 220,
    277–8, 305
Herrmann, W. 40
Hesse, M. 239 n.
Hick, J. 6, 10–12, 25, 29, 34, 37
Higgins, A. J. B. 283 n.
Hilberath, B. J. 219 n.
Hill, E. 309 n.
Hillerbrand, H. J. 309 n.
Himmelfarb, M. 68 n.
Hoffmann, P. 224 n., 228 n., 230 n.
Homrighausen, E. 309 n.

Hooker, M. 14, 16, 72 n.
Hoover, R. W. 17 n., 262 n., 263 n., 273 n., 287 n.
Horbury, W. 50 n.
Horgan, M. P. 283 n.
Horton, D. 309 n.
Howard, W. F. 73 n.
Hume, D. 195-8
Hunsinger, G. O. 239 n.
Hurst, L. D. 287 n.
Hurtado, L. W. 59 n.

Ignatius of Antioch, St 143
Irenaeus of Lyons, St 143-4
Ishmael, Rabbi 121

Jay, M. 145 n.
Jenni, E. 61 n.
Jeremias, J. 14, 176 n.
Jesus Christ:
　ascension of 110-11
　burial of 14-15, 253-7, 276-80
　and Christian ethics 4, 26-7, 45, 326-35, 339-60
　as coming Son of Man 70-3
　crucifixion of 204-5, 347-8
　as divine Glory 70-89
　empty tomb of 13-17, 36-7, 48, 56, 219-20, 221, 253-63
　and the Eucharist 2, 169, 208-12
　and the Holy Spirit 18, 39-40, 165
　incarnation of 145, 182-3, 203-5
　and the preaching of the resurrection 3, 8, 20-1, 308-38
　and the resurrection of creation 49, 51, 55, 56-8, 358-9
　risen appearances of 2, 9-13, 29-35, 37-9, 47, 126-47, 148-83, 220, 227-32, 263-5
　risen body of 24-5, 43-5, 139-40, 163-9, 182-3, 187-8, 237-8, 265 n.
　and special divine action 5, 21-3, 199, 201-6, 225-7, 303-4
　testimony to 2, 14, 19-202, 223-37, 242-8
John XXIII, Pope 242
Johnson, B. A. 274 n.
Johnson, E. A. 25-6
Johnson, L. T. 292 n.
Johnstone, B. V. 3-4, 339-60
Jonge, H. J. de 284 n.
Jonge, M. de 88 n.

Josephus, Flavius 101, 102, 105, 107-10, 113, 114, 122, 252 n., 279-80
Jung, C. 38
Junker-Kenny, M. 12 n.
Justin Martyr, St 143, 208

Kant, I. 198, 235
Käsemann, E. 81, 176 n., 342
Katz, E. 359 n.
Kaufman, G. D. 21 n., 231
Keck, L. E. 88 n., 296
Kee, H. 250 n.
Kelber, W. H. 17 n.
Keller, J. A. 302 n.
Kendall, D. 10, 11 n., 13 n., 15 n., 129 n., 277
Kepler, J. 196, 299
Kessler, H. 9, 216 n.
Kessler, W. T. 10 n.
Kierkegaard, S. 305-6
Kiessling, E. C. 329 n.
Kim, S. 71 n.
King, L. 35
King, M. L. 176-7
Kirk, A. 274 n.
Klappert, B. 25, 26
Kleinhenz, C. 20 n., 320 n.
Klooster, F. H. 216 n.
Kloppenborg, J. 275
Klostermann, E. 273 n.
Koch, K. 68 n.
Koester, H. 274 n., 281 n.
Kosanke, C. 12 n.
Kraus, H.-J. 63 n.
Kreitzer, L. J. 76 n.
Kremer, J. 238 n.
Kretzman, N. 15
Kuhn, T. 195 n.
Küng, H. 13, 14, 36
Künneth, W. 14
Kuntz, J. K. 66 n.
Kurzschenkel, W. 28 n.
Kuschel, K.-J. 219 n.
Kuss, O. 224 n.

Lactantius 257
Laudan, L. 301 n.
Leeuwen, C. van 66
LeMoine, F. 20 n., 320 n.
Lenker, J. N. 309 n.
Léon-Dufour, X. 14, 346 n.
Lessing, G. 217, 233-4

Levenson, J. 51 n.
Levin, S. R. 240-1
Lévinas, E. 235, 345-7
Lightfoot, R. 228 n.
Lincoln, A. T. 79 n.
Lindars, B. 79 n., 273 n., 274 n.
Locke, J. 47
Lohfink, G. 224 n.
Löhrer, M. 237 n.
Lonergan, A. 358 n.
Long, B. O. 65 n.
Lorenzen, T. 221 n.
Lowrie, W. 305 n.
Ludwig, R. 263 n.
Luedemann, G.:
  on the appearances of Jesus 34-5,
    37, 38, 231
  on communion with God 39-40
  on historical explanation 304-5
  on Mark's sources 16-17
  on tomb traditions 274 n.
Luther, M. 308-38

MacIntyre, A. M. 301 n.
Mack, B. 18 n., 291, 293
MacNamara, V. 342
Macquarrie, J. 225 n.
Mahoney, R. 273 n.
Malbon, E. S. 285 n.
Mann, T. W. 62 n.
Manson, T. W. 283 n.
Marcus, J. 283 n.
Maréchal, J. 234
Marshall, I. H. 71 n., 73 n., 284 n.,
    290 n.
Martin, R. 307 n.
Martin-Achard, R. 20
Martini, C. M. 14
Marty, M. 317 n.
Marxsen, W.:
  on the appearances of Jesus 158 n.
  on the cause of Jesus 9, 166 n.
  on faith 152 n., 306
  on historical science 155 n.
  on the risen body 140
Mason, S. 107 n.
McFague, S. 6-9, 10 n., 39, 40,
    359
McGrath, A. E. 17 n.
McKay, D. M. 303 n.
Meeks, W. 60 n., 84 n., 85 n.
Meier, J. P. 18, 297-8, 300, 303-4
Mendelssohn, M. 90

Mettinger, T. N. D. 64 n.
Metz, J.-B. 24 n.
Meyer, B. F. 250 n., 281 n., 300
Meyer, M. W. 274 n.
Meynell, H. 16
Michaelis, W. 129 n., 134 n.
Michalson, G. E. 216 n.
Michelangelo 3
Milbank, J.:
  neglects resurrection 342
  on post-modern philosophies 354
  on social order 356
  on tradition 346
  on violence 347 n., 349
  on virtue of justice 352 n.
Miller, D. G. 283 n.
Minear, P. 50 n., 283 n.
Mollenkott, V. R. 24 n.
Moltmann, J. 26, 342
Moo, D. J. 283 n.
Moody, R. 10
Morgan, R. 287 n., 288 n., 289 n.
Morris, T. V. 21 n.
Morton, R. 274 n.
Mosley, A. 283 n.
Moule, C. F. D. 14, 220 n., 252 n.,
    283 n.
Moulton, J. H. 73 n.
Mowinckel, S. 70 n.
Mudge, L. S. 235 n.
Muilenburg, J. 67 n.
Muller, R. 316 n.
Murphy-O'Connor, J. 14
Mussner, F. 14, 224 n.

Nagel, T. 295 n.
Napoleon Bonaparte 155
Nauck, W. 14
Nehemiah, Rabbi 117, 118
Neirynck, F. 14 n., 274 n.
Neusner, J. 60 n.
Newman, C. C. 59-89, 147 n.
Newton, I. 299
Nickelsburg, G. 20
Nida, E. A. 61 n.
Niditch, S. 66 n.
Niebuhr, R. R. 288
Nietzsche, F. W. 347, 349, 351, 354,
    357
Nineham, D. E. 228 n.
Nixon, R. 292 n.
Noth, M., 63 n.
Nützel, J. 220

Oberlinner, L. 219
O'Collins, G. 3, 5–40, 147 n., 148 n., 307
  on St Augustine 320 n.
  on Karl Barth 318 n.
  on the burial of Jesus 277
  on the crucifixion 348
  on founding Easter faith 217–19
  on Jesus' appearances 129 n., 131, 133 n., 141 n., 160 n., 165 n., 344 n.
  on Marxsen and Bultmann 294 n.
  on the meaning of the resurrection 236–7
  on the resurrection redeeming matter 359
  on risen body 140
  on risen Jesus in art 130 n.
  on the Trinity 349 n.
  on women witnesses 189, 356
Oden, T. 284 n.
O'Donovan, O. 27, 342
Oechsli, L. 359 n.
Ogden, S. 290 n.
Ohlig, K.-H. 222 n.
Origen 189, 231 n.
Ortony, A. 239 n.
Osborne, G. 136 n.
Osiek, C. 14 n.

Padgett, A. G. 273 n., 287–311
Pannenberg, W.:
  apologetic for the resurrection 17 n., 19, 216, 217 n., 231 n.
  on the centre of Christology 25
  on the empty tomb 14
  on faith and history 288
  on seeing the risen Jesus 11 n., 31 n., 35, 127 n.
Paulus, H. E. G. 231 n.
Pearson, B. A. 281 n.
Pearson, S. 307 n.
Pelikan, J. 112 n., 309 n., 338 n.
Percy, W. 10, 12
Peregrinus Proteus 229
Perkins, P. 28 n., 147 n., 293 n.
  on the crucifixion 11 n.
  on the empty tomb 14, 227 n.
  on Jesus' appearances 9, 165 n., 176 n., 227 n.
  on resurrection beliefs 20
Perrin, N.:
  on criterion of dissimilarity 176, 184

  on the disciples' failure 163
  on the Easter narratives 7
  on the empty tomb 13, 14, 36
  on inspired prophets 152 n.
Pesch, R. 14, 16, 219–21
Peters, T. 45–7, 48 n.
Philo Judaeus 102, 105, 279 n.
Pilate, Pontius 252 n., 348
Pinkaers, S. 341
Placher, W. C. 239 n.
Plato 54, 112, 358
  on immortality of the soul 91, 94, 99, 102, 106, 109, 142
Polkinghorne, J. 303 n.
Powell, E. 11 n.
Priebe, D. A. 11 n., 288 n.
Proudfoot, W. 10 n.
Prudentius, Aurelius Clemens 167
Pseudo-Dionysius 358
Ptolemy 195
Puccini, G. 162
Puech, E. 20
Pythagoras 324 n.

Quinn, E. 13 n.

Rahner, K. 2, 19, 234, 238
Rambam 124
Ramberg, B. T. 239 n.
Ranke, L. von 186
Ratzinger, J. 221
Rawls, J. 345 n.
Reimarus, H. S. 36 n., 231 n., 284 n., 289
Rengstorf, K. H. 14
Richards, C. 358 n.
Richards, G. W. 309 n.
Richards, K. H. 283 n.
Richardson, A. 288, 290 n.
Ricoeur, P. 235, 239 n., 241 n., 285 n.
Riley, G. J. 224 n., 238 n.
Robbins, V. K. 16
Robert, H. 70 n.
Roberts, A. 143 n., 144 n.
Roberts, R. C. 290 n.
Robinson, E. 225 n.
Robinson, J. A. T. 76 n.
Robinson, J. M. 281 n.
Romulus 229
Rordorf, W. 208 n., 209 n.
Rorem, P. 51 n.
Rorty, R. 239 n.

Rotelle, J. E. 308 n.
Rowland, C. 208 n.
  on apocalyptic 68 n., 69, 70 n.
  on empty tomb 14
  on resurrection belief 55-7
Rückstuhl, E. 14
Russell, D. S. 69
Russell, R. J. 21 n.

Sacks, S. 239 n.
Sade, Marquis de 162 n.
Sambursky, S. 195 n.
Sanders, E. P.:
  on the crucifixion 347 n.
  on faith and historical science 291,
    293 n.
  on reliability of Gospel tradition 16,
    281 n., 282 n.
  on resurrection experiences 284 n.
Sanders, J. T. 60 n.
Schaff, P. 309 n.
Scheidt, D. L. 309 n.
Schenke, H.-M. 274 n.
Schenke, L. 14
Schillebeeckx, E. 219, 221
Schlatter, A. 288 n., 290 n., 299
Schleiermacher, F. D. E. 231 n., 235
Schmid, J. 224 n.
Schmidt, B. B. 93 n.
Schmitt, J. 14
Schnackenburg, R. 224 n.
Schneider, J. 73 n.
Schneiders, S. 12 n.
Scholla, R. 18 n.
Scholz, G. 273 n.
Schubert, K. 14
Schweizer, E. 14, 16
Scuka, R. F. 240
Searle, J. 240 n.
Seeberg, E. 6 n.
Segal, A. F. 90-125
  on Christianity's break with Judaism
    59 n., 69 n., 84, 87 n.
  on the Jewish Jesus 3
  on resurrection beliefs 20, 57 n.
  on Son of Man 72 n.
Seidensticker, P. 14
Sekeles, E. 278 n.
Selby-Bigge, L. A. 195 n.
Sellars, W. 213 n.
Selwyn, E. G. 74 n.
Setzer, C. 59 n., 60 n.
Sevrin, J.-M. 274 n.

Shannon, W. 356 n.
Shuster, M. 20-1, 308-38
Smith, M. 250
Sobrino, J. 26-7
Soskice, J. M. 3, 41-58, 145 n., 240 n.
Soto, H. de 292
Spohn, W. C. 27 n.
Staats, R. 20 n.
Stanton, G. N. 7 n., 11 n., 28 n.,
    283 n., 284 n., 290 n.
Stoebe, H. 63 n.
Stone, O. 292
Stookey, L. H. 42-3
Strauss, D. F. 29, 32, 36 n., 37, 231,
    289
Strecker, G. 225 n.
Strobel, A. 14
Stuhlmacher, P. 14, 80 n., 284 n.
Stuhlmueller, C. 66 n.
Stump, E. 15 n.
Suger, Abbot 43 n.
Sweet, J. 50 n., 54
Swenson, D. F. 305 n.
Swetnam, J. 16
Swinburne, R. 2, 19, 28 n., 191-212,
    217, 290 n.

Tacitus 252 n.
Talbert, C. H. 289 n.
Taylor, C. 350 n.
Teani, M. 24 n.
Telford, W. R. 281 n.
Theissen, G. 85 n.
Thielicke, H. 308-38
Thurneysen, E. 309 n., 312 n.
Tipler, F. 45-8, 57, 58
Tödt, H. E. 72 n.
Tolson, J. 10 n.
Tracy, D. 233 n.
Trajan, Emperor 208
Trilling, W. 14, 257, 264
Troeltsch, E. 288-9, 291, 301
Turner, M. 73 n., 133 n.
Turner, N. 73 n.

Verweyen, H. 219, 221-2, 231 n.,
    243
Vielhauer, P. 274 n.
Vincent, M. V. 79 n.
Vögtle, A. 14

Waard, Jan de 61 n.
Wainwright, W. J. 47 n.

Walker, P. W. L. 51 n.
Walter, N. 274 n.
Wansbrough, H. 282 n.
Weaver, W. F. 273 n.
Weiser, A. 64 n.
Wengst, K. 225 n.
Wenham, D. 282 n., 283 n.
Werblick, J. 219, 221 n.
Westermann, C. 61 n., 63 n., 288 n.
Wieser, M. 309 n.
Wilckens, U. 14, 220 n.
Wildberger, H. 66 n.
Wiles, M. F. 7 n., 21 n.
Wilken, R. 28 n.
Wilkins, J. 1–4
Wilkins, L. L. 11 n., 288 n.
Willeke, B. H. 224 n.
Wilson, S. G. 59 n.
Winquist, C. E. 285 n.

Wintzer, F. 20 n.
Witherington, B. 281 n., 282 n.
Wolterstorff, N. 47 n.
Woodward, K. 1
Woolf, B. L. 227 n.
Wrede, W. 289 n., 291
Wright, N. T. 287 n.
    on John Dominic Crossan 250 n.,
        268 n.
    on God as King 67 n.
    on Jerusalem 51 n., 52 n., 54
    on the reliability of the Gospel
        tradition 281 n., 282 n., 283 n.
    on the Temple 53, 54

Yarbro Collins, A. 15–17, 20, 276 n.
Yehochanan 278 n.

Zias, J. 278 n.

Printed in the USA/Agawam, MA
September 7, 2011